Unsolicited Submissions

A Memoir

ISBN: 978-0-9846786-1-7

For all children, so that they may be safe and know love.

To Rachel, who loves with all of her heart.
To David, who takes risks.
To Alyssa, who knows herself.
To Lillian, who lives in joy.

Disclaimer

On February 10, 1960, I was born in Pompton Lakes, New Jersey to Harry David and Nancy La Rosa Higham. At that time I had two older sisters; one who was three years old and one who was approximately 14 months old. My mother later gave birth to my two brothers; the twins having been born in February 1963. My younger sister was born in January 1965. Because I understand that each of my siblings have lived their own lives, I have changed their names and avoided telling their stories except to further illuminate my own.

Additionally, my life has been shaped by various people whose past actions may now be causing them some regret and/or other uncomfortable feelings.

Or, perhaps not.

In any event, I have exercised sensitivity and restraint when presenting those situations and people, having changed identifying information in order to allow them contemporary anonymity.

Acknowledgments

As a writer, I am grateful for the works created by many authors whose sole contact to my life involved their published words. Further, I relied heavily upon popular and other types of music as a refuge and for inspiration. To list the authors and artists of such contributions would be an infinite task.

Throughout the years, there have been many who directly contributed to my development as a writer through having suffered my words in their classrooms while I attended Mansfield State College such as the professors Dr. Ira Hindman, Dr. Ellen Blais, Dr. Larry Uffelman, and Dr. Peter Keller. Additionally, my writing effort was given a boost by Walter Sanders, an English professor at Mansfield and writer who endured my short fiction and yielded both instructive and inspirational guidance many decades ago.

Unfortunately, as the years have passed, I have parted ways with others who had contributed to my growth as a writer by reading and critiquing my works with a sensitivity and candor that helped shape my creative voice. Though our lives no longer intertwine, I remain sincerely grateful for their past contributions and support.

Allegra Wong and Nancy Hardin also directly contributed to my growth as a writer by reviewing and working with me in developing my memoir pieces for publication and potential cinematic production, respectively.

Further, I thank my siblings who assisted me in telling my story in a way that respected their adult lives while still capturing the range of our shared experiences. I would be remiss to not acknowledge Cara Furiosi-Clarke for having waded through portions of my admittedly voluminous rough manuscript and encouraging me to pursue editing it. I am sincerely appreciative for the editing of the current book by Jen Bowen.

I appreciate the sacrifices made by my children David, Alyssa, and Lillian so that my words and experiences could find their way into this volume.

Finally, I remain thankful for the input and emotional support provided by my loving wife Rachel as I endeavored to turn a mass of recollections into the work that now inhabits these covers.

1963

Nighty-Night

Mommy put me in bed. Me nighty-night. It's bedtime.
Mommy put me here. Tee-Vee is on. Tee-Vee!
It's bedtime. It's nighty-night!
Mommy says, "Nighty-night," and "Don't let the bed bugs
bite!"
Mommy tucks me in.
Mommy tucks Faith in; she's my big sister.
Mommy tucks Maria in; she's my other sister.
Faith sleeps. Maria sleeps.
Mommy says to the girls, "We love you."
Me up. Me pooped, me pooped, me pooped, me pooped!
Me pooped!
Me pooped in my pee-jays. Me pooped in my bed. Me
pooped on my pillow. Me pooped, me pooped, me pooped!
Me run to the living room.
"Me pooped, Mommy and Daddy."
"You shit your pants?" Daddy asks. "Been in bed ten
minutes and you shit your pants?"
"David, don't yell at him," Mommy says. "You'll wake
the girls!"
Mommy cleans me. Poop is everywhere. Got poopy
belly, poopy toes, poopy face, poopy hair.
"Goddamn you, Poop!" Daddy says. Daddy gots poop on
his hands. "Goddamn you for poopin'," Daddy says. "When are
ya' gonna grow up and stop crappin' all over the place?"
Mommy takes my dirty diaper.

"Throw that the fuck out," Daddy yells. "It's too shitty to wash!"

"David—," Mommy says.

"What? He sat on the toilet for an hour and didn't go. He's in bed ten minutes and he shits all over the damned place." Daddy looks at me. "Poop, poop, poop; that's what you are," Daddy says.

Daddy gots poopy T-shirt, poopy hands, poopy pants.

"Me sorry, Daddy. It's nighty-night."

"If you shit this much when you go to bed, you can sit on the potty 'til you shit."

Daddy picks me up. Takes me to potty. Puts me on potty.

"Fuckin' sit until you shit," he yells. "Shit or get off the pot, Poop. That's what I'm fuckin' callin' you from now on, Poop."

"David, don't yell at the boy."

"He knows when he should take a shit. He shits on purpose so he can watch TV."

Me can't poop.

Maria and Faith walk out.

"You girls go to bed, Johnny had an accident," Mommy says.

"An accident? He fuckin' shit all over the place. His name is Poop," Daddy says.

"Poop," Maria says.

"Poop," Faith says.

Me can't poop.

"Poop held it in all day: look at all this shit," Daddy says. "He can shit all he wants after goin' to bed. Not puttin' up with that anymore."

Me try poopin'.

Me can't.

Me can't poop.

"Poop: that's what you are!" Daddy says. "You girls go to bed."

The girls giggle. "Poop, poop, poop," they say.

"Poop, you woke up the whole fuckin' house!" Daddy yells.

"C'mon girls, get back to bed," Mommy says.

Mommy goes.

Mommy gets the girls.

Mommy kisses them nighty-night and don't let the bedbugs bite.

Me can't poop. Can't poop at all.

Daddy gets mad. Real mad.

He runs at potty.

He grabs me.

He runs to sofa.

He throws me.

He pushes me into sofa.

Me bounce. Like a bouncy ball.

Me cry.

"Fuckin' poop!"

"David, you'll hurt him!" Mommy says.

"I wanna hurt Poop. Wanna scare the shit out of Poop so he never does it again, the little shit."

Me Poop.

Brothers

Me got brothers.

Real small twins.

Mommy says they look different.

Daddy says Mark popped out first. He's got a real big head.

Warren took his time. Daddy said Warren finally 'cided to be born.

Blocks

Daddy's gone. He's in New York. He's a salesman.

Mommy says he'll be home. Soon.

Maria and Faith are gone. Go to nursery school. Lenape Nursery School with Miss Ann.

Mommy's watchin' Tee-Vee. Me playin' blocks. Me build big buildings. Me knock 'em over in big blow-up all over the place!

Ka-boom! Me throw 'em at the wall.

"Play nice," Mommy says. She's watchin' Tee-Vee. Tee-Vee men are talkin'. Talkin' 'bout Pres-dent Kennedy. Somebody hurt him.

In Dallas.

In Texas.

"Who hurt him, Mommy?"

Mommy doesn't say anythin'.

Mommy doesn't say anythin'. The twins are cryin'. She makes 'em bottles. She gets twins from cribs.

Mommy feeds them.

Baby twins need bottles.

The Tee-Vee men are talkin'.

Me playin' with blocks. Buildin' big buildings. Skyscrapers.

Then me knock 'em over.

Boom! Boom! Boom!

Big blow-up all over the place! Ka-boom!

1964

The Econoline

Daddy gots a new Econoline. It's white.

Daddy parks it in the garage. Except when I play. Then he parks it in the driveway.

I'm four now!

I'm a big boy!

I get to play in the garage with the big door shut!

I race 'round on my trike. Maria and Faith and me play racecars in the garage.

We drive real fast.

Drive so fast, drive right to the sky, never come down 'til the Fourth of July!

I go to nursery school with Miss Anne. We play games. She gives us lessons.

I don't sit still.

I'm bad.

I bite. I hit kids.

I didn't bite Miss Anne. I didn't hit Miss Anne.

Daddy said Mafia kids go there.

Daddy says not to talk to Mafia kids.

Daddy says they have dirty money.

Daddy brings me home from nursery school every afternoon. Just 'fore the girls get home. Me and Daddy laugh and laugh at his jokes.

"You're my big boy," he says.

One day Maria and Faith are at school. Daddy parks the Econoline in the driveway. Daddy and me go into the garage. Daddy put me on his shoulders: I pull, pull, pull on the garage door. I pull it shut and Daddy locks it.

Daddy locks the big door.

"Son, you play here."

"Racecars?"

"Yeah."

I get on my trike and I'm racing 'round the raceway.

Daddy stands in the middle, watchin' me. Daddy smiles.

I like to race 'round and 'round the raceway, faster and faster.

'Round and 'round!

Faster and faster!

'Round and 'round!

'Round and 'round!

Faster and faster!

'Round and 'round and 'round and 'round and 'round and 'round and 'round and faster and faster and faster and faster!

So fast, I'm goin' a hun'red miles an hour!

"Son, you play out here," Daddy says. "Play racecars."

I stop.

Daddy smiles.

Daddy goes into the house.

Daddy uses the small door: it goes to the kitchen.

I play racecars.

I go 'round.

And 'round.

'Round and 'round!

Faster and faster!

'Round and 'round!

Faster and faster!

'Round and 'round and 'round and 'round and faster and faster and faster and faster!

So fast, goin' two hun'red miles an hour! I'm racin' everyone in the world, goin' faster and faster! I'm goin' so fast that I'm the fastest person in the whole wide world! I'm the fastest, fastest, fastest, fastest person ever!

Daddy's tellin' Mommy jokes 'cause I hear her laughin' in the kitchen.

'Round and 'round I go. I'm the fastest, fastest, fastest person ever! Must be goin' three hun'red miles an hour!

No, four hun'red miles an hour!

No, five hun'red miles an hour!

No, six hun'red miles an hour!

Goin' fastest in the whole wide world! Faster than the sun! Faster than everything!

Mommy screams.

I stop.

I don't hear Mommy.

I don't hear Daddy.

I run to the kitchen door.

It's locked.

"Mommy? Daddy?"

I don't hear Mommy.

I don't hear Daddy.

I don't hear nobody.

I push the door. It's locked.

"Mommy? Daddy?"

I can't see the Econoline anywheres.

I knock on the kitchen door. Mommy and Daddy must be gone 'cause I can't hear them talkin'. Can't hear them laughin'. Can't hear nothin'.

Mommy and Daddy go away forever!

I knock again.

And again and again and again and again!

I hit the door.

I hit it again and again.

I look at the door.

Mommy and Daddy got to be go away forever 'cause I can't hear 'em. They got to be go away 'cause nobody's home. Got to be going away because there's no one left in the whole wide world anymore!

I kick the door.

I kick it again and again.

I don't wanna play racecars anymore. Don't wanna play anythin' anymore.

Just want Mommy and Daddy.

"Mommy? Daddy?"

Mommy and Daddy gots to be in there 'cause I seen 'em go in the kitchen 'less they ran away without me. 'Less they ran far away with Faith and Maria and Mark and Warren.

"Mom-mee," I scream 'cause she's not hearin' me at all. "Mommy!"

The door opens: it's Daddy! In underwears.

Mommy's on the floor. In underwears.

Daddy's face is all wet.

I run to Mommy.

Daddy grabs me.

"What the hell are you doin'?" Daddy says.

"Me scared."

Daddy pushes me down the step. "Don't be such a big baby, son. Play racecars."

He slams the door and locks it.

I don't want to play racecars.

Mommy laughs and laughs and laughs.

Mommy screams.

I scream.

I scream and scream and scream and scream and scream.

I scream and scream and scream and scream 'til Daddy comes back out. He's all dressed and Mommy's gone.

She's all go away.

"Poop, you woke the twins," he says. Daddy grabs me, then he spanks me so hard I don't wanna play racecars anymore.

"You wanna cry, you can cry in the garage," he says.

He slams the door.

I cry and cry and cry and cry for a hun'red years.

I hear the Econoline go away forever.

Don't want racecars. Just want Mommy, Daddy.

I jump up and down, up and down, up and down for a hun'red years.

I sit on the step forever. I cry and my legs shake.

Just want Mommy and Daddy. Don't want racecars.

Mommy opens the door. She's not in her underwears.

Mommy sits on the steps. She hugs me.

Surprise! Daddy opens the garage door and Faith and Maria are home from school!
I stop crying.

1965

Lassie

We got a babysitter.

Daddy got one. He took Mommy, Mark, and Warren to the hospital.

I went to bed.

Without supper.

Daddy spanked me.

Spanked me with his belt 'til Mommy said we better get the twins to the hospital.

The twins are sick.

The girls are talking to the babysitter. They get to stay up.

Daddy says he's not waitin' for no damned ambul-ants. Says, "Poop is a bad boy," and took Mommy, Mark, and Warren to the hospital.

I didn't do nothin' to the babies. Honest, I didn't.

The girls get to watch *Lassie* on TV. Daddy says they could.

Says I have to stay in bed.

Says no matter what and calls me Holy Mackerel Andy and Jesus Christ. Says Poop knows better.

It's all mixed-up.

Mommy cries.

I didn't do nothin'!

Mark and Warren ain't cryin'; Daddy says I hurt 'em real bad. They ain't cryin' or nothin'.

Just wanted to see 'em drink some ink from Daddy's pen. Just wanted to see 'em with black teeth.

Can't a guy do that?

I'm hungry. Daddy says I have to keep my ass hungry.
'Til breakfast.

Says, "You almost killed the twins!" Says, "Jesus Christ,
Poop, what kinda boy are you?"

Says that a whole bunch of times.

Then throws me on my bed.

Then spanks me again.

Then slams my door.

My bedroom is dark.

Real dark.

Makes me cry.

Bang!

Daddy opens the door and stands there, just stands there.

"Stop cryin' and take it like a man," he says, but I can't
stop cryin' cause I'm scared of the monsters.

"Daddy, turn on the light!"

"No," he says.

"I'm scared of the monsters!"

"You should be. Maybe the monsters should get you."

My bottom hurts real bad.

Bang! He slams the door.

I'm scared of the monsters. They're all over the place.

I can hear *Lassie* on Tee-Vee, but the monsters are
waiting.

Waiting for me to sleep.

Will get me.

But, I ain't gonna sleep.

Not ever.

The Train Yard

Daddy took me to the station. We watch trains goin' up
and down the tracks. Daddy calls the engines dee-sills. I wave at
the cabooses. The men wave back.

We count cars on the trains.

Count cars through the window of the Chevy.

Daddy got the Chevy from the company. They pay him money. He drives all over New York City. He takes food to the A and P grocery stores.

"They pay good money," Daddy says. "Money doesn't grow on trees."

Money on trees?

I'm gonna find a money tree. Plant it in the backyard. I'll always have lots and lots of money.

Daddy says he knows Heinz. Daddy won a contest! Sold the most Heinz Ketchup for six whole months! Was the best salesman in the whole wide company!

He's the best dad in the whole wide world!

Anyways, a whole bunch of dee-sills run by without cars! They honk their horn at us 'cause I was wavin'!

"They like us," Daddy says. He's smokin' a cigarette and wearin' his white shirt. That's what he wears to work. Can see his T-shirt too; that's got no sleeves.

Daddy always got on his black pants and scuffed shoes. When he gets home, he takes off his shirt and loosens his belt so his tummy don't hurt when he lays down for a nap.

I don't like his belt 'cause it hurts me. Hurts me when he spanks me all the time.

"Be quiet, Daddy's sleeping," Mommy says when I'm playing real loud with my sisters.

Me and Faith and Maria shut our mouths or go outside to play 'cause we know better. Mommy says we're the Biggies and the twins are the Little Ones. The twins are just babies. They don't stop cryin', so Mommy just rocks 'em two at a time in the chair.

I play on my trike with Maria and Faith. We hear the train whistle from across town and pretend that I'm the little engine that could!

I pull 'em like we're a train, choo-choo!

Choo-choo!

We run 'round 'till dinner.

"Wash your hands for supper," Mommy says.

Daddy gets mad at us kids when we run inside.

"You kids run around like a bunch of niggers. Why the hell can't you be quiet?" he yells.

15

We hush ourselves and wash real good 'cause we ain't supposed to be dirty at the table or Daddy'll get mad.

Sometimes I stuff my mouth full of yucky food. Then I go to the bathroom, pretendin' to poop when I'm just spittin' out spinach. Faith did it once, but Daddy caught her and spanked her.

Daddy points at the shiny cars sittin' by themselves next to the dee-sills.

"See the transit cars? People ride them into New York," he says.

And I look real hard, but I don't see anyone sittin' in them train-sit cars. There's a guy walkin' 'round the yard, playin' with the track, but the train is empty. People must be hidin' from the dee-sills.

Daddy shoots his cigarette butt into the air like a rocket and takes one from his pack. I got me some candy cigarettes and I suck on one. It tastes really good, just like candy. Daddy got a carton of his cigarettes on the seat. He took me to the store right after dinner. I got a pack of my cigarettes and watch trains with him.

Daddy got real mad at dinner 'cause the twins cried all the time and ruined everythin'. He got mad and swore at them. Called them names and punched the table so hard that my plate jumped ten feet high in the air.

"I'm gettin' some goddamned cigarettes," he said. "Can't eat this slop."

"Daddy, can I go? I finished all my dinner."

He looks at me real long 'cause he knows I'm done.

"Honey—," Mommy says.

"He'll be all right," Daddy says. "Come on, son."

"You're the favorite," Maria says.

"Eat your dinner," Mommy says to Maria. "And you, scrape your plate."

"Better hurry, 'cause I'm not goddamned waitin'," Daddy says. He tucks in his shirt and fixes his belt.

I scrape my plate and hurry: I'm goin' with Daddy!

Daddy's real quiet 'til we get in the company car.

"Fuckin' niggers are no good," he says. "Five percent are good, but the rest of them should go back to Africa."

16

There ain't no niggers anywheres on the street.

He didn't say nothin' the rest of the way down the hill to the store or even at the yard, 'cept swearin' a couple times 'bout niggers. I don't know why he's so upset at niggers 'cause we don't know any 'cept on the TV.

We don't see any niggers at the train yard. Daddy just smokes cigarettes and sits on the hood. We watch trains forever, but the dee-sills never touch the train-sit cars. The sun is 'bout gone before he has his last cigarette and he gets back in the car.

When we get home, the twins are sleepin' in Mommy's arms. She didn't wash the dishes, but Daddy doesn't care. He put his cigarettes on the table.

"I'm sorry, Honey," he says to Mommy.

"It's okay, David," she says and they kiss.

"Mommy, we saw train-sit cars! They're called that 'cause people sit in them goin' into the city! They got big shiny windows!"

Mommy smiles. She's real happy 'cause I tell her all 'bout the train-sit cars.

Farina

Mom yelled last night. Woke me up.

Did she wet the bed?

Daddy was on the phone. "I think it's time," he said.

Mommy was all swollen out. Her tummy looked like a big pillow when the ambu-lants came and took her away. Daddy was still in his Chinese pajamas and held her hand. Daddy calls them "Chinese pajamas" 'cause they gots dragons on 'em.

"Nancy, you'll be alright," he says.

I saw everythin' 'cause I peeked out from my bedroom. Saw everythin'. The nice ambu-lants men took Mommy away. Everybody whispered 'cause they didn't wanna wake the twins. Us Biggies were already up, but we played quietly in our rooms.

I was the first one up. I heard Daddy when he called on the phone. He saw me peekin' out of the bedroom.

"It's okay, son. Mommy is havin' a baby."

Mommy looked really tired.

Yeah! She didn't wet the bed, so she won't get in trouble!

Her hair was all messy like she rolled out of the wrong side of the bed and her pajamas didn't fit right. And it was way too cold for her to be goin' outside without a coat on, so the ambu-lants men put a big heavy blanket on her just like that and she was all set for the baby hospital.

Daddy smoked a cigarette and watched her. I came out and hugged his leg.

"Is Mommy okay?"

"Yes, son. She'll be fine."

The ambu-lants sat in the driveway forever.

"Is she havin' the baby now?"

Daddy patted my head.

"Soon, son. Very soon."

Daddy made Farina. Me and Maria and Faith squished the lumps with our spoons and filled our mouths with the junk, only we never call it that 'cause Daddy gets mad and yells at us to eat it all.

Daddy can't fry eggs or make pancakes. He can't fry bacon or sausage and we don't have no cereal.

Mom always made eggs and bacon. I like eggs in a cup with lots of salt and butter. Mom boils them on the stove, then mixes butter and salt with them 'cause they taste so good.

Daddy turns on the steam kettle and makes lumpy Farina.

"Makes me sick, Daddy," Maria says.

"Well you better eat it 'cause it's all you're gettin'."

The twins don't care because they don't know any better.

"You'll eat poop if I put it in your bowl," Daddy says.

Maria and Me and Faith laugh 'cause Daddy is funny.

We eat Farina a long time 'cause the hospital says Mommy lost a lot of blood and almost lost Baby Rose. Mommy stays in the hospital forever before the doctors say she's strong enough to come home. Daddy says Mommy was so thin that the doctor couldn't find any fat to stitch her back together after they C-sectioned her almost into two parts.

C-sections are for people who almost lost a baby.

Daddy said they had to cut Mommy apart to save Baby Rose.

18

"We almost lost your mother," Daddy says one morning. He makes a funny face like he's gonna cry, but he forces himself to make another face and he doesn't cry at all.

Daddy never cries.

We can't see Mommy 'cause the hospital says she has to rest and get more blood. We eat lots of Farina and the twins don't eat no poop.

Baby Rose

Mommy can't have no more babies 'cause she don't have fat on her tummy for the C-section.

Least that's what Daddy said.

"We almost lost Mommy," he said the night before she comes home from the hospital. "She bled and they couldn't sew her up."

And Daddy makes funny faces again and doesn't cry at all. Daddy made Tee-Vee dinners, but he ain't eatin' nothin'. He's just standin' near the oven, smokin' a cigarette and lookin' at the wall. He's really quiet and just smokes a cigarette.

Me and Faith and Maria are sittin' at the table. The twins are in the playpen 'cause they're still learnin' how to walk.

The next day, Mommy comes home with Baby Rose.

Small Baby Rose!

So small!

She's the smallest thing in the world!

So quiet!

She doesn't even say anything!

Baby Rose doesn't say anything; only cries after a little bit. I touch her and rub her cheeks 'cause she's my itsy-bitsy teeny-weenie baby sister.

Ain't never had one of 'em before, so I have to figure out what to do with her.

"Mommy, are you alright?" I ask.

"Mommy's tired, son," Daddy says. "She needs to get some rest."

Mommy lights a cigarette and Baby Rose cries. Daddy gets to the stove and puts on some water.

Baby Rose cries a lot when she's hungry.

Mommy smokes some more while Daddy gets the bottle ready. He makes formula, then hands Mommy the bottle, but Baby Rose screams a lot 'cause it takes about a hun'red years.

That's a long, long, long, time.

And I can't see no C-section on Mommy or the baby, so I don't worry about it.

I just go and play with my Matchbox cars, making it rain on 'em by spittin' on them, then wiping the rain off with my fingers. I spit on my Matchboxes all night.

1966

Stanhope

Wow, I get my own room!

This place is bigger than the shack we had, at least that's what Dad called the house in Netcong. It's nicer than the one in Denville! And we got a big yard, too!

There's an upstairs too: that's where my room is!

My room is the best room in the whole house! I can look out and see the woods!

The upstairs hall is shaped like a giant letter U with my room at one end in the back looking at the dogs. Faith has her own room, then the twins and Baby Rose in the other corner room, then Maria. Dad and Mom have the bedroom at the other end.

We got woods to play in and two dogs: Tippy is a Collie and we have Dodo. Dad says, "Dodo is a fuckin' Daschound."

That night, we hear Mom laughin', yellin' and screamin' so we all talk to her 'bout it in the mornin' after Dad leaves.

She just gets real red.

"Oh, Daddy poured some rubbing alcohol on my Kitty-Cat," she says "'cause I hurt it."

Me and Faith and Maria know 'bout Kitty-Cats 'cause Mom told us all about 'em and Babymakers one day. We know they can get hurt real easy so you have to be careful touchin' 'em. We all know that only girls have Kitty-Cats and only boys have Babymakers.

Later, when us Biggies were playin' in Maria's room just before dinner, she told us that she looked in Mom and Dad's room and didn't find any rubbing alcohol in there.

"Dad was just tickling Mom," Maria says. "She was laughing just before she screamed."

Maria knows everything. She's very smart.

School

I get to stand right next to Route 206!

"I'm so proud of you, son," Mom says as she holds the camera. I'm in my blue suit carryin' my lunch in a big brown bag. I'm going to Kindergarten 'cause I'm a Kindergartner.

"You're so handsome," Mom says. She takes a picture of me and Faith and Maria. They've been goin' to school for years, so they know what to do. Every year, Mom takes pictures on the first day of school. We get to wear nice clothes and the girls wear ribbons.

Mom cut my hair cut real short 'cause I'm goin' to school now. Me and Faith and Maria are Biggies goin' to school together.

I get my own lunchbox!

I get my own pencil box!

I get to come home early!

The twins and Rose are Little Ones. They don't go to school. Only us Biggies get to go to school!

"I'll be waitin' for you right here when you get back," Mom says. And I know she will 'cause I'm a Biggie.

Dogs

"That asshole is a fucking bastard," Dad says.

"He's a lazy moron," Mom says.

We're eatin' dinner and Mom and Dad are talkin' about the bus driver.

My bus driver.

I'm scared.

Real scared of the dogs.

I'm real scared 'cause I know they're gonna bite me. I'm scared cause they're gonna get me, knock me down on the ground, and bite me into little pieces.

I'm real scared 'cause they always chase me when the bus driver lets me off up the highway and not at our house.

"It's easier on everyone, Ma'am," he says when Mom yells at him one afternoon. She's at the bus stop with the twins and Baby Rose on Route 206 as cars go by really fast.

She just doesn't care 'cause she's mad at the bus driver. She's mad at the lazy moron and is yelling at him with all of her might. She's yelling really loudly and making Baby Rose cry.

"He could get killed out here," Mom yells. "He could get killed because you're not doin' your job!"

"Ma'am, it's easier for everyone if I drop him off up the road. It's just five houses, for Cripes' sake. What's that take for him? He's a big boy. 'Sides, he told me that he can walk."

"Johnny, did you say that?"

I shake my head 'cause it's not good to lie.

Mom looks at me like I just broke somethin' and she's gonna tell Dad when he gets home. She looks like she's gonna beat me to an inch of my life. That's what Dad says when he's really mad.

"He drop John in the right place?" Dad asks at dinner. We're sittin' around the huge dining room table that is held together on Dad's end with a large strap 'cause it broke one time when he got really mad and flipped it over.

"He said it's easier to drop him up the highway," Mom says.

"You tell him that John could get killed out there?"

"He said he's a big boy. Said he could walk."

Dad punches the table. Mom gets quiet.

Dad punches it again, hitting his plate and flipping it into the air. There's spaghetti everywhere and his face is really mad.

Shouldn't have told the driver I could walk. Shouldn't have said anythin' about the dogs. Shouldn't have, but they scared me. They're so big, they could eat me alive if I'm not careful. They're so scary.

It's all my fault.

24

"You tell him we pay our taxes?"

"Yes, Dear."

"Fucking bastard!"

He punches the table again and I pretend I don't hear him 'cause he might get really mad and yell if I look at him.

"That asshole drives that bus all the way up here in the morning!"

Dad lights his cigarette and sucks in some smoke. When he wants to, he can make all sorts of pretty smoke rings one right after another. Mom and Dad do that sometimes 'cause us Biggies like to watch.

"I know he does," Mom says. She reaches for a cigarette.

All that talkin' doesn't do any good 'cause the bus driver makes me get off up the highway and the dogs still chase me.

Picture Day

Dad's gonna be really mad at me, madder than he gets when I wet the bed all the time. He's gonna be so mad at me 'cause I can't wipe any blood off my suit. He told me to be careful this mornin' when I put it on for picture day.

See, I was playin' with a bunch of my friends.

Was playin' with a bunch of my friends on the see-saw.

Was playin' at recess.

They were goin' up and down on the see-saw.

And, I thought I'd be a real funnyman and stand right behind one of 'em.

And, I was goin' up and down right with him.

When he went up, I went up.

When he went down, I went down.

Was jumpin' way up and gettin' real low right with him, makin' everybody stand around and laugh at me 'cause I'm a real funnyman.

Up and down, up and down, up and down.

Then, all of a suddenly, it went up real fast, the see-saw went up real fast. Went up so fast that it went right up to the sky and didn't come down until the Fourth of July and my face started hurtin' really bad and my mouth started hurting really bad and all my friends got really big eyes 'cause the see-saw hit my lip and cut it really bad.

It cut me really, really bad and my blood went all over my suit and I can't clean it off no matter how I try or anything, not even with all the wet paper towels that the nurse gave me and I'm not gonna be in picture day and Dad said, "You be careful in that suit today and don't get it dirty 'cause I'm not made of money and money don't grow on trees," and now it's all ruined and everything 'cause I had to be a really stupid funnyman.

Daddy's gonna be really mad at me 'cause I got my suit all bloody and he's gonna spank me real hard and yell at me and everythin'.

The nurse called Dad 'cause Mom can't come and get me. She don't drive. Wished she did 'cause she wouldn't yell at me 'cause she don't care about money growin' on trees or anythin' like that. She wouldn't spank me. She wouldn't care 'bout the blood. She'd just hug me, say that she loved me.

And Dad's gonna be really mad at me 'cause I'm not gettin' my picture taken 'cause the nurse says I better get to the doctor and get some stitches in my lip 'cause I cut it really, really bad and now Dad's gonna be mad at me for missin' picture day.

Shouldn't have been a stupid funnyman. Never be a funnyman ever again 'cause that just ruins my suit forever and everythin'. It's not even worth it.

But, guess what? When Dad comes and gets me, he's not even mad! He doesn't even say anything about the suit! He talks nice to me the whole time even when I'm expectin' him to be yellin' at me and spankin' me. He's even talkin' nice to me when the nice doctor sticks a needle in my lip and sews up my lip and everythin'! Dad's even nice afterwards when he takes me home and everythin'! Gives me a big hug even after I told him the whole truth 'bout what happened!

The Big Snow

Me and Maria and Faith are ridin' a cardboard box down the stairs. The Little Ones are too small for that, so they just have to watch 'cause they could get really hurt if they ride with us.

We can't ride outside 'cause there's no snow, but the TV man from WCBS said that we're gonna get a big snow.

Big snows don't matter 'cause we ain't gonna live here much longer!

You know why?

'Cause we're movin' to Italy 'cause Mom got this letter from her Aunt. In Palermo. It was in this really, really thin envelope that had Mom's Italian name on it. When Mom opened it, it was a letter written on really, really thin paper.

Mom and Dad looked at it. The words didn't make any sense to me or anyone else!

It didn't make any sense 'cause it was all in Italian words!

Dad took it somewheres when he went to work.

"Your aunt wants you to sign over the land," Dad said when he came back. "Your land."

Mom and Dad are laughin' and dancin', sayin', "Our ship has come in!"

We got land in Italy!

"Holy Mackerel, Andy!" Dad yells. And he's smilin' and dancin' 'cause we're gonna move to Italy and live like Italians. Mom's a hundred percent Italian. She looks it: she's got dark hair and skin. Us kids are only fifty percent Italian, but me and Mark and Maria and Baby Rose look a hundred percent 'cause we got dark skin and hair. Dad's fifty percent French and fifty percent Irish. But, he can live in Italy with Mom and us kids!

So, Dad got on a plane and went to Sicily. He's gonna get us a house there and we're gonna live there forever and ever!

It's nicer than Stanhope, you know.

Me and Maria and Faith are riding the cardboard box down the stairs. Mom sits in the dining room listening to the song *Downtown* on the radio when the phone rings. She turns down the radio.

"Children, be quiet. It's your father."

"Shush," I tell 'em 'cause girls never listen to anybody. We run like a bunch of Crudleys' to the living room and wait to talk to Dad on the phone.

The Crudleys' lives door. Dad calls 'em that. Dad says they're dirty bums. There's a whole bunch of 'em, but they're nice.

"I miss you, Honey," Mom says to Dad. When I hear her say that, it makes my face turn red and everything. My face gets like that when I sing songs too.

Anyways, me and Maria and Faith are sittin' by the phone, listenin' to Mom talk to Dad about Italy. I wanna go there on a boat 'cause there's too much water between New Jersey and Palermo. Better to get on the Queen Mary boat and sail all the way around the world.

We got to wait until after the big snow. It hasn't started yet, but the WCBS man is never wrong.

"Are you alright?" Mom says to Dad. She gots a sad face and I poke Maria 'cause my sister is so smart that she knows everything.

"What's the matter?

"Shush, so I can hear." Only thing, I can't hear nothin' 'cause Mom and Dad must be talkin' in their whisper voices. They talk a bunch like that, but we can't ever hear nothin'.

Mom says, "I love you, David," then hangs up.

Us Biggies look at each other.

"They met your father at the airport," Mom says. She's sad now. "They told him to go home."

Maria and Faith don't say nothin' 'cause they want to ride the cardboard box.

"Who?" I ask Mom.

Mom lights a cigarette.

"The men who stole our land," she says.

"Mom, are we livin' in Italy?"

Mom hugs me and kisses my head. I can tell she's really sad 'cause she does that when she's really sad. Sometimes I see her like that waitin' for Dad at night, just starin' at the curtains and listenin' to music. I always give her some hugs 'cause that's what a boy should do for his mom.

"They forged Mommy's signature on the deed," she says.

I hug her a long time, even after Maria and Faith take my turn on the stairs.

"We'll owe you five rides when you come up here," Maria says.

"Is Dad okay?" I ask Mom.

"Yes. He'll be back the day after tomorrow."

"What's *forged*?"

Mom kisses my head. She says, "Forged is when someone pretends they're you by writing your name on an important piece of paper. It's a big lie."

She gets up and turns off the radio.

I watch Maria and Faith, then look outside. A couple snowflakes fall, but it's too slow for me to tell when the big snow is coming. By the time Dad gets home a few days later, the whole place is covered with lots of snow and nobody knows when school is gonna be open again.

1967

The Monster

It's night.

I hate it.

I hate it 'cause no matter how many places I look, I can't find him.

I look under the bed.

I look out the window.

I even look in the closet.

I look in the closet a lot, but only when I got my light on. I don't open my door and look down the hallway 'cause he might get in and I wouldn't even know it until it was way too late.

Way, way too late!

I look everywhere, but there's no monster. I know he's really, really good at hiding. I know 'cause he only comes out after Dad goes to sleep.

Then the monster rattles my door and I just know that he's gonna get me.

"Dad. . . , Dad-dee," I yell.

I yell and yell and yell.

I yell and yell and yell even when I hear Daddy running like he's a steam engine coming down the hall to my room.

Choo-choo!

Dad runs the all the way past Maria's room, the Little Ones' room, and Faith's room. He runs all the way down the hallway to my room.

Choo-choo!

I scream and shout because I know the monster must be pushing on the closet door. It almost gets me, but Dad turns on

31

my light and chases it away.

"What is it? You wet the damned bed?"

"There's a monster in the closet and he's gonna get me."

Daddy looks at my bed, then looks where I pointed as he pulls at his T-shirt. He stands on his tippy-toes and searches all over my closet.

"There's no monster here," he says.

"He escaped through the wall!"

Daddy looks at me like I'm telling a lie. But I know. I know all about monsters. I know what he's gonna do to me as soon as Daddy leaves. He's gonna climb through the wall, get back in the closet, and wait for me to fall asleep!

None of the other rooms have monsters!

Just my room!

He's gonna get me! He's gonna get me so bad and there's nothin' Daddy can do about it. There's nothin' the Army, Navy or Marines can do about it!

"You hear it, Daddy? You hear it right there?"

Daddy turns his head. He looks like Dodo our dachshund when that mutt hears someone in the backyard. He and Tippy even bark at birds.

The monster runs along the wall!

"Daddy, he's climbing up the side of the house! He's tryin' to escape!"

Daddy looks out the window toward the dogs and the rest of the backyard. He presses his face against the glass, then waves at me.

"C'mere, son."

When I get out of bed and look out there, it's all dark.

"I can't see, Dad."

"Look at the side of the house."

I push my face really hard against the glass. I'm lookin' real hard and can't see anythin' but all the darkness 'cause it's night. I push against the glass even harder and try to look out.

Wait, I see it.

I see something really, really scary.

It's so scary, I just can't believe it!

It's a big black snake that goes all the way from the ground to up and up to the top of the house! It's a big black snake

32

that's jumping back and forth right by my window! The big black snake is going past my window to the roof! It's gonna squeeze the house to death!

"It's a monster snake that's gonna trap us in the house!"

"Son, it's just the antenna wire," Daddy says. "The wind is making it hit the house. You're fine."

"But it sounds like a monster snake that's gonna trap us in the house and squeeze us to death! Gonna squeeze us all to death in our sleep!"

He picks me up and puts me back in bed. He tucks me in and gives me a kiss on the head.

"Lots of things can sound like monsters," he says. "That doesn't make it one. See, there's nothin' there and nothin's gonna get in here. "Not gonna... let anyone hurt you kids or Mom."

He makes a funny face and gives me the biggest hug in the whole wide world!

He turns off my light and walks back down the hall. I keep listening for the monster. I stay awake 'cause I know it's there.

"They're in there," Dad said one night last month when we returned from the Dairy Queen. "They want us to know that they're in there," he said.

We were all in the car. He floored it so we went right past the driveway.

"Is it the Crudleys'?" Maria asked.

We kids sat in the back seat of the company Galaxie 500. Well, us Biggies and the twins did 'cause Mom held Baby Rose on her lap. Maria and Faith always get to sit by a window, so I couldn't see the house. It looked the same to me, but Dad could tell.

Dad knew things like that.

"No, honey it's not the Crudleys'. It's burglars."

"They better not steal my Barbies," Maria said.

"David, should we call the police?"

"Maria, your Barbies are safe." He slowed down after we passed the house.

"Honey, the cops can't help us. You know that."

Dad drove up and down Route 206, turning around in the

parking lot of Wild West City, passing the house, then turning again at the Shop-Rite. I don't know why he kept letting other cars go ahead of him.

"Are we goin' grocery shoppin'?" Faith asked.

"No, Dad's just waiting until the burglars leave."

We drove some more. Dad put on the radio and whispered something to Mom, but I couldn't hear even though I leaned against the seat.

We kids didn't say anything 'cause Dad knew exactly what to do. After awhile, Maria got ants in her pants.

"When are we goin' home?" she asked.

"David, I'm scared," Mom said.

Dad wrapped his arm around Mom's shoulder, "I'm not gonna let anything happen to you or our kids."

Finally, after driving around for a thousand years, Dad finally pulled up the driveway. The headlights showed us Tippy and Dodo. Both dogs pulled at their chains and barked 'cause they were happy to see us. We all went inside and everything looked okay.

"Did they steal my toys?"

"No, son, they didn't take your toys," Dad said.

"They wanted pictures of when Daddy was married before Mommy," Mom said.

Us Biggies got real quiet. Dad never talked about being married before Mom. He got a dee-vorce and never saw the bad lady ever again. Sometimes, Dad and Mom talked about her when we weren't supposed to be listening, mostly late at night when us Biggies sat on the landing and listened to Dad tell Mom not to worry about anything.

"Did you see the burglars, Dad?" Maria asked. "Are they gonna hurt us?"

Instead of getting really, really mad at Maria and spankin' her for talkin' about the burglars, Dad gave her a hug and pat her head!

"No one's ever gonna hurt you," Dad said. "I'll make sure of that. And I didn't see the burglars. They're never gonna bother us again. They're all gone and never comin' back!"

Right after the burglars left, the monster was in my closet, waiting to get me every night.

Sometimes, he was real quiet.

Sometimes, he was real invisible, but then he always made lots of noise.

I yelled for Daddy and he came to chase away the monster!

The monster was scared of Daddy, but he always came back after Daddy left. I turned the light on to chase him away, but if Daddy found out when he went to the bathroom, he'd get real mad.

He'd walk down the hall, turn off my light, and sit on my bed. I could see his outline. He's bigger than any monster, I figured, but it's always quicker.

"Keep off that damned light," he said. "I'm not made of money."

"But the monster will get me, Daddy."

"Told you I won't let any monsters get you."

"Daddy, why do I have to sleep in my own room?"

"You're a big boy," he said, tucking me in. "And a big boy isn't afraid of the dark!"

"But I'm not afraid of the dark. I'm afraid of the monster!"

"Well, a big boy isn't afraid of anything. Are you a big boy?"

"Yeah…, I guess."

Daddy hugged me and closed the door.

Sometimes, I get really scared.

I get so scared that I put my head under the covers and don't ever want to get out of bed because the monster is watching me. Rather be invisible forever under the covers so that the monster will never ever find me.

So he'll never ever get me.

Sometimes, and I don't really mean it, but sometimes when I get really, really scared and hide so far under the covers, I have really big accidents and wet the bed 'cause I have to pee so bad and can't let the monster find me. When Daddy finds out, he says bad words and tells Mom.

"Poop wet the damned bed," he yells, but there's nothin'

else I can do when I hear the monster in my room and I can't yell for Daddy or put the light on 'cause Daddy isn't made of money. There's nothing else I can do to hide from the monster. If I get up and try to run to the bathroom, I know the monster will get me, get me, get me!

Mom comes and helps me change. She never says bad words or yells at me when I have a big accident and wet the bed. She never has to worry 'bout a monster 'cause Dad is in her room all night. She's so lucky that the monster is scared of Dad!

The Turtle Back Zoo

"John, come on, I'll take you home," Mr. Myerson says. I get all my stuff and climb into the back seat of his car. Dad is supposed to pick me up, but he must have got caught in traffic on the George Washington Bridge.

"I have to go back inside the school to get something," Mr. Myerson says.

I wait in the empty parking lot for him.

We had a class trip.

We went to the Turtle Back Zoo.

I rode the train.

Jim House's Mom went with us and she took care of our group.

We rode all the rides and had a big picnic under a big building that had no walls, just a roof.

Jim's Mom took him home at the end of the day. I'm the last one left at the school and Mr. Myerson told me he'd take me home. Then he went back inside.

Mr. Meyerson is the principal.

Mr. Myerson stays in the school a long time.

He said he'd be right back, but I start thinkin' about what Dad said to us Biggies right after the burglars broke in and stole pictures of the lady he was married to before Mom.

Dad said never ride with strangers.

Dad said never talk to strangers.

Dad said that strangers might know the burglars.

Dad said the burglars were bad people.

36

Dad said they were Mafia.

And, I'm thinkin' and thinkin' 'bout what Dad said. It really gets to me 'cause Dad looked right at my face when he said it and said all that stuff over and over again and told me to 'member it 'cause it's very, very important.

What if Mr. Meyerson is making plans to kidnap me?

What if he's gonna hide me away somewheres?

What if he's friends with the burglars?

What if he's Mafia?

I look around the empty school, push open the car door and run away as fast as I can. I saw on TV where the bad guys always chase after you in their cars, so I run right into the woods. I figure I'll have to hike home that way or Mr. Myerson will catch me and get me in no time at all. Of course, he'll figure that I'd be on to him, so he'll have to tie me up to keep me from escaping.

The Mafia isn't gonna kidnap me! No one's ever gonna kidnap me!

I stay off Route 206, following it from the woods. I see a couple of state troopers in cars driving really slowly and looking all around, but I'm not about to let 'em see me 'cause the kidnappers could have told them lies so they could get me.

'Sides Dad said the police can't help us!

No one's gettin' me!

When it gets dark, I walk really slow and stay away from the lights on account of not wanting to be seen. Mr. Myerson probably lied to the police.

"Car 54, be on the lookout for a first-grader named John Higham. He was last seen runnin' away from Mr. Myerson, the elementary school principal."

They'd make it sound like that just to keep me from getting Mr. Myerson in trouble. That's how bad people do things.

It doesn't matter 'cause I'm too late.

When I get home, there's a bunch of state troopers there. I see their cars in the driveway. Some troopers are in the backyard, pointing their flashlights into the woods. Tippy and Dodo bark at them, which is good 'cause then I sneak inside without being kidnapped by the bad state troopers!

Mom is sitting at the kitchen table, crying. Dad looks

really mad when he sees me. Him and a trooper come right at me.
If Dad wasn't there, I'd run as fast as I could into the woods and
escape all over again until the bad state troopers went away!

"Can't a guy even have a drink?" I says.

"Son, how did you get so dirty?" the trooper asks.

"Went through the woods 'cause I figured Mr. Myerson
was looking for me."

Dad sits down and lights a cigarette. He looks right at me
and I gotta tell him everythin'.

"You told me to never ride with strangers," I says. "Mr.
Myerson is a stranger. What if he was a kidnapper?"

"Son— ," Dad says 'fore he swallows hard. "Son, Mr.
Meyerson..., Mr. Meyerson... thought someone... kidnapped
you."

"Naw, no one kidnapped me. No one's ever gonna kidnap
me, Dad! I'm not gonna let 'em!"

Mom gives me a hug and the troopers go outside with
Dad. Mom is still hugging me after all the troopers are gone and
Dad comes back in. He sits at the table smoking a cigarette. He
keeps making faces like he's gonna cry, but instead just swallows
really hard. When he's done smokin', he gives me a hug.

It's the biggest hug in the whole wide world!

I know 'cause he squeezes me so hard I feel like I'm
gonna pop!

Racecars

I slept so hard that I grabbed the pillow and wrapped my
arms all the way around it 'till it forced me asleep.

The monster went away when I squeezed my eyes shut
and I couldn't hear anything.

I was lucky 'cause I didn't have another big accident and
wet the bed.

The girls were up.

"We heard him," Maria says. She always hears him ever
since I could remember. That's because she always picks her ears
and can hear so well that she can hear a pin drop and on a clear
day she can hear all the way to New York.

I'm sitting up in bed rubbing my hands real fast so that they slap back and forth. I'm really, really, really, really happy right now! I'm thinking really fast, like a racecar!

Sometimes I think like a racecar. Sometimes, I think so fast and everythin' 'cause I get so excited 'bout somethin' goin' on in my head when everyone is not excited about anythin' at all. They all look at me like I'm stupid or something but all I'm doin' is bein' real 'cited.

All I'm doin' is I rub my hands really fast or repeat things to myself faster and faster and faster and faster until I'm thinkin' so fast that I just can't stop thinkin'!

And, I can't talk right at all and Dad get's mad at me 'cause my words get all messed up and everythin'.

And my legs bounce and everythin' else 'cause all I am is really, really, really happy about everythin' in the whole wide world and nothin' else and nothin' can make me feel sad at all!

But, everyone is excited tonight! It's really not night: it's mornin'. Really early mornin' 'fore the sunrises and all that! It's Christmas Day in the morning!

We get the twins up, though Baby Rose is already downstairs. Mom must of heard Santa too 'cause she holds my little sister.

Me and Faith and Maria got to be careful on the stairs or we might slip. Our footies are slippery on the wood stairs. Sometimes, we sit on the top of the stairs and bump our butts down each step. Maria always races me, but she always wins. She's just always faster and quicker and I'm just always slower than molasses in January.

It's not January.

Not yet.

The house is cold. The front room looks like it's glowing in the dark, the lights on the tree barely showin' through all the presents. We each got piles of wrapped stuff.

Big, big piles!

Big, big piles of presents piled so high that they'll never come down until the Fourth of July!

Mine is the biggest one in the world!

I got lots of boxes!

Lots of big boxes!

It's still dark outside.

Dad leans against the wall near the little table we sit at in the summer when we have picnics. The Ansco is on the table, but he's too busy laughing to take pictures.

We tear into the presents.

Maria got Barbies. So did Faith.

Rose got a dolly and stuffed toys.

The twins got matching Jeeps and a Tonka car carrier with neat cars.

And me?

I got the neatest thing: I got racecars!

Zoooom, racecars!

Big ones: bigger than my hands. I can barely hold them in my hands. I want to put them right on the track and race them, but instead I open a really big box and find a large battleship!

It's like the battleship Missouri!

It can go in the bathtub or roll on the floor and everything! It's even got a searchlight! And, Santa put in the batteries. I roll it over to the corner and turn on the searchlight. I'm looking all over the ocean for somethin' but can't find nothin'!

I got Lincoln Logs and a big tank that shoots missiles! Warren and Mark got police cars!

Me and twins all got U-Haul trucks that are so big we can sit on them! We can move our house with them! We can stick our heads in them and move all sorts of stuff in there! When it gets nice outside, we can play with them in the dirt! Maybe even take them out in the snow!

"Dad, can I play racecars?" I ask.

"Sure."

I go inside the living room and set up the track. It's really neat. It's not a stupid oval, but a bunch of curves and twists! Even got some bridges so I can make a big figure eight! Got guardrails and all sorts of cool things!

"Can I race you?" Maria asks.

I give Maria the white car. I want the red car. It's my set and I can give her the red car. If I want, I can race the white one. She has to listen to me 'cause I can put it away if I want to.

I plug in the controller.

There's lights flashing and Dad says, "Look at me and smile."

I smile so hard I close my eyes. Maria does too. The cars stop 'cause you have to keep your eyes open to drive or you'll wreck.

"Everyone sit in a big line with your favorite toy," Dad says.

"It's my racecars!"

We all line up like Mac Namera's Band or something like that. Mom watches Dad as he takes pictures of us. He's laughing at us in our homemade bathrobes. Mom made them out of towels and they're so warm!

Mark and Warren got police cars and Rose got her doll and a rolling popcorn popper.

And Faith?

Faith just sits on the sofa without opening anything, staring at us.

"What's the matter?" Dad asks.

Faith just looks at Dad.

"Suit yourself," he says.

Dad takes a picture of us, then one of Faith all by herself in the living room chair.

She's not playin' or anythin'. Maybe after I finish Maria off, I'll let Faith race.

She better watch out!

I can drive really really fast!

The cars are really fast and Maria gets lucky for a while, but then I make the race longer. Mom makes coffee, then the house smells of eggs and bacon.

Dad calls Mom *Venus* but she looks funny in her curlers and cat eyeglasses. She's got bare feet and she's smoking a cigarette.

It's Christmas Day in the morning! It's Christmas Day in the morning!

Dad gets to eat first. We're so busy playing, nobody wants to eat as the sun comes up. We're playing racecars! It's funny 'cause the sirens go off on the police cars: I'm racing so fast I can't hear anything but the racecars on the track. I'm Speed Racer against Maria and she doesn't stand a chance.

Faith comes down from her chair and I show her how to race.

"Whoopi thrills," she says. "Big whoop."

She lets the car sit there on the track. I don't care if she's not racing. I squeeze the controller and blow right past her.

Zoooom!

She's not doing anything but letting me cream her. It's too bad, but there's nothing I can do about it. I'm playing racecars!

She waits until my car swings around the curve into the home stretch.

What?

She floors it and her white car makes a roar!

She slams me into the guardrail, making my car jump the track!

"I'm gonna win," she says as she speeds around the overpass.

"Hey, no fair."

"Oh yeah, it's fair to just keep goin' when I have trouble?"

"You didn't have trouble. You just let it sit there like you're in the pits."

She makes up a lap.

"Better catch up. I'm gettin' way ahead of you."

I put my car on the track as Dad sits down with a plate of dippy eggs and bacon. Mark and Warren sit next to him like hungry dogs. Mom comes out of the kitchen and grabs the Ansco.

"Don't look at me," she says. "Look at your father."

The boys pretend they're starving kids in China. We're laughin' 'cause it's funny. Dad smiles like he's never givin' up his bacon.

After Mom takes the picture, Dad breaks his last piece in two and gives a piece to the twins. The boys suck them right down.

"I win," Faith says.

"Hey, no fair, I was lookin' at Dad."

"No, you were in a pit stop." She laughs and grabs a Barbie. She jumps back into her chair. "I won fair and square."

It doesn't matter 'cause they're my racecars and it's Christmas Day in the morning! I can race all day!

1968

Matchboxes

I have all my Matchboxes on the bed. I spit on them like rain and make tire tracks by pushing down on the blue sheet: it makes a road for the cars and trucks. I can play up here all day long after I come home from school.

I got bad news on the TV.

Somebody shot Martin Luther King. It makes me cry.

The black people are real mad.

Dad never let me watch Martin Luther King on TV 'cause he says he's a bad nigger who don't know nothin' and should go to h-e-double-l. Said he should take Malcolm X with him 'cause Earth ain't got no place for bad niggers.

I know all about Martin Luther King 'cause he was in the *Weekly Reader* and Mrs. Baty told us about him.

I want Martin Luther King to be okay. My tummy hurts, but I'm not thinkin' 'bout that 'cause I'm so sad for him.

I won't say nothin' to Dad 'bout it. Won't even tell him I cried 'bout it or anything.

I'm up here by myself thinkin' 'bout all the bad people who don't like Martin Luther King. I'm playin' Matchboxes on my bed, making highways all over the place and havin' a tummy ache.

"John, Daddy's home," Mom says.

I tear down the stairs, then outside just as he pulls up to the garage. Me and twins all stand around like Mac Namera's Band waiting for him to open the car and step out like he always does. Sometimes, he works real late in New York City and never comes home until almost bedtime. He comes into my room, gives me a hug and tells me to have sweet dreams.

Now, he's so big in his suit. Got a big smile.

"Daddy, they shot Martin Luther King."

Daddy laughs.

"Niggers aren't gonna get me," Dad says. "Look at this."

He shows me the biggest wrench I ever saw. It's as thick as my arm and it's as long as Dad's arm. It's broken at one end, but that part is still attached. Just doesn't work right.

"What's that?"

The twins look at it. They can barely pick it up, but Dad holds it so it won't hurt them.

"My nigger beater," he says, swinging it in the air near the company's Impala. "Any of those niggers get near me, I'll beat the living shit out of them."

I just look at him 'cause I can't figure out why they'd want to get near Dad. He only likes white people.

"It's gonna be burn, baby burn for them," he says. "Stupid niggers."

He put the nigger beater under his front seat, then gets a case of frozen food out of the car.

A big box of Swanson TV dinners.

All Salisbury steaks.

Me and the twins follow him into the house. It's a parade.

Later, all of us Higham kids are sitting around with our TV trays, looking at the Salisbury steak. It's pretty good, but not the carrots! They're like red squares that go mushy in my mouth and 'bout make us all puke! I shovel a whole load into my mouth, then go to the bathroom.

There I spit 'em out with my head real close to the bowl 'cause if Dad finds out I'm spitting out carrots, he'd be really mad at me and spank me with his belt.

"Eat," Mom yells. "Your father had to steal that food from work so that you kids could eat."

Dad gives Mom a bad look like she just had a big accident and wet the bed.

"Damnit, Nancy, I don't want them to know that," Dad says.

"I'm just being funny," Mom says.

We all laugh at her 'cause she makes a funny face.

After dinner, us kids sit in the living room with Dad while Mom washes dishes. I play Matchboxes, but I don't spit on 'em 'cause Mom and Dad get mad when I do.

Sometimes, I hear 'em talkin' late at night, sayin', "What kind of a boy spits on his toys and mumbles all the time? He needs to see a psychiatrist 'cause he's crazy!"

I like to pretend it's raining on the cars and I'm a big cloud making it rain all over the place! And, sometimes, I get really, really excited and my words talk too fast!

Anyways, the girls play Barbie. The twins sit on the rug watching me make highways on the rug. It works just as good as it does on the sheet.

The TV is really bad. Some kind of black people burn Newark: looters. It's all over the news. Race riots, but nobody was playing racecars. Worse than watching the Vietcong War News 'cause this wasn't In-doo-China but New Jersey. I don't even know any looters.

Dad sits on the sofa, drinking a Reingold. "Stupid niggers. Only five percent of that entire race is worth somethin'," he says. Rest of 'em should get their black asses back to Africa."

"Are not," Maria says. "There's some girls in my class and they're real nice to play with."

"That's cause you go to a good school. That's the five percent I'm talkin' about. Their parents work hard and make an honest livin'. Not tryin' to burn things down 'cause they're too damned lazy. Go into the city. You'll see the lazy niggers all over the place, standin' 'round street corners doin' nothing but makin' trouble. Then you'll see what I mean."

I play with my Matchboxes, but I want to go upstairs 'cause my tummy aches. Aches even though I spit out the yucky carrots. Just want the race riots to be over and my tummy ache all gone.

Don't know why Dad says all those things about people all the time. Don't know why he gets so mad 'bout it. Only thing he gets madder at is me when I wet the bed.

The Ansco

Me and Dad are outside. He has the twins standing 'round like a pair of Crudleys'. And Baby Rose is on her tricycle.

"Faith and Maria, get out here," he says.

My sisters wait a long time. Dad doesn't care. He's foolin' with the Ansco.

I climb on my bike. I can ride it anywhere I want 'cause Dad taught me. Showed me how to push off from the big rock near the driveway and ride my bike the whole day.

"Hold it," he says. I sit up straight, leaning the bike over and putting my tippy toes down.

The twins got go-carts. Dad fixed Warren's after I crashed it into the concrete step a few times and broke the steering. Wasn't an accident: I just wanted to break it 'cause car wrecks are cool.

I really like breakin' things. Sometimes, I like smashin' my Matchboxes with rocks.

Dad fixed Warren's go-cart once at the welders, then got real mad at me for smashing it into the step when he brought it back.

"Poop, cut that shit out or I'm sending you to a goddamned psychiatrist," he said. "Why are you always tryin' to break things?"

"Was an accident."

"Bullshit. Now, get out of that car. If I ever catch you playin' in it again, I'll spank you."

That was a month ago and I don't play in Warren's stupid go-cart anymore. Don't need to play with his stupid go-cart 'cause I got a cool bike and I can ride anywhere in the world as long as I stay on the property!

Big boys ride bikes!

Little boys play in stupid go-carts!

Anyways, Dad holds the Ansco right in front of his belly and looks down at the glass top so he can take a picture.

"Move a little closer," he says. "Faith, Maria, get out here!"

He pushes the Ansco's button. It's got a big flash that looks like one of them press jobbies you see in the movies when the reporters run in and take a picture of a bad murder.

It's sunny out, but he still wants to use that flash.

"Move, Johnny. I want to take some pictures of just the twins."

The girls come out of the house with Mom. They all just stand there while Dad points at the twins.

"You guys move together," he says. He takes a couple more pictures as the girls walk toward the garage.

"Don't walk into the picture," Dad yells as he looks at the Ansco. I ain't never looked into the big shiny glass on top of the Ansco, but I figure that it ain't big enough to see the girls: they're way over to the left. It's probably 'cause they're laughin' at Dad tellin' them not to do that. They always do what they're not supposed to 'cause they're the favorites.

The phone rings.

"Honey, get that," Dad says without looking up. He slowly pushes the button on the right side, then winds the picture.

Mom goes into the house.

The girls line up.

"I want all the girls together," he says.

Mom runs out of the house and whispers to Dad.

"Holy mackerel, Andy!" Dad yells to Mom. "I told you we needed to take these pictures. You believe me now?"

Mom hugs Dad like they're on a honeymoon or somethin' but they don't play smacky-mouth or nothin' like that. Mom looks sad, but Dad won't let her stay that way.

48

"It's picture time," he says.

"We're ready," Maria says. The girls are on their bikes, including Baby Rose.

Mom is moving around a lot, like she's nervous or something. She finally puts her hand on Dad's shoulder, but he doesn't mind. He looks down at the Ansco and pushes the button. He takes a couple more pictures.

Of me.

Of the twins.

Of the Little Ones.

Of the girls.

Of us Biggies.

Mom stands right next to him the whole time, wipin' her eyes and blowin' her nose.

Later, the Ansco is on top of the china cabinet in the dining room. We're eatin' spaghetti with meatballs for dinner. Mom started the sauce early in the mornin' and it cooked all day. The whole place smells of yummy sauce.

"Don't talk to any strangers, Dad says again. "And watch out for strange cars."

"Why?" Maria asks. She's always asking questions.

"They gunned down Finnegan," Mom says. "Right in his driveway."

Dad looks at Mom like she had a big accident, but he doesn't yell at her.

Finnegan is the guy who let Dad borrow the Ansco. Sometimes, he comes over to the house and drinks Piels with Dad at the table or in the backyard. He's always laughin' or jokin' 'bout somethin', I think.

He's Daddy's boss.

"Who did?" Maria asks. She never shuts up.

"Mafia," Dad says. "When he came home from work. They were waiting for him in his driveway."

Mom stares at her plate like she's not really hungry. That's not good 'cause Mom says we should *manga, manga* instead of staring. Dad doesn't even try to make her smile 'cause he's telling us Biggies what to do.

"You Biggies look after the Little Ones. Don't leave the property. When you go outside to play, you tell me or your mom."

And Dad is real serious 'bout this, so us Biggies will look after the Little Ones.

Warren bugs me. Bugs me 'cause he eats so slow.

Warren eats so slow that it's a million years before he swallows anythin'. He dangles the spaghetti in the air above his face, then slurps it all up. He doesn't eat like I do. I put my fork right underneath it and cut the spaghetti with my teeth, just like Dad taught me.

"John, do you understand me?"

"Yes sir. You want us to look after the Little Ones and not go outside unless we tell you or Mom."

"And?"

"Stay on the property."

"That includes your bike. You ride it in the back of the house or in the backyard. Not down near the highway unless Mom is watching you, you understand?"

I shake my head up and down 'cause Dad isn't smiling and I don't want to get him mad.

After dinner, Dad runs the Ansco film down to the Rexall. When we get the pictures back, I look really big on my bike. I don't want a stupid go-cart anyways.

Dad puts the photos in the album he and Mom keep in the bookcase. He keeps it there so he can look at me and 'member how he taught me to ride bike.

Oxford

I hate it.

It's a small house.

I have to share my room with Mark and Warren. Their bunkbeds take up the whole place. Maria and Faith and Rose are in the same room. We had to leave Tippy and Dodo. There's no woods to play in and there's no highway. We live way out in the country, but there's only hayfields around us.

We live way out in the hayfields!

Dad says he likes it 'cause Vern lives next door. He's a state trooper. Dad says he's getting us new dogs, Duke and Brutus; they're German Shepards. Says we need dogs in the country.

Mom and Dad don't talk 'bout burglars or Finnegan or Mafia anymore.

I still get scared of monsters and still have big accidents and wet the bed. Faith and Maria pick on me 'bout it. They say, "Johnny wet the bed, Johnny wet the bed" over and over again even after Mom tells 'em to stop pickin' on me.

I wanna punch 'em!

I wanna go back to Stanhope. Even though that bedroom had monsters, it didn't have the twins in it.

I hate them. They're so stupid. All they want to do is bother me. All the time.

Only good things that Oxford got better than Stanhope is Chuckie and Butchie.

Chuckie's got a big HO scale train set in his basement so we can play trains all the time. And, he's got a pool and a stupid sister, Cindy. He's in the second grade and I'm in the third grade. We play together all the time. His dad's a state trooper, too.

Butchie's got a Lionel train set in his basement and a real live fire truck in his barn! We play fire department everyday and pretend we're drivin' that truck forever. Butchie is in the fourth grade and his uncles own lots of farms. He lives with his mom, dad, and his big sister. She's real pretty!

Guess what? Mom lets me walk all the way down the road by myself to play with Butchie and Chuckie! And, the twins have to stay home!

Dad and Lad

Dad and me are at *Dad and Lad*.
The twins aren't here!
Faith and Maria aren't here!
Baby Rose isn't here!
It's just Dad and me!

Just Dad and me are looking at suits!
Dad's buying me a suit!
A brand new suit!
Dad says men wear suits.
The whole place is filled with suits.
I like buying suits with Dad!

Sunday Matinee

See, I got it all figured out. Because there's five of
us—Baby Rose stays at home with Mom—we get lots of money
for popcorn and stuff at the movies! We go every Sunday
afternoon to Hackettstown when Dad takes his big nap. Mom
drops us off, Maria buys the tickets, and we go in and watch the
movie.

I like movies, movies, movies! Everything is so big on the
screen!

Big movies on the screen!

It makes me rub my hands really fast!

Today, we're watching something about monkeys in outer
space! And, a space ship named Hal that talks to this guy before
it kills him. It's got really cool music and it's about the year two-
thousand and one.

We always go to the matinee and eat our popcorn and
watch our movies, movies, movies!

I always want to tell Dad about it, but Faith overheard
Mom on the phone saying that he's terminal. That means that
he's got to take some morphine naps on Sunday afternoon until he
feels better.

Sometimes, Mom and Dad wake up at night. I hear them
whispering at the dining room table. They just whisper 'bout Dad
being tired all the time and goin' to Dr. Heller's office down the
road right next to Chuckie's house.

Mom and Dad always whisper at night. They never
whisper during the day 'cause that's when Dad works or takes
naps.

I can't always hear the words they say, but I can hear them whispering. One night, Dad said he got a will and lots of insurance, so everything will be okay for Mom and us kids.

I wanna tell him 'bout the part in the movie that has screaming monkeys. Maria says he'd probably like that.

Tonka Dune Buggy

"Gees, it's right there in the catalog. I want the Mini Tonka, not the Mighty Tonka. Can I have it? Please, Dad?"

Dad leans on the steering wheel of the company car. I waited until we were in the car to ask him 'cause I don't want anyone else to hear me.

We're in the driveway, waiting. He's not talking as we wait for a car to come up the road from Butchie's house.

Mark is flying a kite in the field next to the house, but there's no one else outside. It's getting cold and the leaves are turning orange.

I've been talkin' to Dad about the Mini Tonka Dune Buggy for at least a month. Maybe even a year. Ever since I saw it on TV during *The Flintstones*. It does all sorts of neat things in the dirt. Does wheelies and stuff like that.

"It's so nice; I'll never play with it in the dirt like I do with all my other cars. And, I won't smash it with rocks. Or spit on it, I promise."

"Pretty soon, we'll have to get our own car," Dad says.

"Wow, we gonna get a Mustang like Chuckie? Or a Camaro? How 'bout a Corvette?"

Dad makes a face and slides on the seat. His face scrunches up and he rubs my hair like I'm Duke. Only thing, I'm not a German Shepherd dog chained to a coup in the backyard. If I was, I wouldn't want a Mini Tonka Dune Buggy!

Mom is inside. She's getting ready to make dinner 'cause that's what moms do. It's been a good summer, but it's all over now. We moved from Stanhope in April 'cause that house had Mafia burglars and monsters. Dad followed Interstate 80 west and moved us here.

Dad waves at a brown Rambler. It's Butchie's Dad, Butchie Senior, comin' up the road. He waves back at Dad. Butchie lives just down the road from the Knapp shoe man. That's not his name, but he's got a big sign near his mailbox sayin' *Knapp Shoes*.

"Those shoes are shit," Dad said the first time he drove by that sign. "Cheap imported shit."

He puts the car into gear and backs out into the road. He's adjustin' the radio 'cause he wants to listen to his music. He pushes the big black buttons and the songs come on. It's WABC from the top of the Empire State Building.

When I turned five in 1965, Dad took me to New York City! We went to the very, very top of the Empire State Building all by ourselves 'cause it was my birthday! We went across the George Washington Bridge 'cause it was so big! It needed to have lights to keep people from accidentally hitting it and dying!

Dad rubs my head again. My hair is growing back. In summers we get buzzcuts so we don't sweat like pigs.

"Dad, what's the name of this place again?"

"We're in Oxford. This is Jane's Chapel road."

"What's the name of the mountain? I forget."

Dad rubs me again and gives the Impala a little gas.

"Mount Bethel," he says. "In Warren County."

"New Jersey," I say.

Dad sings along with Frank Sinatra as he goes down past the Fitzins', Dr. Heller's, and Chuckie's house.

Chuckie has cool model trains!

I don't have any model trains, but I read about 'em all the time. I saw a picture of one in the encyclopedia and I like watching the beginning of *Superman* reruns when the announcer says, "More powerful than a speeding locomotive."

I like watching that passenger train go by real fast.

Dad is sleepy. He's is the strongest man I know! He picked up a tree all by himself and Mom took a picture to prove it! That was last year in Stanhope. Me and Dad and the twins were outside with the guns, posing for pictures with Mom. She took all sorts of pictures of us.

"Dad, 'member when you took all those pictures of us with the war rifle in Stanhope? 'Member we did that last year?"

Dad is too busy drivin' to say anythin'. That's how dads are sometimes 'cause they're too busy worryin' 'bout where our next meal is coming from or how we're gonna make all the ends meet. Least, that's what Mom says.

We drive past a big barn that's 'bout ready to cave in. I'm really scared of it and whenever I ride my bike past it, I go really, really fast. Dad says I'm a chicken-shit for being afraid and I should walk right inside it, but I don't. It looks so bad, it could swallow you up and no one would ever find you!

"Son, that was in sixty-five. Right after we moved from Denville," Dad says. He turns off the radio.

"Fuckin' nigger music," he says.

I like the song, 'specially the part where the guy says, "tighten up" and you can hear the guitar playing. Think it's guitar.

"If we get a new car, we should get a new Mini Tonka Dune Buggy too. I won't play in the dirt with it, I promise. Please?"

Dad laughs. "Think so, huh?"

"Yeah! I'll take really good care of it. Will you get it for me? Otherwise, it's just not fair."

"No, it's not."

Dad gets real quiet and I don't say nothin' 'cause I don't want him thinkin' I should run alone into the scary barn. I just don't look at it 'cause a ghost or monster will come after me next time I ride down to Lichtenstein's Country Store for some fireballs and jawbreakers.

"A dune buggy?"

"Yeah, with a plastic roof."

When we lived in Stanhope, Dad bought me lots of Matchboxes. He bought me lots of Formula One racecars and lots of King Size construction ones. He never got anyone else anything. Sometimes he bought them once a month, sometimes more than that. He'd let me have them and I'd play with them while he watched TV and drank his Rolling Rock. Or, he'd sleep on the sofa right after he got home.

They were too nice to take outside, but I broke most of 'em cause I kept getting real excited and threw 'em around real hard. I kept throwing them at the wall and the floor. Dad says I'm crazy and need a psychiatrist. Mom says I play too rough.

"I won't play with it in the dirt," I say to Dad 'cause I want a Mini Tonka Dune Buggy more than anything else in the whole wide world right now!

"Really?"

Dad gets to the end of our road. Most times, I go to the right 'cause that's Lichtenstein's General Store around the big curve. When Dad drives, we always go left into Hackettstown for somethin'.

It's pretty out here. There's big power lines going across the mountain, but most of the grass is for farms. There's development way over near the city, but there's nothing on this part of the road. It smells like old barns and hay. Nobody's got cows and I never see anyone in the fields.

"Dad, where are we goin'?"

"Post office. Daddy has to mail a letter."

"You write to President Johnson again?"

"No, son."

He doesn't say anythin' for a good couple of miles. He's thinkin', I guess, and I better be quiet. Sometimes he just gets that way and it's better not to say anythin' 'cause he might get real angry at you or start swearing or somethin'.

Or worse, he might take his belt off and spank you for back talking!

He used to get really, really angry and flip over the dinner table, but he doesn't do that anymore. I'm really happy that he never gets really mad anymore.

Just yells sometimes is all.

"Got to mail somethin' to the V.A.," he finally says after we pass the sign for Camp Merry Heart. One of Mark's friends, Ned, lives there. It's for crippled kids, so I never get to go.

"Watcha mailing'?"

"Oh, somethin' from Dr. Heller," he says. "Just a letter to one of their doctors that says how I'm doin'."

"Can't he call 'em?"

"The doctors are very busy."

"What's the letter say?"

"Tells him how I'm doin'."

"How are ya' doin'?"

Dad looks and me and smiles. He turns the radio back on. Glen Campbell is singing 'bout lineman and Daddy starts singing.

"I need a small vacation," he sings along with Glen Campbell.

"Maybe you should take one," I say.

Dad pats and rubs my head. "Hey, Mister Funnyman."

And I pretend I'm drivin' the Impala, but instead, I'm really thinkin' I'm drivin' the Mini Tonka Dune Buggy that he's gonna buy me.

It's a month later. Lots of stuff happened. Dad had to give up the company car 'cause he's not drivin' anymore, but he got a big package in the mail! I know 'cause I get to check the mail when I get home from school.

I'm in third grade now!

Anyways, Dad gets dropped off early that day and is sleepin'. He's taking another nap in his bed and I just run right in with the big envelope 'cause it looks like it's tellin' him that he won the Irish Sweepstakes and that his ship is finally comin' in.

Mom and Dad say that all the time. They say, "Our ship is coming in," but that never makes sense 'cause we don't live near a harbor and there's never any ships nearby. 'Sides, ships can't go on mountains!

Anyway, Dad is in his T-shirt and under the covers, smokin' a cigarette. Only thing, he holds it between his teeth so he can open his envelope.

"Is that from the doctor at the V.A.?"

"Son...," he says. He looks really tired. His hair is pushed up in the air and his mouth talks slow. He's slow all over, but points to his closet.

"Open..., open the closet..., and... get me something."

"What?"

He tries tearing through the brown envelope. It has a big warning on it that says anyone using it for private purposes will be fined three hundred dollars.

"I forget…, but it's… in the closet."

I slide over the door and there's a big box on the floor. Part of it is hidden by the hamper, but I find it 'cause I know what it is: it's a Mighty Tonka Dune Buggy!

"Daddy!"

"Don't play with it in the dirt, okay?"

"Wow!"

I can't believe how big it is! It's bigger than the rest of my trucks! The top comes off and the seats are big enough for one of the girls' Barbies! It's got big black tires! I run it all over Dad's bed as he reads the V.A. papers! He puts on his drugstore reading glasses and stares at the print. The Buggy makes tracks all over the blanket!

"Promise me you'll take care of it so that when you grow up and have a son, you can pass it on to him."

"You bet I will, Dad! Wow, it's great!"

I make tracks with it on the blanket, then go racin' down the hallway to the kitchen to show Mom and the girls!

Playin' with Trains

It's cool. Daddy's smiling as he sits in the chair. He wears pajamas as we rip apart all the wrapping paper and boxes. Mark and Warren are playing with new Tonka trucks, Rose got a Raggedy Anne Doll, and Maria has a Barbie house. Faith has a big sketchpad and lots of artist's pencils.

Me?

Santa got me a train set! A Lionel train set!

It's really neat! Got 0-27 track!

It's bigger than HO scale!

I can make a really big oval with it and there's even a helicopter car that comes with it. It's just like Butchie's train and some day I'm gonna have a big train set in my basement too!

"You figured that out fast," Dad says as he sits in the chair. He's in pajamas. Ever since he came home from work, that's all he wears. Mom says he's got to sleep 'cause he's tired from the morphine medicine.

Oh yeah: he coughs. All the time.

Sometimes he'll start in the middle of the night. It sounds like he's got bad snot in his throat and can't get rid of it. Mom will pat him on the back or fetch a glass of water for him, but he just keeps coughin' for a long time.

I put the train track together and I'm runnin' my train in no time. Santa got me a 0-4-0 engine. That means it's got no leading wheels, two drive wheels, and no trailin' wheels. All the weight sits on the drivers. The wheel arrangement is used by the American Association of Railroads to identify engines, that's how I know.

I know all this stuff 'cause I read about trains all the time.

Anyways, I got a tender. It hooks to the engine with a drawbar, not a knuckle coupler. It holds the coal so that the engine will run. See, coal is fuel that heats the water and makes steam!

Then the coolest part; the cars. The engine pulls a gondola, a boxcar, a coal car, and a Lehigh Valley caboose. The caboose is for the brakeman and the conductor.

The conductor is the boss of the train. What he says goes. If the engineer wants the train to go around a curve through a red signal, he's got to ask the conductor first.

"Wow, Dad, Santa got me everything!"

Dad smiles and puts his head down so that it's tilted back. Mom pats his head.

She's still in her clothes.

You know what, I figured out something tonight, but I'm not tellin' anyone. Tonight, I figured out that Maria and Faith helped Mom wrap presents. Had to be them 'cause I just heard them talkin'.

There is no Santa.

I figured it out.

I figured it out because after the twins fell asleep, I sneaked to my door and put my ear against it.

Was spying on Santa.

Only thing, I heard Mom and Maria and Faith instead of Santa!

"That's good, Maria," Mom said. "Now, tape the ends."

I tried sleeping in my room, really. Didn't sneak out into the hall and stand near Dad's door like I used to 'cause I knew Santa would be coming. Santa would know I was waiting for him.

"You kids get some sleep," Mom said when she tucked us in early last night. She kissed each one of us after we filed into Dad's room and gave him a kiss or a hug. I wouldn't kiss him 'cause Dad says boys don't kiss boys, but I gave him a big hug and a handshake.

"Get some sleep so Santa will come," Dad said.

I took the twins to our bedroom and we went to bed.

"Think Santa will be here before midnight?" Mark asked.

"Shush, get some sleep," I said. We covered our heads with our blankets.

Mom came in and kissed us goodnight, then tucked us in. She tucks us in every night 'cause she's Mom. I like it when she does. Before Dad stayed home all the time, he tucked us in too. He'd come in and sit on my bed, telling us stories about the war or his day in New York.

Daddy's too tired 'cause of the morphine the doctor gives him. Sometimes, he just sleeps all day.

But, he's awake for Christmas!

His eyes are falling asleep in the chair. He wakes up when he starts coughing and I got to wonder if he's ever gonna stop.

Mom helps him sit up.

My train is running in circles as Maria and Mom take Dad to his room.

"Goodnight, Daddy," I yell over the train. He keeps going, but I think he can hear me. He hears me a lot, like when I sneak into his room when he's sleeping during the day and I listen to him. Sometimes, I just sit on the floor with my Mighty Tonka Dune Buggy as he sleeps with his television on.

Sometimes, he wakes up and we play chess.

Maybe I can set the layout up in his room and we can play trains!

That would be so neat!

1969

The Schwinn

Don't tell, okay?

Don't tell Mom and Dad.

Don't tell 'em that I threw a big rock at my crappy bike 'cause I didn't want it anymore. Don't tell them that I rode it real fast right at the garage wall only to jump off at the last minute and—boom—crashed it into the concrete wall.

And don't tell Mom and Dad that I went down the hill to Chuckie's real fast. Really, really fast and slammed on the brakes as hard as I could so that I could skid and wear out the tires.

It's a stupid old bike. Chuckie's bike has five speeds. It's really neat. He has handbrakes, not a stupid coaster brake.

Don't tell Mom and Dad, but I want a Schwinn for my birthday. I'm gonna be nine and I deserve to have a good bike. I'll take really good care of it and everything.

I promise.

Guess what?

Mom and Dad got me a brand new Schwinn for my birthday!

It's the neatest bike in the world!

Dad's Room

Dad's beating me in chess again.

He's awake.

He's in his pajamas, but he's wide-awake and he's beating me fair and square.

I can tell 'cause he's got a bunch of pawns, two rooks, two bishops, his queen, and his king left on the board.

I haven't got anything but my king and a couple of pawns. He took everything else. Not right away, but a little bit at a time. He always does.

"Now, pay attention, Johnny," he says.

He says that a lot, but I can't pay any more attention even if he turns off the TV and I'm not watching cartoons with him on Saturday morning in his bedroom. He's got *The Flintstones* on his black and white Admiral TV. I like *The Flintstones*: Wilma Flintstone is pretty! When I grow up, I'm gonna marry her!

We're playin' chess and he's beating me. Again.

"Do I have to play?" I ask. I always ask him that, 'specially when he's beating me. There's so much to watch. I get confused by all the pieces and everything. It's too hard to concentrate, even when he tells me to.

"Yes, you do!" He says.

"Why? Why do I have to play chess? You always beat me."

He lights a cigarette and looks at me.

"It'll make you a man," he says.

I don't say anything 'cause he keeps beating me with all his pawns, all of his rooks, and all of his bishops. And, especially with his queen.

He beats me all the time with his queen.

There's nothing I can do about it.

See, the queen can move any way you want: she can go diagonally, backwards, forwards, sideways. Only thing, she can't jump like a knight.

Knights can jump.

They do it funny, up-one-two-three.

Then sideways one space.

Sideways either way.

Or, you can make a knight jump one forward or backward.

Then sideways either way, one-two-three.

It's hard to remember how they move.

Dad always beats me. Sometimes, he has all his pieces on the board. Sometimes, I get a few of them before he beats me. Sometimes, he gets real excited just before he beats me 'cause he does something that I didn't even know he could!

"Did you see what I did?" he asks just before he gets me with a rook. "That's called 'checkmate,' because you can't protect the king. You have to protect the king," he says.

I always try to protect my king, but it's hard 'cause all the pieces move funny and I can't do much about it. Sometimes, if *Huntley and Brinkley* is on the TV, I can guess what Dad's gonna do with his pieces. But, I never know what to do about it anyhow 'cause once I escape in the nick of time, he has somethin' else up his bathrobe sleeve and he gets some more of my pieces!

Guess what? Dad only plays chess with me! He won't play with the girls or the twins. He doesn't even play chess with Mom. Mom says that's okay 'cause Dad is teachin' me somethin' I'll use for the rest of my life.

I don't know what rooks and bishops and knights have to do with the rest of my life, but I don't care. He doesn't get out of bed much anymore and sleeps most all of the day. I'm glad he plays with me. He doesn't play with the other kids.

It's neat, he gets to stay home all day and take naps!

Mom is always hushing at us kids to be quiet so we don't wake him up. Mom gives him some morphine so he can sleep all day until the afternoon.

When he wakes up, we play chess for hours.

Little League

See, this is how it works; Chuckie's Dad is the coach. He puts me in the game for the late innings.

"You're just learning," he says.

I get to sit on the bench, pass out sodas, and cheer for my team!

We're the Maroons. That's the color of our shirts and hats. I always wear mine, even to practice. That's the only time I get to play catch.

Dad is sleeping all the time so he can't play catch.

My brothers can't throw. 'Sides, they're still just kids.

At practice, I help Chuckie work on his throwing and catching.

At games, I cheer when he has a hit.

I always cheer for my team!

When I bat, I always strike out 'cause I swing at every pitch, but that's okay because baseball is so much fun!

At games, all the families come to watch, but Mom has to stay home with Dad until he feels better.

Listen, one day I asked Mom about it while we were eating spaghetti and meatballs for dinner.

"Why can't you guys come to a game?"

"I have to make sure Dad's comfortable," Mom said. "That's why you ride in with Chuckie. We have to make sure Daddy's okay."

"Is he gonna sleep forever?"

Mom wiped her eyes and went to the sink. She coughed a few times, then sat down and lit a cigarette.

"Daddy will be better soon."

"Before the season ends? I bet he can really throw the ball!"

His bedroom door opened. We all look there until Dad approached. His hair was all messed up and his pajama pants were pulled up way too tight.

Mom stood up and helped him to the table.

"Dad, you have pillow face," Faith said. Faith is funny, but she's always so quiet like she's watchin' everything around her.

Us kids laughed and Dad smiled as he lit a cigarette. Dad wiped his face, but in slow motion 'cause he was really, really tired. His breath smelled funny and he slumped forward like he was goin' play dead on the table. Mom rubbed his back and helped him sit up. He mumbled something and his head went up and back down.

"Dad, can we play catch… sometime?"

Dad inhaled his cigarette. It took awhile for him to pull the smoke away from the lit end to his mouth, but we all watched him. Only Baby Rose kept eating, but she didn't know any better.

"Dad?"

Mom sat next to Dad, leaning against him.

"Honey, Daddy's very tired."

Dad raised his head, then coughed and wheezed. The ash end of his cigarette fell onto the table, but Mom crushed it before anything caught on fire.

"In... a... little... bit," Dad said.

"After dinner? I'm almost done and I don't have practice tonight. We could play. I don't have any homework."

Dad shook his head as Mom ran her fingers through his hair.

"How about this weekend?"

"We'll... see..., son."

Dad sniffled and his eyes watered. He lurched forward in his chair and banged into the table. Slowly, he stood up. Us kids watched him as he coughed and stumbled to the hall. Mom led him down the hallway and back to his room.

"Dad's gonna play catch with me this weekend."

Maria and Faith looked at each other, then watched the end as the hall as Dad's coughing faded behind his bedroom door.

Dad didn't play catch that weekend.

A couple weeks later, the ambulance men came for him in the afternoon. They made lots of noise, but Dad didn't notice 'cause he was fast asleep the whole time. We could even hear him snoring.

"You play with the twins in your room," Mom told me when the ambulance pulled up.

The twins and me played trains while the ambulance men got Dad onto a stretcher and took him. Took him to the V.A. Hospital so that he won't have to have morphine naps anymore.

Mom was real quiet when they left. It was really strange because they didn't put on the siren. I never saw an ambulance go somewhere with its siren turned off 'specially when someone was ridin' in the back.

Easter Dinner

Good news!

The doctors said Dad can go with us for Easter Dinner!

Mom and me get the Country Sedan Ranch Wagon 500 all clean and ready. I empty all the papers and trash into plastic bags and sweep out all the dirt.

"Now, get your suit on," she says when we're done. She grabs the Ansco and lots of film. She's got rolls and rolls of the stuff. And extra flashbulbs.

The girls get on all their Easter dresses 'cause it's like we're gonna be in an Easter parade! The twins and I are running around like Duke and Brutus chasing our own tails on the living room floor!

"You boys pose for a picture!"

We stand up and adjust our clip-on ties. I stand between the twins, goofing off.

"Now just the twins."

I step back.

Mom looks down at the viewfinder. Maria and Faith come down the hallway behind Mom. They sure look wow-whee pretty! They wear pretty dresses and barrettes in their hair. They smile real pretty and look at Mom.

"Okay, the Little Ones," Mom says as she holds the burnt flashbulb in her fingertips.

I take it from her and ouchy-ouchy it all the way to the garbage can.

Rose and the twins pose in front of the other Admiral TV, Mom adjusting the flash so the light doesn't reflect in the screen.

"Now, the Biggies," she says, blowing on the bulb and putting it on the kitchen table.

Me and Maria and Faith stand together. They always put me in the front 'cause I'm so short, but it doesn't matter.

When Dad gets to the house, he's wearing his suit and a tie! He looks very handsome and smiles! Nobody knows how he got there because all of a sudden, he's just standing on the front lawn, smiling when we see him through the living room window!

He said a friend dropped him off.

Mom takes more pictures.

Us kids stand in front of Dad and around him. He's so tall, he stands at least a foot taller than Faith and Maria! Mom takes pictures of us men, then Dad takes pictures of the ladies while the twins and me stand at ease on the lawn in our suits!

Then Mom takes a picture of Dad and he takes a picture of her. For some reason, she can't make a pretty smile.

We all watch Mom pull the Ford out of the garage, us kids giving her directions as Dad watches. It takes Mom forever to pull out the car and she just about hits the side! Dad is just smiling 'cause he's got to think it's funny as he nods his head! He doesn't even get angry anymore since he's been at the hospital!

And I'm really, really excited 'cause Daddy's home and we're goin' to Easter Dinner and we're all dressed up and everything looks really nice!

We're all dressed in our Easter clothes and everything 'cause the V.A. Hospital doctor said Dad could have Easter dinner with us and we're gonna eat the best dinner in the whole wide world!

We never go out and we're quite a sight!

Last night, Mom said we all had to behave 'cause Daddy could only visit for Easter, then had to get right back to the hospital.

"I'll control my guinea temper, Mom," I promised her. "I promise." Mom calls it that 'cause sometimes I just get really, really mad 'bout things. I get mad and I say mean things and break my toys and hit myself really, really hard. She says it's my guinea temper 'cause I'm Italian and if I don't control it I'm gonna end up in jail someday.

I don't have any guinea temper today. I don't even get mad when Warren steps on my pants. Wasn't his fault: he wanted to get into the car before me 'cause he's excited just like me about Dad and everything about Easter!

Dad waits until we're all in the wagon, then he climbs in. For some reason, it takes him forever to get in the car. He bends funny and makes odd noises because he's all doubled over. Us kids behave perfectly and he finally gets in.

He and Mom sit in the front seat.

"It's really weird: Mom's driving," I say.

Me and the twins laugh so hard 'cause it's so funny seeing Dad in the passenger seat!

The girls sit in the second seat and us boys are in the back.

We go to a real nice restaurant, The Red Shingle. There, I eat chicken. The Little Ones get real cool placemats that make rabbit masks. It's a little kid thing, so I don't get any, but Mark lets me play with his.

Dad doesn't eat much and goes to the bathroom a lot.

"His stomach isn't used to this good food," Mom says.

I forgot to tell you that Mom looks beautiful. Mom is really beautiful! For the first time in a long time, she's wearing make-up and a very beautiful dress! She's so beautiful that she could be Miss America or something! Not only that, she has a scarf that matches her dress and she wears rosy red lipstick!

Dad sits next to her in the booth, just hugging her 'cause he loves her so much!

She's so beautiful that it makes me embarrassed and feel stupid. Guess it's 'cause I love her and Dad so much and she's so happy because we're all dressed up really nice and eating dinner at a real restaurant for a change!

Outside The Red Shingle on Route 46, Dad has us all stand for more pictures. It's like we're Hollywood stars and everybody else just looks at us because we're so beautiful! Dad takes pictures of Mom and the girls, us kids and Mom, then the Biggies, the Little Ones, and the boys.

Mom drives real well. Dad doesn't get upset, not even when she almost runs a stop sign just before Jane's Chapel Road.

Dad's friend is waiting at the house in a car.

"The man from the V.A. is here," Dad says. We all get out of the car and stand on the front yard.

The man is really old, but nice. He smiles at Dad and shakes his hand. Us kids all give Dad a big, big hug. The girls get to give him a kiss and I shake his hand 'cause Dad says boys aren't supposed to kiss boys. Mom gives him a really big hug and a kiss.

We all wave to Dad when he gets into the car. It's really tough for him and he starts coughin' again. The old man helps by putting his hand on Dad's back.

We watch the car as the man slowly drives down the hill past Chuckie's house and takes Dad back to the V.A. Hospital 'cause Easter is all over.

I can hardly wait until Memorial Day!

G.I. Joe

Look, I figured it all out. Even woke up early. As soon as I heard Mom in the kitchen, I got my card and ran out. Got out there even before Faith and Maria, but I heard them up late last night. I knew they wouldn't be up early.

Uncle Lenny is asleep in the living room; I can't believe it! He's sleeping in his T-shirt and dress pants on a chair. Aunt Winnie sleeps on the sofa, her hair all messed up.

Of all the relatives, I like them the best. Lenny was in the war. He fought under Patton. He's bald on the top of his head and he's funny. He's really funny, but he always makes his point without yelling or swearing. And, he's really smart.

And Winnie is nice. She's funny, too.

Mom is at the sink, filling the percolator. I like the way it fills the house with Maxwell House coffee smell. I used to think that every house smelled that way, but Chuckie told me that his house smelled like Eight O' Clock coffee.

Mom doesn't see me at first. I stand there and look at her. She is all dolled-up in curlers and make-up. She smells Avon pretty too.

70

"Happy Mother's Day," I say, giving her the construction paper card I made in Mrs. Baty's class on Friday. I hid it in my lunch box so Mom wouldn't see it, then snuck it out and put it in *Black Beauty*.

Kept it top secret. I didn't even tell the twins, which was kinda tough.

Mrs. Baty made us spell *M-O-T-H-E-R* using each letter for a word to say something we really liked about Mom. I smile as Mom takes the card. She reads it really fast, flipping through it and smiling without even putting down the percolator.

"Mom, why are the relatives here?"

She nods her head. "They're all coming for a visit today," she says. "Thank you for this card. It's so sweet. You're Mommy's little man."

She gives me a big kiss and a hug 'cause I got my card to her first and she really loves me.

Uncle Jessie and Aunt Marion show up after breakfast. Uncle Jessie is real young. Marion is younger than Mom, but she looks like her 'cause she has long black hair and tans real easily.

By the time Jesse and Marion show up, Uncle Lenny is wearing a clean shirt and Aunt Winnie has fixed her hair.

"Uncle Jessie isn't really our uncle," Maria tells me when I'm sitting on the porch playing with my G.I. Joe. She plays with her Barbies. G.I. Joe is visiting Barbie to ask her if she wants to take a Jeep ride in the jungle.

"He's Aunt Marion's *boyfriend*," Maria says.

"What happened to Uncle Joel?"

"Marion divorced him."

Uncle Jimmy shows up with Aunt Palma. Jimmy is old. He's going bald too, but he still has some gray hair.

Maria and me stand up 'cause we don't want Palma to pinch our cheeks, but she does anyway. She stands at the car and makes herself smile funny, then hugs us. Usually, we all hide 'cause we don't like her to pinch our cheeks.

Palma is big and fat and likes to cook. "You're too thin," she always says when she sees Mom, grabbing at her arm and telling her, "You look like skin and bones."

She doesn't say that today. She looks at us and says nothing but, "May God be with you poor kids."

Now, we Highams ain't very religious. We say our In-The-Name-of-The-Father-and-of-The-Son-and-The-Holy-Ghost-Grace at dinner just like we're supposed to and we've all been baptized, but Dad and Mom don't make us go to church like Chuckie's parents make him and Cindy.

Mom comes out to greet Jimmy and Palma. They give each other big hugs. That's when I notice Mom is dressed wrong: she's wearing a really nice dress, high heels, and make-up. I push my Jeep with G.I. Joe and Barbie across the grass to Jimmy's Chevelle.

"Mom, are you going to Church?"

Mom just looks at me. Jimmy and Palma wait for her to say something. Mom looks back at them, then notices G.I. Joe and Barbie.

"You kids go play," she says.

My cousin Martin gave me G.I. Joe: Joe has a broken-off leg. He gave me all his weapons and uniforms, but I couldn't find the missing leg. Most the time, no one can tell 'cause I take one of his boots and use a rubber band to fix it to the bottom of his pants. Works real well like that 'cause he looks perfect. I'm the only one who knows that he's broken.

"Mom, are we goin' to church?"

"No, John," Mom says, "Mommy is visiting Daddy at the hospital. Your relatives are gonna babysit."

"Can I go with you?"

"No, maybe another day."

Palma and Jimmy give Mom the evil eye, but she ignores it and goes inside with them.

"You go play," Mom says before she closes the door behind her.

Uncle Jessie takes a Frisbee out of his Volkswagen station wagon.

Mike and Margie show up. Mike is mean: he swears more than Dad. He's tall and going bald just like Lenny.

Aunt Margie wears make-up and is always dressed in real nice clothes.

Our lawn looks like a reunion.

Mark, Warren, and me are runnin' all over the front lawn, trying to catch the Frisbee. For being just a boyfriend, Jessie can really throw that thing. He gets it to do all sorts of tricks, making it fly backwards, forwards, and over our heads. I put G.I. Joe and Barbie on the porch. They can talk while me and the boys play.

We play forever!

Jessie can throw it all sorts of ways, making it come right back to him, bouncing off the road, and curving it way over the house and coming right at me. At the last minute I jump way, way, way up in the air and catch it!

"John, get the twins," Uncle Mike yells.

Uncle Mike is stupid. Dad says that Mike beats Margie and drinks all the time. Dad says Uncle Mike is a mean coward. Dad used to yell all the time, but he never hits Mom. He only spanks us kids when we're really bad.

When Mike yells, us three boys just stand on the grass, looking at him. We're all sweaty and thirsty, but no one noticed any of that stuff until we stopped.

"What?"

"C'mon, your mother wants you."

"We're playing Frisbee."

Uncle Mike inhales on his cigarette.

"There's plenty of time for that later. She wants to talk to you now. Get inside the house."

We get inside pretty fast because Uncle Mike sounds mean. Once, he and Dad got into a big argument in Stanhope when they were drinking beers. I thought Dad was gonna punch him. Only thing, they were laughing out loud just a minute later. I never know about Uncle Mike.

Never know about him at all.

Inside the house, everyone is quiet when me and the boys come in. We're all sweaty and thirsty from running around like Crudleys'. The relatives are sitting around, drinking coffee and smoking cigarettes.

"Where's Mom?"

Uncle Mike points down the hallway to Mom and Dad's room.

"She said you three should go to your room. She's talking to the girls."

Marion sits with Winnie on the sofa. They're quiet. Lenny, Jimmy, and Mike sit at the kitchen table. It's weird seeing them here 'cause the relatives never visit us. Dad doesn't like 'em.

I clean up by wiping my face on my shirt when I go to my room. Can't figure out what I did wrong. We were just playin' Frisbee on the front lawn, for cryin' out loud!

Me and the twins wait in the room. I sit on my bed. Mark tries to sit next to me, but I chase him away.

"You got your own bed," I tell him.

"I'll sit with Warren."

"Maybe you should."

Mom comes in. She has black circles around her eyes that she wipes with a wad of toilet tissue. The black circles make her face look sad, real sad.

"I'm not visiting your father," she says. "Last night, the hospital called and said that he died."

We sit there for a minute, me and the twins looking at each other. We rub our eyes with our dirty hands.

"He's never gonna play catch with me?" I ask.

"He was a very sick man, John. He had terminal cancer." Mom wipes her eyes.

"I have to go to the hospital and make arrangements for the funeral," she says. "You're the man of the house now, John."

Mom gives us all big hugs and kisses, but it doesn't help 'cause none of us boys can stop crying. All I'm thinkin' is that Dad isn't ever going to play chess with me again.

Or play ball, or even G.I. Joe.

Dad isn't gonna see me play baseball next year like he promised.

We all wipe and rub our eyes.

My nose starts running.

"I love you kids so much," Mom whispers as we hug her.

"We know," I say.

Mom gives us each another bunch of hugs and kisses. Us boys sniffle, snort, and wipe our faces on our shirts.

When I open my door, I see Maria and Faith in the hallway. They stand near their door, looking down and rubbing their eyes. Baby Rose stands between them holding her Raggedy Anne.

"Did Mom tell you?" I ask.

"Yeah," Faith says.

Us kids cry for the rest of the day 'cause there isn't much else to do or even think about. Aunt Marion tries to play chess with me but I can only think about all the times I played with Dad, so I can't even play that well. I stay polite, then go out on the porch and push G.I. Joe's Jeep back and forth.

"You can play with my Barbies if you want," Maria says.

"Naw."

"G.I. Joe doesn't want to talk to anyone. He just wants to sit in his buggy."

Ranch Wagon 500

"Where are we?" Faith asks as she sits up.

"You've got seat face," I say.

Her light brown hair flies around as she rubs her jaw: one cheek has the pattern from the vinyl upholstery.

My oldest sister looks around the car. She sits in the middle seat, a box of colored pencils and a small sketchpad sticking out of her purse. Baby Rose sits next to her: she holds her Raggedy Anne.

Faith is a really good artist. I like her drawings.

Mom is in front, her head barely above the steering wheel. Maria is the navigator, her new maps spread across the dashboard.

Mark and Warren are in the rear seat right behind me. The twins play with Hot Wheels. I'm in the back with them, sitting on blankets and pillows next to the brand new styrofoam ice chest and right above the gas tank.

It scares me: I'm always afraid the gas tank is gonna blow up and burn me to death, but I don't tell anyone that 'cause Mom says I'm The Man of the House now and I have to be brave.

"You're going too fast," Faith yells, putting her head down as another Mack truck rips past us on Interstate 80. "We're gonna die."

"Only doing forty-five," Mom says. She sits with a green bolster behind her 'cause otherwise she can't reach the pedals or the steering wheel. If I move just right, I can see her face and necklace in the rearview mirror.

Warren rolls his Hot Wheels Red Baron Coupe near my feet.

"It snowed on the mountain," he says as he pushes it on the blanket.

I didn't bring my Hot Wheels. They're in the moving van with all my suits and other stuff. I don't play in the car anymore. I'm watching the moving vans right behind our car: I'm the lookout.

Mom changes lanes, but not really: she's having trouble keeping the wagon on the road while she turns on the radio. The moving vans slow down. Mom gets the channel before Faith can get upset again.

On the radio, Tom Jones sings about falling in love.

"Mom, can we listen to somethin' besides morgue music?" I ask.

Faith giggles and looks over the seat and gives me a look. A mean one, like the one she had when she caught me using her Noxzema.

"Son, why'd you say that?" Mom pushes up in her seat and looks over her sunglasses so I can see her eyes. Faith might reach over the middle seat and swat me. She never bullies me or anything, but she's not afraid to speak up.

"'Cause they play it in morgues to keep everyone dead," I say.

Faith laughs, sitting up.

Dad bought the wagon last year. Before Dad got terminal really bad, he taught Mom to drive. Maria said he also taught Mom to use a checkbook. Mom and Dad took us all down to Knechel Ford in Hackettstown and he bought the shiny wagon right off the showroom floor. We all stood around it except Dad: he leaned over the salesman's desk and made funny faces as he wrote a deposit check.

"Why is it blue?" Rose asked as she ran her finger over the nameplate.

Mom gave her a big hug. "Navy blue, Baby Girl, 'cause Daddy was in the Navy."

Faith sketched when Dad drove, even when he took us all the way to the Poconos so we could look at a farm. On the way back, he leaned over the wheel as Mom hugged him. I know 'cause I watched after everyone else fell asleep. Me and Dad were the only ones awake.

"Your father always drove like that," Mom said when I asked her about it.

When Dad died, Mom paid off the car with some of the insurance money.

Mom doesn't like going fast or passing.

"Forty-five is fast enough," she says all the time.

"Are we there yet?" Baby Rose says every once in awhile.

We drive way past the Poconos. The air is hot and everyone stays quiet for a long time. Pennsylvania stays countryside for miles of Interstate 80.

"Go there," Maria says hours later.

"Where is 'there'?" Mom yells, making the car swerve when she looks at Maria.

"We're gonna' die," Faith screams.

Maria points at a ramp without looking up.

"Take that exit," she yells.

Maria used to yell a lot. One time, she got Dad so mad that he had to flip over the dinner table just to quiet her down. Me and Mom picked up the mess 'cause Baby Rose cried so hard Faith had to take her for a walk.

Mom takes the exit and traffic bunches up behind us.

"Merging is terrific," Mark says, making fun of the sign.

Baby Rose drops her doll on the floor and cries. I lean too far over, falling on Faith.

"Mom, John's in my seat."

"Just getting Raggedy Anne. Baby Rose dropped it."

Mom turns around, making our car swerve onto the shoulder. Other cars are honking as she slams on the brakes and makes the car skid.

"Mom, you can't stop here," I yell.

"I'll stop anywhere I damn well please! Get back in your seat!"

The moving vans stop. A big fat mover with a cigar in his mouth gets out and runs along the shoulder as cars honk and speed around him.

"I want a sandwich," Maria says.

Mom turns off Dean Martin: he's singing about love. "You kids have to stick together," she says, taking her cigarette from her mouth. "Stop fighting right now." She hollers in Italian and nobody says anything.

Mom turns, ready to swat. I jump back to my blankets. She swings so hard that her necklace tosses around on her neck. She's got Dad's wedding band on it.

"Stay back there," she yells, tucking in the necklace and playing with the wedding ring.

"I will."

"Where's my sandwich?" Maria asks.

"John, feed your sister."

"Yes, Ma'am."

Mom sticks her head out the window at the mover.

"My children need to eat," she says. "You'll have to wait."

"Lady, we're on an entrance ramp," the mover says.

"My children need to eat and I know where we are."

He runs back to the truck.

I grab Maria's egg salad sandwich from the cooler, then hand out lunches with Cokes. We eat as cars honk, the drivers making faces at Mom. She doesn't care 'cause she's looking out the windshield and smoking Pall Malls like Dad used to.

Maria puts on *Sugar, Sugar* from The Archie's. Maria and Faith sing along. I know the words, but hum to myself.

I like music. I like the way it makes me feel. Sometimes, I can think of a story when a song plays. I can imagine the song playing in my head and the story that I put with it but I don't tell anyone any of that 'cause it's just too stupid and embarrassing.

I don't want anyone to pick on me about it. So, I just get quiet and think of it to myself so I don't get too excited.

Mom finally gets the car going after everyone passes their garbage to me and I put all of it into the ice chest.

Mark forces out some burps and laughs.

"I heard that: what do you say?" Mom asks.

"Excuse me."

"We almost there?" Baby Rose asks. She doesn't want her Coke, so I drink it. Mom never lets us drink soda, but this is a special occasion.

"Yeah, when are we gonna get there?" Faith asks. She's slipping back down in the seat. Maria fumbles with the map, but she's looking at the wrong one. I can tell all the way from the back seat.

"Maria, we left Jersey three hours ago."

"I know that," Maria says. "I'm looking for the interstate."

"It's right there, Maria Marshmellow," Mark yells, pointing out the window.

Even Warren laughs.

"That's not eye-eighty," Maria says. "It's fifteen. We're headed north."

Faith burrows her head into the seat. "How much longer?"

Mark laughs. "Way Mom drives," he says, "I figure I'll be twelve by the time we get there!"

Us kids laugh 'cause Mark's a funnyman right now.

Mom floors it, making me fall onto the twins. We hear dirt being kicked up by the rear wheels. The moving vans wait for traffic to clear on the ramp before racing to catch us.

The car stays quiet for a few miles. Maria folds her map, then says, "Yeah, it's another hour once we get on fourteen. Stay right on fifteen until Trout Run."

Around Williamsport, Pennsylvania changes into a bunch of twisty hills so the builders slapped highways over them. And, there's tractors everywhere. We get stuck in a few long lines when they hog the road. The twins take off their sneakers and Faith sits up.

"You could draw that," I say, pointing to the big hills.

"Don't feel like drawing."

I give the Little Ones their pillows, but it's too hot for the blanket.

It takes hours to go the sixty miles from Williamsport to Troy. We're almost to the New York state line. I discover a train track outside the window. Faith, Baby Rose, and the twins are asleep. The breeze is hot and the late afternoon sun nails us.

I watch Mom drive.

There isn't much to Fassett. The village has a church, a deserted gas station, a bunch of trailers, and old houses. At the corner of Route Fourteen and Roaring Run Road is Owen's Rancho Country Store. It looks like a house with a big sign.

Faith wakes up when Mom leads the moving vans uphill toward our house.

We drive for some more miles. Me and my sister watch our new neighborhood. We pass trailers and houses being fixed up. There are rusting trucks and cars on some front yards. Dogs run out into the road, barking so close to the car that Mom slows down. People sitting on rickety lawn furniture stare as we pass their old trailers.

We cut around a bunch of curves. Mom goes real slow as we enter the hollow. Faith makes herself sit up straight and grabs a hairbrush. She taps Baby Rose. I get the twins going and help them tie their shoes. Mom slows way down as we come out of the woods and we see the house.

Our house!

It's just like in the real estate catalog! It's a lovely brick two-story ranch with an attached garage and two beautiful flagstone fireplaces! It's got three bedrooms, one bath, a paneled den, and an attached garage all sitting on a quarter-acre of lawn and sixteen acres of woods!

80

It could be from Jersey. Only thing, the nearest neighbor is a half-mile away! Can't see them 'cause they're on the other side of the hills!

"We're home," Mom says.

Faith puts her hairbrush back in her purse, ignoring her seat face.

Roaring Run Road

"John, this is your room," Mom says as she stands with Maria, Faith and me in the hallway outside the door to the room.

My room!

All mine. No more twins bugging me all the time!

It's cool 'cause it's on the corner, so I have one window that faces north and one that faces west. I can look at the back yard or the creek across a dirt road!

"No fair, the rest of us have to share a room," Maria says.

"He's The Man of the House. He needs his own room."

The Little Ones' room is across the hall from mine. Faith and Maria have their room down the hall from me.

Us Biggies and Mom got all new furniture! Rose is using her crib, but with the sides pulled down. The Little Ones got a new dresser, but they still have their bunk bed. Mom figured it all out.

Our brand new house sits back from the intersection of Roaring Run Road and Kinney Road. It's on the edge of the woods.

Our woods!

Mom says we own sixteen acres.

We never owned this much land in our entire lives!

Roaring Run is paved.

Kinney is dirt.

If you go on Kinney, it takes you along our property. Between Kinney and the woods is our strip of flagstone. Actually, the flagstones start just after the brook, which is between our back yard and our woods. That rock strip is about a hundred feet wide from the road to the woods.

Across Kinney and Roaring Run are creeks.

We live in a hollow! That means the hills surround us and we don't see our neighbors Dale English to the east and Bobby English to the west. We see their names on the mailboxes when Mom was driving around.

Our new house is brick.

It's two stories because part of the front yard slopes down like a giant *U* so that the basement door is just like anybody's front door. There are picture windows downstairs on that side of the house, but the rest of those windows are tiny basement ones.

Down in the basement is a tongue-and-groove paneled den and a flagstone fireplace!

There's another flagstone fireplace upstairs in the living room! That's got a cool view: not only does it look out over the front yard, but it's high enough up to give us a great view of the opposite hillside where the power lines cut across!

Guess what? Our new house has three bedrooms and one bathroom!

Mom says that's okay, because she's gonna take the inheritance money and pay a contractor to build two more bedrooms and another bathroom in the basement! There's enough room down there to have a second living room even after all that construction is done! It'll be neat, 'cause me and the twins will have our own part of the house! Mom and the girls will have the upstairs to themselves!

Right now, Mom tells the movers to set up her bed and dresser in what will become the dining room. It's only temporary until the renovation is over, then she'll take my room.

I get my own room!

I even get my own TV set; the Admiral that was in Mom and Dad's room in Oxford!

The twins' room is cool 'cause it has two doors; one goes to the kitchen and the other goes to the hall right across from my room!

Like I said, my room is on the corner.

I can look out at the backyard or can see the intersection of Roaring Run and Kinney! I haven't had my own room since Stanhope!

I get a brand new big bed, a dresser with a mirror, and a night table! And, there's plenty of space for me to play with my trains!

And, it's my room, so if I don't want anyone in here, I can tell 'em to get out—and close the door!

The dining room table fits into the kitchen. All that's temporary. Mom's gonna have wall-to-wall carpeting put in real soon, then have the basement all changed like I just said.

Mom bought all new stuff for the kitchen: an electric stove where she can cook, a side-by-side refrigerator just like the ones you see on *Let's Make a Deal*, a new Broyhill Tavern Pine table with matching chairs so we can eat together, and a dishwasher so she doesn't have to wash dishes anymore.

She even bought a brand new washer and dryer for downstairs!

She got a new sofa, a matching chair and a coffee table, and a Lazy-Boy recliner that has a footrest that goes up; we never even had a recliner before!

Our house looks like a furniture showroom!

It's beautiful outside, too!

When we stand on the lawn, we see people driving past slowly as the movers unload the truck. Us kids help out, but we don't carry the new stuff; we don't want to drop it by accident. The men take the new things out of their boxes on our front yard before bringing in all the brand new stuff!

Everything is shiny!

Everything is new!

It's gonna be even more beautiful inside with all these nice things in our new home!

The people look at us and drive by real slow in their Crudley cars and trucks. The people nod and smile. I bet they never saw so many new things in their lives!

Inside our house, the movers set up Mom's bed, dresser, and night table. She can see the living room and kitchen when she sits in bed.

And guess what?

She also bought a brand new Singer sewing machine that she told the movers to put in her bedroom!

Mom bought lots of two-foot tall plaster statues of half-naked ladies holding candy dishes and flowerpots! They go on the living table and the matching end tables!

She even bought a two-foot high plaster statue of a man and a woman standing next to each other! She says it's called, "The Lovers." She put that right on top of the Magnavox in the living room.

She bought all sorts of figurines that she put on the flagstone shelves near the fireplace. All the new lamps have plastic on their lampshades, but the movers leave them on.

"It makes them easier to dust," Mom says.

Everything is new. And very nice. We never ever had any new things before!

The Magnavox

It sits in front of the picture window in the living room, centered. Mom put "The Lovers" on top of it. Take a look at the controls that are hidden underneath one of the sliding pecan-finished panels. It's like a James Bond thing: Mom bought a brand new Magnavox that has a color television, an AM/FM radio, a phonograph, and could have an 8-track player.

It's not a TV, it's called an Entertainment Center, but Mom calls it "The Magnavox."

Only thing, Mom doesn't like 8-tracks.

Look at it—it's got a twenty-seven inch *color* screen and it's got a pecan finish! It's got sliding front doors with handles so that when you're not watching TV, you can cover the screen and it's just another beautiful piece of furniture. It's as tall as my waist and it took three movers to get it inside!

The speakers are bigger than my head!

Guess what? Mom bought a Channel Master that turns the antenna on the roof. You know what? We can still watch the same shows we did when we lived in New Jersey!

We can watch WOR and WPIX and WABC and WCBS and WNBC out of New York City! And, we live hundreds of miles away from there! We can also watch TV stations from Elmira and Binghamton just by turning the dial and adjusting the Channel Master!

Mom likes to listen to music. She bought a whole bunch of records just before we moved here. She likes that mushy stuff like Tom Jones, Englebert Humperdink, and Glen Campbell. She sits on her bed reading the latest issue of *Cosmopolitan,* smoking her cigarette, and listening to that mushy music.

Or worse, she gets really happy when she hears it and wants to dance.

"Dance, Johnny," she says, coming into my room when she has one of her songs playing. It doesn't matter if I'm watching WBNG on my TV and playing with my brand new Lego blocks. She's really happy and she really wants to dance.

"Mom, it's embarrassing."

She takes my hand and I go with her. Not 'cause I want to, but 'cause she really wants to. She's got a big smile as I go down the hall into the living room.

"Follow my lead," she says. "This is a simple box step."

We make our way around the Lazy Boy and the matching coffee table. The largest space is right in front of the fireplace, not too far from her bed.

"Johnny, you lead," she says.

I'm laughin' 'cause I feel kinda funny. Everyone is watching. My brothers and sisters are sitting on the sofa and the recliner as I try the stupid box step.

It's stupid. Really stupid.

"Johnny's blushing," Maria says.

"He's doing fine," Mom says. Mom leans really close to me and whispers, "You're becoming quite a young man. Your father is proud of you."

She gets real sad for a moment, then gets really happy again. I go along with it even though I hate dancing.

When the song ends, everyone claps and Mom goes to the Magnavox. She adjusts it so that the tone arm moves back to that mushy Tom Jones song. It can play the same mushy song forever.

"Do I have to?"

"Johnny, you lead," she says.

Mom holds me tight as I try to make boxed steps with her in front of the fireplace. She keeps whispering stuff about Dad.

It makes her sad and happy over and over again.

1970

Mom's Chair

I don't know why Frank English always visits Mom. He's here when we get home from school. He and Mom are sitting at the kitchen table, just looking at each other. And, he's sitting in Mom's chair!

It's a nice chair: It's got wooden arms and everything. It's called a Captain's Chair and Frank sits in it like it's his! For instance, if he's eating dinner and sitting in Mom's chair, he just smiles and eats without saying much.

And Mom? Mom runs around like a chicken with her head cut off, getting him everything.

"He's a coot," Maria says behind his back.

"He is not. Don't talk like that," Mom says. "Show a little respect."

I don't think he wants to be our dad. I mean, he takes us on trips to Watkins Glen and stuff like that, but that's 'cause there's nothin' else for him to do. He's got people to run his farm for him. 'Sides, Mom and him never hold hands or nothin' like that. Never seen him even hug her or shake her hand.

"They're just friends," I tell Maria. Us Biggies are sittin' in my room watching *Mike Douglas* and playin' Lego blocks one afternoon just before dinner. Max is busy tearing apart the paneling in the downstairs den. Mom hired him to renovate the basement. The noise is so bad I have to turn up the sound on the Admiral. He's almost done for the day, so it'll be quiet in just a little bit.

"Coot comin' over?" Maria asks like she's Cora Mae. You know, Maria's talkin' like she's never been out of Fassett for her entire life. Cora Mae runs The Rancho that's at the end of the road on Route 14. "He's one fine piece o' man there, that Coot!"

Faith is sittin' on the bed, so she laughs about it. It's kinda funny 'cause Maria gets going with it. This is what the girls do when they're feeling good: they make fun of Cora Mae and Coot. They'd never act that way in front of them 'cause Mom says we have to have manners and be nice to people.

These people up here are different: they're all related to each other.

And, all the people up here have light skin like Faith and Warren. They have Dad's skin coloring. Warren looks like Dad. One time, I played a trick on him; I got an old picture of Dad when he was a boy wearing a suit. I showed it to Warren.

"Where'd you get that neat suit?" I asked him.

And Warren just looked and looked at the picture 'cause he didn't know it was Dad. Instead he just looked and looked at it!

Anyways, Faith's making fun of Cora Mae. She says, "Frank's finer than my Petie, don't cha' know?"

Faith does a really good Cora Mae impersonation. Maria's isn't bad, but Faith can say things using Cora's raspy voice.

This is what us Biggies like to do: sit in my room, watch *Mike Douglas* and make fun of Cora Mae. Maria keeps talkin' 'cause she's picking on Frank. Only thing, Mom better not hear us, 'cause she'll get mad at Maria and yell at her, especially when Maria calls him Coot.

Maria laughs at Faith's pretendin' to be Cora Mae. She takes a handful of Lego blocks and builds a little box.

"I'm makin' me a little dish for my dog Pookie and my man Pete," she says. "Petie, ya' git over here to the store and git your dinner 'fore Pookie eats it!"

"Petie, ya' ain't that fine hunk of man like Frank is!" Faith says in her Cora Mae voice. "That there widower is quite a catch!"

I just laugh and laugh as I build a Lego battleship.

Anyways, about a week ago, Frank took us all to Watkins Glen and we're looking off the stone pathway at the top of the gorge, trying to figure out which way to go.

We're all in line. I'm at the end, making sure that no one gets lost 'cause we're in the middle of nowhere.

Frank's at the head of the line. He's wearing a baseball hat that makes his ears stick out.

Maria turns around and whispers to me, "He's got donkey ears." I laugh 'cause they stick out from his head. Never seen ears like that before, but never noticed them until we walked on the path on top of Watkins Glen.

"Looks like Dumbo," Faith says and us Biggies laugh about it.

Frank looks back at us and we just smile.

"Can he fly?" Maria whispers. He can't hear us 'cause of the rushing water, but we don't want to take any chances. If he's got ears that big, he could hear us plain as day and then he'll tell Mom.

Frank's truck is usually in the driveway when we get home from school; that's how I know he's gonna be sitting in Mom's chair. When he's there, Mom usually sits right next to him. They're always sitting at the kitchen table drinking coffee and smoking cigarettes. Mom doesn't let any of us kids drink coffee 'cause she says it will stunt our growth. And, I'm never gonna smoke cigarettes 'cause that's what killed Dad.

Sometimes Max is workin' in the basement, but mostly it's just Mom and Frank sittin' at the table listening to Tom Jones or Englebert Humperdink or Glen Campbell playin' on the Magnavox. Mom sits next to him where Maria usually sits, but Maria never complains 'bout it 'cause my sister then sits on the other end of the table all the way across from Frank. She just stares at him, but he ignores her.

We always greet Frank when we come home from school. Mom says that the front door is only for guests, so we have to use the side door through the garage into the kitchen. When we're done greeting Mom and Frank we go to our rooms to change our clothes.

"Coot likes that morgue music," Maria whispers to me one day when we're going to our rooms after school. We always do that 'cause Mom makes us change out of our school clothes. Not supposed to get them dirty, so we change into our play clothes. When we lived in New Jersey, everyone changed out of their school clothes after they got home. In Pennsylvania, no one else we know has special clothes for school; around here, everyone has special clothes for church!

Us Highams don't need any church clothes 'cause we don't go to church!

When we're done gettin' changed, Frank is usually standing up 'cause it's almost time for him to get chores done on his farm. 'Sides, it's time for Mom to make dinner.

Frank's Farm

Me and Ed English are helpin' Frank with milkin'. He lives up the road from us. Bobby is Ed's Dad and Frank is Ed's grandfather.

Listen, Ed is really short.

And strong. He can do lots of pull-ups in gym.

And, he's really dark. He gets as dark as me.

Ed's in the fourth grade with me at Gillett Elementary School. The school is so small that it only has one fourth grade class. And, it doesn't have a sixth grade or high school.

And, not only that, but part of it is made of wood!

Anyways, Ed and me are helpin' Frank do chores on his farm. You have to close all the gates so that the cows don't figure out how to escape.

Cows poop.

Everywhere.

They don't care if you're standing near their butts. Ed tells me to watch their tails 'cause if you see their tales goin' up in the air, it means they're gonna poop and pee all over the place.

They just don't care.

And Frank is yelling at them 'cause although they're big, they get scared real easy and you have to chase 'em all over the place to get 'em where you want 'em. Sounds like Frank is gonna hurt them when he yells, so they run like crazy on the concrete barn floor to get into their stanchions.

Ed's strong and can shut the stanchion so that the cow's head is caught near the water dish and its butt is over the manure trough. I can't do that 'cause I ain't that strong. I try throwing my body into it, but I just can't do it.

Frank and Ed milk by hand. The teat feels funny to me; slippery and disgusting. I'm supposed to squeeze it up top and pull it down toward the bucket. Frank and Ed can do it so that the squirting milk sounds like a song.

I can't do it 'cause it feels gross.

Real gross.

Not only that, but I don't want to hurt the cow. I mean, what if I snap it off by accident? Besides, what if the cow poops and pees when I'm kneeling down by it? I watch Frank and he's not afraid to push the cows. Ed does the same thing, but my cow feels too funny to touch.

It's gross.

Cows have really big heads and *moo* out loud when they're really, really angry.

Frank and his wife had a big farm, but she died. Mom says that he's a widower.

He's a widower cow farmer with grown-up kids.

Mom's a widow with us six kids.

They must have a lot to talk about.

The Woods

Me and Ed and the twins are in the woods playing Hide and Seek. When you play Hide and Seek in the woods, you can hide in all sorts of places because there's so many trees and ravines. Ed's so good at hiding because he can climb up a tree before anyone can spot him. Sometimes we play in the dirt in the backyard right outside my window that goes up to the brook. That brook is dry during the summer.

Anyways, Mom lets us boys play in the dirt there. We play with our Tonka trucks building an interstate highway and a city, too.

92

Ed is my new best friend. We play together every day.

When we play Hide and Seek, it doesn't matter if I find him 'cause he's so fast he can run to Home Free before I can catch him. And, it doesn't matter if I'm right on him, he can outrun me.

He's says he's gonna go hunting with his Dad in two years when he turns 12. He says maybe I can go with him. We're gonna take the Hunter Safety course together. Mom says I can. Sometimes Ed comes with Frank on the weekend when his grandfather visits Mom. Sometimes, he comes over to our house and we play in the dirt.

Even when me and Ed and the twins aren't playing Hide and Seek, I like walking in the woods. It's kinda' stupid, but the place has really neat sounds and smells. I like it there 'cause it's quiet, no one else is there, and I can hear and smell the place living.

It's beautiful.

1971

Stony Fork

Coot's camper stinks. I only call him that when he gets me mad. I never say that to his face 'cause that's not right. I'm calling him that right now 'cause his camper stinks. The girls stand under its canopy, Maria's looking like she's goin' on a date. Faith looks like she could be getting ready for a school field trip. Mom runs around the campsite with a cigarette in her mouth and curlers in her hair.

"Where's Coot?" Maria asks.

Mom raises a hand toward my sister. "His name is Frank." She swings and misses Maria, who just looks at her. Oh yeah, that's another reason why I don't ever call him that name to his face or say it out loud; I don't want to make Mom mad.

Mom's kinda upset with Frank anyhow.

She's upset with him 'cause of Ann of The South. Least that's what Frank calls her. See, this woman named Ann lives in Florida and wants Frank to visit her.

Frank calls Mom Nan of The North. Says he's just friends with Ann of The South and has known her for years. Sometimes, it makes Mom upset after Frank leaves her at night and calls Ann.

It's afternoon right now, but Frank left the campsite.

Faith stands, waiting. "Yeah, Frank took his farm truck and went somewhere," she says. "I told you."

"He's shopping," Mom says. Maria and Faith walk toward the road.

"Don't go too far," Mom says. "I'm making dinner soon."

"No, we won't go anywhere... except down the road."

Me and Mark and Warren sit in lawn chairs 'cause Coot's camper stinks. Me and Mark talk about everythin' and nothin' while Warren plays with some toys soldiers. Mom sits at the picnic table, smoking a cigarette and watching Baby Rose.

"So, this is camping," Warren says just as he makes one of his toy soldiers stab the other one with the bayonet on his rifle.

Me and Mark laugh like hell 'cause Warren is pretty funny. Warren isn't like Mark. Mark speaks his mind and is always getting Maria and Mom mad. Warren on the other hand keeps a lot of things to himself, but he's always watching everything.

The twins are both pretty smart.

Us boys sit and look at the woods surrounding the camp ground. They're marked by *No Trespassing* signs nailed to trees.

The idiots who put them there don't realize the tree will pop out the nails as the bark grows. Never saw a tree tolerate having nails driven into it. Dead trees are worse 'cause the wood splits and won't hold the nail.

I know about trees and nails 'cause the twins and I posted our woods last hunting season. Nailed signs into the bark and found them all down in the spring. Didn't find a single footprint, so I know the bark popped them out. The signs dropped onto the forest floor where everybody stepped on them and ignored them.

Mark and me are ignoring everything right now 'cause we're on vacation.

"How'd everybody like to go on vacation?" Frank asked a month ago. We sat at the kitchen table with our strawberry shortcake. Mom made it, but Maria didn't eat any. My sister sat in her seat, looking at her bowl and pushing her cake around with her spoon. She kept her mouth shut even when Mom and me carried the cake up the basement stairs.

"C'mon, everybody sing *Happy Birthday*," Mom said.

Maria looked at her fingernails, but me and Mom led everyone else.

Frank smiled and nodded his head. He kissed Mom on the cheek.

"Nancy, that's a wonderful-looking cake," he said after he blew out the candle.

Mom hugged him and gave him a big knife. He sliced the cake and dished out strawberries.

"I hate strawberries," Maria said, but she took a heap on her cake. I watched her play with it.

Frank picked up a card and read it. It had a picture of flowers on the front. Mom gave it to me to sign just before he got there. Inside, every one of us kids had signed it except Maria. Mom signed it for Maria 'cause she was afraid Maria would start yelling at her if she asked her.

Maria doesn't like Frank. She calls him Coot and The Benefactor, but I don't know what that last name means. Maria is really smart and uses big words all the time that I don't understand. Maria is like Mark 'cause she always says what's on her mind.

Faith is smart too, but she's just like Warren. She keeps it all in her head or says something really funny under her breath. She's an artist, too. She's always sketching pictures.

I'm not that smart and I keep lots of stuff in my head 'cause I don't want to get embarrassed.

Anyways, we were all eating shortcake with Frank.

"I think we should all go camping," Frank said. "This family needs a vacation."

"I don't like camping," Maria said.

"That's a wonderful idea," Mom said. "Where should we go?"

"I know a place that's just right for the kids. Over to Wellsboro. Got waterfalls, swimming holes and hiking trails. We'll take my camper."

And last week, I helped Coot hitch the camper to his pick-up. The twins and I stood ankle deep in manure near the barn as he yanked it from the lower barnyard with his Massey Ferguson. There wasn't much to it. It was a Nomad, but someone had taken something sharp and creased the side door.

It smelled of manure and mildew: it stunk!

"You boys clean it up," he said after he pulled it onto his front yard.

We scrubbed it, but the dirt stayed right on it. We wiped it with soapy rags.

"Might as well piss on it," Mark said after we scrubbed a

patch and the metal stayed dull.

"We're cleanin' Coot's camper," Warren said.

Me and Mark just laughed 'cause Warren never called him that name before.

The Magnavox

Mom is listening to Englebert Humperdink.

Again.

Damn, I hate it when she listens to him 'cause she just sits in her bed and stares at the kitchen.

The basement was supposed to be done, but Mom said that Max had to work on something else, so her entire bedroom is still where our dining room should be. Her queen-sized bed takes up most of the space, making it hard for us to squeeze between it and her double dresser. Near the head of her bed is a matching night table. At the foot of her bed is the large Singer sewing machine, but she never uses that anymore. If Maria didn't dust, the whole place would be a mess.

When Mom sits up in bed, she looks right at the kitchen. That's what she's doing right now. She isn't even inhaling when she smokes; there's a long red tip on the cigarette in her hand.

She only gets up to tap the cigarette on her ash tray and go to the Magnavox. She pushes the Magnavox's tone arm over so that the same song keeps playing over and over.

"Every day I wake up, then I start to break up," Englebert sings.

Mom goes back to bed. She just stares at the kitchen.

It's not any better when she makes me dance 'cause she just whispers stuff in my ear about love and being a fool. Then, she whispers about Dad and Coot and Ann of The South. She doesn't really dance but just holds onto me and tells me all that damned love stuff.

Maria tries to talk to her, but Mom yells at her. Maria yells back and then they're off arguing about dumb stuff like money.

It's a mess.

Finally, Maria gets mad and goes to her room.

Mom just sits in bed and stares at the kitchen.

Englebert keeps singing, but it doesn't make any difference to Mom. Nothin' makes any difference to Mom.

Cosmopolitan

My sisters get *Cosmopolitan*, but I know what to do. I wait until they've read it, then I sneak it into my room late at night when everyone is asleep. Then, I block my door and read all about sex.

Before I started reading it, I looked up the word *sex* in the dictionary, but it didn't tell me anything, so I decided I'd read about it in the magazine. It says right on cover all sorts of things about sex and it has sex stories in it. I read it several times and learn all sorts of sex stuff, then put it back in the morning when I go to wake Mom up.

I return it 'cause I don't want anyone to find out that I've been reading about sex. It's none of their business.

The Panasonic

After everyone goes to sleep at night, I play with toys on my bed. Sometimes, I sit with Lego blocks scattered all over the place making battleships, fighter planes, tanks, and bombers. I play war by putting all the tanks on my bed and throwing marbles at them, making them explode.

"Ka-boom, bang, bang," I whisper to myself. Sometimes I get so excited that my arms and legs are moving real fast back and forth 'cause I can imagine all the explosions and stuff going on during the battle. I make noises with my mouth like munitions are going off as I throw marbles at my ships; that makes the blocks fly all over the place!

"Red alert, red alert: this is not a drill! We are under attack. I repeat: we are under attack!"

Dad was in World War Two. He was on a destroyer. As a Gunner's Mate. Got blown off a couple of ships.

"I repeat: we are under attack!"

Sometimes I play Fort Apache; I set it up so that the Lionel train runs through the center of the fort. I pretend that the Indians take over the train, kill all the soldiers at the fort and take it over for themselves.

Don't tell anybody, but one time when I was really excited and playing war with ships I made from Lego blocks, I threw a steel marble really hard at one of them. I stood all the way near my bedroom door and put my arm way back and threw that marble with all my might like I was a baseball pitcher.

I threw it as hard as I could right at the battleship!

And, do you know what happened?

The marble missed! I couldn't believe that the marble missed the battleship and hit my TV set instead!

It made a loud noise, like a gunshot!

And, the picture tube got a big chip in it! When Mom asked me about it, I didn't say anything about the marble or the battleship. I didn't say anything about playin' war or anythin' that. I just told her that it did it all on its own.

She believed me, but told me to unplug it so it wouldn't explode.

TV sets don't explode; they implode. That means they blow in, not up!

Anyway, I don't play with the steel marbles anymore.

No matter what I play, I keep the radio on AM Radio 1230 WENY from Elmira.

They play good music. I have my Panasonic cassette recorder right next to Dad's clock radio. When a good song comes on, I hit the Pause button, then Record and Play.

Sometimes I listen to the same song for hours, rewinding it when it ends. Like, I was listening to *Someday We'll Be Together* 'cause it makes me think about Dad so much that it makes me cry.

It makes me wish he could be here 'cause Mom sits in bed all day, staring at the kitchen.

Sometimes, she doesn't even listen to Englebert, Glen Campbell, Johnny Cash, Dean Martin, or Tony Bennet.

It doesn't matter, 'cause all she does is sit in bed and either stare at the kitchen or listen to all her sad songs.

Mom got me the Panasonic from the Century Store in Elmira. I asked her for it one day when she was taking a nap. It was a couple months after Frank stopped coming around and Max had to stop working on the basement.

"Max took all my money and didn't finish the job," Mom said when I asked her about the renovation.

Anyways, Mom was sleeping in bed in the afternoon and I woke her up.

"Mom, can I have a Panasonic tape recorder?"

"No, Johnnie, let me sleep."

"But I really want it. Want to record my favorite songs."

"You can hear them on the Magnavox."

"You let the girls join the Columbia Record Club. They get to listen to songs on their own record player!"

"Let me take a nap."

Mom rolled over so that she faced the wall. I got real mad right then and started jumping up and down real hard.

"Stop throwing a shit-fit," she yelled. "I'm tryin' to take a nap."

"I want a Panasonic cassette recorder from the Century Store in Elmira!" I'm jumping up and down and punching myself real hard in the chest 'cause I'm mad as hell and throwing a first class shit-fit over it 'cause I don't get anything I want and the girls get everything!

Mom yelled at me a few times, then rolled over in bed and lit a cigarette.

I kept jumping and started swearing about the damned girls getting whatever they wanted.

Mom sat up and gave me the Evil Eye.

I didn't care.

I figured that if she came after me, I'd run to my room and block the door shut. 'Sides, she'd finally get out of her bed!

"Whoa, right there!" she yelled. "If you don't stop, I'm gonna beat you to an inch of your life! An inch of your life! That goddamned guinea temper of yours is gonna get you in jail!"

Mom can't hit that hard; she can't hit like Dad could.

"I want a Panasonic cassette recorder!"

"I said, 'no'. Go outside."

I jumped some more 'cause I really wanted the Panasonic. She was too tired to get me, so she just looked at me. I kept jumping up and down and telling her to get me the Panasonic.

"You're not gonna let me sleep, are you?" she finally after 'bout a half-hour.

"You should get out of bed anyhow. You stay in bed too damned much!"

"Don't you swear at me."

"That's all you do; stay in bed ever since Frank stopped comin' around."

"Mommy's tired, John."

"Should still get out of bed."

"Just let me sleep a couple more minutes."

"Get out of bed!"

She says that crap every morning when I try to wake her to make breakfast before us kids go to school. Every damned morning, I stand by her bed, tryin' to wake her up 'cause she told me to do that.

Told me to do that the night before.

Told me to wake her up so that she can make breakfast for us kids.

You know what?

One morning, I stood right by her bed when her Big Ben alarm clock went off and she didn't even move.

Didn't move one damned bit!

She's not moving now: she's just staring at me.

"Not until you give me a Panasonic cassette recorder. It's only twenty dollars at the Century Store in Elmira."

Mom slid out of bed and straightened her hair.

"Go ahead and get your shoes and wait in the car. I'll get you one if you promise not to swear again."

"Okay."

And, you know what? For the first time in about a month, she got out of bed long enough to drive to Elmira, buy me the Panasonic, and take me to McDonald's!

I like the Panasonic. I like sitting up late at night and listening to my cassette tapes and playing toys in my room. I block the door to keep everyone out. I like my privacy.

Burning Barrel

The best time to burn garbage is right after dinner 'cause the girls are doin' homework and Mom is back in bed reading a *Philly Inquirer* or *Cosmopolitan*. The way our house was built, there's no way they can see me and the twins sneakin' lawnmower gas from the garage to the old oil drum across the side lawn that sits near one of Dale English's pastures. Me and the twins fill old hand lotion bottles with gas and spray it all over the trash. On a cold fall day like this, Mom keeps the windows shut, so no one would even smell the gas burning.

The envelopes burn quickest, even the ones with the clear plastic windows that Mom never opens. We make houses with them. It's cool to watch 'em burning like a son-of-a-bitch.

The twins want to play, too. I watch 'em real closely 'cause gas and fire are dangerous. Once, when I was real young, I made them drink ink from Dad's fountain pen. He got mad at me and spanked me 'cause of it.

"He beat you within an inch of your life," Mom says when she talks about it.

Even though the ink didn't kill them, I learned never to give them anything dangerous to play with again. It's the same with lawnmower gas: it's just too dangerous.

We like to make gas fuses on the lawn. What we do is get a whole bunch of gas and spray a line from the burning barrel all the way across the side lawn to a piece of scrap wood from the heap Max made when he gutted the basement. Have to make sure that we soak the board. Then what we do is light one end and watch the flame race across the lawn to the burning barrel; the fire climbs up the barrel to the garbage and burns the shit out of everything!

"Cool," Mark says.

Warren likes it too, but doesn't say anything. He stands there and watches it, taking it all in.

The twins and I are playing with gas and fire the day that Maria says Mom is going crazy. Me and Mark set up a house made of windowed envelopes from Sears, JC Penny's, and MasterCard. We take a bunch of dry leaves and small twigs and arrange them all like a pretty fence around some bills and milk cartons. Mark and me make gas fuses all the way up the lawn to Brutus' coup. The dog doesn't mind and we don't put any gas near him.

Warren isn't here 'cause he went inside to pee. He stays so long that Mark goes after him. I mean, what's the point of making a big fire if no one can see it?

I stay outside and keep the fuse wet because if I let the fuse dry out, it won't burn all the way to the burning barrel. Most people don't know that you have to keep the fuses soaked if you want them to burn really fast.

Anyways, Mark comes out and says, "Mom wants you."

That really bugs me 'cause I've been soaking the fuse and I don't want him to light it until after I get back. 'Sides, he's got to keep it soaked or it'll burn poorly.

"Keep it soaked and don't light it until I get back," I say. I take the matches with me even though I trust him.

When I get inside, Mom is yelling on the phone. She's real upset. I take my coat off 'cause I know I gotta stay there and be her man of the house.

"I don't give a damn," she yells into the phone, "You're not to send your goddamned son down here to spy on us," she says. "He's not welcome at my house."

She slams down the phone.

Maria runs into the kitchen, looking real mad. Maria always gets mad about some crap. Like yesterday, she got royally angry when she found a bunch of envelopes in the garbage that Mom hadn't opened. I was home and Mom was reading *Ladies Home Journal* in bed. Maria waved some bills in Mom's face.

"Aren't you gonna open these?" Maria yelled.

"I called the companies," Mom said.

"They can ruin your credit if you don't pay them. They can repossess everything."

"I called and got it all taken care of."

"How? You don't have a job. You don't even get out bed."

"Never you mind."

Maria reached into the kitchen garbage can and—this is really gross—she picked out a bill that had an old chicken bone stuck to it. Usually, we feed scraps to the dog, but you can't let a dog have chicken bones.

Maria didn't care about the bone. She opened the envelope and read it just like it was sent to her instead of Mom.

"They're going to send this to collections if you don't pay."

"I already took care of that," Mom yelled back at Maria. Maria didn't care; she just kept right on going. Mom isn't feelin' well 'cause Frank doesn't visit anymore and Maria just bitches at her.

All Maria does is bitch, bitch, bitch. Can't shut her up for nothin'. She shouldn't say anythin' cause she doesn't know nothin' about anythin'. She bitches at Mom all the time.

So, anyway, Maria threw the bills all over the kitchen, then ran to her room and slammed the door behind her. That bitch!

I started picking up the bills and Mom came over to me.

"Son, make sure you burn the garbage every day."

"Yes, Mom."

She gave me a big hug and a kiss, then went back to her bed and her *Ladies Home Journal*.

Mom doesn't look like she's gonna hug and kiss anybody right now. Instead, she slaps the table real hard. She looks at me like I did somethin' wrong, but it's hard to tell 'cause Bitch is there in the kitchen. She is Bitch; that's her new name.

Mom yells at me, "You're not to talk to Ed anymore. He's been spyin' on us."

"They're not spyin' on us," Bitch yells.

"What the hell do you know?" Mom yells back. Mom gets really close to Bitch like she's gonna hit her; that makes Bitch back away.

"Shut up, Bitch!" I yell.

"You heard your brother," Mom says. "Shut up or I'll beat you to an inch of your life."

"Mom, I think you need to see someone," Bitch says. "No one's spying on us and I think you're depressed."

I wanna get the twins 'cause I need back-up. Bitch and Mom stare at each other as they walk around the table like they're gonna fight. Baby Rose comes out of her room, holding Raggedy Anne.

"Rose honey, go play in your room," Mom says. "You're sister is just complaining."

Bitch just looks at Rose. Bitch knows she's messin' things up, but instead of being nice, she just keeps being a bitch.

"Mom, no one's spyin' on us. You're crazy," she says. "Why do you think that anyway?"

"First of all, how do you explain that Dale's cows have broken lose every day this week? How do you explain that they've been on our yard, shitting all over the place?"

Mom's right, they did break out every day and shit all over our yard!

"You think that's a coincidence?" Mom asks.

"Yes," Bitch says.

"And how do you explain the fact that our mail gets dropped off real late in the day? You'd think it would be on time unless someone was steaming open the envelopes, reading what's inside, then resealing them."

Baby Rose goes back to her room and closes the door. Mom doesn't notice 'cause she's too busy trying to make Bitch listen.

"And, how do you explain that Cora Mae knows everything I've been doing to the house up here? She knows all about the renovation work that Max did before he took all my money. Don't even get me started with how he stole all our money! And, he won't even finish the job!"

Mom's right; Max never finished the job. Oh yeah, he tore everything apart and started fixing some of it, but never finished anything. I never thought about all this stuff, but Mom makes sense. These people are out to get us.

Why can't Bitch understand that?

"Yeah, Bitch, explain all that!"

Bitch gives me a look like I'm makin' her puke. She doesn't care; she goes against Mom 'cause she wants to be right and in charge.

"We live in the country, Mom," Bitch says. "The mail is always late."

Mom's shaking her off. "No, no, no," she screams. "I followed the mailman yesterday. Waited for him in the garage, then followed him after he dropped off our mail, watching him the whole time, pretending to look for cows. And, you know what? He didn't have any mail for anyone else!"

"Yeah, Bitch!"

"Maybe they weren't supposed to get any mail."

"Exactly. And you know why?" Mom asks. "Because they already got it earlier in the day! Maria, these people are all related! We're outsiders and they want to take you kids away from me! They want the Board of Health to come and take you kids! Is that what you want?"

"Yeah, Bitch, is that what you want?"

I get so mad at her that I punch her a couple of times, but then she gets really mad and digs her fingernails into my arms, making me bleed.

"You're gonna give him skin cancer!" Mom yells.

By now, it's all messed up 'cause Faith runs out of her room and slaps me. It's okay, though, 'cause I punch her in the back so hard that she runs cryin' to her room.

Bitch kicks me in the leg 'cause I'm too fast for her punches, but she's ripped open my arms and I'm bleeding all over the place.

"You're gonna give Johnny skin cancer!" Mom yells.

I'm bleedin' like a sonofabitch. Mark comes in and starts punchin' Bitch in her stomach. That slows her down until she pushes him away.

Mom slams the table like a judge, making everyone stop.

"This is exactly what they want," she yells. "They want to split us apart! We have to stick together until we can get out of here! I'm putting the house on the market! We're moving back to New Jersey! None of you kids are allowed to talk to anyone anymore: they can't be trusted! That includes you, John!"

Mom looks right at me. I'm really mad at myself 'cause I should never have trusted Ed and now everything is ruined 'cause of me.

I'm kinda sad, too. I really like Ed and thought he was a friend. Guess I can't trust anyone.

"I won't talk to him anymore, Mom."

It really bugs me that my best friend is an enemy spy.

Me and Mark go outside. We soak our fuses again, then light them. We watch the fire trail burn all the way down from Brutus' coop past the side of the house to the burning barrel. In the barrel, Mom's unopened bills are like a village that is now going up in flames. When it's done burning, I go back inside the house and go straight to my room.

There, I turn on my radio and punch myself a few times in the chest.

I'm mad at myself for messin' everythin' up.

It was stupid to trust Ed. I'm supposed to take care of my family and got careless by being his friend. Now, the Board of Health might come and take us away from Mom.

I punch myself a few more times in the chest 'cause I just hate myself so much.

Bitch, Old Lady, Blimp, Rosie, Cheeky, and Ear

When us kids fight, it's pretty simple: Maria is Bitch 'cause she bitches at Mom all the time. She never shuts her mouth for anything.

Faith is Old Lady 'cause she acts scared like an old lady all the time and she can't hit that hard. Mark and me chant, "Old Lady sitting in a corner; Old Lady sitting in a chair; Old Lady don't know what to do."

Rose is Blimp 'cause she's fat. Like the Goodyear blimp. We say, "Blimp, Blimp, Blimp," really fast and stick out our arms and puff out our cheeks to get her mad but nobody ever hits her 'cause she's just a baby.

Bitch and Old Lady call me Chink, Rosie, or Chairman Mao because my eyes look slanted when I smile or laugh. They also pick on me by saying that I'm rowing a boat back to China. Or they say, "Rosie is leading the Revolutionary Army!" They say it with a fake Chinese accent. It gets me real mad 'cause I'm not Chinese. I'm Italian and French!

We call Warren Cheeky because he takes forever to eat steak and puts that meat in his checks. It can stay there for hours while he plays.

"Ohh, Cheeky!" we say while making our faces look like we have buck teeth.

And Mark is Ear 'cause he's always picking his ears.

Listen, nobody ever calls anybody these names when we're out in public 'cause that's none of their business.

Mom hates it when we call each other names, but there's nothing she can do about it. Bitch and Old Lady keep trying to attack her, but me and twins aren't gonna let them win.

This is Mom's house and I have to protect her and the kids, no matter what.

I have to help Mom protect all of the kids.

The Bus

"Highams are pigs," Ed says.

"We're humans," Maria yells back.

Maria should shut up. If she ignores them, they'll get tired of it and leave us alone. Ed and everyone else on the bus has been picking on us since we got on this morning.

They hicks yelled at us all the way into school and now they're doing it all the way home. I wish they would leave us the hell alone. They're only doing it 'cause Mom called Ed's mom last night and said he was a spy. His cover is blown and now they're all out to get us.

"Highams are niggers," someone yells.

"The Niger is a river in Africa and we're Italian," Maria yells back.

"Then you should go back to Africa. Or New Jersey," someone else yells.

Joe the bus driver stares out the windshield, paying attention only to the road as the attack continues.

Fuck him.

Fuck everyone.

We're being ambushed on this fuckin' bus. Ed's mom probably called everyone and warned them that Mom caught Ed spying on us. Now everyone hates us 'cause we know the truth about them.

"Highams are niggers," someone else yells. "Niggers belong in the jungle."

"The Niger is a river in Africa and we're Italian," Maria yells.

The six of us sit together. Faith and Maria are in one seat. Me and Mark are together, then Warren and Rose. I am watching Joe's face in his mirror, but he's not looking at us. He knows what's going on and isn't doing anything about it. He's part of the attack on my family, aiding the enemy.

Fuck, he is the enemy!

We are outnumbered and surrounded by enemy forces. If we try to hit them, they can claim self-defense and destroy us in a quick counter-attack.

"Highams are pigs," Ed yells.

"You people are white trash."

Why does Maria say anything? It's only making it worse.

It's like how Pearl Harbor was attacked. It's better to stay low and avoid getting hit instead of counter-attacking. We're outnumbered. I read in one of my books about the Communists in Vietnam. They've learned to use guerilla warfare against the United States. They know how to lie low and let the attack continue when they're outnumbered. They only counter-attack when the conditions are right and they can demoralize the enemy.

"At least my mom's not crazy," someone yells.

Maria says nothing. Shit, Bitch believes that. She's like our own fuckin' Hanoi Jane. She can't say anything to that 'cause she believes that Mom is a nutcase. A fuckin' nutcase!

That proves it: Ed must've been spying if he knows what Maria said last night. Must have somehow found a way to bug the house and get that from Maria. She played right into their hands, that stupid Bitch!

The attack continues even as we get off the bus, Ed swearing at us out the window as the vehicle pulls away.

WENY AM RADIO 1230

It's after midnight and I'm listening to WENY AM Radio 1230. Everyone else is in bed. I should be in bed, but Mom woke me up a few hours ago just like she has every night after she caught Ed spying on us about a month ago.

"Johnny," she said before turning on my light, "wake up."

"What?"

"The hit men are here," she said.

"Again?"

"Yeah. They're in the woods."

Mom stands at my window, the one that looks out at the back yard where me and Ed used to play in the dirt. She looks right out there and points.

"The hit men are there, Johnny."

I couldn't see them a month ago.

I still can't see 'em.

Can't see squat. Sure, Mom's got that floodlight on, but all I see is the backyard and the woods at the very edge of the lawn. The trees are all dark 'cause the light can't reach that far.

"Mom, I'm tired."

"Johnny, stay awake and protect us. You're The Man of the House: you have to protect us," she says.

"Okay, I'll protect you. Want me to tuck you in?"

She stands there for moment, looking out the window and smoking her cigarette. She's real afraid like she's gonna die. I can feel how afraid she is; she reminds me of how I felt in Stanhope when I was afraid of monsters and Dad chased them away by searching my room. Only now, I'm like Dad 'cause I chase away the hit men.

"Yes, Johnny, tuck me in. Please."

I walk her back through the darkened living room to her bed. She climbs under the covers and I give her a kiss on the forehead.

"Nighty-night," I whisper.

She smiles and grabs my neck, pulling me close to her. I smell cigarettes on her breath and look at her tired face as she whispers.

"If you fall asleep, Johnny, they'll break in! They're break in and kill all of us in our sleep! Please don't let the hit men kill us in our sleep!"

She watches my eyes.

"Promise you won't fall asleep! Promise, Johnny, that you won't let them kill us!"

"Okay, Momma, I promise I won't let anyone get us. I won't fall asleep."

She smiles and kisses my cheek.

"That's a good boy, Johnny. Daddy is so proud of you."

She hugs me.

"Nighty-night, Mom."

"Nighty-night."

I go back to my room. I stay up all night, staring out the window at the woods. Those bastards are pretty clever. They always know I'm watching them.

They don't move at all.

The first couple times when Mom saw the hit men, she called Bill the sheriff and he came out. He walked all over the backyard, shining his flashlight on the ground, but said he didn't find anything. Mom called him every night, but then his wife started saying that he wasn't home.

"They're paying him off," Mom said when I asked her about it. "Paying him off so that the hit men can wait until you fall asleep and kill us."

Every night after all the kids have gone to sleep, Mom gets really scared when she sees the hit men. She is really scared when she tells me about them and makes me promise that I'll never fall asleep.

Only then does she let me tuck her in.

Only then can I kiss her goodnight and say, "Nighty-night."

Only then does she feel safe.

Then, I go back to my room. I sit on my bed and pretend to play, but I'm really watching. I'm watching everything out my windows and listening for the hit men to make their move.

I don't wanna play.

I wanna sleep.

But, I gotta protect my family from the Mafia men hiding in the woods just beyond the edge of the lawn. I'm really just watching out the window in the middle of the night. Mom said I should just act natural so they don't think I'm watching them.

I gotta wonder if it's really hit men in the woods every night. Sometimes, I think it's the kids on the bus and their parents who want to get us, getting into position for the final attack. They're just like the goddamned Vietcong; they own the night.

What keeps them away is the back floodlight. They know they have to run at least two hundred feet across open lawn from the woods to reach the house.

The side of the house next to Dale's field is the weakest part of the outer perimeter. That's why Brutus is there. He'll tear the shit out of any intruder if they step into his circle.

Can't count on the assholes doing that. I figure they've reconnoitered us. They know the dog's circle doesn't cover the whole side yard. And, if they use signals like me and the twins, they're gonna use Brutus' barking as a cover.

The garage blocks that part of the lawn from view. It doesn't matter 'cause the floodlights don't reach that far. The front door and Mom's bedroom are on that side of the house.

I timed it. Running as fast as I could, it takes me seven seconds to sprint from that fence to the garage. They can probably do it in five. What me and the boys do is train to run to the side window in the living room as soon as we hear the dog barking. We flip on the lights and as soon as they're on, it's a different story: we can watch that side.

The enemy never attacks. They just get upwind of Brutus and get him going. It's their way of wearing us down. Sometimes, I'm thinking it would be nice to get out the war rifle—Dad's M1 Garand—and fire a few shots. I'd fire above their heads 'cause it's not self-defense if they're out of the house.

Sometimes, I decide I'd rather just wait for them to breach the perimeter so that I can end this cold war and prove Bitch and Old Lady wrong. The girls don't think there's anyone waiting in the woods, but Mom and me know better.

W.R. Croman Elementary School

Wow, how'd I get in classes with all the smart kids? I'm in sixth grade and somebody put me in with all the smart kids. We have a whole bunch of different teachers; one for each subject. I have a bunch of books.

And, guess what? I got more friends! There's David and Derek and Robin and Mark! They're funny. Sometimes, we plan to drop our pencils at the same time in English class: that's David's idea.

He's funny and smart. He says that he wants to be a carpenter when he grows up 'cause he doesn't want to go to college for the rest of his life.

And Derek is teaching himself Spanish! All by himself. He's translating words all the time and saying them out loud.

My friends live all around. David and Derek live in Troy. Robin lives in Big Pond and Mark lives in Columbia Cross Roads.

None of them ride my bus, which is good 'cause they'd probably turn against me and my family.

War Rifle

Right after dinner when *Bonanza* comes on, Mom takes Bitch, Old Lady, and Blimp down to The Rancho for coffee. Me and the twins watch the Ford turn around in the driveway, pretend to watch the show for a few minutes in case Mom comes back early to get something she forgot, then we open the living room closet.

There's lot of shit in there: Dad's private papers, Mom's old dresses, and all of our weapons. That's why we go in her closet; we get out weapons for training.

I got me a target I made out of paper. I pin it on the tree at the edge of the woods.

Gotta be safe like I learned at the Hunter Safety course. Never point at anything you don't wanna kill. That's the first thing I taught the boys 'cause it's the most important lesson. Every weapon should be handled like it's loaded. You have no room for error once a shell is in the chamber. And it doesn't matter if you think the safety's on.

We go outside to where the back yard meets the woods. That's where I put up the target.

I make the twins stand back behind the shooter. Once they get more experience, they can stand alongside.

We're careful.

Sometimes we take Frank's Marlin. The .22 has a pump action. It's a great gun. Someday Frank'll come back for it. I'd like to see him try. He better come with Bill.

Anyways, it takes long rifle shells. We got plenty of those.

Frank left a 16-gauge, too. We use birdshot for that. You can adjust the scatter of the shot by turning a ring at the end of the barrel.

Mark likes that one. Recoil is a son-of-a-bitch, but it's a good gun. It also makes a lot of noise.

I like the Marlin better 'cause its shot isn't as spread out. If we could get slugs, I'd like the shotgun better. Well, probably not 'cause it's not a double barrel and you can only fire one shot before havin' to slip another bullet in the chamber. The Marlin holds a ton of bullets. A .22 can take someone down just as good as birdshot or slugs provided that you aim for the head or the heart.

I handle the war rifle. Mom calls it that because Dad picked it up at Anzio. It's a M1-Garand. That's the neatest one 'cause it's got a range of five miles and the clip holds eight shells. Mom says it's Italian, but the words on the box of clips are all English. It hasn't got any recoil pad and Vern the state trooper told Dad that it'll knock anyone on his ass when they fire it.

I always load it and pretend to sight it in. I learned in Hunter Safety to fire a rifle by standing with one leg back and off a little to one side. That way, the kick won't knock me on my ass. I don't fire it, though, 'cause we can't afford the bullets.

The trick to making a Molotov cocktail is the rag. You gotta make sure it's long so you have enough time. When I practice using them, I always make sure that the rag is long enough. If it goes off too early, it can explode before it hits the target. You gotta let the rag burn a little bit, too, 'cause otherwise the fuse'll go out and it'll just splatter gasoline over everything.

I make mine so they burn for a couple seconds before I throw the sucker toward the brook. Can hear that son-of-a-bitch for miles; it's louder than the shotgun. I got a whole supply of gasoline 'cause I mow the lawn. And we can get gas without anyone knowing that we're stockpiling weapons.

When me and my brothers go out on a raid, we take along a pair of wire cutters. I found a pair in a box Mom bought at an antique store. They're big and old, but they're tougher than snot. They cut through barbed wire. Gotta be careful with that 'cause if the wires are pulled tight, they can fly back at me when I cut them. First time I did that, it barely missed my face. Of course, the trick to cutting wire is to target rusty strands. Any asshole knows that new wire isn't gonna snap.

First time we raided, we messed up 'cause we pulled the wire out of the post. All the assholes had to do to fix it was to staple it.

Other thing, we never raid near our house. Instead, we go into the woods and make our way onto the farms, cutting the wires on the far ends of the pastures. Hell, a couple times we even cut some near cornfields and chased the fuckin' cows in there.

"Cows are stupid," Warren said.

Me and Mark had a good laugh over that.

As part of weapons training, I also teach the boys to aim their weapons correctly to make a kill.

"Close-casket the deal," I tell them. "Aim for the face, that way it's self-defense."

The war rifle is our nuclear warhead. In close range, it won't leave much behind. The Molotov cocktails are good, but we can't use them inside 'cause if the house caught on fire, the volunteer fire department assholes would just watch from their trucks.

Dad's Bowie knife stays in the sheath. Me and the twins have looked at it, but we figure if something were to happen, we'd need to hit the intruders with gunshot. If it comes to hand to hand combat, we'd surely die 'cause there's no way these farmers are gonna lose. They work chores all day and they're much stronger than we could ever be.

Trouble is, we need ammunition. There's no stores here. Can't get any in Elmira 'cause Mom never buys sporting goods. Maybe we could get some on a bike trip, but I don't want anyone finding out that we bought the shells: that way they'd be saying that any killing we did was premeditated.

I tell the boys, "Remember, you can't fire unless they penetrate the inner perimeter; they gotta be inside the house. Then, it's self-defense. But, you have to shoot them in the face or chest."

Warren doesn't like weapons training. He bitches like a pussy 'bout it.

Fuck him.

I just punch him a couple of times and tell not to say anything about it.

He shuts his mouth and listens 'cause he's a good soldier.

Mom always returns right after *Bonanza* ends. By then, we got everything back in her closet and behind all of her dresses from the forties, we got our hands washed ('cause we don't want to smell like gunpowder or gasoline), and got ourselves just sittin' in the livin' room watchin' TV and mindin' our own business just like weapons training never happened.

Sometimes late at night when Mom has ordered me to sit up and watch for hit men, I think I might tell her 'bout weapons training, but I don't want to upset her. Worse, she might take away my weapons. Then I won't be able to defend our house when we're attacked. It's just that I'm thinkin' if the men in the woods saw me with my M1, they would leave us the hell alone 'cause then they'd know that I meant business.

1972

The Snake

Old Lady found the snake. She found it this morning when she went down to the basement to get some clothes out of the dryer.

We never had any snakes there before and because she is such a pussy, she screamed and yelled like an Old Lady.

I was in my room, playin' Fort Apache when I heard her screaming. Even though she and Bitch are my enemies, I have a duty to protect every Higham in my house. Since I wasn't fightin' with her, I figured something bad happened, so I ran out to the living room.

Mom's sitting in bed, reading *Better Homes and Gardens.*

"There's a snake in the basement," Old Lady yells.

I go to the kitchen and head down the stairs. There it is right in front of the dryer.

"Johnny, kill that snake," Mom says. "They broke into the house and put it there to kill us in our sleep."

I order Mark to guard it while I fetch a shovel from the garage. Then, I club the shit out of it.

"Cut the head off and put it in a can filled with vinegar," Mom says. "It's a rattler. Or water moccasin. It won't die unless its head is kept away from the body for a whole day."

Bitch, thinking she's cool, runs downstairs and looks at it.

"It's a harmless garter snake," she says.

I don't believe her, but that doesn't matter 'cause Mom yells, "Maria, we have to stick together. You want the state to come and take me away? You want the Board of Health to come? You want to be split up and spend the rest of your lives in an orphanage?"

Mom starts to cry. I hate Bitch 'cause she makes Mom cry all the time.

"Bitch, they're not putting us in an orphanage," I say. I punch her a few times 'cause Mom is gettin' really upset. That's Bitch; she just fuckin' bitches at Mom!

"Aw, Rosie protects the Chairman," Old Lady says.

"Shut up, Old Lady," Mark yells. "Old Lady, sittin' in the corner; Old Lady, sittin' in a chair!"

I punch her real hard in the back and she cries like a pussy. A big fuckin' pussy.

I cut off the snake's head by hitting the damned thing with edge of the shovel, put that part in an empty Maxwell House coffee can, pour in some Heinz vinegar, then take everything outside. Out there, I snap on the plastic lid and weigh it all down with a rock.

Mom watches me. "That's the only way to keep it from getting back to its body and biting us in our sleep," Mom says.

I know she's right 'cause I don't ever see another snake in the basement.

The Sun

It's almost summer when Mom sees Dad. Mom was taking a nap on a Saturday afternoon. Us kids were watching *Charlie Chan Theater* on the Magnavox when she woke up. I watched her stand up on her bed and look out her window onto the porch.

"It's your father," she says.

Me and the troops look right away; we stare out the window.

"Your father is the sun," Mom says. And she cries really hard, but she's smiling and pointing at Dad's Navy picture that hangs on the wall over the sofa. "His eyes are always watching us, protecting us. His loving-kindness blesses us!"

"Dad's not the sun," Bitch says.

"Shut your fuckin' mouth," I yell.

"Hush, children. Your father is talking. He's talking to me, saying we have to stay inside because his rays will burn us all. He'll burn us all to Hell."

I look out the window and try seeing Dad out there. I only see the empty front yard.

"You have to look right at the sun to see him," Mom says like she's giving us instructions.

"Don't look at the sun, it'll make you blind," Bitch says.

"Blind to all evil," Mom says. "Blind to bad things. Your father will protect you. See, watch his eyes in the picture, they follow you." Mom points at the picture of him that she put on the living room wall.

She's right: Dad's eyes do follow me when I move around!

He is watching us!

"What's he say, Mom?"

Mom pats my head.

"We have to make the house safe so that when they come for us, you won't let them in. You're The Man of the House. Dad wants you to help me."

"Dad isn't the sun," Bitch yells.

"Shut up, Bitch," I yell back.

So, me and Mom move the piano in front of the downstairs window and tie the basement windows. I push real hard as she takes baler twine and ties the window handles shut, then I loop the twine around the legs of the upright.

I take a few nails and drive them through the downstairs door into the casing.

The enemy can still get in, of course, but they'll have to breech the front door just off the porch. There isn't anything we can do about that except to make sure that the floodlights are on every night. That's also our regular operating response during an attack. We have no more than five seconds from the time Brutus barks to scramble to turn on the light, load the weapons, and engage the enemy.

The rear flank is much tougher to defend. The switch to that floodlight is in the garage. During a surprise attack, we won't be able to get to it in time and will have to settle for patrols to secure the back. Because that light can give away our troops' positions, the garage will be a sure suicide mission for any soldier who volunteers for it.

Any soldier on that patrol will only have his wits to guard him from the dangers lurking in the darkness. Hell, that soldier could be killed and his body dragged off into the woods without anyone knowing, except for our dog and the bastards who did it!

The only good thing about our rear flank is that we know that it's impossible to defend. It's logical that the enemy will try to use it to launch their attack against our house. We know the bastards will be invading in that direction! Our efforts in that area involve making sure that anyone who reaches the house's rear cannot breech the inner perimeter. They must be stopped dead or we'll be defeated; that's all there is to it.

On this Saturday evening after Dad went over the hill so that his rays could no longer incinerate us, me and Mom go outside and drive three eight-penny nails into each wooden storm window in the back of the house, securing them into the sills. We fortify the two kitchen windows like this and also the one in the twins' room, then my two windows. Bitch yells at us when we nail shut one of her windows.

"You're crazy," she says.

See, her and Old Lady's room is at the corner of the house, overlooking the front yard. Their side window can be easily reached by anyone coming down Kinney Road, but the attackers will need a ladder to reach their front window.

"If there's a fire, we'll burn up," Bitch says to Mom and me. Her yelling stops Mom.

"Johnny, what would we do if there's a fire?" Mom asks.

What a stupid question! I lift my hammer and pretend to swing it at the window.

"As long as I keep a hammer in my room, we can just break the glass, Mom."

Mom gives me a hug 'cause she loves me. She knows that I'm not gonna let anything happen to our family. She knows that I'll keep our family safe.

Bitch keeps bitching, but we ignore her at first, then I confront her.

"If Mom's wrong, how come you didn't go outside during the day? You knew Dad would burn you up 'cause you argued with Mom."

"No, it was just too hot," Bitch says. "I'll go outside tomorrow."

Mom smiles. "Tomorrow, his rays won't kill anyone," she says, laughing.

I laugh too 'cause Bitch really believes Mom and just can't admit it. That's how Bitch is. I've got her all figured out. Pretty soon, Bitch will stop fighting Mom and help me defend the house against the enemy. Then, no one can harm us! As long as Bitch and Old Lady oppose Mom and me, the enemy will use our civil war as a distraction. They'll continue to reinforce their positions just beyond the perimeter!

Bitch doesn't understand any of that. She doesn't understand the first thing about war, the first thing about combat. She's just thinking of herself, but she's gonna ruin my family. Her kind of thinking isn't good for the family.

Nighty-Night

That same night after Dad was the sun, Mom stopped an attack all by herself! She came to my room around midnight.

"Johnny, I chased the hit men away!" she said.

"What did you do?"

"Well, I was looking out the kitchen window and saw the men run across the backyard, so I ran into the garage and turned on the floodlight."

"What happened?"

"They ran into the woods." She smiled and inhaled on her cigarette. "Watch 'em Johnny," she ordered. "They're hiding in the woods."

It was really scary 'cause they managed to advance on the house and retreat to the woods without making their scent known to Brutus. Only thing I figured was that they stayed downwind and covered themselves with blood. Animals can be fooled by the smell of blood, I think.

"See 'em in the trees, Johnny?" Mom asked.

I look out real hard through an opening in my curtains and remember reading about Nazis hiding in the trees during World War II. When I remembered that, I could see the enemy in the trees, high up in the branches.

"One, two, three, four, five, six, seven, eight, Mom," I said, counting those bastards.

She stands next to me at the window.

"If they come any closer, break out the weapons and get the twins up. Don't let them take the kids away."

"I'll get 'em."

I stayed on full-alert all night, listening to the Panasonic, watching the men in the trees, and playing Solitaire.

Sometimes, I get a little tired at night when I'm on guard duty, but I just ignore it and it goes away. It's kind of funny 'cause when I go without sleep, I feel like I could stay up all the next day.

Around one in the morning, I went out to the living room. Mom was sitting up in her bed, her *Cosmopolitan* in her lap. When I got closer, I could tell that she was sleepin' 'cause her eyes were closed. I took off her glasses, slid her down the sheet, then kissed her nighty-night. I didn't tell Bitch or Old Lady or even my troops, but Mom was ready for the attack that morning.

She looked at me and smiled.

"Are we safe?"

"Yeah. Nighty-night."

She smiled at me and kissed me.

"Nighty-night."

When I hugged her, I found the meat cleaver under her pillow. She's real smart, figuring that the attackers would look through the window and see her sitting like that. They'd figure that she was sleepin' when she was just playing opossum!

Mom sat up when I picked up the cleaver.

"Mom, I chased them away. Saw them go home. They're not gonna attack."

"Son, put that cleaver away! That guinea temper of yours is going to land you in jail. You have to learn to control it!"

"I will."

"I mean it. You get so mad and lose your temper."

"I'm sorry."

"I don't want you to go to jail for losing your temper."

"I'll control my temper."

"Give me a kiss."

I kissed her forehead. She smiled and laid back down. It was like when you're a baby and all ready for bed and Mom and Dad smile at you because they're so proud of you and everything is going to be all right. They know nothing is going to hurt you 'cause they'll protect you.

That's how Mom's looking at me; she knows that I'll protect her and our family. Makes me feel real proud.

"Make sure they don't come back, Johnny," she said. "I love you."

"I love you, Mom. Nighty-night."

"Nighty-night."

I kiss her nighty-night, then put the meat cleaver in the drawer.

Afterwards, I made eight slices of French toast 'cause I was hungry. I sat in Mom's chair at the kitchen table and just watched her sleep. Felt good knowing that I kept her and everyone else safe.

The Bus

It's Monday afternoon and I'm real tired 'cause I was up all night again after Mom told me about more men in the trees. I can't let myself fall asleep on the bus. Have to stay awake 'cause Ed started another attack when we got on it this morning.

"Highams are pigs," he said.

And, damnit, Bitch took the bait.

"We are not," Bitch yells.

She always argues with them. They outnumber us and could beat the shit out us at any time. If we act defeated and like we just don't exist, they'll stop attacking us. They'll get bored and ignore us. But Bitch doesn't care, she always has to stand up for herself!

"Are too, that's why you're called 'Hig-hams,'" Ed yells.

"It's *High-am*," Bitch says.

And so on and so on. Back and fuckin' forth, Ed and Bitch lobbing word shells. Only thing, everyone takes Ed's side and soon the whole fuckin' bus is yelling at us again.

All the way to school.

All the way home.

Why can't Bitch just shut her fuckin' mouth? It's just getting them really angry and making them want to attack the house when they think we're sleeping!

Sunday

It's just like any other Sunday. Bitch gets up bright and early and starts on Mom. Actually, she makes bitchin' noises all day until around noon when she steals Mom's checkbook!

That's an attack on Mom! I rush out to Mom's bedroom and punch Bitch. She digs her claws into my arms and gets blood all over my shirt, that fuckin' Bitch!

"That's none of your business, Bitch."

She kicks me, so I retaliate by punching her and spitting on her. Old Lady tries to help Bitch by punchin' me in the back.

"Mark and Warren, I need back-up!" I yell.

Mark arrives and gives me help, but Bitch and Old Lady are faster. They knock Mark against Mom's dresser. Warren just fuckin' stands there.

"You fuckin' pussy, help me," I yell.

It's no good. Warren doesn't give a shit. He's like Sweden was in World War II: neutral and useless. He can't fight.

Maria cuts my arms pretty badly. I get really angry and everything feels strange. I yell 'cause my head hurts from where Bitch punched me. I try punching her a couple of times, but I can't fuckin' hurt her. Things feel really strange, like in a dream.

I retreat to my room and block my door.

The house gets quiet. So quiet, I can hear Mom turn the pages of her *Cosmopolitan* and Rose playing with her Tumblina doll. That's the good thing about fightin'; it calms everyone down so they can relax for a little bit.

About an hour later, me and the twins regroup to play Hot Wheels on the living room floor while Mom takes her afternoon nap.

I'm not tired, even though I've been awake for most of two days. I know I should sleep, but I want to occupy the living room in case Bitch and Old Lady try to attack Mom again. If I need to, I'll grab the meat cleaver and stand guard in front of Mom to protect her.

Stories

"Johnnie," Darla, the pretty girl from the cover of the Coed *magazine says, "Are we all right?"*

Darla picks me up from the ground and burps me. "Are we all right, huh, little Johnnie-Donnie?"

"Goo-goo," I say 'cause I'm just a baby.

She opens my diaper and peeks in, then stops.

See, we're standin' in the middle of a field and she hears an airplane coming, so she runs like crazy. It's out in the Midwest. It's a bi-plane coming at her, the sound of the engine straining as it comes straight at us. Like in that movie, 'North by Northwest.'

She runs, ducking and dodging as bullets bounce near her in the soil. They tear apart the ears of corn all around us. She holds me tight against her.

"Wah-wah," I say.

"It's okay, little Johnnie-Donnie, Darla will get you back to your mommy."

The plane zooms overhead, its shots barely missing her. No, the plane zooms past just above the corn stalks. Are they stalks?

Shit, I don't know.

"It's okay, Johnnie-Donnie, Darla will get you back to your mommy."

The plane fires more shots as it comes closer to her. She stumbles, falling forward. As she does, she clenches me in her arms to protect me as the bullets make the dirt around her dance.

"Wah-wah."

The plane climbs and turns, making the engine strain.
"Wah-wah."
Darla sits up among the stalks. She thinks for a minute.
Naw, wait a second: Darla's not gonna have a minute with the plane comin' right back at her. She's got to think fast.
Okay, I know what I'll say.
She thinks for a moment, then puts me on the ground.
"Johnnie, you wait right here."
The plane sounds stronger as it levels off, then dives right at Darla and baby Johnnie. Darla uproots a few stalks and groups them together, holds them together, bundles them together, wraps them together—
Bullets fly through the air, landing in the dirt all around her. As the plane comes closer, it builds speed and dives closer to the field until its wings are almost brushing the tops of the corn.
Darla sees the plane approaching.
She is waiting.
Waiting.
Waiting until—
Waiting until all she can see is the wings and the propeller, the plane blocking out the sun—
She—
No, she waits until she can see the whites of the pilot's eyes, then she—
THROWS THE CLUMP OF CORN PLANTS RIGHT AT HIM!
THEY HIT HIM IN THE FACE!!!
HE KNOCKS THEM AWAY—
He turns and laughs at Darla—
Causing him to accidentally fly RIGHT INTO THE GROUND!
KA-BOOM, KA-BOOM, it explodes into a fireball that kills the pilot!!!
Darla yells, "Little Johnnie is safe!"
"Little Johnnie is safe," Bitch yells from the hallway outside of my bedroom, laughing. Even though my windows are nailed tight and my door is blocked shut, my face is red 'cause I feel like my bunker's perimeter has been breached. I poke my face out from under my covers as Bitch knocks on my door.

"Little Rosie is safe!" Old Lady says. "Chairman Mao has saved all the babies for the People's Army!

I sit up and look over the end of the bed. Right near my Fort Apache is the copy of *Coed* with Darla on the cover. I grab the magazine and shove it under the bed with the rest of them.

"Chairman Mao is ready to march his troops to the sea," Bitch yells through the door.

"Fuck you, Bitch!" I yell.

Bitch punches my door a few times, making it bend inward when she does. Each time, Mom yells *whoa* from her bed.

Mom won't be getting up. She fuckin' stays in bed all day now. Sure, she'll yell at Bitch and Old Lady, but she just stays in bed lookin' sad all the time. She's not even fuckin' eatin'.

Hell, when we're not fighting, us Biggies are runnin' this damned house.

"Who's Darla, Chink?" Old Lady yells, laughing. "The Chairman's Geisha?"

They laugh like assholes and I wish that I would've whispered the story. Sometimes, I get so excited that I move my legs back and forth and make all my characters talk out loud. I forget 'cause I'm only thinking 'bout the story. It's the only thing that matters 'cause I can imagine it all taking place just as I say it.

"Rosie, maybe you should get a new rickshaw," Bitch says.

She punches and kicks my door again, making Mom yell *whoa* again, but the door holds. I got it blocked shut with my books. I'm barricaded in. No one gets in my bunker unless I let them.

"Fuck you," I yell.

Fuck them. I'll whisper my stories to myself from now on. Stupid fucking Bitch and Old Lady can go to hell for interrupting my story.

They're my stories. Won't ever write them down 'cause Bitch and Old Lady might find 'em and use 'em against me. Or even worse, Ed might break in and find them, picking on me about 'em in front of everyone on the bus. In this house, everything can become a weapon.

Fuck, I'll just hide under the covers and tell them to myself. I'll whisper.

Gotta fuckin' remember to whisper my stories.

Gotta remember that I can't tell anybody anythin'.

It's hard to remember that 'cause I get excited tellin' them to myself.

I'm not gonna stop tellin' myself stories just 'cause of Bitch, Old Lady, or Ed. I like tellin' them to myself and pretendin' that I'm in 'em. It's like watchin' a movie while bein' in it at the same time.

Uncle Lenny's Ventura

Everything is okay now.
It's really strange.
There's no more hit men.
There's no more kids on the bus.
There's no more civil war.

See, Faith and me got a real sweet deal. We've got our own rooms. Uncle Lenny and Aunt Winnie let us stay up as late as want to as long as we get to bed before midnight. Oh yeah, they live in the woods at Berkley Heights outside of New York City that has all sorts of neat paths and stuff. This is the best summer vacation in the world!

Well, not really. I mean, because Lenny works at the Linden GM plant on the night shift, we have to eat dinner when we really should be eating lunch. And, Winnie likes lima beans; they're gross.

It's different now. It got all different right after school ended. Maria sneaked a phone call to Uncle Mike when Mom was fast asleep and I was in my room.

Maria called him and told him everything.

Said that Mom was crazy.

Said that Mom was crazy for thinking that there were men hiding in the woods.

Said that Mom was crazy for thinking that there were hit men after us.

Said that Mom was crazy for thinking that Ed English was spying on us.

Said that Mom was crazy for thinking that Dad was the sun.

Maria told Uncle Mike everything.

The next day, all of our uncles came up: Lenny brought Mike in his Ventura. Jimmy drove his Oldsmobile 88. They came all the way from Jersey to rescue Mom from being crazy. Made us Higham kids put some clothes in garbage bags to bring with us.

Took us back to New Jersey

I rode back with Mike and Lenny. They told me that I was The Man of the House and that my family had too many chiefs and not enough Indians.

"Johnny, you have to teach those kids the meaning of respect," Uncle Mike said.

"I know."

"You have to be a man for your mom. These kids have to obey her and you."

"I know."

Mark only respects me 'cause I beat him up when he doesn't listen. I beat up Warren, too, but he stays the exact same way, not changing one bit. He doesn't say anything when I punch him. Mark tries to fight me, but I can easily beat him up. Then I have to hit him again 'cause he doesn't listen to me.

The girls don't listen to anyone, but that doesn't matter.

Mike and Lenny said that Maria is disrespectful. I thought about telling them about how I beat the twins and call Maria "Bitch," but that's none of their business. Mom doesn't trust them anyway; that's why she moved away from New Jersey.

Listen, Maria and Rose are staying with Uncle Jimmy and Aunt Palma. They live in Lodi right across from the inspection station. It's a fuckin' development. The air smells like chemicals and they have plastic slipcovers on the carpet and the furniture.

The twins are with Uncle Mike and Aunt Margie. Our cousin Barbara lives there with our other cousin, Martin. They have a French poodle that I want to stomp on until it's dead.

It fuckin' yaps all the time.

The twins hate it there 'cause Mike tells them to sit on the stoop all the time.

Faith and me, though, we got it good. Lenny lives in the woods and even though it's raining all the time because of Tropical Storm Agnes, we're having a blast. Lenny takes us to the plazas. He lets us ride in the backseat of his brand new Ventura. He and Winnie sit in the front.

Faith and me make jokes about everything, but we don't tell the adults 'cause it's none of their fuckin' business.

Maria says she saw Mom today. She went to Bergen Pines Mental Hospital and stood outside, waving at the building. Mom was way up on the tenth floor or something and waved at Maria through the bars in the windows.

Lenny said that Mom might have a weekend pass in a few days. Then, if she does real well, we can all go back home to Pennsylvania. At least until she sells the house and we can move back to New Jersey for good.

Maria says that Mom had to have electric-shock therapy or something like that. I don't know what the heck that is. Maria said that they put electricity through Mom's brain. She was so depressed that no medication in the world could make her feel better. Maria said we shouldn't talk about it with Mom 'cause Mom's mind is real slow right now.

Maria was right.

When us kids visited with Mom at Jimmy's house, she was real quiet and talked really slow. She stared a lot, too, and barely talked.

"Children..., I'm sorry... for... what... I... put... you through," she said.

We told her that it was all right, but she kept talking.

"I really... thought... they... were... spying... on... us," she said. "But..., I had... a chemical... imbalance."

We told her that she was better now.

"Johnny..., there... were... no men... in the... woods," she said. "I'm sorry... I did that... to you."

We told her that we were all behaving really well and looking forward to her getting out of the hospital.

"The doctors... say... I'm... manic-depressive," she said.

We told her that we were looking forward to her getting out of the hospital.

"That means... that sometimes... that... I get... really sad..., really happy," she said.

She said a bunch of other stuff, but none of it mattered 'cause the electro-shock got rid of her manic-depression. She said that she loved us. She said that she's taking good medication and will always take it.

She didn't even cry, not even when she said mushy stuff that used to make her cry all the time. She didn't seem happy either; just tired. I guess that's what electro-shock does: it makes you so tired it takes away your manic-depression.

I don't care.

I just want to go home.

Roaring Run Road

Everything's a mess.

Tropical Storm Agnes flooded Elmira. The National Guard is there. Williamsport got hit too, but not as badly.

'Cause our house is up on a hill, we didn't have any flooding.

It doesn't matter; Brutus is gone. We figured that Bill took him to the ASPCA.

And Mom?

Mom is just like she was when we moved here from New Jersey. She's happy all the time, talking to us kids about enjoying our summer. She's talking to us about what we like to do and everything.

It's like the men in the woods never even existed. Or, that Dad was never the sun. It's like she forgot all about that bad stuff.

Just like that, it's all gone. I don't have to sit up anymore and watch the woods at night. And, 'cause it's summer, we don't have to ride the school bus right now.

And, the civil war is over! Maria and Faith and I are
friends! We sit up all night, talking in my room like all that bad
stuff never happened. And you know, they're pretty cool sisters!

It's odd when I go to bed. I expect Mom to wake me up,
but she just sleeps all night!

Sometimes, I wake up at night and stare out the windows.
I wonder if the hit men are hiding in the woods, but I can never
see them.

It's all strange 'cause Mom's getting up in the morning to
make us kids breakfast! She sits in the living room and watches
TV with us! She even talks to us and listens to us!

I love Mom. I'm glad they cured her manic-depression!

Troy Junior High School

I'm not sure how it happened, but I'm in one of the top
sections again with the really smart kids.

I'm in seventh grade!

I'm in high school!

All my friends from sixth grade are here and I've got even
more friends now! There's Mark and Dick and Fuzzy and a
bunch of other kids.

They're so smart. They always do their homework and do
really good on tests.

And, you know what's really strange?

They think I'm just as smart as they are.

Math Homework

I am holding it, pulling the sides down to make the head
swell shiny. On the bed next to some Kleenex I stole from the
bathroom is the *Alden's Spring Catalog* on top of my Algebra
book and my tablet. The underwear models are looking at me.
Some smile, some are serious.

It's quadratic equation shit. Mrs. Williams went over a
few examples in class, but it doesn't make sense. I took lots of
notes, but I can't read my own writing. Shit, why didn't I write

neater notes?

I'm holding it late at night when I shut the curtains, the kids are asleep, and the door is blocked. Ain't no way anyone is gonna walk in. When I'm done, I'll do my math homework.

Got the radio on, it's playin' *Sundown* and I'm thinkin' 'bout Sundown coming 'round my backstairs. She's in a cotton dress.

And she's pretty, really beautiful like the girls in *Coed*. She's got long brown hair. And pretty eyes.

Someone's in the hallway. I stop, listening to the sound above the clock radio. The clock reads almost midnight.

Someone taps on the door and the knob turns.

"John, are you okay?"

"Yeah, Mom."

"Why aren't you in bed? What are you doing?"

My other schoolbooks are blocking my door. Mom can't get in; that's how I usually do it. Forget the bathroom: the girls always want in there. I thought about going up in the woods, but I can't go there at night.

"Homework, Mom."

"Don't stay up too late."

"I won't."

I listen to her leave. I pull at myself again, but the purple is gone. I pull and pull and look at the catalog.

I'm not even halfway done with my homework. Shit, there's no way I'm gonna get through these problems unless I finish first.

Sundown is over.

"It's a minute before midnight," the DJ on the radio says. "That means I'll be out of here until tomorrow night."

I pull some more, but it's useless. I've got to get my work done. Mrs. Williams gets really mad if we're not done and makes a big stink in front of the class. The DJ won't shut up.

I reach under the bed and pull out this month's *Cosmopolitan*. The real sexy one with the lady on the cover. She's showing a lot of breast through her evening gown. Her breasts are pushed together.

I stole it from the bookcase even before Maria and Faith could read it. They yelled at Mom because they couldn't find it. I

136

was gonna return it, but the cover was so good, I kept it. When I'm done with it, I'll take it out to the burning barrel.

I stop when I hear Mom turn off the TV and climb into her bed.

I wonder if she heard me and got scared.

I'm okay. I checked everything out. I can't get VD as long as I wash my hands, though I thought I got syphilis and asked Mom to get me some penicillin. The syphilis wasn't that bad and went away when I stopped doing it for a week. I didn't tell anyone 'cause I don't want them to take me to the Board of Health.

When I'm done, I take the dirty tissues out to the burning barrel. Nobody knows what I'm doing. When I started, I messed up my underwear. Mom made a big thing out of it, coming to my room and asking me stupid questions. She waited until late when everyone was sleeping and knocked on my door when I was looking at my catalogs. She wouldn't go away and I had to wipe all my stuff on an old t-shirt that I burned the next day.

"John, is there anything you want to know about sex?"

"No, I already know everything," I said.

"You do? Where did you learn about it?"

"From books, Mom."

I don't ruin my underwear anymore. I just steal a couple Kleenex and burn them when I take out the trash.

"This is W-E-N-Y radio, twelve-thirty AM on your dial. It's midnight," the DJ announces. The news theme kicks in.

I lean back on my elbow and pull hard, stretching myself, then rubbing. With my free hand, I turn the pages in the catalog to the negligee section. I think I can see the *Cosmo* lady's nipples. They're not as easy to see as the outline of her thighs, but I can see them.

I pull the sides down and the head swells shiny.

Gotta hurry 'cause I wanna do my homework.

There's no time in the morning and I don't want to ruin my grade.

Wood Shop

I like shop.

I'm finishing a mahogany foot stool.

It's cool making things with my hands. I never made anything before.

I used the table saw to cut the pieces from stock, clamps to glue the pieces together, then the planer to smooth the surface.

After that, I used a scroll saw to cut out the opening for the cross member.

And, of course, I did all the sanding and finishing.

Ranch Wagon 500

We're sitting, Mom and me, in the front seat of the Ford.

She drinks her cup of coffee.

I have my regular meal; a Quarter Pounder with Cheese, fries, and a chocolate shake.

We do this every day after school.

I have a half day 'cause they're renovating the high school, so I go in the morning. Maria and Faith go in the afternoon. When I come home around one, Mom takes me to McDonald's in Southport at the W.T. Grant Plaza. We talk about almost everything like school, my friends, and my classes. We always talk about things in the Ranch Wagon.

When we get home, Mom usually sits on the sofa, smokes a cigarette, and watches TV while I do my homework. I leave my door open and we talk about all sorts of things.

The Bus

It doesn't matter what the kids say anymore 'cause I can hear them without looking at them. I can see them without looking at them.

I'm reading.

Last week, it was *Guadalcanal Diary*.

This week, it's *The Rise and Fall of the Third Reich*. I can read while I watch them.

I realized something.

I realized it this morning when Ed was calling us niggers and telling us to get back to Africa.

They can't hurt us.

They just say things.

The same old stupid things.

They call us the same old names and try to get us going.

They don't get me going.

I can sit here and be quiet.

Their words bounce off me like I'm a Panzer tank and they're firing a Luger at me.

Even when Maria argues with them, I'm not afraid anymore.

They're stupid; they're all in the stupid sections in school.

They're cowards; they won't hit us.

They'll never break into our house.

They'll never hit us.

They want us to be afraid.

I can put up with their words.

I'm not gonna live here forever.

I'm not stuck here. I'm going to move away when I grow up.

They're pathetic.

Troy Junior High School

I know what I am: a thief.

I don't know why I steal except that I like to. I like to pretend that everything is normal when I'm just planning on stealing something else. Some things are so easy to steal that I stop doing it after a few times.

I just get bored.

Like library books: I just rip out the card pocket and carry the book out like I came in with it. Of course, I make sure that the librarian is away from the check-out desk when I go past. The student helpers never stop me.

It's more fun to steal tapes from the language lab. I can take a whole box of them at a time.

I like being a thief: It's the most exciting part of school.

Princess and Snappy

It snowed and I can't find Snappy.

Princess is running around in her dog circle. She's always glad to see me. She's where Brutus used to be.

But, I can't find Snappy. The snow is deep and it's blowing hard. The opening to Snappy's coop is covered by snow. It snowed last night and there are drifts around this side of the house.

Brutus is long gone, Bill having taken him to the dog pound after our uncles took us to New Jersey six months ago. I don't blame the sheriff; that poor boy was probably starving and Bill was just looking out for him.

Snappy's coop is right next to the garage. I'm digging around in the snow with my foot when I find a big, thick lump behind the coop.

It's Snappy's frozen body.

The dogs were Mom's idea. Us kids were so broken up when we returned home with her from Bergen Pines at the end of June and found Brutus gone that Mom decided to get two dogs.

"I'll breed German Shepherds and sell the pups for money," she said. Faith wanted Snappy. She went with Mom and they came back with him and Princess. Mom had A.K.C. papers to prove that they were purebred.

Faith named the guy Snappy. He was her dog. She took care of him, played with him every day, and fed him.

I had Princess. She took Brutus' coop and was in the backyard. They were just pups when we got them.

Yesterday, Snappy didn't look right. Mom thought she had a cold. Maria and Faith tried to tell Mom to take him to the vet.

"I don't have any money for that," Mom said.

"Can't you keep him inside then?" Faith asked.

Snappy isn't house-trained and I know exactly who would be cleaning it up when he pooped, so I wasn't thrilled about that.

"No," Mom said. "He'll be okay."

Mom has been doing really good since her shock therapy. She's been leaving me alone at night and hasn't seen the men at all.

But she changed.

She talked about being poor.

She got us on food stamps.

She said we couldn't afford to pay for fuel oil, so we had to heat the house by turning on the electric oven and leaving the oven door open.

She couldn't even get us any new school clothes and she hardly ever went to The Rancho for coffee.

So, what did Maria do?

She complained.

She complained about not having things, complained about not having food, and complained at Mom for not taking Snappy to the vet.

Maria complains a lot. Even though she's got a boyfriend who drives a car, she's always complaining. At least when she's not on a date with Kevin.

Faith doesn't have a boyfriend. She never talks about any friends at school and she never has anyone over to visit. Snappy is Faith's only friend.

I pat Snappy's head. It's hard and cold. Guess he's been frozen for a long time. When I clear out the snow, I can tell that he must have laid down to die.

I go back inside. Faith is at the kitchen table, eating cereal. She looks at me a certain way 'cause she knows something is wrong. Faith can always tell when something is wrong. She can just feel it, I guess. Sometimes, I think she's psychic like Jeane Dixon.

Mom is sitting on her bed reading an old *Philadelphia Inquirer*.

"How's Snappy?" Faith asks.

"He's dead. Think he died in his sleep."

"Are you sure?"

"He's... frozen solid."

Faith looks at Mom.

"You should've taken him to the vet," Faith says, crying. I want to hug her 'cause I know she's got to feel as bad I as did when Dad died and everything felt terrible inside me. She's got to feel like puking up all her guts.

Mom looks up from her newspaper. "Don't have any money for that."

Faith looks at her cereal bowl and eats real slow for a few minutes. It gets real warm in the house. Well, not really, but I'm getting real warm 'cause I dug Snappy out of a snowdrift. I'm all sweaty and everything. I want to hug Faith or go outside, but I'm waiting for Mom to tell me what to do.

If Maria comes out of her room and complains, I'll just tell her to mind her own business.

That's all there is to it. I'll just tell her that.

"Bury Snappy, son," Mom says.

"Do I have to?"

"Yes."

"But, the ground's frozen."

"Use the pickaxe."

I look at Faith, but she won't look at me. She won't look at Mom, either. She only looks at her cereal bowl and sniffles.

I feel sorry for her 'cause I know how much she loves Snappy. It's like her best friend just died.

Hell, her only friend.

I want to hug her and tell her that everything will be okay. I don't want her to be sad about Snappy.

"Go ahead and use the pickaxe, son," Mom says.

I step out into the cold garage, find a snow saucer, a pickaxe, and a shovel.

Outside, I wrestle Snappy's hard, frozen body onto the saucer. I drag the saucer uphill through the back yard to where the woods start near Dale's pasture. In the summer, this part of the yard always becomes overgrown with weeds; I figure I'll make it into a nice memorial in the spring.

It's hard to dig because my tears keep freezing and my hands are cold. I dig for hours, chipping away at the frozen ground with an antique pickaxe Mom had bought at some rummage sale. The point shoots dirt pellets in my eyes, my tears mixing with it to make my face dirty. My hands are useless as long as I wear gloves 'cause the handle keeps sliding, making the pickaxe bounce away from me.

When I break off a piece of ground, I pick up the shovel and try to scoop it away from the grave. Then, I grab the pickaxe and do it all over again.

All the while, Snappy's frozen body is on the saucer. I think about setting it on fire with gasoline, but that would really upset Faith. I think about burning the ground to soften it, but I decide not to.

Instead, I just chip away with the pickaxe and scoop with the shovel, taking lots of breaks to wipe my eyes.

It's almost dark by the time I slide Snappy off the saucer and into the grave. I say a few words to myself and Snappy, then shovel chunks of frozen ground over him. I stop every couple of minutes to stomp the dirt down, then go back to shoveling until I make a mound of frozen dirt.

Sears

Hell, it's almost Christmas.

Tonight is Christmas Eve.

You can't tell in this house. We haven't got a tree or any crap like that.

We're just too poor.

Maria is yellin' again. When she's not with Kevin, she's yellin'. Faith is right behind her, the pair of them yelling at Mom.

I push Faith a few times, but Maria becomes Claw Lady and tears into my arms. I retreat 'cause my arms are bleeding.

Where the hell is Mark? I need reinforcements!

Mom doesn't care. She keeps the house real cold, but her ass is in bed under the covers. I know we got oil in the tank 'cause I keep an eye on it, reading the gauge every day.

Maria runs toward the thermostat. "Leave that the hell alone," Mom yells at her.

"The pipes'll burst."

Maria doesn't give a shit about the pipes. She only cares about herself.

I run into Mark's room. He's playin' with Lego blocks. "Get in my room."

I grab him, throw him into my room, and slam the door.

"What the hell were you doin' when Claw Lady was slicing my arms?"

"Was playin'."

I punch the shit out of him 'cause he just sat in his room when he should've been helpin' me out.

Stupid fucker. How am I supposed to defend myself when he's disobeying my orders?

It's 'bout noon 'fore Mom gets out of bed and sits on the sofa. It doesn't matter 'cause no matter what she does, Maria is ready to pounce on her.

It's just like the school bus. Anything we do gets pounced on by the hicks. I can ignore them, though.

It's getting kind of tough to ignore Maria yellin' at Mom.

"What, you want to spend time with us?" Maria sarcastically asks Mom. "Why would you do that?"

"Why the hell are you here?" Mom asks. "Thought you'd be spending Christmas with Kevin's family. You practically live there."

"'Cause Christmas is supposed to be special. 'Course you couldn't tell by lookin' at this house. You haven't even gotten a goddamned tree."

"Leave her the hell alone," I yell, punching Maria in the head. I get one shot off 'cause she turns around and nails me in the arms with her fucking claws. It doesn't take much and I'm fuckin' bleeding again.

"You're gonna give him cancer, skin cancer!" Mom screams.

Mom's a mess. Her hair is all pushed to one side and her clothes are messed up from her sleepin' in them. Faith rushes out from her bedroom. I could hear her coming 'cause her Neil Diamond record gets louder when she opens the bedroom door to rush out. I'd break that record if I didn't want to record some songs off the album.

It doesn't matter. Maria is digging her nails into my arms and beatin' the shit out of me.

"Goddamnit, it's Christmas Eve," Mom says, pointin' her cigarette at us as her yellin' becomes a bunch of coughin'. It's that same kinda shit Dad used to have. Maria looks at her while she holds me with her claws.

"When are you gonna see a doctor?" Maria asks.

"Never mind that. Get in the car."

"Why? Are you finally taking us Christmas shopping?"

Mom nods and lights a cigarette.

It takes Maria and Faith forever to get ready. They have to get all sorts of make-up on and do their hair. I leave them alone 'cause we have to hurry if we want to get to Elmira before the stores close.

Mom pulls me aside. I sit on her bed and watch her smoke.

"When we get to Sears, you take the Little Ones around the store." She hugs me and whispers, "They still believe, don't they?"

"Yeah. You want me and the twins to cut down a tree from the woods?"

"No, I'll pick one up."

In the car, I'm leaning over the seat and keepin' an eye on Maria and Faith.

"People's Army is on patrol," Faith says.

I'm goin' pull her hair, but Mom watches me in the mirror, so instead I just whisper, "Old Lady, sitting in a corner; Old Lady, with a bug up her ass; Old Lady, so fuckin' stupid; Old Lady, ya' gonna get beat."

"Chairman Mao threatens the Caucasian Lady. So scary. So-o-o scary," Old Lady says in that accent.

At Sears, I look in one of the mirrors and realize my pants are too short and my coat is too tight. It's the same for the Little Ones; we look like the Crudleys'. Bitch and Old Lady go off by themselves. I walk around the store with the Little Ones 'cause that's my assignment.

People are buying things like crazy. We walk around the toy department and I see the NFL electric football game I always wanted. It's got everything and it's nice. Mom shows up. Her clothes are all wrinkled, but at least she combed her hair. She don't look too bad except compared to other Moms.

She looks like a Crudley, too.

"I hope Santa brings me this NFL electric football game. That would be real neat."

"Johnny you need a winter coat," she says. "They have some nice parkas."

"No I don't. This one'll last."

146

"Johnny, it's a summer coat. You'll catch pneumonia and die in the winter."

"I want this fuckin' game."

Some of the other people look at me like they got a bug up their ass.

"You watch that mouth of yours," Mom says. She looks at the twins. "What do you boys want Santa to bring you for Christmas?"

The stupid assholes point at Hot Wheels and Matchboxes and Lincoln Logs and Lego sets. Shit, Mom hasn't got enough money for food: they'll be lucky to get anything.

"And what about you, Rose?"

She doesn't fuckin' understand either. She points at all the Barbies and dolls. She just doesn't know 'cause she's just a fuckin' kid and thinks that all this nice shit grows on trees.

Mom plays along with her only 'cause she doesn't want Rose to find out that Santa is dead.

The kids look at the toys like they mean something. Fuckin' kids don't know shit. Think that just lookin' means Santa's gonna make everything all right.

"And I want Santa to bring me this," I say, pointing at the football game. Mom looks at it, examining the price tag, thinking.

"I'll tell Santa, but don't be surprised if he brings you a coat."

"Don't want a coat. I want this fuckin' game."

Mom whispers in my ear. "That guinea temper of yours is gonna get you in jail. You want to spend Christmas in jail?"

"They don't arrest people for swearin', Mom."

"Disorderly conduct."

I take Baby Rose's hand and lead the Little Ones away from Mom.

When we get back to the car, I'm keep an eye on Old Lady. It's no fuckin' fair 'cause she and Bitch each have two bags of shit. Mom had the store wrap the Little Ones' shit in extra bags so they can't see it. They don't care. They're goin' on about all the toys they're getting, but they're not getting shit.

Mom put it all on her fuckin' credit card. I'll be burning that bill next month and the collection notices starting in February. She doesn't pay for shit anymore.

It's almost closing time when she stops at The Rancho. There's a few shitty trees out front and she points one out to Pete. Like always, he smells of watered-down gasoline and grease. He's got that shit-eating grin. He's always fuckin' happy 'bout something.

"Merry Christmas, kids," he says, smiling his big fuckin' smile.

"What do you kids say?" Mom asks.

The Little Ones jump around like they got ants in their pants. "Merry Christmas, Pete."

At home, me and Mom take down the tree from the top of the car. It's a real piece of shit: all the branches on one side are pressed upward.

"Do we have to put it up?" I ask.

"It's Christmas, John," Mom says.

When I reach for it, I hear a ripping sound. I don't tell Mom 'cause I don't want her to know. I got cold air coming in under my arm and the coat's stuffing falls onto the garage floor. I kick it under the car and hold my arm tight so she won't see it and start bitchin' at me.

Bitch and Old Lady have the Little Ones in bed. We got all the presents on the floor and we're wrappin' all the shit at once. Its nighttime and we got one string of lights on the tree. Mom moved the tree so that its bad side is against the wall. Bitch takes a picture with her Instamatic after I wrap my football game.

We leave the lights on. Mom climbs back into her bed, a cigarette in her hand. Bitch and Old Lady go to their room and I sneak *Cosmopolitan* into mine. I fall asleep in my clothes; it's too cold to even beat off.

Merry Christmas, everyone. Merry fuckin' Christmas!

1973

WENY 1230 AM Radio

Fuck, that didn't take long. I'm in bed tryin' to get sleep when Mom comes in.

"The hit men are back," she says.

I get out of bed and look out at the backyard at the snow. I can't see any footprints. Just like last year, the floodlight reaches the bare trees at the edge of the yard.

"Princess isn't barking."

"They've found a way to avoid giving off a scent," she says.

Fuck, I know what I have to do. I walk with Mom through the darkened house to her bed and tuck her in. She's got the meat cleaver next to her. Shit, it's on the other pillow like it fuckin' belongs there.

"Mom, can I put that away? No one will hurt you."

She grabs the cleaver and carefully hands it toward me.

"You'll protect us, Johnny," she says.

I take the cleaver and tuck Mom in.

"Nighty-night," I say.

"Nighty-night," she says.

I put the cleaver away in the kitchen.

So, I'm listening to music again at night. I'm fuckin' tired, but I can't let the men get in and kill everyone.

Mom's depending on me.

The Elmira Branch

"We hate the Highams, we hate the Highams," the kids chant. When I look at Joe without raising my head from my book, I see the driver watching the highway. He's running in fourth gear, but the bus ride takes forever because the stupid kids are in charge now. I get to listen to them every school morning and afternoon.

I'm re-reading *The Rise and Fall of the Third Reich*. When I move my eyes to see my sisters, they are reading and talking to each other. I read and watch them because Agnes came and destroyed the Elmira branch, so I can't look for any trains.

The bus takes forever to go from the high school in Troy to Fassett. On a map, it's only sixteen miles, but the kids make it last forever. I sit very still when they start, pretending that I'm not even on the bus and like I'm invisible.

Sometimes, they start before the bus leaves Troy as we wait in the heat for the cop to wave us through the intersection onto Route 14. The kids walking past on the street from Maria's or Faith's class will yell something or someone on the bus will start.

"Fuck the Highams," they yell. "Niggers. Go back to Jersey, fuckin' niggers."

"White trash," Maria yells back.

Why can't she shut up? She doesn't have to egg them on. Why can't she just sit there and take it like Faith and me? She only makes it worse.

We can't win.

Joe sits there, the fat old fuck, looking in the overhead mirror. Fuck, he never yells at anybody.

It's because his grandson rides the bus.

And his nephews.

Fuck, these stupid white trash assholes are all inbred. Get into an argument with one of them and they all attack.

I don't see any of them at school, except for gym class, but Mr. Berry doesn't put up with shit there.

But now, I'm watching them. They don't even know it. They think that I'm just reading my book, but I'm watching every single thing that they do.

They attack in large numbers 'cause they're stupid cowards. When I see any of them in school, they look away 'cause they know they can't do anything. I look right at them 'cause I want them to know that I know how stupid they are.

Those dumb fuckers never have any homework. They all plan to work at the A&P plant in Horseheads and have kids before they graduate. They'll buy their trailers, fuck their second cousins, and live happily ever after.

"We hate the Highams, we hate the Highams," I can hear the girls chanting. Some of them are pretty girls with pretty voices. Dumb fucking bitches, though. To them, we're niggers, pigs, or assholes, depending on the day. Fridays are worse. No, Mondays.

Hell, I don't know anymore.

Time-wise, Gillett Elementary is the halfway point. In the morning, we get on the bus second, right after Ed. Sometimes he starts, though most of the other kids are neutral like Sweden until then. Once he starts, he'll keep going until Lyman gets on after the Congdons. Barb is pretty and Mark has a crush on Tonya. Lyman and Maria are in the same grade, but Lyman never brings home any books. He's pretty fucking mean.

They all are.

When the De Witts get on is when it really gets going. Ed has a crush on Julie and the pair of them get going. From there, it keeps going the rest of the way down the hill until we get to the elementary school. It's mostly the big kids yelling at us.

There's Rod, the Weaver boys, the Riley girl, the Leonards, and Bobby. They all hate our guts. Jimmy and Bev get on just before the last stop, but so does Ron.

Ron sometimes sits next to me. He's a good guy and never joins in the attacks. He never sticks up for us Highams, but he's never mean to any of us.

He's got it tough 'cause his father killed himself last year. We talk about all kinds of stuff when he comes to school. He's got it real bad. He's got seven brothers and sisters and he always wears the same clothes. He takes his bath just before the bus comes.

"Why you do that?" I asked him.

"Cause we ain't got a lot of hot water."

"Good morning," and "Good night," is all Joe ever says. No, sometimes, he'll talk about deer hunting or some other white trash shit, but he's not gonna do anything.

"Blood is thicker than water," Mom said one time when I told her about him not doing anything. "These hicks are so inbred. Well, let me tell you, Mister, there's plenty more of us where we came from."

It reminds me of the siege of Stalingrad. We are being bombarded and attacked every single day without any end in sight. But like Stalingrad, we're not going to surrender to these assholes even if it means we have to put up with them every school day for the next five years until I graduate.

I look around the bus without turning my head, just my eyes. These assholes think I'm deep into my book, but I'm watching them. I keep my head down 'cause if anyone sees me looking, they'll just pick and pick, going on until they start chanting or calling names. I hate it when they start 'cause nothing stops them. We wait until the bus stops at their shacks and trailers, though sometimes they yell at us from outside if they see us looking.

It's worse 'cause the Little Ones sometimes cry. One time this kid named Fish Face pushed Rose, but Maria pulled him out of the seat.

"Pussy John has to have his sister protect him," he yelled.

The rail line extends from Elmira through Fassett, Gillett, Snederkerville, Columbia Cross Roads, and into Troy. There, it crosses the highway as it winds through the narrowing valley toward Canton and Trout Run onto Williamsport.

Agnes destroyed most of the tracks. I can see where the Penn Central has propped up some washed-out sections with stacks of ties.

Maybe they'll fix that track. They'll cut away all the weeds and let the trains run again. They'll upgrade the rail so it can become a mainline for hotshot freights. I'll be able to watch from the bus window.

Every day, I look for the cranes and dozers the company will use to repair the line. I know Penn Central will fix it: they have to.

I like trains. I like thinkin' about where they're headed and where they've been. I like watching them pass through the countryside. Nothing can stop them as long as the rails are in good shape.

Playin' with Trains

It's spring and I'm excited!

I'm so excited that my legs are bouncing, bouncing up and down as I'm sitting on my bed! My legs are bouncing and my arms are waving all over the place 'cause I'm just so excited about everything in the whole wide world!

I got war maps all over the walls of my room!

This is my bunker!

This is my command post!

I've got maps of New Jersey, maps of Pennsylvania. I got 'em all over my walls.

I got Coed and Cosmopolitan magazines under my bed.

I got catalogs under my bed.

I got bags of chips under there.

I got a hammer in my room.

I got the M1-Garand in Mom's closet.

154

I got a load of soda bottles and rags.

I got lots of gasoline in the garage.

My leg is bouncing, bouncing, bouncing and I'm getting ready again. I'm getting so fuckin' ready that my legs are bouncing and my arms are waving like crazy and I'm rocking back and forth like crazy on my bed, looking down at all the toys that are on my bedroom floor.

Okay, the door is locked.

The radio is playing: It makes enough noise.

I know it makes enough noise 'cause I checked by standing in the hallway with my bedroom door shut.

The trick is simple; it only took me a little while to get it all straightened out.

See, the idea came to me while I was playin' with trains. After being attacked on the school bus one day a couple of months ago, Bitch and Old Lady got into another fight with me. I had enough of their shit, so I retreated to my room and blocked the door.

I was angry.

Was fuckin' angry.

Was so fuckin' angry that I kicked a couple holes in the wall before I could calm down.

Fuck.

That's how it is: I can't calm down until I kick or punch the shit out of the wall or punch myself. When I fuck up the wall, I cover the holes up with pictures I cut out of *Newsweek*.

Now, I'm excited. I'm so fuckin' excited that my legs just keep bouncing, my arms keep waving and I'm rocking back and forth on the bed just thinking about how I got everything the way I want it so that Mom will be able to take care of things when I'm gone.

Fuck!

Listen, it's really weird how I figured it out. How I figured everything out.

Was playin'.

Was playin' with trains.

Was playin' with my Lionel train and when I tripped over the cord to the power pack.

I accidentally pulled the plug out of the wall.

Then, I saw the mahogany footstool.

You know, the one I made in shop class.

That's right, I saw the power pack and the mahogany footstool that I made in shop class.

And, I knew. I knew right then what was so obvious that I laughed 'cause I never even thought about it before.

It all made sense. It all made perfect sense. Perfect fuckin' sense. It's like putting two and two together to get a perfect way to deal with the wars, a way to win all these endless fuckin' wars.

My legs are bouncing, my arms are waving and my body is rocking back and forth.

Everything is all set.

Listen: I figured that if I tied the power pack cord around my neck, threw the power pack over the top of the closet door and closed it while I'm standing on the mahogany footstool I made in shop class, I had my own gallows.

My own fuckin' gallows!

Fuck, that's cool!

Listen, suicide is honorable. I read in my books how Japanese soldiers in World War II killed themselves instead of surrendering.

I won't surrender.

Not to Bitch.

Not to Old Lady.

Not to the kids on the bus.

Not to the men in the woods who are coming around again almost every night.

Hanging myself is not the same as surrendering. It will get me the fuck out of these wars I just can't win. There's nothing wrong with admitting that I'm beat.

I'm beat in so many fucking different ways. There's nothing else I can do.

Wait: I didn't do it. I mean, every day I've stood on the footstool, tied the cord, and threw the power pack over the top of the door and got ready to hang myself.

But, I didn't kick the foot stool away!

Fuck, I tried.

I've tried so hard.

Shit, a botched suicide is worse than a successful one.
There would be cops, the ambulance crew, and an investigation.
They would put me away or something and say that I was crazy.

Crazy?

Crazy, fuckin' crazy!

Yeah, Bitch would then say Mom and me are crazy.
She'd fuckin' call Uncle Mike and have me electro-shocked to
cure my manic-depression, but the only thing about that is no one
can cure anything except make it go away for a little bit.

Am I crazy?

Am I crazy for knowing that I can't win a civil war against
Bitch and Old Lady while fighting a war against the hit men and a
war against the neighbors? Not to mention fighting another war
at the same time against the kids on the bus?

No, I'm not crazy.

Not crazy, not crazy, not fuckin' crazy!

So, what I do is practice. Every day for the last couple of
months, I planned what I was going to do and stockpiled weapons
for Mom to use after I'm gone. I thought about it while the kids
on the bus yelled and swore at us. I thought about it in school. I
thought about it at night. I thought about it in math class and
when I did my homework.

I thought about it 'cause thinking about it makes me feel
so good that I'm not gonna be here much longer. I'm gonna be
free!

Didn't tell anyone about it 'cause no one can help me. I'm
on my own!

Only thing, I can't struggle once I kick out the foot stool
'cause then everyone will hear me and they'll come get me. I
have to be quiet for at least five minutes, I figure, but I don't
know for sure 'cause I can't find anything that tells me how long
it takes to die by hanging.

My legs are bouncing, bouncing, bouncing right now.

Every day, I plan to kill myself.

And, I practice.

I block my door, turn on my radio or the Panasonic and
assemble my gallows. I stand on the footstool, tie the cord around
my neck, stand with my back against the closet door, prepare to
kick the stool, and go away for good.

The best time to practice is right after dinner, right after I burn trash and feed the dog. Everyone is in their rooms, so no one will be buggin' me.

Only thing, I can't do it. I can't because I know that the police will conduct an autopsy. They'll find all the magazines under my bed and get suspicious. And they'll know that I pull the sides down and make the head shiny. They'll say that I did that.

I tie the cord on days I don't have math homework, but it doesn't matter. I know that they'll find the magazines under my bed and say that about me.

I tie the cord the day after I burned all the magazines.

That didn't matter either. I figured that the cops would ask Mom all sorts of questions about me acting strange or having strange things happen and she'll tell them about my asking her about penicillin and the missing magazines. They're cops; they'll investigate everything and conduct some sort of scientific test on the burning barrel ashes and figure everything out.

I keep tying the cord anyway. I keep tying it and trying to figure out a way that the cops will never find out what I've done. Sometimes, I stay up at night and get really mad at myself for being such a fuckin' chicken!

Sounds stupid, but I like how the cord feels against my neck. I like knowing that I can step off the edge of my footstool and never have to deal with Bitch, Old Lady, the kids on the bus or the men in the woods ever again.

I can if I want to!

I will if I want to!

I play with trains every day just after feeding Princess. I stand up there, thinking about kicking it away. Thinking about being away from everyone once and for all. Once, the song "Without You" by Nilsson was playing on my radio. That's how I feel about Dad: "I can't live if living is without you."

And, Mom says that I'm The Man of the House!

Fuck, I'm no man and this stopped being a house a long time ago!

I'm like Hitler while Berlin is being attacked by the Russians and the Americans, fighting a war on two fronts. But, I'm worse than Hitler 'cause I'm losing on both fronts and I'm losing a civil war!

All of a sudden, I'm depressed.

My legs stop bouncing.

My arms stop waving.

My body stops rocking.

Everything feels bad.

I feel real bad like I've been punched really hard in my gut. Punched so hard that I ain't got no guts left.

Everything is bad, real bad. Feels like the kids on the bus are never gonna stop, the hit men are gonna over-run the house, that Bitch is never gonna leave Mom alone, and the Board of Health is gonna try to take Mom away and split up my family.

I feel so bad that my guts hurt like I'm gonna puke up everything I ever ate.

Sometimes, I write letters to Chuckie. I tell him all about how much I miss playin' with him. Sometimes, I tell him goodbye and tell him how much I miss everything about New Jersey.

I always burn those letters. Once, I almost sent one, but I decided at the last minute to burn it.

It's better if no one knows what I'm thinking.

Now, my legs aren't bouncing and my arms aren't waving. I'm not rocking anymore, just staring at my stupid toys and my stupid gallows.

I'm so fucking stupid.

I punch myself really hard in the chest 'cause it's the only thing I can do.

It's the only thing I can do right and it feels good to punch myself so hard that my chest and my hands hurt. Only thing, it makes my guts feel better.

Nighty-Night

I listen for the men in the woods, but I can't hear them.

I can't play with trains now 'cause Mom would blame the men and she'd be mad at me for falling asleep and letting them penetrate the perimeter.

Worse, if I did it now and the men saw me, they would breach the perimeter and kill everyone. Anyway, it's better to try it right after dinner when the kids are awake so they know that they're safe and sound from the men in the woods.

I'm tired, so I whisper to myself. I whisper real softly 'cause I don't want the men to hear me. I don't want them to know about my stories. I don't want them to know that I'm just a tired boy lying in bed in the middle of night telling himself stories 'cause he's got no one to talk to.

The pillow feels good, even though it's hot and the house is stuffy.

I'm whispering.

I like whispering.

I like it so much because I'm the only one who can hear it.

I'm here, but I'm lost.

In the woods.

During the day.

In the summer.

Deborah is looking for me. And she looks just like the girl on the cover of Cosmopolitan*. She's really pretty, but she's not wearing an evening gown.*

She's in a pair of jeans and a shirt. With sneakers.

I can see her, but I just stay lost in the woods. I don't want her to find me 'cause—

Two bad men are watching her: I can see them.

They plan on hurting her when she finds me.

No: They plan on killing her when she finds me.

I'm just a kid. Maybe three years old.

No: Five years old. Just like when I thought Mr. Meyerson was kidnapping me. Yes, I'm five and I'm lost in the woods, but now I'm hiding from the bad men that are following Deborah.

I want to help her, but if I say anything, they'll kill her.

She slowly turns around—

The men hide behind some trees so she can't see them. I can see them!

She turns back around and keeps walking. They wait a few moments, then they step out from behind the tree. She quickly turns around—

And scares them out of their wits! They run away, falling off a cliff a thousand feet to a river below. There, they are carried away and are never seen again!

And, before I know it, Deborah finds me and scoops me up in her arms. Suddenly, the woods look beautiful!

Playin' with Trains

I'm here again, looking down at my Lionel train set.

It's set up on the floor, but without the power pack. That's over the top of the closet door with the cord tied around my neck.

I've barricaded my door with books.

I'm ready.

I'm ready to go away.

Everyone is fast asleep. I got mad a few minutes ago and punched myself in the chest a couple of times.

I got mad 'cause I miss Dad. It's stupid to miss him 'cause he's never comin' back; there's nothing I can do about that.

Should just kick away the stool, but I'm scared.

A chicken.

A scared chicken.

Don't want people talkin' about me. Just want to disappear. Want to go away.

I stand up here, thinkin' about going away. I think about it a long time, but it doesn't matter.

I open the closet door and hold onto the power pack. I hold it next to me as I step down from the foot stool, then untie the cord from my neck and plug it in. I attach the wires to it so that I can run the train in a circle.

I lay on the floor and watch it go 'round and 'round, then turn it off and climb into bed.

I turn off the light.

I am whispering now.

Felicia holds my hand.

I'm just a kid. I'm about eight years old.

We are walking along a sidewalk in a city. It's a big beautiful city, like New York. It's in the spring and Felicia is walking with me. She's looking after me: she's my babysitter.

I'm just a boy and Felicia is walking with me in New York. She very pretty and she's holding my hand.

I'm about eight years old. Yeah, I'm eight and she's taking care of me.

A couple of blocks away, a car is racing through the streets. It's going fast, way too fast. And, it's running red lights, making people jump back and everything else.

My legs are moving back and forth a little bit.

Yeah, it's making the cops chase it. They're all chasing after it now, their lights are flashing and the cops are firing shots at the car as it's going faster and faster and faster and faster. It's going so fast, that the streets are just a blur to the driver.

Everything is just a blur.

It's going so fast that not even the fastest police cars in the world can catch up to it, instead falling farther and farther behind as the driver makes the car go faster, even faster and faster toward—

My arms are moving back and forth with my legs.

Felicia, who is strolling down the street with me. She's leading me down the street. We're window shopping. We're taking it easy and enjoying ourselves.

BANG! Blocks away, cars crash as they swerve to avoid that really fast car.

My arms and legs are bouncing really, really fast as I'm whispering my story. They're bouncing just like the car does in my story when it hits every bump in the pavement!

The car is getting closer to Felicia and me. It's going faster and faster. And faster. It's going so fast, that the people on the street can't see it except for a second as it screeches past!

Meanwhile, Felicia and me are talking.

"Johnnie, isn't the street just beautiful?"

And she's really pretty and she smiles at me. And I smile back at her 'cause I have a crush on her.

"Johnnie, isn't the city beautiful?"

And she keeps smiling at me. I keep smiling at her.

"Johnnie, isn't it just a beautiful day?"

"Yes, it's beautiful."

She laughs and we keep walking down the street.

The car is going faster and faster and faster and faster and faster and faster and faster and faster and faster and faster and faster! It's going so fast that it's almost going the speed of light! It's going so fast it looks like a light beam!

The car turns down a street.

IT'S THE SAME STREET THAT FELICIA AND ME ARE WALKING DOWN! IT'S COMING RIGHT AT US! FROM BEHIND US SO FELICIA CAN'T SEE IT!

IT'S GONNA GET US!

My head is bouncing up and down!

So is my chest!

My whole body is bouncing up and down on the bed!

I can imagine the whole story! Can imagine what the sky looks like. Can imagine the way the street sounds like! I can imagine everything!

And my whole body is bouncing up and down on my bed! My body is rolling around and I can hear the car screeching down the street, bearing down on Felicia as she holds my hand and she doesn't know that the car is coming!

I DON'T SEE THE CAR COMING!

FELICIA DOESN'T SEE THE CAR COMING!

My head is bouncing against my pillow. I'm bouncing up and down.

"Johnnie, isn't it a wonderful day?"

"Yeah."

"Lookout!"

Felicia grabs my hand—

My whole body is bouncing on the bed. I'm bouncing up and down really, really fast. My arms and legs are everywhere in the bed. There's just so much goin' on!

THE CAR ZOOMS RIGHT AT US AND SLAMS INTO THE BUILDING—BOOM!

IT EXPLODES ALL OVER THE PLACE! AND, BECAUSE IT HITS THE BUILDING SO HARD, THAT EXPLODES TOO!

EVERYBODY COMES RUNNING AND SEES THE WRECK!

THERE'S DUST EVERYWHERE. THE CAR HIT THE BUILDING SO HARD THAT IT'S NOTHING BUT DUST!

THE PEOPLE ARE TRYING TO SEE WHAT HAPPENED! THEY'RE TRYING TO FIGURE OUT WHAT HAPPENED TO FELCIA AND ME 'CAUSE THEY SAW US STANDING RIGHT WHERE THE CAR CRASHED INTO THE BUILDING!

THEY'RE ALL STANDING AROUND, TALKING!

"WHAT HAPPENED?" A GUY ASKS.

"I DON'T KNOW," A WOMAN SAYS.

AND THEN—

FELICIA STEPS OUT OF THE DUST, HOLDING ME IN HER ARMS! WE'RE COVERED IN DUST!

"Are you okay?" Felicia asks me.

"Yeah, I'm okay."

"Yeah, I'm okay," I whisper.

The Birch

The twins don't know shit. They don't know shit about trees, they don't know shit about axes, and they don't know shit about the woods.

Fuck, look at 'em, they stand there like pussies while I'm swingin' Mom's dull antique axe at this birch tree.

She got it from a yard sale over to Millerton. That's when she used to get out of bed and do shit. She doesn't get out of bed anymore.

Another thing; she no longer smiles. Her face looks so sad in the morning. Hell, it looks sad all day long. Makes me angry when I think about it 'cause I'm doin' everything I can to help, but it's not making any fuckin' difference.

Anyway, I'm swinging the axe real hard, but the rusty blade just bounces off the wood.

Thunk!

Mark laughs.

I drop the axe and punch that pussy a couple of times, knocking him onto the ground. Goddamned kids don't understand nothin' about hard work. Don't understand, instead thinkin' that life is all fuckin' fun and games.

"Leave me the fuck alone," he says, trying to roll away. I grab his arm and yank it real hard.

Warren? Warren just watches and takes everything in. He's not helping me out at all! At least he doesn't give me any lip the way that Mark does. Mark will backtalk unless I beat him. Sometimes, I just punch the shit out of him to keep him in line. He tries fighting back, but he's just a pussy. One big fuckin' pussy.

I pull Mark up off the ground. Wanna beat the shit out of him, but I haven't got all day for beatin' up pussies; we've got a tree to cut down.

I pick up the axe and swing again.

Thunk!

See, the trick to cutting down a tree is to make the first cut real low; that's where you want the tree to fall. Then, you go to the other side and make a little higher cut across from the low cut. That's using the tree to bring itself down. Any lumberjack knows that.

We're about a quarter mile away from the house. Mom never goes outside anyhow, so I'm not afraid of her finding out. Even if she heard it, I'd just tell her that someone was cutting trees on Dale's property.

"You leave that axe in the basement," she yelled last week when she saw me carrying it over my shoulder. "We need that if anyone tries to break in through those windows."

"I know, Mom. I'm just gonna sharpen it."

"You're not to use that in the woods. That's how people get killed."

"I'll put it back behind the furnace."

And I did. Only thing, I snuck it out the next day when she was taking a nap. Shit, she's always taking naps.

Anyway, the twins and I ran into the woods with it. No way we could build anything without it. We raided all the building supplies in the basement and got a ton of nails. I found an old antique claw hammer. All we need now for our cabin is wood.

It's gonna be beautiful. It's gonna have two floors; the basement and the lookout. I'm gonna build it just in the woods past the brook above all the flagstone. When it's in place, I'll have an observation post that will allow our forces to watch the woods at night.

Thunk, thunk, thunk the axe goes against the birch.

The woods smell of summer, but that's still a couple weeks away. The trees protect us from most of the heat. We located this birch about a hundred feet east of a big maple tree I call Point X. That's the thing, we have to build this in secret. Not even the Kinney kids can see us so we duck when we hear their F-100 drive by on their road. They're not spies, but they might let something slip that our enemies could use against us. In World War II, they had a saying about loose lips sinking ships. It's better not to let the cat out of the bag.

Once the fort is finished, we'll man it every night and protect our rear flank from attack.

After the truck passes, I grab the axe. I swing it with all my might.

Thunk!

Bits of bark and the tree's gut wood fly off.

"See, it's a matter of tilting the axe so it hits the wood at an angle," I say. I gotta instruct the boys so that they know what to do if something would ever happen to me and they would have to take care of Mom. I wish they would understand that someone needs to take care of Mom and the kids.

Thunk..., thunk..., thunk!

More pieces of the bark and gut wood shoot off the tree.

Mark pushes at the birch.

"It's too early," I tell him. "Wait until I make the second cut on the other side."

Thunk..., thunk..., thunk!

The chunks of wood are bigger now as I slam into gut wood. My blade is chopping at the tree. Bits and pieces of its guts fly past me.

"Fuckin' bitch!"

I jump to the other side and cut another slice that's about twelve inches long and three inches deep.

The twins move as more gut wood flies out of the tree's body and covers the ground. The birch leans and creaks; the fucker is comin' down!

166

The way I figure it, we have to build the lookout on the ridge. If we don't, our rear flank will remain open to attack. Sooner or later, the bastards in the woods at night are goin' figure out that they can launch their attack when they have enough troops. Mom hasn't bought any ammunition and I'm not old enough to buy it. The enemy has got to know that when they gather enough troops, they could storm the house, kill us, and retreat before sunrise without anyone knowing who did it.

"The People's Army prepares for war," Bitch says when she looks into my bunker at the house and sees my maps all over my walls. She doesn't realize that I keep watch every night. She doesn't realize that I patrol the perimeter at dawn to look for signs of the enemy who moved in and out of position during the night.

When everyone is sleeping, I make French toast or eggs during my watch. I check on Mom and the kids. Hell, I even listen to make sure that Bitch and Old Lady are okay. I'm what stands between the enemy and my family.

Why can't Bitch understand that?

At dawn, I patrol the perimeter from the front lawn to just inside the woods. Most of the time I only find fresh tire tracks on Kinney Road. Sometimes, they get careless and leave empty beer cans or cigarette butts. Often, late at night, I can hear their cars up Kinney Road. They sit up there, idling their engines, waiting for me to fall asleep. I keep my lights out, listening to the Panasonic or WENY radio, but I can hear 'em. The music is a diversion: I want them to think I'm sleeping like a baby when I'm really just sitting near the window, watching the road and the woods.

Those stupid assholes haven't figured out that I don't need that much sleep. I can make it up on Saturday and Sunday by sleeping until noon. Sometimes Princess picks up their noises, but then they just keep the cars running to cover their advance through the woods.

"Timber!" I yell.

The twins run like pussies even though the birch is cut to fall away from them.

The tree? It now stands still though I'm not sure why it's not falling. It's got nothing to connect it to the ground, nothing to connect to its source of nourishment. It can't stand on its own even though it still looks healthy.

Every living thing needs roots to keep it alive, but this tree just keeps on living without anything to help it.

It's funny: a tree like this could do anything. Could stand until a slight breeze pushes it over. Or, it could kick out, slam hard into the ground, or fall just right. I can't tell what it's going to do.

We don't know what it's going to do.

It could collapse in a split second. Yeah, just tumble right down 'cause it's got nothing to hold it to the ground. Nothin' to attach it. It's disconnected from the forest that raised it and protected it. It's got to fall.

"Watch out, boys, it's gonna fall hard," I yell.

We're all watching this tree, but the boys are far away from it.

Anyway, the fuckin' birch just acts like it's in the wind and sways, then rubs against another tree. It's still standing!

"It's pretending it's not chopped apart," I yell. "Doesn't know that it's dead."

The twins are far away, but they eventually return to the fall zone. The tree looks likes it's hinged, like it's still getting nourishment from its roots. Anyone can see that it's severed and could fall in any direction. Even a gentle wind can cause it to fall and take out more trees.

"What the fuck are ya' gonna do?" Mark asks.

I punch the birch with the backside of the axe, making it jump off the stump and slam upright into the dirt.

Fuckin' tree!

I hit it a couple times with the axe, but it doesn't do anything but take it. It's acting just like Warren does when I punch him.

"Now it knows it's been cut: it's trying to grow its own roots. Trying to act like it's still alive when it's actually dead," I tell the twins. "It's worse than dead. It's trying to fake being alive even though there's nothing feeding it but itself."

"Couldn't it kick out and kill you?" Warren asks. "Look how it's leaning. Couldn't it hurt you?"

I look at it, examining its chopped end that's buried about eight inches deep into the woods' soft floor. Warren is right; it could kick out of the dirt and pretty much fall in any direction including right onto me!

"It's not falling down," Mark says.

That's it! I've had enough of his shit!

I drop the axe and beat the shit out of Mark for giving me lip. He breaks away after I punch his gut a couple times, but then I catch the asshole and pin him against another birch.

"You fuckin' sonofabitch, it's gonna fall down! We have to get it chopped into beams for the cabin! 'Sides, it can't stand on its own. It's got nothing to connect it to its roots."

It's too bad I can't punch him in the face. Mom would see that bruise and paddle my ass real hard. So instead, I punch him in the stomach. Not hard enough to make him puke, but enough to shut him up. A man has to think; the last thing I need is his insubordination!

"You fuckin' pussy," I yell. "Shut up."

It's the only thing that works. If I let him go on, he'll give Warren bad ideas and nothing will get done. They have to know who's in charge.

My clothes are soaked. Should've put ice water in the Thermoses, but fuck it. Our mission was to escape the house undetected. Didn't want Bitch and Old Lady saying anything that would've made Mom suspicious.

"Warren, get the rope from garage. If Mom says anything, tell her that we need it to make a path."

Warren runs out of the woods toward Kinney Road. Mark and me watch him run down that road toward the house.

"Ya' gonna pull the bottom out?" Mark asks. He's a smart kid when he's not arguing with me.

"Yeah."

Warren gets back with the rope. He reports that he got it without anyone seeing him. He's sure. Me and the twins take the clothesline and wrap it around the bottom of the trunk three inches above the ground.

The son-of-a-bitch is stuck pretty tight. I can't move it with the axe and I ain't choppin' it again.

"Stand over there with this end," I order Mark as I hand him one end of the rope. I tell Warren the same thing, only he stands about eight feet from Mark. From above, the rope makes a letter *V* with the twins at the top of the letter and the tree at the bottom. Way I figure, we can persuade the tree to fall. I'll punch it with the axe while the twins pull the rope.

"You guys have to pull exactly the same or it'll kick into the stronger one."

I dig a little ditch behind the buried end to give it a straight path right between the twins. That way, it'll kick straight back.

"Don't let go when it starts kicking out or it'll kill the one still holding the rope."

The twins wrap their ends around their hands. They're fuckin' sweaty.

And scared.

Shit, they should be. Nothin' wrong with bein' scared, it's what you do with it. They gotta be brave.

It must be about noon 'cause I can't see the sun through the leaves.

"Ready? Let's go."

They grunt like pussies and I punch the tree with my axe. They yank and yank. The rope stretches, then snaps on Mark's side. He was pulling so fucking hard that he falls onto the ground.

"Warren, you didn't pull hard enough! And, why'd you get shitty rope? Get your ass to the house and get the fuckin' better rope!"

He just stands there like a pussy asshole, so I chase after him. He runs like a pussy through the woods, then I let up a bit. I have to save my strength for the birch tree.

Mark and I examine the rope: it snapped near the tree.

"Yeah, this tree thinks it's still alive," I tell him. "Thinks it can stand forever on its own."

I spit on the tree.

Mark looks up at its crown.

"It's caught up there," he says. "The other trees are holding it up."

I look with him and see that the fuckin' pussy is right: the birch's upper branches are tangled with the other trees around it.

170

It's all screwed up.

"Shit, it doesn't know it's dead and it shouldn't be doing that," I say. "Should just fall down and let us chop it apart. Thinks it can grow new roots and start growin' again, but it can't. It can't go on livin' anymore. There's nothin' to feed it."

Mark nods his head 'cause he knows I'm right.

"Not only that, the living trees around it don't realize that it's dead. When they discover it's dead, they should let it fall down. That might take forever."

Me and Mark stare at it forever. That's how long it takes Warren to get us the good rope. It takes another forever for us to pull down the birch, but we finally accomplish that part of the mission.

The Cabin

Eight feet of freshly-cut birch is too heavy to lift, so I tell the twins that we have to drag each section down the rock hill to the edge of the woods. We then have to roll it about a hundred feet down the rock hill. Once we get there, we have to take the sucker down Kinney Road to just below the power line, then drag it up the hill thirty or so feet to the ridge.

I tell the men what we're gonna do as we're examining the fallen birch.

"Can't we have lunch?" Mark asks.

"Fuck no."

I slam the axe into the severed tree just above a mark I made with a stone. It's always better to cut wood a little larger than it needs to be. I chop through the log quickly and we try lifting the sucker. It's too heavy, so we drag it through the woods. Our shirts get all dirty and soaked, but we don't care 'cause we're making progress. Shit, every day I read about the Vietcong who make highway bridges with their bare hands; we can build one fuckin' cabin.

We roll the beam from the forest onto the flagstone-covered hillside. The log bounces over the rocks to the road. It slams into the ditch, but doesn't splinter.

"That's birch. It's a hard wood," I tell the twins.

We grunt and groan like old farts trying to get it out of the
drainage ditch. The ditch is a foot lower that the road and we
can't get the rope around the log at first, so I use the axe as a lever
beneath it until Mark gets it around.

Warren gives it a yank and we got it on the road. I stand
in front, acting like a brake as the twins give it a push. We roll it
down the hill, stopping before it gathers speed.

What we do at the ridge is throw the rope around a tree at
the top and use that as a pulley. I pull the rope as the twins push
the beam up the ridge. It's a pain in the ass because the flagstones
are loose and they give away, creating rockslides that make the
twins fall. The rope holds the log: it's tied tightly.

After we get it on top, I run to the house and grab a shovel.

"John, what are doing?" Mom asks through the closed
kitchen door when she hears me in the garage.

I poke my head into the kitchen and see her sitting at the
table having a cup of coffee and smoking a cigarette.

"Just diggin' a hole in the woods."

"The twins with you?"

"Yeah."

"Well, you be careful," she says.

"Yes, Mom."

The boys look like beat dogs when I get back.

"You men sit in the shade while I dig," I tell them, "then
we'll get this one in place and call it a day." They're quiet as I
poke around the rocks and dig. Because I'm digging on the
western side of the ridge, the sun nails me. Too, it's hard because
the slope is steep.

I dig 'bout six, eight, then twelve inches. We then wrestle
the beam into place and it leans toward Kinney Road.

It's gonna fall, taking the twins with it!

Mark saves it by throwing himself against it, even though
it could send him thirty feet down if it tumbles!

Warren and I throw dirt around the bottom like crazy and
stomp our feet to tamp it in.

"Hurry the fuck up!" Mark yells.

We stomp like crazy and it holds.

The next morning, I get the twins out of bed early. I'm sore as hell, but it's better to get the next beam up before it gets too hot. My axe makes echoes as I cut the next beam from the birch. It's not as big and it's easier to handle.

We get that beam into place. Then I chop smaller beams that anchor the main ones into the hill. It looks like a dock, but there's no water, only a good view of Kinney road from our house to the north end of our property.

I take the last boxes of nails from the basement and nail cut branches perpendicular to the two floor beams. It's just wide enough for us, say about two feet. In some ways, it's like the bridges we built across the brook.

We cover the sides and top with some tarpaper we found in the garage. The outpost is fully operational in a week.

It's a secret, so we don't tell anyone about it. We sit in it for hours in the hot sun, watching for movements on the road. I sit up there all the time when I got nothing else to do.

Next week, I'm gonna use it as my night post.

Doug's Impala

Doug is such an asshole. There's not many cars with six circular taillights in a straight line. He thinks that coasting past the house with just his parking lights on makes him invisible. On the bus when he rides to his friend's house, he's just another hillbilly hick not saying anything until someone braver jumps in and starts on us.

Tonight, I hear him out there. He must have a few of his buddies with him. Maybe three or four them drag what sounds like a heavy chain all the way up the rock hill to the fort.

I'm in my room, playin' with Lego blocks and my train, acting like I don't hear his engine runnin' and wishin' he would wait until I went to bed. That way I could grab the .22 and fire a pussy shot. That's one that's not aimed at anyone, but nobody knows that.

Asshole; I can even hear his Impala's radio and his giggling. Can hear him and his friends as they climb up the hill. One of them must have fallen 'cause I hear them.

"Motherfucking niggers," he says. "Too bad they live in a brick house. Brick don't burn."

I stand still just inside my cotton curtains. They are plain white, but they hide me as long as I stand off to one side. I figure they probably have a lookout watching my room.

The back floodlight is off, so anything could be going on but as long as his car radio plays, I don't have anything to worry about.

Someone lets off the Impala's brake and I hear the partially bald tires rolling against the dusty road.

The assholes are silent and then they giggle like pussies. Darkness makes cowards brave.

I hear the main beams splinter just before the whole fort crashes down the side of the hill.

Doug lives on the other side of the valley from Fassett. For us to retaliate would be a very dangerous mission. To hike to his house would take a long time, at least five hours. There's no way the twins and I could sneak out and avoid Mom for that long.

At school, he parks his car at the building and though I could probably steal enough sugar from Mom to poison his gas tank, that lot is in clear sight of the building.

The pussies giggle as they peel out.

"Fuck you," one of them yells as the car disappears into the night. I go into the twins' room.

"They just tore down the cabin."

At sunrise, I go out and find a pile of cigarette butts and a couple soda bottles. What's left of the cabin is in the roadside ditch, a jumbled mass of twisted wood, torn tarpaper, and bent nails. I don't find any strange footprints on the path that leads from the cabin to the brook behind our house. They must have thought we were completely unsuspecting. I don't like people thinking I'm stupid.

I'm not stupid.

When the twins wake up, we examine the wreckage.

"Get the gasoline," I tell Mark.

He runs to the garage and returns with the red metal can. We set the wreckage on fire, the tarpaper making thick black smoke. By accident, the flames spread to some of the weeds at the bottom of the rock hill.

"Get on it, boys!" I yell. We three shovel like hell to keep the blaze from spreading down the hill and into the woods. We're tossing dirt all over the place, but we manage to contain it.

On Monday, I'm sitting a few seats behind Doug on the bus. He's visiting one of his friends, or he wouldn't even be on our bus.

"It's a good thing that cabin fell," I tell Mark.

"Yeah."

"Yeah, with those beams being as rotten as they were it probably would've killed us all if we were in it when it collapsed."

I ignore Doug as I walk to the door.

He's so stupid.

Ranch Wagon 500

The army sergeant puts his hand on my chest and forces me to the ground.

"Son, get down," he yells.

I cover my eyes 'cause the sun gets in the way. When I turn my head toward the interstate, I see a lady standing on the shoulder. She holds a baby on each arm.

Next to her is a man in a suit.

Next to him, a group of kids stand in front of their mom and dad.

On the other side of the median strip, some army soldiers climb out of their jeeps. From as far as I could see west, the convoy is stopped on the shoulder.

The sergeant pulls Mom from the wreckage. He yanks on the door and I hear steel twist. Something had pushed the Ranch Wagon's fender into the door.

Mom stumbles into the grass and holds her head. I stand up and look at the windshield. Mom's side is fine, but Maria's side looks like a rock slammed into it… from the inside.

Warren screams and some soldiers cautiously approach the tailgate. The side window is all busted out. I can see the seats are bloody. Rose's Raggedy Anne is on the median strip. Rose, crying, stands near Faith on the grass.

Though neither of them are bleeding, Faith has seat face.

My mouth tastes salty. When I wipe it, I feel a wet flap of skin on my nose. My arm turns red and wet when I wipe it against my face.

The sergeant puts one hand on my chest and one on my back.

"Son, I said to get down," he says, pushing me against the grass on the median strip. They sky is so blue and everything feels so quiet. I can't believe everything is quiet for a few moments.

Then I hear Warren.

I hear Warren crying.

I never heard Warren cry before.

He never cries when I beat him or yell at him or call him names, but I can tell it's him crying right now. He's wailin' real hard.

I hear an ambulance. The sergeant and his men run toward the Ranch Wagon's tailgate.

There's a Pennsylvania State Police Car on the shoulder, its lights flashing. The trooper is close by, talking with Mom.

"My license is expired, officer," I hear Mom say to the Trooper. "For God's sake, you can't arrest me. I'm a widow with six children. Who will take care of my children?"

I watch the lady with the babies climb back into her car, though the rest of the audience just stands on the shoulder of the interstate. Mom leans against our car, crying. She runs toward Warren when the volunteer fireman pry open the tailgate. That sounds like twisting metal as they tear it open.

"What's wrong with him?" one of the firemen asks the sergeant while pointing at me.

"Facial lacerations, I think," the sergeant says. "Think he put his face through the side window.

I look at the side window right near where I was sitting. It's the broken one.

"Any bone damage?"

The sergeant shakes his head.

"Don't think so." He gets real quiet, "But the one in the

back sounds pretty bad."

Some soldiers help the troopers route traffic around the rescue vehicles when a fire truck arrives.

Mom is crying, yelling, "Warren, Warren!"

"Hurts… to… breathe, Mommy," he says.

My eyes sting and my arm turns red again when I wipe my face with it. My tongue runs over my teeth. The front of my mouth is numb. My face is numb and wet. Wetter than sweat. I sneeze blood and feel dizzy when I try to get up. I have to get up and help Warren. He's my brother and he needs my help.

"Son, stay down," the sergeant says.

Even from the ground, I can see that something had dented the car's roof. Faith's door rests a few feet off the ground, even though the Ranch Wagon's rear end is bent upward. Her door hangs open: it can't close anymore.

The firemen carefully take Warren from the back of the wagon, get him onto a stretcher, and lift him. Mom is crying and clutching her purse. A second trooper arrives and gets the other kids into his car.

A fireman kneels down beside me and looks at my face.

"Where does it hurt?" he says.

"What's wrong with Warren?"

"He's gonna be all right," he says, trying to convince me. He feels my face with hand and traces the outline of my jaw, making my face hurt. "We need another stretcher," he yells.

A group of firemen rushes Warren to the ambulance, a Cadillac. My brother is coughing and screaming.

Another group place a stretcher on the ground next to me.

"I can walk." I say. When I look at my hand, I see that it's covered with blood.

"Not yet. We better make sure you're all right," the fireman says.

They roll me onto a stretcher and I look at our wrecked car as the fireman carry me to the ambulance. There, they slide me in next to Warren and the driver puts a Band-Aid on my nose.

"Warren, it's me. They're letting me ride with you."

He's wheezing on the stretcher and his head is fastened so tight that he can't turn it. I sit up and lean over toward him and try not to cry.

I look at Warren's face. I've never seen him so scared in my life.

Mom climbs into the front. The driver makes the tires kick dirt and rocks against the car when he floors it. He switches on the siren and pulls onto the road. I sit up and watch the Caddy pass all the cars that pull over as we race to the hospital.

"John..., am I... gonna be... okay?" Warren asks.

I don't know. I don't anything right now, so I hold his hand. I hold it tight and tell myself that he'll be okay. I tell myself that he has to be okay, that he's just a kid and he shouldn't die.

We cry together for the second time today.

Earlier today, us kids and Mom sat in the Ranch Wagon. Mom had shut off the engine, but Johnny Cash was singing on the radio.

The cemetery was quiet.

"I always forget to get flowers," Mom said as she turned off the radio. We sat on the road at the park's edge for a few minutes, then Mom got out and wandered through the cemetery, stopping a couple of times.

At the wrong graves.

"She always forgets Dad's plot," Maria said, unbuckling her belt. She got out of the front seat and helped Mom look for Dad.

I reached out the opened back window and grabbed the handle, opening the tailgate. The rest of us kids stood around the car and looked at the headstones.

Dad only had a marker. Mom couldn't afford a headstone.

Mom and Maria looked for his VFW marker and his faded miniature American flag. The grounds were filled with them. Some stood next to headstones and statues. Others, like Dad's, stood above a plot.

Maria found it a ways from where Mom was looking.

"Here it is," she said.

She waved Mom over. The rest of us walked past the headstones toward Maria, being careful not to step on anyone's grave.

We stood at the Dad's miniature flag and looked at the ground. Mom closed her eyes and I cried 'cause I missed Dad so much. So many things have gone wrong since he died and it got to me standing at his grave and thinking about how bad things were.

Sometimes, it hurts my guts if I don't cry when I have to. It always makes my guts feel better.

"He was a good man," Mom whispered.

"Yes…, he was," I said.

We stood together around Dad's marker a mile from the house on Mt. Bethel. And two hundred miles from Fassett. Us kids and Mom stood together and we cried. We weren't Bitch and Old Lady and Chink and Cheeky and Ear and Blimp just then. They weren't any hit men in the woods, mahogany foot stools, or kids on the bus.

They were all gone right then, erased for a moment 'cause we all missed Dad so much.

We had taken Interstate 80 East to get back there. We always did on Memorial Day when we visited the grave. Maria rode shotgun. Faith hid in the second seat with Baby Rose next to her. The twins sat in the back with me, but I kept my spot between the second and third seats above the gas tank.

"C'mon, let's get going," Mom said that morning. Maria and Mom had made sandwiches the night before. Now, we ran like hell around the house to get toys to play with in the car.

I never took anything 'cause we always came back home the same day. Once we stayed with the Fitzens down the road, but Mr. Fitzen smoked cigars that made our clothes smell funny.

When we reached Jersey, we took the exit for Route 46 and followed the river past Old King Cole's Hot Dog Cove and Hot Dog Johnny's.

"We'll stop on the way back," Mom said.

The stories started at the foot of Mt. Bethel.

"Mr. Peterson died that morning his milk truck wrecked," Mom said. "Told your father and me that his brakes felt squishy. Daddy told him to get them fixed. We made Mr. Peterson promise to get them fixed."

She slowed down while climbing the hill to point at the new guardrail.

"That's where he went over the edge."

I tried to see the truck, but the trees and leaves covered it up. Butchie told me that the fire company and the cops decided to just leave it there.

"Nothing left to it 'cause it blew right up," he said.

We stopped in front of the old house. Mom left the car's engine running as she stayed in the road.

I looked at Butchie's house. It seemed like a thousand years ago that we played fire truck in his barn.

"Can't we see if he's home?"

"Honey, it's a holiday. People have family picnics on Memorial Day. Butchie probably wants to be with his family."

She gave it a little gas and we went down the hill past Barbara's house, the Fitzens, Dr. Heller's, Chuckie's, and the Kalendovich's.

We passed the farm with the scary barn and the country store and then we were at Cemetery Road.

They are waiting for Warren at the local hospital. By now, he quiets down and I watch the nurses gently lift him out of the ambulance. He lets go of my hand when he has to, which wasn't until they take him in for x-rays.

A nurse pours alcohol on a rag and rubs my nose. I wince, then she makes a bandage. A minister comes out and shakes Mom's hand, but she sends him away.

Three hours later we all sit in the waiting room without Warren, reading *Life* and *People*.

I have a headache and my face hurts.

Cemetery Road stretched a few miles past some farms and scattered woods. The road went up and down the hills.

"They had a color guard at your father's funeral," Mom said over John Cash's *I Walk the Line*. "Ha, full military honors. They had a couple of drunk wops."

"It's right up there," Maria said.

The top of the hill had been cleared into a field, then made into a cemetery. A stone wall separated it from the road, though

180

the parts away from the pavement and the main entrance were open.

Mom pulled into the side entrance. There were cars all over the place, people carrying flowers and plants in their hands walking slowly to the headstones. Mom never brought anything but us kids to the cemetery.

In the hospital, Maria puts down her *People* magazine and whispers something to Mom.

"At least they're not arresting me," Mom says, "But they gave me a warning."

"You better get those glasses," Maria says.

"I'm not paying for new glasses just to drive. That's ridiculous. I'm not made of money and I can see perfectly with this pair. Besides, I didn't need special glasses in New Jersey."

"Can't you take the test with those glasses?" Maria asks, not believing her.

"No, I have to get an appointment with an optometrist."

"Well, you better get it done."

Maria opens another *People* and reads about Elton John.

"Can I have that when you're done?" I ask.

"Sure, Bro."

The Ranch Wagon stayed quiet between the cemetery and Hot Dog Johnny's on the way to I-80. I ate a hot dog and fries, then drank birch beer just like everyone else, except Mom. She smoked a cigarette and watched Baby Rose swinging.

Once in Pennsylvania on Interstate 80, we watched an eastbound Army convoy. Somewhere west of the Poconos, the frame on the Ranch Wagon spread. Mom lost control of the car and it slammed into the median strip. Mom hit the windshield, Warren bounced like a ping-pong ball in the back and I put my face through the side window when the car hit the median strip and stopped dead.

Fearing the car would explode, I jumped over my sister and got out, then ran around the totaled wagon trying to rescue my family until the sergeant grabbed me by the shirt and forced me to the ground.

All of us look up when we hear footsteps coming down the hallway. We look up and see a doctor. Next to him, a nurse is pushing a wheelchair with Warren in it.

"He's just been knocked around a little bit," the doctor says. "He'll be sore for a couple days, but he didn't break anything."

The nurse wheels Warren out the door.

The doctor lets Warren walk to the taxi, an Impala. Four of us sit in the back. Mom rides in front and talks all the way home. She holds Baby Rose on her lap, who holds onto her Raggedy Anne.

It's been one hell of a Memorial Day.

Satellite Sebring Wagon: Summer

Smell that? That's a cool smell: it's the smell of a car that hasn't been ruined by someone sitting in it yet!

And look at that color! It's blue! Sure, it's lighter than the Ranch Wagon, but it's faster, handles better, and doesn't use as much gas!

And it seats eight! The back seat faces toward the back of the car. Not like in the Ranch Wagon! Those seats faced each other.

It's so neat.

And, guess what?

It doesn't cost that much.

Faith's gonna learn to drive on this car. She's almost 18! It'll be so cool!

We're at Elmira Chrysler Plymouth in Elmira and Mom's buying us all a brand new car!

Satellite Sebring Wagon: Fall

The men come a few nights before Halloween. We don't celebrate it anymore 'cause Mom can't afford costumes and her Singer is buried beneath old *Inquirers* and other shit at the foot of her bed.

They don't even knock, just pulling their car up to the house and opening our garage door.

Princess barks and we flip on the lights. I look out and see them in their white shirts and dark ties.

"Mom, what do hit men look like?"

Bitch goes off when she sees them.

"You pay the fucking car bill?"

Mom fumbles with a cigarette and puts down an old copy of *Redbook*. She's real careful with it, putting it face down so that it's opened to the page she was reading.

Bitch grabs the checkbook. Old Lady starts her shit, bitching about losing the car.

"You don't know what the fuck you're talkin' about," I yell, trying to grab the checkbook. Bitch grabs my arm, cutting into me with her claws.

"She hasn't paid a fucking thing," she says.

Mom stands and looks in the mirror. She straightens the waist of her wrinkled Capri pants and combs her hair as we hear the men walk into the garage.

"Mom, they're stealing the car!" Warren says.

"If they don't get their money for it, they can sue us for the difference. Especially since you never got that dent fixed," Bitch says.

A few months ago, some asshole in Elmira cut Mom off and dented the front fender. He drove away and Mom couldn't report it to the police because she doesn't have a license. Oh yeah, I broke the side mirror when I threw a snowball in the garage a few weeks ago, but the dealer fixed it 'cause Mom lied and said it just broke like that when she hit a pothole.

Anyway, Mom goes into the garage. Bitch goes out with her. Me and the twins stand right near the kitchen door just in case Mom needs us.

"Don't fuckin' believe this shit," Old Lady says.

"Shut up, so we can hear," I say.

We listen to Mom beg the men.

"But I'm a widow with six children," she says. Her voice is real sad. And tired. "The nearest grocery store is twelve miles away in Elmira. How am I gonna feed them?"

The man says he's sorry, but the bank needs its money. He says Mom agreed to pay the bill and the bank needs its money. Says he's just doing his job and maybe everything will work out.

"I was in the hospital and got behind. The doctor said I had to get electro-shock. Said I had a chemical imbalance. And my brother stole all my money. I tried to get it back, but I couldn't make the police believe me."

The man says he's sorry, but Mom will have to talk to the bank. He says that he has a family, too, and he won't get paid if he lets her keep the car.

Mom doesn't say anything.

The kitchen door swings open. Mom comes in, a cigarette hanging from her mouth. She fumbles with her shoulder bag and opens her key purse. When she opens it, the leather seams split open and it breaks into three pieces. She takes the Plymouth's keys and walks outside.

Me and Mark see the Ford key in her key purse.

"Shit, she never turned that in? Wonder if that'll fit in any Ford," Mark says, pocketing it.

"Give me that," I say, punching the little bastard a couple times. He gives it up 'cause he knows he better not fuck with me.

The man thanks Mom and says that he's sorry. He says that he hopes that she talks to the bank and works everything out.

The man starts the Plymouth. We watch it as it takes him forever to pull it out. Mom has it in there all fucked up and the guy has to be careful he doesn't take any more chrome off it.

Princess barks, but it's because of the men.

"At least we don't have to get the dent fixed," Warren says. I want to punch him, but I get distracted. Bitch is bitching as soon as she puts down the garage door. I go out and stare at the empty garage.

"What are we gonna do for food?" Bitch yells. Mom is straightening all the rakes and shit like that. "You don't pay the goddamned bills and now we don't have any fucking car! How are we supposed to get food?"

"Me and the twins'll ride to the store, Bitch."

"It's twelve miles to fucking Elmira. Rosie takes fucking People's Army on a Great March!"

I punch Bitch real hard in the back. She swings around and hooks my arms with her nails. Fuck her! She kicks me in the legs and pushes me against the wall.

Mom doesn't give a fuck. She wanders back inside.

Mark helps me out, punching Bitch in the shoulder. She kicks him in the ankles and he cries like a pussy.

"Fucking Rosie and his army gonna ride their rickshaws down steep mountain to get supplies at store," Bitch yells.

"It's better than bitchin', Bitch."

Bitch slaps me, giving me a nosebleed. She hooks her nails back into my arms and slams me against the wall.

Mom runs at Bitch, screaming like crazy. "Will you stop it?" she yells. "Stop it this minute or I'll beat you within an inch of your lives." She slaps Bitch a few times. "You're gonna give him cancer. Skin cancer with those nails! You already lost your father to cancer: you want to lose him too? I swear to God, I'm gonna cut off your hands while you're sleeping!"

"He hit me first," Bitch says. She's always blaming Mom and me for all sorts of shit we didn't cause.

"Rosie always wants to fight," Old Lady says in her fake Chinese voice. She makes that oriental voice when she wants to get me real mad.

"Rosie Rickshaw and People's Army will ride their rickshaws to store and get us much-needed supplies."

"Fuck you, Old Lady."

I try kicking Old Lady, but Bitch has her claws in my arms.

Fuck them. I won't let my family starve.

Supply Line

Things are bad now.

Real bad.

Our provisions are low.

Maria and Kevin bring us some groceries when they go out on a date, but Mom doesn't have a lot of money to give them.

The Little Ones aren't getting enough to eat. To help out, I go without food. I mean, I just miss a meal or two each day.

It's no big thing: It's not like I'm starving or anything.

If I don't think about food, I stop being hungry.

Mom's staying in bed all day. It's like she doesn't fuckin' care or anything. I figure that I'm gonna have to establish and man a supply line to The Rancho.

'Cause if I don't, the kids are gonna starve and I can't let that happen.

Princess

My dog is in the dirt. I got the flashlight on her, but she's real sick. I smell guts and dog piss. When she exhales, I can see her breath. Mom gave me lots of old blankets and a big kettle filled with hot water.

"Just let nature takes its course," she says.

My gloves are all bloody from trying to wipe Princess dry. She whimpers for a minute.

Shit, I don't remember when I caught that stray in her circle. It was sometime in the summer, I guess. The air smelled funny and I heard some yelping. I ran out and threw rocks at the bastard fuck, but I was too late. The mutt had finished and ran off into the woods.

I went into the house and ate breakfast.

"Goddamned hicks let their fucking dogs run free," I told Old Lady at the breakfast table.

"She's a purebred," Mom says as she pours out more pancake batter. "I have the papers to prove it."

"Yeah, and she got fucked by a purebred... mutt."

Mark laughs, but Mom got mad and slapped my face.

"You watch your mouth."

I'm laughing so hard 'cause I'm funny.

"Should've got her spade," Bitch said.

"She was gonna breed them, remember?" Old Lady said. "Until she let Snappy die."

"She didn't fuckin' let him die."

"She knew he was sick," Old Lady said.

Mom stood at the stove, turning pancakes. "The vet didn't believe me. Said he'd be okay."

"Should've brought him inside," Bitch said, pouring the Aunt Jemimiah syrup, then putting down the empty bottle. She always took the last of everything.

That was when we had a car and it didn't matter that we lived in the middle nowhere. We could escape as long as Mom put gas in it.

Nothing matters anymore. Over the past couple of weeks, Princess got real big and started digging in the dirt with her front paws. Now, she lies on her side, it's cold as fuck, and Bitch is inside doing homework.

I'm the only fucking one out here in the dark.

I take a blanket and spread it out on the ground, then take my dog and roll her onto to it. She lets me rub her neck, but her fur is cold.

"Fuck them, honey."

Princess is giving birth. Her circle and coop are away from the windows on the dark side of the garage. The floodlight barely reaches us. If I stand the wrong way, I cast a shadow over everything. The Ray-O-Vac battery in the flashlight is old and the light is dim.

Princess gets quiet, then I hear something. She reaches around with her mouth and chews at herself. I reach along her back legs and under her tail. I see steam rising from her. It's so fucking cold, I take my hands and dip them in the water, rubbing my fingers all over the thing.

The pup becomes still and after Princess chews through the cord; it's a lump of wet fur in my hands. My dog turns around and eats some of the steaming stuff as I hold the puppy. I try dipping the thing in water, but it's limp in my hand.

I cover Princess, then fetch the pickaxe from the garage while I hold the wet fur ball in my hand: it is dark and its snoot is long like my dog's.

I trudge to Snappy's grave. The earth isn't frozen when I get to it. Isn't frozen at all. Doesn't matter if it is 'cause I have the pot of hot water Mom poured me.

I do what I have to, then get my ass back inside.

Mom and Faith are waiting for me.

"She lost the baby," I say.

"What did it look like?" Old Lady asks.

"A mutt. It's a good thing."

Old Lady nods.

I wash my hands in the bathroom, but they still stink. I use a bunch of Mom's *Vaseline Intensive Care Lotion*, but it doesn't get rid of the stench.

It takes a few days to wear off.

1974

The Schwinn

Let me tell you what; the downhill ride is easy. It's getting the milk back to the house before it goes bad that's the problem. It's hot as hell, even this early in the morning, and I have to keep stopping because the milk containers keep sliding off the front fork of my bike.

Mark and Warren ride with me. They've got groceries tied to front of their bikes too, but it's tough to peddle with all that stuff. Actually, I've got the heaviest load. The boys are bringing cereal and bread.

We're out of food 'cause Maria went with Kevin's family on their summer vacation for a few weeks. I don't blame her for going. It's not her fault that we don't have a car.

'Sides, they've been getting' us food all winter, so I don't blame 'em.

That's why me and the boys went to get milk and some other stuff. Everything is so expensive at The Rancho, but we're not starving.

The milk is warm by the time we get it home. Maybe next time I should tie the ice chest to the Schwinn's back fender. I'll have to figure out how I'm gonna do that.

Frank Buck

I'm in my room playin' with trains this morning. I got the power pack cord around my neck when I hear Mom yelling at Maria.

Maria must have enjoyed her vacation 'cause she has a nice tan and was nice for one whole day before she started bitchin' again.

Now, she's bitchin' all the time.

She's bitchin' about Mom staying in bed.

Bitchin' about us being poor.

Bitchin' about us not havin' food.

I'm really sad. Been locking myself in my room and punching myself in the chest.

I've also been crying. Been crying like a fucking pussy. I just don't know what else to do. I can't keep the supply line open.

Things are getting worse.

It's really bad.

I've never seen it like this. We are totally surrounded and running out of provisions. To save food for the Little Ones, I'm eating one meal every couple of days. Sometimes, I pick food out of the garbage.

Not only that, I'm expecting the enemy to attack the house any night now. We'll probably sustain heavy losses when that happens because my men are weak and run-down.

I don't how things will ever get any better.

I have failed to protect my family. If I could only get a job and bring in some money so I could buy a car and get some food. Mark and me entered a contest to win mini-bikes. We figured if we won, we could ride through the woods to Elmira and get food that way.

We didn't win the mini-bikes. That's why I'm standing on the foot stool today.

I'm really thinking I'm gonna kick away the stool when I hear Bitch fuckin' starting in on Mom.

Fuck! I just want to kick away the stool! I'm so tired of fighting!

Fuck! I don't want to do anything, but someone has to keep Bitch in line. Most the time, she just needs a good punch or two in the back. She'll dig her claws into my arms and it'll all be over real soon.

I step down from the foot stool and untie the cord.

I always stand in the mirror and look at my neck after I

loosen the cord. If anyone sees the marks on my neck and figures out what I'm thinkin' about, they'll probably put me in jail or the nuthouse. If that happens, I'm pretty sure that the enemy will step up their invasion timetable. I'm the last soldier in this joint.

Besides, I don't want anyone to know anything like that about me. I've seen what they've done to Mom.

"You put that phone down!" Mom yells.

I stand in the mirror, rubbing my neck.

Shit! I pulled the cord too tight this time and it left an ugly red line that goes all around my throat. In front, it's between my jaw and my Adam's apple. Real straight.

I reach under my bed and pull out a pump bottle of *Vaseline Intensive Care Lotion*, putting some on my red skin. They'll all think I've been playin' with myself, but I don't give a shit. Teenagers are supposed to play with their peckers.

I hear the kitchen door slam and I run into the living room, leaning on the Magnavox to look out the window. I watch Bitch run down the driveway. And, get this, she's wearing her nightgown! What a stupid bitch!

When I get into the kitchen, I see Mom standing with a cigarette in one hand and the meat cleaver in the other. Faith is sitting at the table, clearly upset.

"Maria tried to kill me with this," she says, waving the cleaver. "She's goin' to the Board of Health and tell them lies about me. They'll come and take me away. All you kids will be put in an orphanage."

Faith stares at Mom 'cause she's disgusted with Bitch.

"That fuckin' bitch. Mark and Warren!"

The twins stumble out of the room. They carry a couple of Matchbox cars. They look like Crudleys'. Fuck, at least the Curdleys' had food.

"Maria just tried to kill Mom. She's running away to tell lies."

Mom puts away the cleaver just like did she when she finished making veal parmesan. We haven't had that in a long time. She rarely cooks anymore because we have nothing to cook. We mostly have cereal, but the mice get into that so Mark and me hunt down the little fuckers and beat them to death with the fireplace poker and shovel.

192

"Go get her, Johnnie," Mom says.

"I'll bring her back alive, Mom. Just like Frank Buck. We'll all bring her back alive."

Mom slaps me, knockin' me against the wall.

"You better son, or the cops are gonna come and split you children up, sayin' I'm an unfit mother." She inhales cigarette smoke and watches it as she tilts her head back and blows circles at the ceiling.

"I'll bring her back, Mom, I promise."

I fetch a bunch of rope from the garage. I use some of it to tie a Thermos to the front fork of my bike and I loop the rest over my shoulder. I figure she's got to be somewhere in the woods along the dirt road.

I figure that she probably won't come easy. The boys and I will have to tie the prisoner's hands together, then tie her to my bike.

It takes the twins about an hour to get the lead out of their asses before we can hunt Bitch. We ride up Kinney Road past Point X. I can't make any speed 'cause the twins are slow fucks.

"Why can't we call the police?" Warren asks.

I punch him once or twice to shut him the fuck up. Sometimes that works. Now, he just sits on his bike and he shuts his fuckin' mouth. He drags way behind and I have to kick him in the shins to get him goin'.

"She could be anywhere," Mark says when we finally climb past Point X. It's hot as hell.

We go all over the place. I ride my Schwinn ahead of the twins, lettin' them cover my rear flank.

That's how we patrol. I let them drop back to look for any counter-patrol. In this case, they keep a sharp eye in case Bitch decides to double back and kill Mom.

She's probably in the woods whispering "Chink" or "Rosie" as we pass. Could be anywhere. The woods are so thick, she may have just run into Dale's woods to hide until we're gone.

I raise my hand, signaling the twins to stop and yell to Mark.

"Shit, think she might have doubled back? She's gotta know that Mom would've sent us out. Maybe she wants us away from the house so she can sneak back and kill Mom."

"Faith wouldn't let her," Warren says.

"Bitch and Old Lady are allies, asshole," I say. "With us out of the way, they could even frame it on us."

"Maria would never do that." Mark says. "She just bitches. She'd never kill Mom. She's never even hit Mom."

"So, you think Mom's a liar?"

"No, just that Maria wouldn't try to kill her."

I punch Mark. He swings at me, but I just slug him again. Mark fuckin' tries to fight back. That's insubordination and if I wasn't trying to capture Bitch, I'd beat him to an inch of his life!

"Mom wouldn't lie," I yell. "Bitch tried to kill her with a cleaver. Or, don't you pussies believe the truth?"

They get real quiet and look at the dusty road 'cause they now know the fuckin' truth about Bitch trying to kill Mom.

"So, what should we do?" I ask.

"Find Bitch and bring her back alive," Mark says.

"That's more like it."

We get back on our bikes and ride.

Bitch is lucky that I know all about prisoners. When I capture her, she will be treated according to The Geneva Convention. That's for prisoners of war. That's what she will be. I'm not gonna let her get away with trying to kill Mom. She's getting too strong and too dangerous.

She will be punished.

The sun is goin' down by the time we decide to go home. By now, we've patrolled Kinney Road, Wheeler Road, part of Christian Hollow Road, and most of Roaring Run Road up to Frank's farm. Our last stretch is the downhill section from Frank's near Seymours' and past Ed's home to our house.

We stop just after Seymour's where the asphalt levels out a bit and the bumps aren't so bad. From there, we can see the road in both directions for 'bout a half mile before it goes over the top of the hill near Frank's farm and dips into a hollow. I figure I better tell the twins what to expect.

I ride over to them and take a hard look at them. Shit, they're just kids; nine year-old boys. I was still a kid at their age for a little bit until Dad died and everything got all messed up. I figure that I better tell them the truth.

"Men, we'll probably never see each other once we get to the house," I say. "The Board of Health should be waiting to place us in foster homes. Bitch probably got to them and told them all her fuckin' lies."

Warren cries. He always fuckin' cries.

"Men, it's my fault," I say. "I fucked up. As your leader, I should have known where Bitch hid. I'm sorry."

I get on my Schwinn and ride ahead of my men 'cause I don't want them to see me crying.

We take off down the hill just like we had a thousand times before when we pedaled like hell and dodged the potholes. Only this time, we don't pedal at all, standing as we ride our coaster brakes and drift downhill past Ed's, then over the curving rise and across the bottom of Kinney Road into our driveway.

I get off my bike after I pedal up to the garage. That place stinks 'cause Mom stopped paying the garbage men and we stack all the trash in there. It's infested with mice and rats.

My Thermos is empty, but I've got plenty of energy. I go into the house, ready to surrender.

"Mom?"

She sits in bed with her hair all pretty and stuff. She's smoking a cigarette and reading an old copy of *Better Homes and Gardens*. The TV is on and Baby Rose is playing with Faith.

Mom looks up at me.

"We didn't find her. I'm sorry," I say.

"Don't worry about it." Mom says, without looking up from her magazine.

"Did she come back?"

"No." She looks at us. "You boys hungry?"

"Yeah."

Mom goes to the kitchen and gets out some bread, vanilla, and eggs. She grabs an almost empty milk carton from the fridge, then a Pyrex mixing bowl. She makes up French toast, but there's not enough bread for me. Besides, my men need food more than I do.

I go to my room and block my door. I stand and look at myself in the mirror.

I punch myself in the chest a few times because I failed in

my mission and now my family is in danger.

I punch myself again.

And again.

And again.

I find my power pack and tie the cord tightly around my neck. In less than five minutes, I'm where I was when Bitch tried to kill Mom 12 hours ago even though the red mark is gone. I'm thinkin' it's more honorable for me than surrendering to the Board of Health.

I stand on the foot stool a long time, punchin' myself every once in a while.

I fuckin' chicken out again, instead staying up all night waiting for The Board of Health to raid the house.

They never show up. Not even when Bitch comes home the next morning. She acts like nothing happened, but I decide to keep an eye on her.

I don't trust her.

War Rifle

On July 3, 1974 at 2320 hours, an unknown number of guerillas penetrate our house's outer perimeter. Our forces are enjoying R and R when the first rounds slam into our compound. General quarters are immediately sounded when Princess barks.

Mom gives the order to mobilize.

"This is it. They're gonna kill me and split you kids up. Get the guns, boys."

I am fourteen and ready for war. I have been preparing for this day during the past three years.

Because the enemy is smart, they have waited until we were weak before attacking. We have very few provisions and our ammunition stores are dangerously low. We're in a dangerous situation because if they lay us to siege, we'll have to attack them and inflict casualties that will probably not be considered self-defense. I'm hoping they make a mistake and attempt to invade our house.

"You heard her, boys," I yell. "And get those damned lights off. Everybody hit the dirt. This is not a drill. I repeat, this is not a drill: we are being attacked."

Maria and Faith run to Rose's room and fetch my baby sister. The girls huddle in the living room near the Magnavox as *Action News* ends. I follow Mom into the kitchen.

"Mom, what are you doing?"

"Calling the State Troopers."

"The barracks is an hour away."

Mom lights a Winston.

"Protect us, Johnny. Hold them off until the troopers can get here."

The enemy fires more rounds that slam into the front door near Mom's bed. The girls scream and cry.

"Shit, those are rifle shots: they can penetrate the brick," I yell.

The bastards planned well. They had the coordinates and could be anywhere out of the range of the floodlight. They sit on their asses in the woods on the hill across the road, ready to pick us off.

The backyard remains dark, its perimeter guarded by a second floodlight activated by a switch in the garage. That is now off-limits to our forces.

Shit, that's why Doug tore down the fort!

The weakest part of the compound is still our rear flank, especially at night. One sniper strategically placed in the woods at the edge of the backyard can draw fire while a second shooter humps along our dry brook's bed and down the hill to the twin's room. From there he can easily pull the nails anchoring the wooden storm windows, breach the inner perimeter, and neutralize us.

Mark runs to a front window and lifts the sash.

"Fuck you, we've got weapons!"

The enemy responds with a burst of gunfire that hits the garage. I grab Mark and knock him down in front of the Magnavox.

"Soldier, I need you alive. Get to your post."

"We should fire back!" Mark yells.

I punch him a few times.

"Asshole, who's gonna believe this in court? It's not self-defense unless they get inside the perimeter, inside this house. We are in enemy territory. We can't return fire unless they breach the house's inner perimeter. Then, it's self defense!"

I hump over the carpet to the closet door.

"Turn off those goddamned lights," I yell.

"I'll get them," Mom yells. "The troopers are on the way."

"Mark, Warren; come with me," I yell.

Illuminated by the glow of *The Tonight Show's* opening credits, we hump toward the flagstone fireplace. At 2330 hours, we open the ammunition closet, push aside Mom's dresses, and assemble our gear. I slide the .22 Marlin pump to Warren. Mark takes the 16 gauge and loads it with birdshot. I snap a clip into Dad's M-1 Garand.

"This is not a drill. Don't fire until you see the whites of their eyes. Do you understand me?"

"Yes, Sir," the twins say.

"Good. Warren, you guard the girls and Mom. Keep everyone down. If you hear anything, what do you say?"

"Who goes there, friend or foe?"

"Good job, soldier."

"Mark, take up a position in the kitchen and train your weapon on the door to the garage. Take the safety off. Fire only when the door is breached."

"Yes, Sir."

"I'll be in the hallway by my room, watching the other doorway to your room."

"Yes, Sir."

"We'll hump on our bellies, just like we trained. There will be no walking."

The soldiers take their weapons and hump to their posts. Mom sits on the sofa, smoking her cigarette. I hump across the living room. It's fucked: the TV gives away our positions, allowing the enemy a clear view of our troops and civilians. The girls huddle against the wall. Warren sits on his knees, the Marlin in his lap.

"Mom, can you turn off the set?" I ask.

"But, Carson is so funny," she says.

"Mom, get down. We don't want them… don't want them… to… get you."

"Oh, Johnny, you'll protect us and Carson is so funny. His monologues always make me laugh."

"We… don't… want to… lose you," I say.

She puts her feet up on the coffee table.

"You'll protect us."

I hump past Mom's bedroom to the kitchen. Mark sits with his back wedged against the wall and faces the door. He aims his weapon at the door, the barrel choke adjusted to spray birdshot in a loose pattern. He holds a box of shells in his lap. Two years ago, it had been full. Tonight, it's almost empty.

We had conducted almost daily weapons training when Mom took the girls to The Rancho for coffee after dinner. That's when she still had a car. Back then, we were prepared for the attack.

But, the enemy patiently waited. They've got to know how weak we are. I hope they attack so that we can finally kill them.

"Are. . . the troopers coming?" Mark asks me.

We hear Mom laughing at Carson.

I punch Mark in the chest.

"Of course. These hicks probably thought we would fire back by now. Bastards planned this. Were running recon, waiting. They're coming in and we're gonna have to… stop them inside the house… so our case will stand up in court."

I hump back through the living room. Warren peers out the picture window.

"I'm so proud of you kids," Mom says, wiping her eyes when I hump toward the back hallway. "Your father is looking after us."

I take up my post in the hall between the twins' room and mine. From there, I survey all the bedrooms, the bathroom, and the back part of the compound. I crouch in the corner, hiding in the shadow.

At 0100 hours on July 4, Maria humps across the carpet with Faith and Rose.

"Can we sleep in your room tonight?" She asks. "It's the safest room in the house."

"Permission granted."

They move into my room, pushing aside my Fort Apache and Lionel train set. They spread out pillows and blankets on the floor and bivouac there.

At 0110 hours, the twins hump to my bunker. They are exhausted.

"It's okay," I say. "I'll take first watch. You guys sleep next to the girls. If I need you, I'll mobilize you."

The boys put their loaded weapons on my bed, then lay down on the floor next to their sisters.

At 0130 hours, I patrol the interior, then hump across the carpet to the living room, where I observe Mom asleep on the sofa. The TV test pattern lights the room.

"Keep it on," she yells when my hand reaches for the dial.

"Mom, you're not safe."

"It helps me sleep. Can't I get any rest in this goddamned house?"

I return to my position.

At approximately 0220 hours, Princess stops barking. Dogs can be fooled when shifting wind takes away an intruder's scent. I figure that they are out there, quietly sitting in the woods and the creek bed, waiting. I wrap my hands around the M-1's barrel and slip on the safety.

I know they're coming for us.

At 0300 hours, the internal perimeter is breached! As I had predicted, the bastards slip in through the twins' window.

I hear the intruder when he steps on one of my brothers' Matchboxes. That room is completely dark except for a red glowing dot that slowly moves toward me.

The hicks are making a big fucking mistake; they're smoking cigarettes!

I slowly slide up the wall, shoulder my weapon, and sight in. I aim it toward the red dot near twin's bunks in the pitch black room.

"Who goes there, friend or foe?" I ask.

Such a stupid question: everyone from the outside is a foe.

The intruder steps closer, then pauses. I glance at my family sleeping behind me on my floor. The bastards must have been watching the house 'cause they know exactly where to go.

"Halt. Who goes there, friend or foe?"

I brace for the M-1's recoil and, at approximately 0310 hours, prepare for my first kill.

He's just another kid, I figure.

I know it's Ed, the spy that started this war. It's all about to end and it will be self-defense.

Self-fuckin' defense.

I can finally end this war! Sure, the cops will arrest me and charge me with murder, but the facts will set me free. I'm pretty confident that any jury will understand that I was defending myself and my family.

I squint down the sight and my finger finds the trigger.

"I'm not fuckin' kiddin': who goes there: friend or foe?"

The enemy continues to approach. I hear his stocking feet push aside my brothers' Matchboxes. We had played with them at 1900 hours. Now, the cars and track pinpoint the enemy.

"Who goes there? Sonofabitch, I'm not asking again."

I take the safety off.

I decide to wait to see his face before I fire. I aim the rifle toward the red dot, then move the weapon up so that it points at Ed's face.

"Who goes there: friend or foe?"

A hand gently pushes the weapon's barrel toward my bedroom door when Mom emerges from the darkness.

"Your goddamned guinea temper is gonna land you in jail," she says. She inhales her cigarette, making the tip burn bright red.

"Oh my God..., Mom..., I... almost... killed you. Thought... you were... an intruder. Why... didn't you answer?"

"You and your goddamned guinea temper."

She raises her hand to slap me, but stops.

"I'm not... mad, Mom..., honest. I..., almost killed... you. Thought you... were... Ed. Honest..., Mom."

She looks into my room and sees everybody sleeping on the floor.

"You're always breaking things. If you don't control that goddamned temper, you're gonna end up in jail."

She takes a drag on her cigarette, letting the smoke drift from her nostrils.

"Mom..., why didn't you answer? You didn't answer."

"Goodnight," she says, disappearing into the living room. I hear her climb into the bed and click on her light. I put on the rifle's safety and open the bolt.

I wipe my face.

I wipe my eyes a couple of times.

I'm sweaty like I ran a thousand miles in sand. My legs and arms hurt. My stomach hurts so bad that I want to puke.

I turn around and see the kids sleeping on the floor next to the Lionel train. They are huddled together like a bunch of bodies.

I just stare at 'em for awhile: these are my siblings, my brothers and sisters.

I almost killed our mother.

Almost shot her in the head.

Point blank.

Knowing that makes my guts ache.

I sit on my bed, watching my siblings sleep on the floor next to my toys while I rest the war rifle across my legs. After awhile, I carry my weapon into the living room and turn off the Magnavox. Mom sits in bed, reading a worn *Cosmopolitan.*

"I'm sorry, Mom."

She looks up from the magazine.

"State Troopers ever arrive?" she asks.

"No..., not yet."

She lowers the magazine. I kiss her forehead and pull her blanket over her shoulders, pointing the weapon's barrel toward the floor.

"Nighty-night," I say.

"Nighty-night."

I turn off her light.

I play Solitaire on my bed, keeping the loaded weapons next to me. My siblings sleep on the floor all night.

Around 5:30 AM, I open the kitchen door. I walk around the lawn as the sun rises over the southern hill. Near the front door, I find bits of paper and burnt matches. Everything smells of gunpowder. Next to the garage door, I also find singed wadding.

I check Princess.

"Screwing with us, Princess, just screwing with us." I say, petting her. I give her fresh water while I survey the battleground. "Bet you knew all along... and tried to tell us, didn't you?"

At 6:30 AM, I tell Mom what I found. She is in the kitchen, smoking a cigarette and drinking coffee.

"They just threw firecrackers. Just being assholes," I tell her.

She smiles and shakes her head.

"No. They were testing us," she says. "They wanted to see if we could drive them back." She smiles and pours herself another cup. "And you chased them away after they broke in."

At 7:00 AM, I fall asleep on my bed next to the loaded weapons. When I wake up at noon, I unload them and put them away. The boys help me box the ammunition, then we play with Matchboxes and Lego blocks. We stop for dinner, then go back to playing afterwards. I tell them that we're done with weapons training.

Doug's Impala

I stand in the dark downstairs near the piano I tied to the window. The floodlight doesn't stop them and I won't use the rifle.

There are two of them. I can tell as the car cuts doughnuts on the lawn. The bastard driver revs his engine, tearing apart the grass.

"Should throw a rock at the fuckers," Mark says. "Dent their shack mobile."

"They'll stop coming once it snows."

Today we raked all the leaves into pile and took turns jumping. Even Maria and Faith came out and played for awhile. Us kids played as Mom sat in her bed. When we were done, Maria made sandwiches for the Little Ones. The twins and I raked the pile back together.

I thought about hiding in that pile with the war rifle, shooting out their tires. What would the bastards say then?

In the morning, we see their tire tracks. They sliced up the lawn and smeared mud all over the leaves.

Mom is still in bed when I tell her. It's Sunday, so she usually doesn't get up until almost sunset. She sits in bed, drinking a little coffee, reading old copies of *Cosmopolitan*, and smoking Winston's. She's always smoking Winston's.

"Can we call the State Police?"

She laughs.

"Johnny, call them all you want: they don't believe Crazy Nancy." She reads a worn page, slowly turning it.

At night, the boys come back. It's just before dinner this time. They drive a little faster and hardly spend any time in the driveway. Me and Mark stand in the dark basement near the piano, watching them.

"Have to do something," he says. "Fuckers are just gonna keep coming back."

"Can't shoot at them. 'Sides, they might have weapons. Can't do anything unless they come in the house."

We watch them as the Chevy—I can tell by the headlights that it's an old Impala like Dad used to drive—leans to the passenger side as rocks and dirt hits the house. The driver revs it, making the car's big ass shake like a son-of-a-bitch.

We watch them leave.

"You fuckers!" Mark yells.

"Shush. If they think it gets us mad, they'll just do it longer," I say, punching him in the arm. He doesn't say shit 'cause he knows he better not give me lip.

Mom is sitting in her bed when we race upstairs.

204

"Mom, they're just gonna keep coming back."

"Johnny, the police don't believe us anymore," she says from her bed, a cigarette hanging from her mouth. "They'll get tired of it and stop. We'll turn off the floodlight and they'll leave us alone."

"Goddamned hicks," Old Lady says from the living room.

"It's Doug," I say. "He's got a Chevy Impala."

Mom reads her magazine. "Johnny, how can you be sure? Be a good boy and do your homework."

"We gotta do something or they'll just keep coming back. Can't we call the police?"

"No," Mom says.

"Fuck the cops. Should shoot them," Mark yells.

"And the Board of Health will come and split you kids up," Mom says calmly as she reads her horoscope. Shit, that stuff doesn't matter 'cause the magazine is two years old. I don't tell her that.

Can't tell Mom shit anymore.

"Doug's the asshole who pulled down the cabin, Mom. He and his buddies drive by in the morning and give us the finger before the bus comes. Stupid hick fuck. First asshole with a car and he thinks he's so fucking cool."

"Shit, we should blow up the car," Mark says, giggling. "One little Molotov and the fucking dumb hick will have to ride on the bus. He's too fucking dumb to figure it out."

Mom turns the page and reads an article about how women can get sexy-looking for a man. She's read it before, but she looks at it like it's news.

"You boys go play," she says.

Playin' with Trains

The music is on the radio and I can hear crickets in the backyard. Sometimes, when I look out the window into the black toward the trees, I see fireflies.

When I was younger, Mom read me *Sam and the Firefly*, a story about a firefly who saved the world or something by making signs with his light.

Sometimes, when Mom looks out into the backyard, she sees the men moving in the woods, waiting for me to fall asleep.

There are Lego blocks on the floor next to Fort Apache. This afternoon, I set up the Lionel so that the track ran through the fort's gates.

The power pack cord hangs over the closet door.

Ringo Starr sings *Photograph* on the Panasonic and I'm crying 'cause of that line that says, "All I got is a photograph and I realize you're not coming back anymore." It makes me think about Dad.

I fuckin' hate myself for being such a coward.

Tomorrow, I'll be braver. Tomorrow, I'll kick the foot stool away. I promise.

I keep getting mad at myself for breaking my own promise.

I'm such a stupid fuck-up.

Why the hell do I stand up there like a fucking idiot? I'll just pound the shit out of myself instead. At least I have the guts to do that!

I punch myself really hard in the chest until I feel better and I can get some rest.

Stories

It's night, the house is quiet, my chest still hurts from when I beat myself up, and I'm waiting for Mom to warn me about the hit men. I turned off my light and I'm pretending to be asleep, but I'm really just whispering to myself 'cause I feel like telling myself a story. I like telling myself stories, like living in those worlds I create.

It's me.

I'm standing on a city street, walking. I'm working, but nobody notices 'cause I'm cool just like Steve McQueen.

A lady is following me.

No, wait.

A woman is following me. And she's pretty and tough. Her name is Linda and she looks just like the woman on the cover of Coed *that I have under my bed.*

We're both cops. Undercover.

It's just another day in the city. It could be any city street with lots of people. I'm walking with everyone, but I notice everything .

Just like Dirty Harry wearing sunglasses.

Suddenly, I stop.

I can tell something is gonna happen. I can just feel it. Linda can feel it, too.

No, that's not it.

I'm walking just like everyone else when I hear—Gunshots!

No, wait a minute.

I'm walking toward a bus stop when, all of sudden I hear— BANG! BANG! BANG! BANG!

Women scream and men dive for cover. A sports car races down the street and I run right toward it.

No, c'mon, John, think about it.

Women scream and men dive for cover. Suddenly, I see a sports car way down the street. It's a few blocks away and it's coming closer really fast. I run at it.

Linda follows me.

No, that's not right.

Women scream and men dive for cover. Suddenly, I see a speeding Corvette way down the street. It's coming right at me!

"Stop him," someone down there yells. I can see that he's a bank security guard. He runs into the street and points his gun at the speeding Corvette. Just as he's ready to fire, there's a—

BANG!

The bad guy in the Corvette shoots him dead!

I run toward the Corvette as it continues to speed right at me. The Corvette is speeding right at me, the driver picking up speed.

I take my big handgun and point it right at the windshield of the Corvette as it's bearing right down on me.

BANG!

The gun flies from my hand 'cause the bad guy shot it!

No, that's not it.

Just as I'm aiming it right at the driver's head, Linda runs in front of me, gets to the Corvette, reaches into the driver's

*window AND DRAGS THE BAD GUY FROM THE CAR! THE
SPEEDING CORVETTE BARELY MISSES ME AND CRASHES
INTO A GARBAGE TRUCK!*

*I run to Linda and before I can say anything, she slams the
bad guy to the pavement and yells, "You have the right to remain
silent."*

I open my eyes and see the outline of my bedroom
furniture in the dark. It's around two AM. Mom must be
sleeping pretty well because she should be here by now. I'm
hungry, but I'm not gonna cook anything because I don't want to
wake her up and hear about the hit men.

I'm tired and I'm hungry.

Instead, I go back to telling myself the story.

*Linda yells, "Anything you say can and will be used
against you in a court of law."*

WENY, 1230 AM Radio

It's almost noon the day after I told myself the story about
Linda and I'm listening to the radio, writing down all the words to
Hello, It's Me that's playing on WENY out of Elmira. I'm
listening to it because I have to write down all the words right
now because I have to know all the words right now.

I'm listening and writing down the words because of what
Maria found this morning when Mom wouldn't wake up.

When Mom couldn't wake up.

I'm writing all the words down really neatly, even neater
than I've written in all my life because I have to do this right now.
I have to do it alone in my room right now before someone gets
here and takes us all away.

Before they split us up.

Faith's seventeen, but she's too young to be our mom and
we don't have any car. We don't have any food and we don't
have any money.

I'm writing down all the words that are in that song right
now because Maria found Mom's empty pill bottles. She found
them this morning when Mom didn't wake up, when none of us
could wake Mom up.

None of us could wake Mom up.

None of us could wake Mom up when Mom was still, completely still and barely breathing in bed.

She was barely breathing in bed, even though her chest was still.

Her chest was really still. It wasn't moving at all.

I had to listen really hard with my head against her chest to hear her breathing, but she was hardly breathing and I'm making myself listen to all the words of this song locked in my room with maps on the walls and the door blocked shut and my power pack cord hanging from the closet door because I have to listen to the words of this song so that I can write them down on the back of the envelope that I was going to send to Chuckie yesterday when I stood on that fucking stool and instead was a chicken shit for not kicking it away.

I have to write everything down.

Have to make sure I hear every single word of this song so I don't hear the ambulance idling in the driveway as the ambulance people try to get Mom to start breathing again.

As the ambulance people resuscitate her, try to bring her back.

I have to write it all down right now. I have to write it all down now so I can know these words to this song so I can hear the words in my head instead of the ambulance in the driveway right now.

I just have to.

I have to right now.

I have to so that when the song is over, I can say the words to myself and in my stories so that I don't have to hear the ambulance in the driveway or walk by Mom's empty bed or see her piles of yellowed *Philadelphia Inquirers* on the floor.

Or, listen to her barely breathing. Shit, she was barely breathing. I don't think I even really heard her breathing.

I have to know these words. I have to know them without anyone else talking to me, being near me, or even being around me.

Fuck, I want to be so alone right now 'cause, when the song is over, I have the memory of the song, the memory of everything.

I'm so tired of memories…

Phyl-Carlo Restaurant

Coffee: black, with cream, or with cream and sugar.
Eggs: fried, scrambled, hard-boiled, or soft-boiled.
Toast: slightly brown or French toast.
Bacon, sausage, or scrapple.
Pancakes or waffles.
I'm in bed thinking about telling myself stories and I can smell it all.
When I open my eyes, I see car models: there are Mustangs, Corvettes, Thunderbirds, Chargers, and everything else on shelves that Carl built into one of the walls of his son's room.
And, I can hear the restaurant. I can hear the truckers talking with the locals. Can hear the traffic on Route 14 as it goes through the village.
It's summer and I'm living in the house that's attached to the back of the Phyl-Carlo Restaurant in Gillett, about five miles south of Fassett. Phyllis and Carl Oldroyd own the place. They took Faith and me in until things get settled down. The twins are in the village staying with another family. Maria and Rose are with Woody Oldroyd's family. He owns the country store.
It's sunny and I can smell every single breakfast that's cooking in the kitchen. It smells great.
I hear birds outside my window. When I look out, I see the empty elementary school playground. It's vacation!
It's better than New Jersey was two years ago. Hell, the relatives don't even know about Mom. If they knew, they'd be here fighting over us, telling us that we had to go with them back there. They'd want to know everything 'cause they're so nosy.
I don't know what happened.
Maria says Mom attempted suicide.
Mom says she has a chemical imbalance that made her go to sleep.
Maria says Mom died before the ambulance left the driveway.

Mom says the chemical imbalance made her sleep so deeply that she almost died in the ambulance.

Maria says the ambulance guys resuscitated Mom but couldn't immediately get her pulse or heartbeat.

Mom says she was just sleeping.

Maria says Mom died from the overdose, but the ambulance men revived her.

It doesn't matter.

Either way, I fucked up.

Thud. I punch myself in the chest 'cause I'm so stupid for not protecting Mom. For not knowing that she had a chemical imbalance that could put her to sleep like that. For not knowing that she was even thinking of killing herself. Was so busy feeling sorry for myself that I didn't even think of her.

I'm so fucking stupid!

The walls in the room are painted. There's no holes anywhere. It's not like my room; it's really nice.

Thud.

Nobody can hear me 'cause they're all out in the kitchen. Faith's probably sitting at the counter, eating breakfast. They'll make me breakfast when I get dressed and get out there. I don't have to make my own breakfast.

Thud... thud... thud.

Us kids were really scared, but it's all okay now and we don't have to say anything else about it 'cause she's got the chemical imbalance fixed and she's gonna be all better.

That's what Maria says.

That's what Mom says.

They both say that the doctors at the Psychiatric Unit in Sayre are gonna let Mom come home real soon. They're fixing her imbalance so that she never sleeps like that or attempts suicide ever again.

Thud... thud... thud.

Maria and Mom say that the doctors know what they're doing. They told them that Mom has Manic-Depressive disease and her chemicals are out of whack. That made her sleep all the time and think that she saw Dad on the front yard. Manic-Depression made Mom think that Dad was the sun.

Maria says Mom doesn't think like that anymore.

Mom says that she doesn't want to stay in bed all day anymore. Says she wants to come home and be with us 'cause we're her children and she's our mom and she needs to take care of us 'cause she's all we've got to raise us up right.

Thud... thud... thud.

Maria says Mom says all that stuff.

I guess I believe her. Mom's coming home today and we're all going back home.

Thud... thud... thud.

I'm so fucking stupid 'cause I just stood in my room listening to a song while Mom died. I'm stupid for just blocking my door and listening to the radio instead of helping the ambulance men save Mom.

I'm stupid for trying to kill myself when Mom tried to kill herself 'cause then no one would be able to look after the kids.

Thud, thud, thud, thud.

I will never let that happen again.

I climb out of bed and rub my chest. It's sore again. Sometimes, I get so mad at myself that I just want to beat the shit out of me. I always feel better when I'm done 'cause it gets rid of everything for awhile.

1975

Broyhill Premier Collection

My hand deposits a ball of gray hair in the glass ashtray.
Mom's hand holds the cigarette against the tangled mass, igniting
it. The scent of burnt hair fills my nose as I glance from her bed
to the kitchen.

"Please, Johnny? It's tomorrow."

She is tucked in, sitting up, an old *Ladies Home Journal*
by her side. She wears cat-eye glasses, a wrinkled blouse and a
pair of worn Capri pants. Her left hand holds a lit Winston; her
right rests on her swollen stomach.

She looks pregnant. No, more like a starving African
refugee.

She leans toward me and I tug at her head. I pull a few
infested strands. The parasites have turned her long black hair a
waxy gray. They crawl on her head and pillow.

Christ, they're everywhere.

She waits with her cigarette, inhaling as I lower another
ball into the ashtray.

"I'd really like that," she says.

She touches the red tip to the hair. We watch the strands
turn to flame beneath the plastic-wrapped light shade. The cover
has yellowed and become hard, cracking along the bottom where
Mom's working arm touches it.

Her right arm slides off her belly, making her wince.

"Bursitis," she said one afternoon a few months ago.
"Reached too far for my paper."

She sat in bed that day, probably dressed in the same

214

outfit. She grabbed a year-old *Philadelphia Inquirer* from the pile at the foot of her bed. I heard her at night when I cleaned up after my algebra homework. She sat up in bed and adjusted her bad arm so she could read and smoke a cigarette.

"Mom, you okay?"

She patted her bed and I sat beside her.

"You want some toast?"

I watched her read and put a little butter on the slices after they popped out of the Proctor-Silex. She took a couple of bites, then handed me the plate.

I tucked her in and kissed her goodnight.

"Make sure no one breaks in," she said.

"I will. Nighty-night."

I watched her fall asleep, then wolfed down the rest of her toast in my room.

A couple hours later, I helped Faith and Maria get the twins and Rose ready for school. Us Biggies kinda get the Little Ones around. Rose likes Lucky Charms; the twins, Frosted Flakes. If Maria and Kevin went to the store on their date we had plenty of food, but never enough milk.

We always need milk.

The parasites are my fault. I let one of the kids in gym class borrow my comb. Should've let him keep it, but Mom couldn't afford a new one. Maria bought me a fine-tooth one a couple weeks ago. I comb my hair over an old *Inquirer* each night after everyone's asleep, but it doesn't help: they keep coming back.

Maria and Faith use *A-200*, but there isn't enough to share. I understand 'cause they have long hair.

I try teaching the twins to comb over the *Inquirer*, but they don't listen.

"We ain't got any lice," Mark said.

Mom ignites another clump.

It's odd being up this late with somebody. Usually I listen to WENY. Sometimes I stand near the front door and watch Mom sleep. It's been almost six years since the movers arranged her Broyhill Premier queen-sized bed, dresser, and night table in the dining room. It was supposed to be temporary until the carpenters renovated the basement, but the Maison de Ville Collection set in a pecan finish now belongs between the kitchen and living room.

Mom lowers her head toward my chest, and I curl my fingers around the waxy strands. It doesn't take much to uproot them. We have a routine: her cigarette hand accompanies the strand to the ashtray, she ignites it, then leans toward me so I can pull.

"I'll make sure you get to school on time," she says.

"I have an algebra test."

Mom takes a drag. My fingers grab more strands.

Last week, I fell in Mr. Edsell's biology class. I'm in 9B with the smart kids. They're taking turns reading the library's only copy of *Bury My Heart at Wounded Knee*. Somehow, I stumbled out of my chair and hit the floor. We were watching some gross film about diseases.

Mrs. White, the school nurse, checked me for a fever and took my pulse while staring at my face.

"You eat breakfast?" she asked as I rested my head on the pillow, fighting the urge to scratch. The thing is to ignore them until you're alone, then get the fine tooth comb and a piece of paper. It doesn't kill them, but at least you look clean.

"No, Ma'am."

"Why not?"

"I forgot."

Us Biggies sent the Little Ones outside to play when Mrs. White came to the house. Maria had talked to her in school and told her all about Mom's arm. Anyway, the nurse carefully moved past the kitchen table to Mom's bed. She gently touched Mom's lame right arm and swollen belly. Mom tried to stand but almost fell.

"Better get you looked at," Mrs. White said.

"What about my children?"

Mom lowers her head again and I pull. The parasites cling to her hair. We can't kill them without *A-200*. Mom stopped driving after the men repossessed the car, and it takes me all day to ride my bike to Elmira. Maria usually gets some groceries when Kevin takes her out, but they saw *Jaws* last weekend.

Mom raises her head. Her eyes are large, larger than I remember. Her smile is gone.

"They'll let you ride in the ambulance with me to Sayre," Mom says. "Mrs. White can take you back to school."

"Want to see my friends. Before summer vacation. What time are they coming?"

I remove another clump. We both watch me lower it to the ashtray.

"About nine."

I look at the Big Ben next to the ashtray. A few years ago, when I started staying up, I stood next to it and watched her sleep as it rang for five minutes.

I thought she was dead.

"Mom, it's time to get up," I said. "We have to go to school."

She still made breakfast then. She cooked eggs in the middle, French toast, and bacon. We smelled it before getting out of bed. I remember how good it smelled.

Mom straightened our rooms after we went to school and had dinner waiting on the table. Sometimes she stayed up late but she always woke up with us.

Now, we kiss her forehead before we go out the door. She usually gets up when we go to bed. See, with her bad arm, she can't do much except smoke and look at an old *Inquirer*.

Mom puts the cigarette tip against the waxy mass.

"Sure you can't?"

"Mom, it's move-up day. Have to meet my 10th grade teachers."

"Please, Johnny. I'm really scared."

She puts her head up as I'm pulling, and I grab more hair than I wanted, but she doesn't wince.

"Please?"

"I have to hand in a term paper."

She adjusted her remaining pillow. Just last month, she stood in my doorway after midnight. I had dozed off while listening to the radio. I like listening to songs.

"Johnny, there's snakes in my pillow."

I sat up.

"What kind?"

"Rattlers. You have to burn 'em. Once a snake finds a home, it always comes back."

I used a snow shovel to lift the pillow from her bed.

"Burn it in the side yard," she yelled from the front door.

The air smelled of spring until I doused the pillow with gasoline and struck a match. I watched the foam turn black in the flames.

"Kill it with the shovel," she yelled from the porch.

I repeatedly slammed the shovel against the melted gob.

Mom was in bed reading an old *Glamour* when I came back inside.

"It's gone. I cremated it."

She smiled and kept reading.

It didn't matter what was inside the pillow. If I failed to find her snake, she would have me burn something else. Lying made her relax.

I pull out another clump. They come easier. The secret is to pull steady, not jerking the hair.

"Your father loves you, Johnny."

"I know."

"He tells me all the time."

"Yeah, I know."

She puts the cigarette out and slides down in the bed. Her useless arm makes it tough, but I lift the blankets out of her way. I take her glasses off.

"Get some sleep," I say. "I'll see you in the morning."

I reach for the faded plastic lamp cover.

"Leave it on. I promise I won't read," she says.

"Nighty-night."

I kiss her forehead and walk to my room. My light and radio are on. *Philadelphia Freedom* is playing. I close my door and sit on the bed, taking out my comb and an *Inquirer*.

I comb until sunrise, then help the Little Ones get ready for school. Mom is sitting up when I kiss her for the last time.

218

"You behave while I'm in the hospital," she says.

"Yeah, I will."

I grab my books and walk down the driveway.

The Church People

Me and the other kids are sitting near the brook on the edge of our woods in our backyard. The driveway is filled with cars I've never seen before and our house is filled with people I've never seen before.

Except Mrs. White, the school nurse. She's the one who got Mom into the hospital and now she's helping to clean our house. She stands near us and looks down at our home.

"This house is so dirty that we need a bulldozer to clean it," she says. "How could anyone live in this filth?"

A group of men are pulling out all the nails out from the storm windows and putting up the screens. They are moving the piano away from the basement door and cutting the ropes away from the basement windows. They're taking all the old garbage bags that filled the garage and throwing them into a garbage truck. Some of those bags have been in there for awhile.

The church women found my collection of *Coed* and *Cosmopolitan* magazines under my bed. They packed away my train set and dusted my foot stool.

And, they're washing everything to get rid of the lice.

"You kids can't stay here," Mrs. White says. "There's no food and there's no one to take care of you until your mom gets better."

We kinda know that, but no one says anything. The church people are too busy cleaning to listen to a bunch of dirty Crudley kids.

Betty's Camper

The rain makes the canvas damp and the lightning lights everything despite the zippered windows. When it thunders, the shitty thing rocks back and forth.

I sit huddled under the covers. The trucks roar through the village. The lights fill the canvas room, then the thunder cracks and trucks on the highway go away... for awhile.

"John, you'll be safe," Betty said yesterday. "In the fall when Scott goes to college, you can have his room."

Betty is a big lady who has lots of kids. She and Jack are church people. They're talking my family in until Mom comes home from the hospital. They have seven kids; five girls and two older boys. Betty is short and Jack is huge, but he's not fat.

Yesterday, their second oldest son Scott grabbed the camper by the hitch and yanked this thing out of the barn. The twins and I watched him lug it up the lawn to the side of the house where the dirt driveway turned to grass.

"You'll be outside. She can't check up on you," Mark said.

"Betty's okay," I said. "I'm glad she took us all in. We're not getting split up."

Scott positioned the camper where the driveway meets the lawn. He held the tongue high enough for me to put a thick piece of old four by four underneath it.

"Move it over to the left," he said.

I did.

"A little more."

He lowered the camper, then walked to the house. When the twins and I saw him close the kitchen door, we grabbed the camper's hitch.

And pulled.

"Shit," Mark said.

"Fuckin' shit."

We all pulled, but the thing seemed nailed to the four by four. Scott is only two years older than me, but he looks like a pro football player.

Inside smelled of Coot's camper. There were spiders in the bedding. The canvas sides were wet.

"I wish Betty would let me sleep out here," Mark said, unzipping the window. The air rushed in, got mixed up with the mildew, and then stayed until all the air in the camper smelled.

"If I was out here, I'd sneak across the Agway lot to Marty's barn. They'd never see me. Could get into that building down the street or run up those tracks.

Warren smiled. "You still have your own room!"

I laugh because Warren is right.

"Yeah, I guess I do."

It really doesn't matter that I have my own room. I'm too busy thinking about Mom and the hospital. Too busy thinking what we'll do for food when we get back home. Too busy thinking about how we're gonna survive when Mom comes home.

Columbia Cross Roads

The kids on this new bus are nice. Not only that, but we only ride a couple minutes on Bus 4 before it stops at Betty's. We're the first stop up Route 14 from Troy. It's only a mile from Spaulding's Tastee Freeze. If we were on our old bus, we'd still have an hour ride ahead of us.

Columbia Cross Roads is only ten miles from Fassett, but it's another world. Seems strange to be here. It's like Fassett doesn't exist.

That's how it is when Mom gets sick; us kids go to a nicer world for a little bit, then we go back home until everything goes bad again.

Anyway, we now get off the bus with Betty's kids. There's too many girls to name. Scott is at football practice, so he'll come home later.

Betty is waiting for us in the front yard.

"You kids stay right there," Betty says, pointing to us. She lets her kids go into the house from the front porch.

"You kids follow me."

The seven of us walk past my camper in their driveway: I throw my books in there.

"Don't go in there," she says. "You follow me."

We go along the side lawn to the kitchen entrance, coming in through the pantry past the chest freezer and stopping at the kitchen sink. She has a collection of *A-200* bottles there.

"We're washing hair," she says. "Starting with the boys. "Not gonna have lice infest my house."

I go first. She bends me over the sink and scrubs my hair, pouring the soap all over. It smells of kerosene and burns my eyes.

"Stand still," she says as she sprays water all over the place. She hands me a towel and a fine-tooth hard plastic comb.

"Now, go sit on the porch and comb nits."

I start toward the living room 'cause I hear her girls watching TV.

"Not that way," she yells. "You're not spreading your lice in my house. You go out the back door."

I do what she says.

Hell, it's a nice day and I sit on the front porch with my feet up on the railing as I comb my hair. From her porch, I see the feed mill in the center of town and the abandoned Penn Central branch that connected Elmira to Williamsport, the Elmira Branch. I can imagine a train coming through the village and that thought makes me smile.

They call the place Columbia Cross Roads 'cause the road to Sayre comes down off the eastern hill. It continues west through the village to Austinville and onto Sylvania, intersecting with State Route 14 right near Judson's Feed Mill. That road follows the railroad tracks between Elmira and Williamsport.

There's not much to the village 'cause the milk plant just the other side of the tracks is abandoned and the tractor outlet up on the highway doesn't see much business. There's a gas station across the highway from the combination general store and library that's just up the street from here. Down the main street around the curve is a deserted three-story building that looks as though it was once some sort of factory. I can't imagine it as an office building.

Just past that end of Main Street is the First Methodist Church; that's Betty's church. Next to that is the township garage and the old elementary school. Then the village peters out in a collection of farms.

Mark and I walked Main Street two days ago after I set up my camper. He was excited 'cause his friend Marty lives on the other side of the mill. We're not supposed to be trespassing

222

through the mill to get to Marty's, but we sneaked along the old rail bed to get there.

Maybe we'll sneak again.

After a little while, Mark comes out and sits next to me, putting up his feet and combing.

"Bet I have more lice than you do?" He says.

I laugh.

A big Crudley-mobile pulls up. There's a shitload of kids in it who look poor as hell. The car barely runs and the kids look stupid but happy. Everyone seems happy here.

"Welcome wagon," I say.

A big fat mom gets out. She wears an old dress and has big fat arms. She's carrying a glass casserole dish topped with aluminum foil.

Maria comes around the side of the house.

"Can I help you?" My sister asks.

"Are you those Higham kids we heard about?" the woman asks.

"Yeah."

"Well, I made you kids a little somethin' for dinner."

"Thank you," Maria says.

Then I notice the kids' faces. They aren't that smart, but they're nice. I see 'em at school in the other sections. Hell, I had gym once with one of the boys, but I don't remember his name.

The lady rings the doorbell like she's some sort of guest. She smiles at us as we hide our combs.

Maria sits next to me and unwraps her long hair from the towel without even thinking about the whole carload of Crudley kids watching her. Her hair stinks of kerosene as she combs. She starts at the ends, leaning forward over the wood floor. It's all tangled 'cause of the shampoo, but she works at it. Maria works at everything 'till she gets it.

Betty opens the door.

"Look at this, Mrs. Gleason made a potato casserole," she says. Mrs. Gleason beams at us.

"Thank you," Maria says again.

I just nod 'cause I'm not really happy right now. I feel dirty and poor, worse than a Crudley. I figure Mrs. White must have told everybody about the dirty starving Higham kids and their sick mom who stayed in bed all day.

Makes me angry when I think about it, but we're not gonna stay here forever, just until Mom gets better and comes home from the hospital.

Because of all that, I keep quiet.

"You're welcome," Mrs. Gleason says. She climbs back into her Crudley-mobile. "God bless you kids," she says.

Mark leans over toward me.

"Welcome wagon," he says.

"Looks that way, doesn't it?"

Soon, we're all out on the porch, combing our nits. Betty leaves us out here and a couple of her kids are watching us as they play catch on the side yard. Only thing, they have to move each time a car pulls into the drive. It's like all the church people got together and decided to make casseroles. They show up with their families, their kids sitting in their cars watching us as we sit on the porch and we comb out our nits.

"We're the fucking freak show," I say during a lull.

"They're just being nice," Maria says. "Wanna help us out."

"Don't need their help. Just want to get back home."

We comb until our hands ache, but still our heads are itchy. The white waxy nits are all over the place and Betty tells us to sweep them into the dirt.

"They'll die there because they live on the protein in your hair."

The shampoo ruins our hair. It makes it all stiff and shit.

Each night after school, we sit on the porch, combing out nits and being nice to the churchwomen bringing us casseroles.

When Mom gets better and we return home, we'll tell her all about the nice people who came to Betty's house to drop off a casserole so they could watch the freak show.

224

The Elmira Branch

The creek bed smells of creosote, the rails hanging over the gap in the roadbed where Tropical Storm Agnes tore away the grass and the soil underneath.

I stink of perspiration and my legs ache. My hair is wet. My skin shines. I am out of breath from running down the track, half-stumbling along the ties and tripping over the twisted rails.

It hurts to exhale and there's not enough air in the world to fill my lungs. It smells of spring, but it's really not any season right now.

I smell creosote from the old ties that someone piled under the rails. The ties are neatly stacked, criss-crossed over the creek. There aren't enough to support a train and are just barely enough to hold up the track.

The water in the creek is only a few inches deep.

Maria and Faith made me run. They chased me from their room at Betty's, down the stairs, out onto the front porch, past the camper, and toward the railroad track. Maria almost caught up to me, but I lost her when I hit the ties and ran as fast as I could, her words falling behind me.

What they said didn't surprise me.

No, Mom surprised me. When we visited her in Sayre, all I saw in the hospital was her bed, her blue hair cap, and her really short hair. Someone else's swollen belly sat beneath her chest, and a tank of oxygen sat by her bed. A clear plastic tube went from that tank to her nose, which seemed stuck to her drawn face on either side of her bony cheeks.

The nurses tried to be quiet, but I heard them. I could hear everything that day.

"Those are *the* kids," they said as we stood around the bed and tried to be brave. In the ward, we gathered around what was left of Mom: Maria, Faith and Rose stood to her right. The twins stood to her left. I leaned against the foot of her bed and felt my chest collapse as I struggled to breathe.

I could smell the room's antiseptic cleaner and Mom's death.

Betty had placed a copy of *The Way* on Mom's night table and announced, "Well, I'll be outside so you can all visit."

We smiled on cue and talked.

"It's getting warmer outside," Maria said.

Mom smiled and broke into a cough. The hacking lasted forever as it lived in her lungs and rattled her. My guts felt bad and I got all sweaty 'cause I was staring at that thing that was growing in her belly.

Hell, she looked pregnant; the doctor said the tumor in her stomach would continue to grow. It's the only part of her that's growing anymore. When I thought about it, the edges of the room turned gray, then black around the edges. My legs shook.

I ran out to the hallway. I stopped myself from crying 'cause a nurse was there, watching us kids trying to talk to Mom before her body disappeared beneath the tumor.

"She looks so gross," I said. "I can't believe she made me sick."

The hallway smelled of antiseptic. The nurse looked at me and put her arm over my shoulder.

"You have to be strong... for her. You kids are all she's got."

She walked me back into the room.

"And everyone brought food," Maria said.

"I can't believe I fainted, Mom."

"Don't be upset, Johnny," Mom said, trying to lean forward in bed. Without her cigarettes and *Cosmopolitan*, she wasn't anyone anymore. Life was finished with her.

There are no nurses by the creek bed, just the sound of my sisters' voices that had chased me out here. Their words hang in my mind as they had when my sisters pulled me aside upstairs.

Among furniture from Maria and Faith's room, we sat in one of Betty and Jack's bedrooms that they let Maria and Rose use. I looked out the dirty old windows at the Agway and the camper as I sat on the floor.

The room smelled of Betty's deodorant soap.

Maria and Faith sat on the bed.

The Little Ones played downstairs.

It was almost shampoo time.

"The doctors don't think Mom has much longer," Maria said.

"We have to make sure we see her every day... while we can," Faith said.

"Mom changed her will so we can stay here."

"How long are they giving her?" I asked.

"Not long. Before the end of the summer," Maria said.

I punched myself once or twice in the chest and swore. I don't remember running, but I did. I ran until my feet found the Elmira Branch goin' north towards Fassett. I couldn't see anything when I sprinted and bobbed along the twisted rails and undermined ties. They felt slippery like the hospital linoleum, but I held true.

I punched myself a few times under the creosote bridge and cried alone. I wanted to stay there until I no longer smelled Mom or the hospital, but Betty yelled for me an hour later.

"John, come along now," she said.

"I'm sorry, Mom," I whisper. I punch my chest until my hands ache.

I walk back toward the camper and my new life.

Sheet cake

Everyone ran like hell when we heard Scott coming in the kitchen door. We were watching *The Brady Bunch* when we heard that door swing open.

Mark and I escaped through the side door to my camper.

Maria and Rose went up the front stairs to their room.

Warren followed Karen, Polly, and Carol to the kitchen staircase at the back of the house, hanging out with Betty's daughters in their room while Scott threw his shit-fit.

"Where's my sheet cake?" Scott yelled as he moved the kitchen chair away from in front of the fridge and opened the cabinets above that appliance in search of Betty's sheet cake.

"In our stomachs," Mark yelled, laughing like hell.

A few hours earlier, I had used a kitchen chair to get into the cabinet above the fridge so that I could steal pieces of the snack.

When Mark found me, I had to give him a chunk.

Warren wandered out sometime after *Sanford and Son*, so we had to give him a couple of pieces.

When Rose showed up and caught us, we gave her some to keep her from tattling. After we cleared the first cookie sheet, we stopped cutting. Instead, we broke pieces off each time we pretended to use the toilet.

Betty and Jack's kids stayed in the living room, watching the set as us Highams took our turns. On the last sheet we used the knife again, slicing it by two inches, then one inch, then slivers, until only about a square inch remained.

Outside, I was fighting with Mark 'cause he wanted to hide in the camper with me while Scott yelled in the kitchen.

"You stay out. You have your own room," I said.

"He'll kill me," my brother said. We had chocolate all over our hands and faces, wiping some on our pants.

Betty's daughters turned on their bedroom lights. They were safe. After some trucks tore through the village, I heard the steel cookie pans hit the wall as Scott threw them one last time before stomping up the stairs to his room in the back of the house.

"Okay, get in," I said to Mark.

I unzipped the top of one window. With the light out, the streetlight poured in.

We heard nothing but the trucks on the highway as they slowed entering the curve outside the village, then belched dirt and noise when they roared along this side of the valley.

The pans were on the floor when I used the bathroom around midnight. I found that last square of sheet cake still on one, so I ate it.

Vacation Bible School

Us Higham kids are sitting in the kitchen, eating. I've got a ham sandwich with mayonnaise, just like the twins. Maria eats a small salad. Faith is visiting a college downstate. Rose is eating a ham sandwich. Betty's kids are either upstairs or outside, I guess.

"You kids better eat," Betty says. "You're not goin' anywhere until you do."

Warren always eats so fuckin' slow. He chews like a goddamned cow, his mouth moving real slow as he munches. Once in New Jersey he didn't finish his steak after sitting at the table for an hour, so Mom made him keep a couple bites in his mouth.

We couldn't play tag or anything 'cause Mom didn't want him to choke on it, so the twins and I played with my Lionel train. We watched it go around in circles between our beds.

"What else did the hospital say?" Maria asks.

Betty stands at the counter, watching us. She's got her Bible open and there's some old man talking on her cassette tape, telling us all about Jesus. We just heard all this at Vacation Bible School this week.

Heard it all there.

At the church they split us apart; Maria and I went to the teen class, the twins went to the youth class, and Baby Rose went to the kiddie class.

She came home with a coloring book. It has pictures of the story of Jesus. Showed him being born in the manger, making water into wine, being betrayed and crucified, then rising up from the dead.

"How's Mom doing?" Maria asks. She's the only one of us smart enough and brave enough to ask.

"It doesn't matter, you're not going anywhere until you're all done eating," Betty says, turning Bible pages like she's reading along to one of those filmstrips that beep when it wants you to see the next picture.

"But what did they say?" Maria asks.

Betty moves her lips as she reads along. I can see her over the counter, the cabinets that divide the kitchen from the dining room making it look like her face above her eyes has been cut off.

"They said that she lapsed into a coma."

Warren stops chewing. Stupid asshole.

"When did they call?" Maria asks.

Betty sings, "There's a river of life flowing out from me," as I see her eyes closing real quick, then opening. She looks at Maria.

"About an hour ago," Betty says.

"It's an hour drive!" Mark says.

"That's why you kids have to hurry up and finish your lunch!"

"Why didn't you get us from Bible School?" Mark asks just like she stole his Timex watch.

"It makes the lame to walk and the blind to see," Betty sings with her eyes closed.

Fuckin' Warren just eats slower and slower like a cow chewing cud at the Troy Fair. He ain't got anything goin' there: pisses me off 'cause we're never goin' see Mom 'cause of him.

Betty opens her eyes and smiles.

"You kids need Jesus," she says. "That's why all this happened to you. The Bible says that when you don't have a personal relationship with Jesus, only bad things will happen. Your mom didn't accept Jesus as her Personal Savior. That's why she's in a coma right now."

Rose smiles at Betty.

"We can't tell Mom about Jesus if we're not by her side," Maria says.

"That's why you should eat your lunch instead of arguing with me," Betty says, whispering. "The only thing you can do right now is pray for your mom's soul. That's the only chance she's got. Pray for her salvation."

230

Betty closes her eyes and keeps whispering shit, calling Mom Nancy Higham and wishing some Holy Spirit shit to make her realize her sins and save her soul from eternal damnation.

Warren's sandwich isn't even fuckin' half done. He's got so much to eat that I'm hoping that he stuffs it in his cheek and carries it there for the rest of the fuckin' day.

The phone rings in the living room.

Betty smiles and keeps praying.

It rings again.

Her girls don't answer it.

It rings again.

Betty finishes her prayer.

It rings again.

Betty walks out of the kitchen to answer it.

It keeps ringing. Fuck it; it might as well ring forever 'cause it doesn't matter anymore. We got to finish our meal 'fore she's even gonna let us leave her kitchen whether we're hungry or not.

Finally, she walks out of the kitchen.

The phone rings again.

She picks up the phone in the living room.

"Hello," she says.

We're all listening.

She's not talking, just listening.

"Thank you," she finally says.

She hangs it up and slowly walks back into the kitchen. She stands near her Bible.

"That was the hospital," she says, closing her eyes and turning a page. "You kids need Jesus now more than ever." She whispers, "Bless you, Jesus," a few times then opens her eyes.

"When can we see Mom?" Mark asks.

"You kids will have to miss Bible school tomorrow," she says. She turns up the tape recorder and closes her eyes again, whispering some shit and raising her hands. She keeps blessin' Jesus.

"Ask Jesus to forgive your sins," the man on the tape says, "and ask Jesus to be your Personal Savior." He says some other shit, but I'm not listening anymore 'cause I'm not in the mood to hear that kind of shit.

Uncle Lenny's Ventura

We're three cars back. Uncle Mike's Impala is right in front of us. In front of him is Jimmy's Oldsmobile.

Maria sits in back of Lenny's Ventura with me. I know my brother and sisters are scattered among the other cars. I wonder what they're talking about.

Who they're talking with.

It really doesn't matter though because everything is gone.

There's no hit men in the woods.

There's no need for me to ride my bike to the store.

There's no fights.

There's no kids on the bus.

There's no manic-depression.

There's no lice.

There's no Mom.

There's nothing, nothing at all.

There's nothing but Uncle Lenny's Ventura and this back road in New Jersey. It's strange how quickly everything has changed. Everyone's acting like none of that stuff in Fassett ever happened.

We barely talk about it.

"Do you like hot dogs?" I say, imitating the hot dog ad from TV. Everyone laughs.

Lenny nods his bald head.

"Armor hot dogs?"

Winnie nods her head.

Maria stares out the window.

"What kinds of kids eat Armor hot dogs?" I ask.

Maria turns and looks at me.

"Fat kids?" she asks, imitating the ad.

I'm giggling. "Skinny kids." That ad on TV always makes me laugh.

Last night, us Higham kids were the only ones in the funeral home basement when the lights went out.

"Show 'em, Mom," Faith whispered. A half-hour before, we arrived like Orphan Royalty and made our way past the fucking sign-in book. Do people read that on the toilet afterwards trying to figure out why John makes his "J" with a sloppy leaning hook? Does anyone review the pages to see if any mysterious strangers attended?

"Get the twins together, I want a picture," Palma said.

The boys did as they were told, kneeling in prayer for the first time in their lives. They kneeled before the white box that held what was left of Mom. Sure it was open casket, but the view was messed up. Mom looked too thin; somebody had removed her stomach tumor so she no longer looked pregnant. The same thief gave her a shiny black polyester wig that now hid what had become her waxy short hair. After the cancer drained all the life out of her, the undertakers did the same with all her blood and gave her too much blush in return.

"She looks so peaceful," Margie said.

Dead people look peaceful because they are peaceful: they should be. They have nothing to worry about. A dead person isn't a person; just a body. A thing. Death makes people into things. Looking at a dead person is just like looking at a piece of furniture or a pile of wood.

They put her in an insulated box and flew her from Pennsy to the funeral home in Hackettstown so she could return to David.

Return to David?

Return to Dad?

In the cemetery?

In the ground?

That's not Dad. It's what's left of his body. Another piece of furniture. Another pile of wood.

That's not David.

Her David? He's the guy who had the picture with the

eyes that followed all of us as he watched over us, protecting us. He was the one who was proud of me for taking care of the family.

Shit. If he was really watching over us, how come everything kept getting fucked up all the time? Mom never explained any of that.

It didn't matter anymore.

It's all messed up.

After the photo shoot with the twins, those of us who remembered Mom with her head full of lice and her body full of cancer as she spent her last days on her bed intently reading a yellowed copy of the *Philadelphia Inquirer* went to the funeral home's finished basement. Maria and I started talking.

"Remember when the twins and I and went after you?" I asked. "You know, I promised Mom... that I would bring you back alive."

Maria looked puzzled.

"You remember. Was the time when you went after Mom with the meat cleaver? Last summer, I think."

Maria shook her head.

"I never went after Mom with a meat cleaver."

"Yeah..., you did. And, afterwards, you ran away in your nightgown."

Maria remembered.

"No, that was the time Mom came after *me*. She came after *me* with the meat cleaver."

"Really?"

Faith nodded her head.

"But, Mom told me that you were trying to kill her," I said.

Maria and Faith shook their heads.

"No, Mom tried to kill Maria," Faith said. "She chased Maria around the kitchen table, swinging it at her. Was sayin' paranoid shit about her."

"Yeah, she was trying to kill me, John."

"Shit... "

Maria gets really quiet. We all do.

234

Then, a thunderstorm erupted and shot daggers of lightening at Hackettstown, knocking out the power.

"Mom's had about enough of this bullshit," Faith said. The rest of us laughed at her joke.

We sat in the darkness forever, but it was okay 'cause us kids were all together the way Mom wanted us. We could've died right then and it would have been okay.

We heard an electrical popping noise, then the lights came back on.

"What are you kids up to?" Uncle Jimmy bellowed. He stood on the top of the stairs, but couldn't see us.

"Shush," Faith whispered. "If we're real quiet, he'll leave us the fuck alone."

We giggled but didn't answer our uncle. We didn't say a word.

Nobody upstairs at the wake really wanted to hear us anyway and our fighting was over. That became obsolete the day Mom went to the hospital for the last time. Things had been bad before and she had always managed to come back, but not this time.

We obeyed Faith like we were pioneers in a storm cellar during a twister. We held our breaths and waited for Uncle Jimmy to disappear.

"You kids down there?"

None of us wanted to go back upstairs and see Fake Mom in the Box. No one wanted to listen to the aunts go on about how terrible it all was or listen to the uncles talk about what Mom should've done.

Everything seemed to move fast-forward until here I am in Lenny's Ventura.

Here I am.

Here I am.

Here, I am. My mind is moving fast, so fast that everything seems a blur. It's all so much to think about, so much to understand that I just can't stand it. It feels like my head is gonna explode and everything that I am is going come out of me in a thousand different directions and there's nothing I can do about it.

I'm trying to figure out what Maria and Faith said last night at the funeral home. That Mom tried to kill Maria. That means Mom lied to me. But, she really thought that Maria was trying to kill her. Believed it without any doubt, without any question.

What else did Mom believe... that wasn't real?

It didn't matter, because I believed everything she said. I never questioned her, never thought she was wrong or making anything up. I was her Loyal Man of The House.

It's all a mess even though it's all over. There's no more hit men in the woods or kids on the bus chanting that they hate the Highams. It's all over and I don't miss any of it.

Except Mom. I miss her so much right now.

And Dad. I miss him too.

I'm an orphan now. I'm no one now.

And Maria is talking, Maria is laughing at my joke about hot dogs.

And Lenny is driving, bald-headed driving the Ventura and Winnie is laughing with him and we're all just laughing along three cars behind the car.

Three cars behind *that* car.

Three cars behind *that* car that holds *that* box that holds *that* piece of furniture. The car that holds the box that holds the furniture, the car that holds the box that holds the pile of wood.

That car that holds that box.

It's all right there and it doesn't matter anymore.

"Everybody loves hot dogs," I say.

Winnie giggles.

"Armour hot dogs."

I wanna get out of the Ventura. I wanna go away as far as I can. I wanna run away from my life and the car that holds that box.

Four cars bear right just before the turn that could lead to Mount Bethel and the house where I lived before Dad died.

Shit, I stopped living a long time ago.

"Armour hot dogs!" I yell.

236

I see the power line that eventually runs to Camp Merry Heart where Mark's friend used to live. He still lives there, but Mark will never be his friend anymore. Death makes you think about things that don't happen anymore. It makes everything odd 'cause all you can see is what's gone.

And what's gone from my life wasn't all that good. Hell, it was all pretty bad. It's like all the wars just ended and I don't have to fight any more battles.

There's nothing to life now.

I'm gonna stay. I'm not gonna run. I have nowhere to go, anyhow. But, it's all driving me crazy. It's driving me crazy that Mom went after Maria with a meat cleaver, that Mom wanted to kill Maria.

Wanted to kill her own daughter: she *was* crazy!

It's driving me crazy that there weren't any hit men, that no one ever breached the inner perimeter! It's driving me crazy that I believed Mom! That I believed everything that crazy woman said. That I believed her about Dad being the sun, the hit men, and Ed being a spy.

I believed her and fought for her. Shit, fuck, shit, I believed everything she said, everything her crazy mind made up! I sat up each night, afraid of the woods, afraid of the spies. I lived in terror, defending my family against the enemies she created in her mind. They were my enemies, too.

This is all too much and nothing seems real. I mean, I feel like I'm suddenly in a movie or something like that. I feel like I'm watching a movie and I'm in it at the same time. I don't feel like I'm myself anymore, like I'll never be myself from now on.

"What kinds of kids like Armour hot dogs?" I ask.

Lenny laughs.

"Fat kids, skinny kids," he says, imitating the TV ad.

"Kids who climb on rocks," Winnie says.

And I'm laughing 'cause I don't know what else to do.

There's an old barn hidden back from Cemetery Road. If you didn't read the sign, you wouldn't ever know where the road leads until you get there. It winds over some creeks, past a few large farms that got broken-down barns and dirty tractors. When they built the road, they squeezed the pavement over some cow paths, making it twist through the woods before it comes out at the base of the hill.

"A hot dog a day keeps the doctor away," I say. We all laugh as we emerge from the woods and see the headstones outlined on the hill above us. They seem to rise out of the field surrounding the cemetery.

"Save a hot dog for a rainy day," Maria says. "A hot dog in the hand is worth two in the bun."

We laugh again as the cars climb the lane. In the distance is the power line. I look at the wires as they run westward toward God knows where.

Boxed Fake Mom is up front. They put her in the lead car this morning and we drove the ten miles from Hackettstown. My uncles carried the box from the funeral home to the car.

Somehow, we're now out of the cars, watching our uncles carry that box from the car to the gravesite.

That's what they do.

Faith, Maria, Mark, Warren, Rose and I watch. It's all we can do now.

There's a little tent set up over a hole someone neatly dug.

Someone covered the dirt with a black blanket. It's all done for us and Fake Mom.

Someone got a priest. He says Mom's name as if he said it every day and sprinkles some shit on her box when he's done. Mom was never Catholic. I mean, I think she only went to church once in Fassett, but that was a Methodist place.

I'm standing in the back, my hands on Mark's shoulders. Rose is there and Maria's got her arms around her sister's neck. I rub shoulders with my older sister 'cause I'm swaying a little bit in the breeze.

I wonder if Palma is taking pictures now. I can hear birds and all sorts of shit, including a car speeding past on the lane. I can hear everything.

And Fake Mom is in the box going into the ground next to David. Her David. When we're all done, they'll be shoveling dirt on her and we'll be getting back to our uncles' cars and be gone.

It's like taking broken furniture to the landfill. It's like putting dirt over a pile of sticks. It's like a thousand other things that don't mean much.

238

Doesn't mean shit.

Shit!

It's all shit!

No, it's not.

It's not like that at all, no matter how many times I tell myself that it is.

My shirt is suddenly wet as the coffin is lowered into the ground. My face is soaked and I can't see anything.

"I tried... so hard, Mom..., to protect you," I whisper to no one. "I'm sorry... I failed." I hold Mark's shoulders tightly as he stares at the disappearing coffin.

"Don't be ashamed, John," Lenny says. "Don't be ashamed to cry."

Maria hugs me after I throw a rose on the disappearing box. She guides me back to the Ventura 'cause I can only see tears. Winnie holds me too 'cause my knees are loose and my guts feel funny.

"Don't be ashamed to cry," she says as I try stopping it by holding my breath and gasping.

It's not that at all. I want to tell them what's bothering me, but it would take too long. My brothers and sisters watch me, hug me, and then go to their cars. I want to tell them how I fucked up, how I'm sorry I can't protect Mom anymore. I want to tell them but I can't say anything 'cause all I can do is ride in Lenny's Ventura and wait for him to drive the hell away from Fake Mom.

Aunt Palma's Kitchen

Between the time that Mom first underwent electro-shock therapy and before my older sisters and I stand along the load-bearing wall dividing it from the rest of the house, someone had renovated Aunt Palma's kitchen. They put in new cabinets, counters, and a larger sink. They made the dining area larger by building into the garage. They installed a television set on a rotating base that hung from the ceiling. They wired more fluorescent lights and laid new linoleum.

It's Palma's kitchen. To look around the fixtures and not see her standing near the stove or hovering by the fridge seems unusual. The television needs to be turned on: *Let's Make A Deal* should be filling the room.

On the counter, her pastries sit on plates, swaddled in layers of Saran Wrap. They remind me of a bakery's version of those instant families made by fertility drugs. Instead of children, my aunt gave birth to a stack of funnel cakes. They look like pastry angel's wings that have been broken off by confectionery wind.

The room smells odd. Usually the scent of tomato paste and sauce wafted from a pot on the range where the sausage and meatballs played. Now, cigarette smoke drifts from the table toward the ceiling. East Jersey overcast illuminates the room.

Palma has vacated her domain for the living room to be with the Little Ones. She, Aunt Marion, and Aunt Winnie watch them as Faith, Maria, and I remember to keep our shoulders off the wall and not slouch as our hands seek a hiding place. Our area accommodates no more standees, and we shift before our uncles.

They sit in a small arc at the table's far end. Jimmy sits on the end of the row of brothers. He owns the house and its miserable little backyard. In the past, that area had held his above-ground pool and a Sears garden shed. He swore at the Sears men he paid to install the chain link fence that had white and red aluminum filler strips. In '72, my brothers and I enjoyed poking and denting the strips with sharp sticks. The fence kept his dog in the yard, though the mongrel spent much of its life scratching the door and dodging Jimmy's kicks.

Next to Jimmy is Lenny. My sister and I had joked that his wife Winnie's smile was so plastic it reached all the way to her ass. Winnie now plays with my brothers and younger sister. She keeps my other aunts company in the living room, though the only plastic in that room covers Palma's furniture. Another piece forms a runway on the carpet from the front door to the kitchen, intersecting with a section everyone used when going to the back of the house.

I whisper no jokes in Palma's kitchen.

Uncle Mike looks tired and out of place without a beer can. He leans forward on his elbows. Once, I thought he was Phil Silvers, but that notion passed. His face is puffy and, like his brothers, he holds a lit Pall Mall in his hand.

Jimmy had summoned us. In some way, this was his duty: we were guests in his plastic slip-covered and carpet-runnered castle. His brothers allow him to speak first.

"Why didn't you know?" he asks, looking at our faces that feel bigger than we want them to be. If we can, we might melt like candles, oozing across the floor and out into the dog run.

Mike taps his cigarette against the ashtray.

"Jimmy's right," he says. "Anyone could tell. Something like that doesn't happen overnight." He nods, staring. "People can beat it now."

Mike's voice punches the air. His tone has a certain note of urgent anger, sort of how a cop with a nightstick might sound when beating up a pregnant woman.

"Well, how come you kids didn't know? Jesus Christ, everybody knows what to look for. Why didn't you catch it?"

"She wasn't different," Maria says. "She acted the same."

Mike's face twists. "You're telling me that my sister had terminal Cancer and you couldn't tell? She was riddled with that crap and wasn't different?"

"That's right, she didn't do anything differently," Maria says.

"Alright, Barbara," he says, raising his voice. "You all know my Barbara. She's a teenager just like you. Knows when I have a goddamned cold for Christ's sake. You know why she knows?"

Faith and I are safe: we know to be quiet. What can Maria say?

Mike doesn't care: he answers himself.

"She knows because she's a good kid. She's a good kid who loves her parents."

"Maria, her body was filled with the crap," Jimmy says, leaning back casually. "What the hell were you kids doing up there? Why the hell didn't you tell us? We could've helped."

"We didn't know anything was wrong," I say.

"So, she go crazy again? She have those funny whack-o thoughts?"

"No."

"Then, you should've known," Lenny says. "A healthy woman doesn't get sick like that overnight. For crying out loud, we all know that. It's like what your Uncle Mike said about Barbara."

The brothers nod and inhale their cigarette smoke. They remain seated, occasionally looking at their niece and nephews through the doorway to the living room. At those times, they smile. I watch my uncles only briefly, then study the tops of my worn Keds.

I hear the Little Ones on the sofa, watching television and playing with Marion, Winnie, and Palma. Our aunts speak to them in reassuring whispers sprinkled with hugs and kisses.

Our uncles suck smoke out of their cigarettes and expel the clouds into the air that hangs above the table.

"And what was that shit at the wake?" Mike asks. "Christ almighty, didn't it matter that your mother, my sister, was being paid last respects? Why'd you go downstairs when the lights went out?"

"Damned right," Jimmy says. "Let me tell you something: my sister loved you kids, though only God knows why." He lowers his head and puts out his cigarette, then reaches for the pack. "Only God knows why she loved you kids. You kids did whatever you wanted to up there in the woods. You were wild."

Lenny shifts in his chair, then brings his elbows against the table.

"The bottom line is that you should've known. You're the Biggies and should've kept an eye on things. Like Mike's Barbara," he says, taking another puff.

I watch them nod in agreement as they take turns inhaling and blowing out cigarette smoke. They look around the room, avoiding us with their eyes.

"Now, you kids get the hell out of here," Jimmy finally says. "Go out and play for Christ's sake."

We leave the kitchen without touching Palma's pastries. I sit on the front stoop and punch myself in the chest until my hand hurts. Later, when Palma calls me into the fully-lit kitchen, I stand along the same firing squad wall and watch the Little Ones joke as they sit at the table's far end and watch the TV show *Wonderama*. Palma smiles like a proud mama as she carefully unwraps a plate and presents her pastry to her nieces and nephews.

"No thank you, Palma," I say when she pauses with her broken angel wings.

"C'mon, Johnny, you're a growing boy," she says. "Manga, manga."

"Yeah, I know. Just wanna go outside."

"Outside? You have to set a good example for the Little Ones, Johnny. Eat."

She wraps her pudgy fingers around one piece and places it on a napkin, then lowers it into my hand.

"You eat that outside"

"Okay," I say, lying.

Roaring Run Road

The inner perimeter has been breached. Today, our enemies have taken over the house. It makes me think of how the Romans must have felt when the Vandals and the Goths overwhelmed the great city. Instead of those tribes, however, everything that I fought so hard to defend and protect is being carried away by the hicks. They're everywhere: they've parked their cars all over our lawn, they're walking through our house, and they're swarming as they pillage and loot my home.

"What am I bid for this box of tools?" The auctioneer's voice says over the loudspeakers. "Let me see, we have some old pliers here, a hammer, and what looks to be an antique axe."

The enemies from the bus are here with their parents, standing and chatting on the front lawn where Doug drove his Impala just a couple months ago. Oh yeah, he's here with Ed and Frank. Other enemies walk through Mom's room and stare at her disassembled bed. Everything—and I mean everything—has a tag on it. The exterminator made sure of that after he sprayed all the furniture this morning.

Me and Bobby are in the basement. Bobby teaches in Troy. Faith and Maria had him for history class. He lives in Mansfield with June, who works at the college. He's helping what's left of my family.

Anyway, as the enemies walk through my house, Bobby and I are putting stuff in boxes. We are hurrying because we are paying the auctioneer by the hour and we want to save as much money as we can.

I guess I didn't realize that we had so much stuff. At first, I watched the helpers bring out items. I saw entire boxes of books, knickknacks, and Mom's clothes get sold for a few bucks each. The winners celebrated by shouting as they carried their loot to their Crudley-mobiles.

Everything went quickly. I watched the plaster statues, the Channel Master, and the living room sofa disappear into the beds of rusting pick-ups. I watched the Lazy Boy get tied to the roof of a dented car and the lamps being placed in dusty trunks for the short trip down the road to their new life in a trailer.

By the afternoon, the looters had taken most of the furniture. Two nights ago, Jack and I had moved most of us kids' bedroom furniture to Columbia Cross Roads only to discover the next morning that someone had broken in and stole all of the weapons except Dad's .22 rifle. They also broke all of the garage windows. Jack called the state police and filed a report, but it didn't matter because those weapons were now unnecessary.

"At least they didn't burn it down," Betty said. "You kids should be thankful for that."

I wish *I* can burn it down. This place is not my home anymore. I want it empty so we can get the hell out of here. It reminds me of the evacuation of Saigon: we're happy to get out of hell. Anything we can bring with us is good, but we're getting out of hell.

Soon, the only piece of furniture left is Mom's bed. The dusty headboard, footboard, and side rails now stand on the front yard right near the auctioneer's podium. The mattress and box spring are inside propped up against one of the walls that was until a few weeks ago her bedroom.

"Frank, you should buy that," someone yells.

Everyone laughs, including the auctioneer. I stand in the basement door with a box in my arms and stare at Frank and Ed 'cause I don't think it was funny.

"Well," Frank says.

Nobody bids against Frank and he buys it for a hundred bucks.

Our enemies stand around in the front yard beneath the floodlights that I had once used to keep them away. They're all here, smiling and having a fuckin' party as they loot.

I hate them.

Bobby helps us save a box of Dad's papers and old pictures. We save all his service records and his stamp album.

We take down pictures of Dad, but his eyes stare straight at us. Nothing lives here anymore.

That's why my enemies are celebrating. Doug and Ed are playing catch with my football on the side yard. I see them just on the other side of the refreshment tent. Few people go there and I hear someone complaining that the prices are too damned high.

Bobby comes up behind me and taps me on the shoulder. He's carrying a box, but I don't care about that.

"Bobby, they have my football."

He rubs my shoulder.

"I'll get you another one," he said. "Someone must have taken that box when I wasn't looking."

After the auction, Jack and I scrub the garage floor with disinfectant just before we lock it up. We load a few remaining boxes of clothes and dishes and small appliances into his station wagon.

As the day ends, we see my old belongings in scattered piles on the front lawn as my enemies finish loading it into their pickups and cars.

In the fading summer light, Roaring Run Road becomes a memory.

Goodbye Yellow Brick Road

I smell Betty's Mary Kay perfume as I stand outside of her sewing room.

Betty is yelling and screaming.

I can't look at Betty's kids in the living room as we listen to her yelling. Instead, I see the cover of *Goodbye Yellow Brick Road* that is on the table near the black plastic phonograph. On the cover, Elton John steps onto a yellow brick road, his back to me.

Faith is yelling and screaming.

Faith is screaming and kicking her legs. In between her screams, Betty punches and slaps my sister, her voice loud.

"You will go," Betty screams. "This is my house."

I don't have any one favorite song on the album. I like most of them from *Funeral For a Friend* to *Bennie and the Jets*. Once, I memorized the words from *Harmony* and recited them to Mom as she sat in her bed.

"You're a poet, son. You should write that down."

That was last year before she stopped getting up during the day.

It's Faith's album.

As Betty continues to beat Faith, Mark grabs my arm and nods at the door. I am still.

I like *Goodbye Norma Jean* and *All The Young Girls Like Alice*, even though I don't know what that second song is about. When Mom would take the girls to the store for coffee, I'd play it on the Magnavox, making a cassette on my Panasonic as I watched for the Ranch Wagon 500 out the window.

The album somehow escaped being stolen or auctioned off with the rest of our lives earlier this week and made its way here. It's with us now.

"You kids had this happen because you didn't believe in Christ," Betty yells. "Jesus brought you here." Betty slaps Faith, making my sister scream and sob in pain. "I will not let Satan take you."

Mark grabs my arm. I can't look at him. Can't look at anyone right now, even though he pulls at me. After a moment, he drops my arm and moves toward the door.

I block his path.

Once, Mark and I played in the dirt in the backyard at Fassett. We pretended we were building a highway. "Your sister can't twist, but she can rock and roll," I said, quoting a line from that Elton John song.

"That's from that album," Mark said, using his toy steam shovel to dig a hole in the side of the hill.

That was so long ago.

Betty's kids watch us as I shake my head. It stops Mark.

"Fuck you and fuck your church," Faith screams.

"Satan, get thee behind me," Betty yells.

Mark makes a fist, but I put my hand over it before anyone sees it. Jack comes down the stairs, his dress shirt buttoned. His tails hang out and he carries his Sunday best shoes.

"You kids get ready for church," he orders. His kids back away as I stare at him.

We all hear Betty slapping Faith. That woman storms out the door and looks at me. Her polyester cream blouse is messed-up and her Mary Kay make-up needs fixing.

"Jesus is stronger than your rebellion," she says, pointing her finger at me. "He will break your evil spirit."

"I'm not goin' to your fuckin' church," Faith screams.

"What are you staring at?" Betty yells at Mark and me. "Get ready for church."

Betty leaves the living room with Jack, who hugs her.

Mark and I stand in the doorway, listening to Faith's sobbing. I'm still looking at the album cover near the phonograph.

The church smells musty.

Our pew is in the front.

In the center.

The parishioners watch us and smile as the Higham orphans, sans Faith, enter. As usual, we say nothing as we sit with our feet on the floor and hands in our laps. When the collection plate comes to us, we each put in the dollar Betty gave us.

This is Betty's church. After Sunday school and the sermon, we go to a dinner held in the church's basement. There, nice old ladies pat our heads and encourage us to eat more.

"You're just a growing boy," they say as they come over with their dishes to pass.

We bow our heads and move our lips during that prayer, just like we always do.

We're the Orphan Higham Children. The Poor, Godless Orphan Higham Children who Betty and Jack will save from Eternal Damnation.

After we return from the dinner, Mark is sitting in my camper as I change into Wranglers.

"We should kill the bitch," he says.

"Yeah we *should*," I say. "But, we can't do anything. No one's gonna adopt six kids."

"She's gonna do it again next week."

"Faith should just go."

"Fuck you. You sound like you're buying Betty's shit."

I want to punch Mark a few times in the arm just to get his attention. Not hard enough to hurt him or beat him like I used to, but hard enough to make him think.

"Asshole, we have to let her think she's winning. We're outnumbered and she's in charge."

"Fuck you. I can kill her."

I'm still thinking about punching him, this time nailing him in the chest to knock him down so he'll listen to me. I want to, but I don't 'cause all that punching I did before didn't make a difference.

"You do anything, they'll have you declared delinquent and dump your ass in foster care. They'll split us up in the name of Jesus or something."

"I'd rather be in foster care than this shithole."

"We have to stay together."

"You Biggies should have done something. We're fuckin' slaves. You heard her, she thinks we're Satan."

"We have to stay together."

"I'm gonna kill her," he says. "I'll burn down this fuckin' house while she's sleeping. Burn her and her fuckin' family in their goddamned sleep!"

"I'm sorry," Maria says as she sits on her bed. I try not looking at Faith. Not her face or her bruised legs, not anything. The sewing room smells musty. "I didn't know she was like that."

See, this is how we came here; Maria is friends with one of Betty's daughters and Mrs. White belongs to their church. We can't live with our relatives 'cause they'll split us up.

"Mark wants to kill her," I say.

"You guys didn't do anything," Faith says. "She's beating the living shit out of me and you guys just stood by and watched."

I look at the worn wooden floor.

"What could we do?" Maria says. "The caseworker is coming Thursday. If he finds out that we hit her, they could split us up."

"We have to get out of here," Faith says.

Maria nods her head, encouraging Faith.

"We don't belong here. We're not part of this life or this family. Betty doesn't give a shit about us; she just wants to save our fucking souls."

"I know, but I don't know who will take us," Maria says.

"We'll have find someone who wants six kids," Faith says. "They have to take *all* of us."

"Yeah," Maria says, "We can't let anyone split us up like they did with Mom's family."

Fuck. Mom's family was sent into an orphanage when she was young. Grandma La Rosa committed suicide after Grandpa La Rosa died. Mom and the relatives were sent to an orphanage run by the Catholic Church. That's why she always told us to stick together, no matter what.

Dad didn't have it much better. He was born out of wedlock and his parents put him in an orphanage right after he was born. He wasn't adopted until he was three years old!

"I'm not telling the Little Ones," I say. "They might let it slip."

Faith agrees. "Hell, Mark would tell Betty in spite."

It's true.

"I'll take care of Mark," I say. "I can keep him in line."

The canvas in the camper smells damp late at night. I zip up the windows and turn out the light, sitting still. After midnight, when the echo of passing trucks on State Route 14 fills the village, I punch myself in the chest until my hands hurt. Hell, I beat myself until everything hurts. It's the only beating I can do right now 'cause if I hit Betty, I know that the state will split us up.

I also know that if I let myself hit Betty once, I won't stop. I won't stop until she's dead. How dare that ignorant redneck bitch do that to my sister!

I can't let myself think about hurting her because I have to help keep us kids together. Mom said we have to stay together.

It's up to us Biggies to get the family out of here.

Together.

Faith's right; we don't belong here.

Windows

After Faith's beating, there's nothing left to me. My guts feel all hollowed out. I spent the morning sitting in the camper until just before lunch, but then I went inside and back-talked to Betty when she pissed me off.

"You go to hell and take Jesus with you," I said when she told me to go outside. Was just sitting in the living room was all. I wasn't even watching TV.

"You're not goin' sass me," she said. "Come here."

I come there to the kitchen where she's got a big aluminum kettle in the sink. I can see the twins weedin' the garden with Maria. Baby Rose sits at the table, coloring yellow rays of light from Jesus' face in that damned coloring book. She hasn't moved since breakfast.

Betty pours some vinegar. I know 'cause it stinks like all get out.

"Grab yourself some newspapers," she says.

Newspapers? Hell, she only reads the *Pennysaver* and the *Elmira Star Gazette*. Those aren't newspapers.

"Carry that kettle."

I carry that big kettle and follow her upstairs.

"You spill that water and I'll make you mop the floor," she yells.

Don't know why she couldn't fill it in the tub in the upstairs bathroom; that would've made more sense. I wouldn't have to carry it up the steps if she filled it in the tub.

"Come here," she says, going into the front bedroom. That's where Maria and Rose live 'cause Faith went to college last week: she's going to orientation or something.

Betty grabs a rag and dips it in the hot water. She then takes it and wipes the glass.

"Watch," she says, grabbing a couple *Star Gazette* pages. She rubs the window until all the grime is gone. I look around the room and figure that four windows with eight panes is thirty-two panes, sixty-four sides.

"When you're done here, you go to the other rooms until you're all done."

She hands me the rag. It's wet and cold. The vinegar smell makes me sick. She watches me as I stick my hand in the water and wipe the next pane.

"Now, wipe it with the newspaper."

I spend the afternoon dipping, rubbing, and wiping. My hands get wrinkled. The sweat makes the ink run all over my arms. It gets my face black when I wipe away sweat.

Her kids are playing tag on the front yard. I can see them from the window. Can also see the feed mill as it empties out at the end of the day.

Jack comes home with a carrier of milk bottles, his Penelec shirt hanging open to show his dirty T-shirt. I can see him through the window Betty showed me how to clean in my sisters' bedroom. It's real clean now, even if the rest of the windows aren't. In fact, it's the only clean window in the whole damned house.

The Front Stairs

"Brat," Betty says as she tries to slap my face.

We are near the top of the front stairs.

We are standing together.

I ran up here after I called her a bitch. Before I could escape, she ran up them two at a time, grabbed at my collar and tried to slap me.

I grabbed her hands, pulling them apart. She almost fell backwards, but I stopped her.

"Let go," she says.

"Fuck you, Bitch."

She tries pushing me over, but I lift my foot up to the next stair and spread her arms wide. She is unsteady in my hands. She tries escaping, but I hold her away with all my strength. Her flabby arms can't pull her hands closer together to allow her to break free from me and escape.

We are standing together near the top of the stairs, my hands restraining her.

"How do you like it?" I ask. "Don't like it when other people control you, do you?"

She struggles some more, but I'm not letting go of her wrists.

I have her on the stairs. We are far enough up so I can throw her down and fucking kill her. I have been cleaning windows every single day for the past two weeks. Every day, she rides my ass and finds something wrong with me, so she makes me clean more windows.

And, I argued with her. I've argued with her over every stupid insult, every ignorant comment about breaking my evil spirit, every self-righteous statement she's made about dragging me to Jesus.

And, she never hit me. Never even tried.

Until now.

Until she ran up the stairs with that face. That same face I saw when I looked into the sewing room while she was beating Faith.

I can see her anger now, but I only feel *my* rage. It's weird right now because my mind is racing, yet I'm feeling incredibly calm as I stare at her terrified face.

I can't believe how calm I feel.

And strong. It feels good to be this strong. I've never felt this strong before. I know that I can kill her right now. That thought doesn't even bother me.

In fact, it makes me feel strong, so strong that it makes everything all right.

For the second time in my life, I'm ready to kill someone else, though this time I know who it is and what I'm going to do.

The enemy is Betty. It's not God or Jesus; it's Betty.

And, I'm thinking about pushing her down the stairs.

My thoughts become words as I remain calm and completely in control.

"I'll listen to your sermons…, pray to your God…, and find out about your Jesus…, but you will not… hit me. You're not…, you're not…, you are not… gonna beat me up… like Faith. You will not… treat me like that: I'm not… ever… gonna let that happen."

She glares at me and I squeeze her wrists even harder. She squirms as she again tries to escape.

"You don't like that…, do you? Don't like it… when I stop you, huh?"

"Let go of me," she orders.

"When you agree… not to hit me."

No one is in the house. Sure, they might come after I push her down the stairs, but that'll be too late for Betty. I'll just lie and say that she fell. I've just figured it all out. One way or another, she's not going to hurt me.

No, I won't lie. I'll tell the truth. I'll tell them that I did it on purpose.

Lying is wrong.

I will kill her, though; I know that as I hold her wrists.

"You will obey me," she says, struggling to break free. She's not breaking free because I'm not going to let her escape. I'm holding onto her with all my might as I stare right through her. She keeps trying to grab my face and pull her hands together, but I firmly hold them apart.

I control her right now.

"Like I *fucking* said, I'll go… to your church, I'll listen… to your sermons… and I'll pray… to your Jesus, but you *will not ever*… hit me."

I can kill her. Fuck, I can kill her so easily. I can let go and fix her so that she'll never walk, never talk, never fucking breathe without a machine, never live again.

All I have to do is push while I let go.

She struggles and I squeeze harder.

"You're hurting me."

"Did *you* understand… what *I* said?"

Because I stand a step above her, she can't get any

leverage to pull her hands together. It doesn't matter, the next time she tries to hit me, I'm punching the fucking bitch in the throat. That's how you kill someone; it breaks the fucking windpipe.

She nods her head and stops struggling long enough for us to hear a car drive past. The house is completely quiet.

It's peaceful.

"Okay. I'm gonna let go. If you *ever*... try to hit me, I'm gonna stop you... and I'm gonna hurt you. I'm gonna hurt you real bad. So bad... that you'll *never*... be able to hurt me again."

I slowly open my fingers and watch her hands. She pulls away, then raises her right hand as if to slap me. My left hand shadows it and I prepare to push her with my right. I stare through her.

Our eyes meet and her slapping hand freezes in mid-air.

"You... get your kettle. You... get your vinegar. And, you get your newspapers," she yells. "You are not going to swear at me."

"Yes, Ma'am."

I remain on my step as she slowly retreats down the stairs. Only when she reaches the ground floor do I walk up a few steps to the hall, go down that, then take the backstairs to kitchen where I fetch my kettle, my vinegar, and my newspapers.

I spend the rest of the day cleaning her windows.

That night, for the first time in weeks, I don't beat myself before falling asleep.

East Smithfield Dairy

Bang!

Bang!

Bang, bang, bang!

It sounds just like gunshots when the milk bottles hit the tiled walls. The Bailey boys have cornered Mark and I inside the locker room of the East Smithfield Dairy, those fuckers firing an endless supply of cream bottles against the steel door.

"Fuck you," Mark yells, pushing a ripped desk chair through the doorway as a diversion.

He runs in the opposite direct and the stupid fucks throw behind him. He ducks behind a stainless steel milk tank. That acts like a shield and the bottles explode harmlessly against it.

"John's still in there," Randy yells. He's bigger, fatter, older and smarter than his brother Billy. It doesn't matter 'cause it's our milk plant.

"Fuck you, you'll never take us alive, asshole," I yell.

I push the steel desk against the door, shutting it as another barrage slams into it. Hell, it's only a matter of time before they go after Mark. And he ain't got any ammo 'cause they have their fat asses on the pile of bottles.

The cream bottles are the best. Sure, the half gallons are bigger and hit harder, but they're a bitch to throw. Can't get any distance on them. They're best for lobbing like a hand grenade.

Fat Ass Randy hits the door, but nothing budges. Not yet.

The windows in the locker room won't open far enough for me to sneak out. And the doors to the backside of the plant and the loading docks are both locked. I slam myself against them a few times, but they don't budge.

"I got those keys, asshole," Randy says.

I should've fuckin' taken them when I had a chance. They were in the locks yesterday. Mark and I found them when we came across a bunch of water-soaked *Penthouse* and *Playboy* magazines.

"Fuck you, fat ass."

I punch a locker, denting it. I take someone's white coverall out and search the pockets 'cause sometimes people leave keys behind.

Slam!

Billy hits the door. The fat asses are slamming into it, making the desk move. Though I push it back, I can see their eyes through the opening. They have a few loaded racks in their hands.

Bang, bang, bang, bang, bang!

I hear some bottles exploding, the glass shooting into the room through the opening.

"Leave him the fuck alone, assholes," Mark yells.

Shit, he must've captured the bottle supply and he's tossing cream bottles as fast as he fuckin' can. Right at the door! He hits near the boys and the fat asses are screaming like pussies.

Bang, bang, bang, bang!

"Fuck you, fat asses," I yell.

I open the door as Mark tosses more bottles at the boys. They scamper their fat asses toward the cooling tank as Mark keeps them under heavy fire. When I join in by throwing bottles, we flush the fat fucks from the building and chase them out into the sunny day.

We take off after them and run right into Neil. He owns the gas station on the other side of Route 14.

We don't throw any cream bottles at him, but it doesn't matter.

"You boys get over here," he yells.

We're sitting in Neil's Garage, looking at the abandoned dairy across the highway. Trucks rip through the village, barely slowing down before they continue along the valley. Mark and I are sweating and my face is bleeding, though I don't know how I was injured.

"You those Hig-ham boys?"

"Yes, sir," I say.

"You boys tore up that building pretty bad."

I nod 'cause I know that our asses are grass and Neil is the lawnmower. For all I know, he could've called the State Troopers in Towanda and is just keeping us here 'til they pull up in a big fuckin' Plymouth Fury III.

It's our plant. Me and Mark claimed it a week ago. The Bailey boys were the ones who started throwing the bottles. Shit, they almost hit me in the face. We were only defending ourselves.

"You boys just committed a serious crime," he says.

A Ford F-100 pickup pulls in, ringing the air chime. Neil stares at us a moment, goes out there.

Mark and I look at each other. We have glass slivers on out shirts and in our hair.

"Think he's gonna tell Betty?" he whispers.

"Probably, if we don't act sorry. Best to just admit everything and hope he doesn't talk. We probably should act scared. Real scared."

"Was our building. Fuckin' Bailey boys."

"Shush. Look at your feet."

Mark and I look at our shoes.

Neil walks into the office with a twenty-dollar bill. We watch him put it into his full cash register, get change, then walk back out.

"Shit, you see how much he's got in the register?" Mark asks. "Got enough for us to escape to California."

"We gotta stay together."

"Shit, we could all escape."

"Shush."

We get real quiet when Neil comes back in. He tucks a greasy rag into his pocket and smells like gasoline as he leans against the wall. He knows me and Mark have been talking.

"So, you're the orphans, ain't you?

We nod our heads.

"Living with Betty and Jack?"

We nod.

"They're good people."

"Yes, sir," I say while looking at the dirt on Neil's shoes. It's all grease and oil with dirt caked right on.

I'm thinking that I better not to look at him. Better to stare at the floor and be all humble and shit or he'll get really self-righteous and feel that he has to punish us sinners.

Don't think he goes to church. Never saw him on Sunday.

"Think your Mom and Dad are looking down on you from Heaven and feelin' real proud 'bout what you just done?"

"Done nothing wrong. Got to prove that in court," Mark yells.

"You shut your mouth right now," I say, quickly glaring at Mark, then looking back at the floor. Better to act like a beat dog right now instead of telling Neil to go to hell. Better to pretend that what we did was wrong or he'll get angry at us and call the troopers. Better to act sorry.

"He caught us red-handed, Mark. He's right. We've done the wrong thing and should be punished for it. We trespassed and vandalized that milk plant."

Mark shuts the fuck up just like he should. He's lucky that Neil's here or I'd beat the shit out of him.

Neil lights a cigarette. He's not supposed to be smoking near gasoline 'cause it could start a fire. He smokes it forever while Mark and I stare at his greasy boots. I agree with Mark: it's a deserted building and it wasn't our idea to throw the bottles. Fucking Baileys started it: we just ended it.

Neil finishes the cigarette by snuffing out the butt against the wall.

"You boys run on home to Jack and Betty and wait for the State Police. I put a call in and ain't got no time to babysit a couple of juvies. And don't try running away unless you wanna end up being wards of the state."

"Yes, sir," I say.

I glare at Mark.

"Yes sir," he finally says.

Mark and I are quiet as we cross the highway and walk to the house. I go to the camper and arrange my stuff so that Betty can put it in storage after the troopers arrest me and take me down to Towanda. Mark says he's thinking of running away, but he's right there at the breakfast table the next morning.

Mr. Estep's Massey-Ferguson

The next morning, Mr. Estep picks me up outside the house. His Jeep weaves over the road as he zips from Betty's home to a few miles up the road. Neil never called the cops and I made Mark promise that he'd never go back to the milk plant.

Now, I'm working for Mr. Estep.

At his farm, I see Bruce standing around Mr. Estep's Massey-Ferguson. The tractor is hooked to a baler and a hay wagon.

"You need the money," Betty said this morning when she knocked on the door of the pop-up camper. It's been my bedroom for the past two months. Betty says that I'll move into the house when the weather turns cold and Scott goes to college in the fall.

259

She and Jack have seven of their own kids, but Little Jack is in the Navy. It doesn't matter because I get to sleep in the pop-up and listen to the highway.

Betty's lying 'bout the money. We get Social Security money, V.A. money, and Mom's inheritance. I know 'cause I saw some papers for all that stuff.

She told me the lie when she stood at the counter, listening to her born-again tapes and reading her Bible that was so dirty with food stains I joked about it.

"Is that *The Jesus Cookbook?*

"How dare you mock Your Lord," she said, getting right next to me. "You will accept Jesus as your Personal Savior if it's the last thing I do."

Then, she got on the phone. When she saw me listening, she yelled.

"You get around. Mr. Estep needs help with hayin'."

Mr. Estep is a nice man from the church. He doesn't have any kids and 'sides, he treats me likes a hired hand, lettin' me stow my Thermos and sandwich in the barn out of the sun. There's no beer in his barn fridge: I checked.

He's got a wide front Massey-Ferguson that kicks out a lot of smoke when he starts it. Behind that, he's hooked a John Deere bailer and then a crappy wooden wagon to catch the bales off the kicker.

His fields are all cut and raked, the hay set out in rows just waiting for him to drive the bailer into it.

The wagon is the place to be. Mr. Estep drives 'cause he knows every single woodchuck hole and swampy area.

Bruce gets to work the wagon. He was in my gym class. He's a strong kid and wears leather gloves.

"You're the chaser," he says.

Bruce has done this before. He waits until the kicker sends a bale flying from the baler and snags it by the twine with his hands. He's got his shirt off, but he's sweating like crazy.

Me, I'm picking up the stray bales, then running after the wagon with them leaning against my thighs. Every time the Massey turns a corner, the bailer tosses one into the field. I can lift the son-of-a-bitches pretty easily at first, but the twine quickly wears through my palms and makes my hands bleed.

260

No one talks much during haying. It's pointless. You can't hear over the baler and the tractor. Even the hay wagon makes noise as it creaks and leans with the load. It's not until the wagon gets back to the barn does anyone talk.

When we unload the first wagon at the barn, Mr. Estep gives me some rags to wrap around my hands.

"A farmhand needs gloves," Bruce says, pushing his on tighter by interlocking his fingers. "Should get a pair."

There's a machine that lifts the bales up to the loft. At the barn, my job is pick up each bale from where Bruce has thrown it onto the floor and place it on the machine's steel belt. It then rides up to Mr. Estep in the loft, who stacks it.

Only thing, I'm really tired and I stumble each time.

"Use your whole body," Bruce says, "not just your arms. Way you're doin' it, you won't last 'till noon." He shows me how to plant one leg and push up with my other thigh while leaning back and pushing the bale away from my chest.

"Just throw the motherfucker," he says when Mr. Estep can't hear him.

It works okay until we get back onto the field, then I keep stumbling and can't pull any bales up 'cause my chest is lower than the wagon floor. I have to push with my chest to get the bales loaded unless Bruce can help.

I chase the wagon and work on curves. Mr. Estep stops the tractor and waits while Bruce looks at me and I run like a woodchuck in the field from bale to bale.

When the wagon is loaded, Bruce pulls me up so I can lean against the slats while Mr. Estep takes the load back to the barn.

Quickly, the rags get all wet with my blood. They're useless and my hands hurt.

It's after five when Mr. Estep pulls into Betty's driveway.

"Might want to wrap those up," he says looking at my hands and giving me a twenty. "We got plenty more hayin' to do."

"You don't have to get me tomorrow," I tell him.

"Is that so?"

"Yeah, but thanks for hiring me today."

Twenty minutes later, my bleeding hands ache while I'm taking a bath. I'm soaking in the tub when I hear the phone ring. Someone runs up the stairs and the bathroom door slams open.

Betty runs in. I'm too tired to care about her seeing me naked. Shit, she has kids of her own anyway.

"You tell Mr. Estep you're not working tomorrow?" she yells.

"Yeah, that's right. I cut my hands real bad— "

I hold them up to show her, but she turns around without looking.

"Get out of that tub," she yells, "I have something for you to do. Get out of that tub right now!"

I stand up without even thinking and she runs down the hall, yelling, "Get dressed and get to that kitchen right now!"

I consider walking downstairs naked, but instead grab my dirty clothes. When I put them on, they stick to my wet skin.

In the kitchen, I watch Betty. She grabs some vinegar and my kettle.

"Grab your stack of papers!"

She takes my kettle and a jug of vinegar and stares right at me. She looks mad as hell and for a moment I'm thinking that she might take a swing at me.

I sure hope she doesn't. I'm not in the mood for that crap and don't feel like punching her in the face 'cause my hands hurt too much.

"Come with me," she yells.

I follow her up the backstairs to the bathroom. I hear *The Adventures of Superman* coming on the downstairs TV. It's a re-run. The twins and Rose are watching it with some of Betty's girls.

In the bathroom, the tub is still wet.

"Put that in there," she says, pointing to the kettle.

I do and she turns on just the hot water. As the water fills the kettle and makes steam, I look at her: her face is really red.

"You can't afford to turn down work," she yells over the water. "You need the money! You will not turn down work, you understand?"

I don't say or do anything 'cause I'm too tired and too sore to argue.

I watch the steaming water rise in the kettle.

"Pour in the vinegar."

I open the cap and let it out of the bottle.

"Now, stick your hand in there and mix it."

Without pausing, I stare at her face then lean over the tub and lower my hand into the water. When I glance down, I see that my blood is making the water pink. The air smells of Ivory soap and vinegar. She looks at me and I stare back at her face, my hand working like a washing machine agitator.

It burns like hell, but I'm not gonna wince for Bitch. I'm not gonna let her know how much my hands hurt.

I'm not gonna cry for Bitch, either.

She turns off the water.

I continue agitating the water without flinching.

"You know what to do. Start in my room." She says, watching me as I gather my stuff and go toward her bedroom.

Washing windows turns the water a pinkish grey. The newsprint blackens my hands and arms.

Betty allows me to take a break for dinner, then I go back to cleaning windows until long after sunset.

At night, I sit on the steps of the camper, pouring rubbing alcohol over my wrinkled palms and wiping my eyes with my forearms. The air smells of freshly cut hay and I hear the trucks roar through the village.

I can't do anything with my hands 'cause my palms are all cut open. Can't even beat off, so I just look at one of the *Penthouse* magazines Mark and I found in the milk plant.

I sit outside of my camper on the side lawn for about an hour after all the lights go off in the house, smelling the hay just like when I was a kid.

That sweet scent fills the village the next morning as I stir another batch of window wash. My washing machine hands mix the hot water all day, but it's okay 'cause I steal some more rubbing alcohol and listen to the trucks later that night.

I even manage to get a few Band-Aids.

The Garden

Holy shit!

I'm sitting in the dirt, weeding around the lettuce in the garden when I see Betty chasing Mark from the barn. She's waving a large stick at him.

Even though Mark is barefoot, he's outrunning her.

"Fuck you, Bitch," he yells as he runs past.

Karen walks out of the barn. She's much younger than Mark and rubs her shoulder. She's crying as she approaches the garden.

"Mark, what did you do?" I yell.

Betty stops and waves the stick in my face. "Never you mind! Get to work and weed this row," she says before resuming her chase. By now Mark has run down the street, his swearing echoing through the village.

"He can't get far. He don't have any shoes," Karen says, rubbing her arm.

"You kids fightin'?" I ask while pulling some grass, shaking a clod of soil, then placing it in a pile between the rows.

"He threw a rock at me. Lookit."

She shows me the bruise: it's a purple circle on her upper arm.

"Why'd he do that?"

"Because he's evil," Betty says. "All you kids got bad spirits." Betty towers over me, waving the stick. "Jesus is more powerful than all your demons. I will teach you kids how to live in The Lord."

I return to weeding. The best way is to dig my fingers into the soil and pull hard, loosen the dirt, then yanking the weed free of the Earth. Then, I shake it until the dirt drops off in clumps.

Betty watches me for a moment, then takes Karen inside. Karen is wearing new Converse sneakers and a new jumpsuit.

Mark's sneaker broke a few days ago; the sole split in half.

"I'm not getting you new ones," Betty announced during dinner after seeing it. "You kids have to take care of what you have."

When I remember to weed, I start next to the house and follow the shade. Today, Betty chased me out of the camper early before I could pretend to do a chore.

That's my trick; get involved in a chore before Betty gets upset and hunts me down. If I wait until she's looking for me, I know she's gonna assign me something and hover over me.

"You want me to do windows?" I asked after breakfast.

"No, you'll just sit in the bedrooms and listen to music," she said. "I want you where I can see you. I'm going to be at the sink. You start right there," she said, pointing at the garden's north end, way beyond the morning shadow.

Pretty soon, Betty brought out Warren, Mark, Rose and Maria. We weeded until the sun moved over the house.

Betty's daughters, Karen, Amy and Polly played tag in the yard.

"We're fuckin' slaves," Mark said under his breath. When he weeds, he tears out everything he grabs. His side of the row is always strewn with lettuce and weeds. He also spits on the plants before moving along the row, hiding it by turning his back toward Betty's vantage point.

When I get hot, my sweat makes my hands muddy. I rinse them when I can sneak off to the spigot neat the kitchen door. That's when I sneak a few sips of water.

Betty's pretty easy to figure out. She thinks she can break my spirit through this type of work. She doesn't understand that I can go without sleep and food. That I learned to stay in control even when I felt like I'm gonna die. That I attempted suicide daily for over a year without telling anyone. What I went through in Fassett was much worse than this bullshit.

Hell, there's no hit men hiding in the woods waiting to kill me and my family if I fall asleep!

There's no kids on the bus calling me names and watching everything I do.

And, there's no civil war with my sisters. Not only that, Faith turned 18 last week. If Betty hits her now, my sister will probably have Bitch arrested.

I'm 15 and have gotten through more shit than most adults.

Bitch thinks she can break my spirit?

Bitch thinks she can defeat me?

With what? Weeding and window-washing? C'mon! If that's all I have to do to keep the stupid bitch off my back, I'll weed and do windows all goddamned day!

At lunch time, Betty came out.

"Wash up and come eat," she said.

The kitchen smelled of raw hamburger and I heard the Jacob Brothers singing about that old time religion. Betty read *The Way*: she propped it open next to her cookbook. We Highams didn't say anything because the music made it impossible to talk. Besides, when Betty was reading the Bible, it was better to keep quiet. That way, she wouldn't start on how evil and dirty we were. It was better to eat in silence than listen to her preaching.

Mark and me finished lunch early, then talked in the camper for a few minutes.

"I'm gonna slit Bitch's throat. From behind," he said. "And kill all of her punks." He sat on a seat, his dirty socks sticking out of his broken sneakers. His jeans were torn, his shirt sweaty.

"Not weeding Bitch's garden while the punks play tag."

"I know it's unfair, man, but you have to be cool. Don't

give Bitch a reason to split us up. Everyone thinks she's cool for taking us. If she says you're terrible, the county will believe her and have us declared delinquents. We're all we have."

Mark punched the cabinet.

"Don't fucking believe you guys aren't doing anything," he said. "Did you know that Bitch took her fucking girls shopping at *Iszards*? Spent our Social Security on clothes for her kids and my fuckin' sneakers are falling apart? Look at these fuckin' things! Even when Mom was on welfare, we had nicer stuff."

"What did Bitch say?"

"'You kids have to take care of things'," he mocked, "'You better tape it.' Fuck her!"

We heard the screen door to the kitchen open and slam.

Mark looked at me.

"Mark, get out here and finish weeding my garden," Betty yelled. "John, get back to weedin'."

"Fuck you," Mark yelled. "Us slaves ain't doin' no more work on Miss Betty's plantation."

"Mark, no!"

"Fuck you, Bitch!"

The camper door swung opened and Betty grabbed him, dragging him down the steps and dislodging his sneakers. Mark swore and pushed her down. Karen ran to her mother's aid.

Mark broke away from Betty and charged at Karen. That poor girl was afraid of my brother and should be. He's got a guinea temper far worse than me and was swearing at her as he chased her into the barn.

"Fuck you and your little punks, Bitch," he yelled.

Betty picked up a stick and ran after him. "No one talks to me like that. John, you get to that garden and start weeding."

"Yes, Ma'am."

I obey Betty. I mean, I could take her. I could really hurt her. Hell, I could kill her because I hate her so much, but then someone would call the cops, I'd be sitting in detention or prison somewhere, and they'd split us up for sure. There's no reasoning with her 'cause she sees everything as good and evil.

And, she's good.

I hate her for what she did to Faith. I hate her for trying to break our spirits while taking our Social Security money and treating us slaves. But, I really hate her for what she said about Mom and stopping us from visiting her.

That's the one thing that gets me really mad about Bitch; standing so fuckin' self-righteously between us and Mom.

I can't honestly think about that one too long 'cause then I get really angry to the point that all of Mark's reasons for killing Bitch make sense.

She didn't have to do that; that was pure meanness masquerading as Christianity.

If I had the chance to kill her without hurting my family, I would. I've thought about it and I would strangle her while I watched her die.

But, I can't kill her or even let Mark kill her. That would ruin the only thing going for us right now; our family. Wish Mark would understand that.

This is a war we just can't win. We have to get out alive. It's like we're prisoners of war and have to escape.

Together.

Karen, Mark, and Betty ran into the barn as I walked over to the garden and kicked a head of cabbage into the neighbor's yard. I plopped down in the dirt and started weeding near the lettuce. I listened to the fight in the barn as I yank at the grass strands.

In a few minutes, Mark runs toward the garden. He's barefoot now.

Betty is far enough behind him that she won't catch him unless he stops. He isn't about to do that. Betty looks as though she'll use that stick on him if he does stop, so I don't blame him.

Mark swears and laughs at her. He runs through the garden, kicking at the cabbage. Betty tries to catch him, but she can barely jump over the rows of plants.

"Fuck you, you fuckin' hypocrite," Mark yells at Betty.

I want to laugh. Hell, I want to knock Betty's ass to the ground and start beating the fucking shit out of her, but instead I just weed.

268

Mark runs down the street, leaving Betty at the edge of the lawn. She's all sweaty and gasping for air. She stumbles back to the garden.

"John, clean up this mess," she screams.

"Yes, Ma'am," I say.

She stands across from me. "You kids *will* know the word of Jesus. Satan, get thee behind me."

"Yes, Ma'am."

Mark stays away from the house through the afternoon, even after Jack comes home from work. From the garden, I hear Jack's utility truck stop and idle as he climbs down.

He's a good man who really believes in God and Jesus; I can tell. He's not self-righteous and mean like Betty.

And, he's happy, really happy. He's always smiling at the end of his day when he comes home. I can tell that he loves his family. If he was the only parent, I wouldn't mind living here.

By now, I've almost made it to the shade and have cleaned up all the plants Mark ruined during his escape.

I pretend to use the toilet, then make my way to the living room because I want to hear what Bitch is telling Jack. Also, Mark's place is not set at the dinner table. In fact, no one talks about him, not even my siblings. After working me all day, Betty allows me to relax after dinner, so I sit in my camper and try figuring out where Mark might be. I don't think Betty has called the police 'cause they haven't come to the house. And, Jack didn't go anywhere in the family car looking for my brother.

The sun sets and Mark is still missing. I get ready for bed. I don't wear pajamas anymore 'cause I don't have any. 'Sides, I don't want to worry about Betty coming in here, so I sleep in my clothes. It's easier that way to run into the house in the morning when she yells for me.

"John," Mark whispers through the camper's screening.

He's back!

We sit in the camper and whisper.

"You're gonna have to apologize," I say. "And not do it again."

"Bitch really pisses me off."

"Jack's probably pissed. Bitch I don't care about, but if
Jack thinks you're a wild boy who doesn't listen to Betty, he'll
probably have you sent away. He can't be here during the day
and if he thinks you're gonna hurt Bitch or the punks, he'll have
to do something about it."

"She a fuckin' bitch."

"Yeah, she is. But, she's in charge and we're just slaves,
like you said."

"Why can't you guys do anything about this? Why are we
stuck here?"

"'Cause we are."

"Can't you guys get us out of here?"

"No. Nobody wants six kids, Mark."

"Have you guys even tried?"

"Yeah."

"Who'd you ask?"

"Never mind. Nobody wants six kids."

"Fuck you. You guys didn't even try."

"Nobody wants six kids. We have to stay together. We
can't let them split us up."

"I hate it here."

"So do I."

"Why didn't you stop her?"

"I'm not goin' to jail. Or detention."

"I hate this place."

"You have to apologize or they'll split us apart."

"I don't want to."

"I don't fuckin' care what you want. You have to
apologize."

Mark sits there, mad as hell. I want to tell him that Maria,
Faith and I are trying to figure out who to ask, trying to find
people who would want the six of us, trying with all of our might
to find anyone, anywhere who can take all of us. Anyone who
could take care of us better than Betty.

I want to tell Mark everything, but I can't. I can't risk it.
He gets so mad and says the first thing that comes to his mind.

We can't let Betty and Jack know what we're planning.
Us Biggies don't trust Betty. All she has to do is make one phone
call and complain about us.

Then we're gone; we're nothing.

"Okay," Mark finally says.

I want to hug him and tell him that it's gonna be all right, but I can't. I have to go in there with him and see what Betty and Jack say and do. I have to figure out what they're gonna do so I can make my next move. If they're really upset, they might just send him away.

I walk in with him. By now, Betty is in bed.

Jack comes out of their bedroom wearing his gray work pants and a T-shirt. He holds a belt in his hand. I follow him into Mark's room. My brother lays face down on his bed.

I realize for the first time since he returned that his clothes are dirty and torn. The soles of his feet are filthy. Not only that, but he's exhausted and hungry.

Jack walks into the room, doubles over the belt, and prepares to whip my brother.

"It's only gonna make it worse," I say to Jack as I sit on the edge of my brother's bed, blocking Jack.

"Well, sometimes things have to get worse for a boy to learn a lesson," Jack says.

"Jack, he just lost his mom. And, he has no Dad. You can't expect him to pretend that everything's great."

Jack moves closer to Mark and me.

"That's not gonna help things," I say, pleading.

I know what's gonna happen if Jack hits him. Hell, Mark punches me back; he's not gonna lie there and take it. He'll fight Jack with everything he's got and Jack'll have to hit him hard, real hard, to knock him down.

I'm not gonna let Jack hurt Mark. I can't do that, so I look around and notice that there's a Bic pen on the night table next to Mark's bed. I'll have one chance, but I think I can grab it and stab Jack in the throat. He's a big guy, but I'll kill him if he touches my brother.

"He swore and pushed Betty."

"Yeah, he did. That's wrong, but he's just a kid and he told me that he was sorry."

Jack pauses.

"Mark?"

Mark just lies there.

"Mark?"

I tap my brother's leg.

"Mark, Jack's talking to you."

"What?" my brother asks without moving. I can tell that he's getting ready to spring up at Jack. I can tell that Mark is mad, madder than hell at Jack and Betty. He's madder than hell at everyone.

If he jumps at Jack, I'm gonna have to hit Mark real hard to knock him down. Gotta show Jack that I got Mark under control so he can go to work in the morning and not be afraid that Mark'll kill Betty.

"John tells me that you feel sorry for hitting and swearing at Betty. Is that true?"

Mark remains still on the bed.

"Mark, tell Jack. Tell Jack what you said."

Mark nods his head without looking at Jack.

"Are you gonna do it again?" Jack asks.

Mark shakes his head. "No," he says. "I won't do it again."

Jack and I watch each other in the dim room while my brother lays still on the bed behind me. We look at each other for a long time, then Jack unloops his belt and goes back to his room.

I rest my hand on my Mark's back for awhile, then return to my camper and listen to the trucks as they pass through the village.

The Ninety-Eight

Bobby and June's Oldsmobile Ninety-Eight smells new. I can see where the sticker was on the side window. The seats reminded me of the Lazy Boy as the car glided over the highway 'cause it's that smooth!

Right now, the Little Ones and I are sitting in the backseat, waiting for Maria and Faith to come out of Bobby and June's house. I'm waiting to hear what's happening in the house after the girls asked them about us.

When Bobby picked us up in Columbia Cross Roads a few hours ago, he popped an opera tape into the built-in cassette player.

"You kids behave," Betty said as we were getting ready. It was her idea for us to wear our Sunday best, even though it was Saturday. Bobby took us over the hill through Sylvania and across Armenia Mountain on U.S. Route Six.

The Ninety-Eight sped along the narrow highway to his house in Mansfield. We've never been here before. It's on Spring Hill. The new house sits on a hill overlooking the valley. In the modern kitchen—there aren't any food-stained Bibles anywhere—June was waiting with home-made Lasagna.

We took our shoes off when we came through the front door and Melville Dewey, the couple's Miniature Schnauzer, leapt on us.

"Melville, down," Bobby said.

The dog obeyed. We stood huddled near the door, waiting.

"People can come in," June said from the top of the stairs. The stairs have square steel bars running from the basement two stories to the counter near the kitchen. It's all very modern.

"Wow," Mark said. "Nice place."

We make it to the top of the stairs and stand on the floor, our stained socks slipping on the polished hardwood. Except for their den and one of the bathrooms, the area is open and one wall is mostly made up of sliding glass doors through which we could see a valley stretching out for miles.

The house sits in a thick stand of woods on top of one of the hills surrounding Mansfield.

"Bobby, you don't have a lawn to mow," Mark said.

Bobby laughed. "We designed it that way. I hate mowing."

At dinner, we used "please" and "thank you," put our napkins on our laps, and listened to Bobby and June. We ate all of the lasagna, then took a tour of the house. At the end of the evening, we said goodnight before I took the Little Ones out to the car.

That's how Faith, Maria and I planned it. While they asked Bobby and June if we could live with them, I was supposed to wait in the car with the Little Ones. It's almost September and we want to move in before school starts.

The Little Ones are tired. Warren and Mark stare at Bobby's kitchen through the Ninety-Eight's windshield. Rose sits quietly next to Warren, who looks sleepy.

"What's taking them so long?" Mark asks. "Bitch is gonna make us go right to bed when we get back to the plantation. Except you," he says, looking at me.

"Listen guys," I say, "The girls are talking with June and Bobby."

"About what? Bitch?"

"Yeah." I swallow hard and try not to cry. "Maria and Faith are... asking Bobby and June... if they..., if they... will... take us... all of us. If they want us... to live with them. We're gonna try to get all of us... out of Betty's house."

The Little Ones smile and cheer while I make a face and keep from crying.

"Really?" Mark says. "I fuckin' knew it. That's why you kept telling me to knock off the shit."

Rose and Warren squirm in their seats. I hug the three of them as we look at the house for any sign of the girls and Bobby.

"We can't let Betty know, especially now."

"Damned right, Bitch might call welfare and split us up," Mark says.

"We're like pilgrims," Warren says. "We want to be free."

Mark laughs and rubs his hands together. "We're gonna be free from Bitch and her fuckin' punks."

"Gotta make sure we don't talk about this at Betty's house, okay? Not even mention it."

They nod their heads.

"Mark, I mean it. Not even when you're really pissed off at Bitch."

He laughs. "John, prison just got a whole lot easier knowing we're gonna be released."

"Stay calm. We don't know if Bobby and June want us."

"June made us dinner," Rose says, "She can be my mom."

"Yeah, but there's six of us. It's a small house. They might not have the room for us."

"I'll kill Bitch if we don't leave," Mark says.

The Little Ones get quiet.

"Mark, it's gonna happen. It just might take some time."

I look at the house, wondering if Maria and Faith were pleading, arguing, or both.

"You mean you don't want to live in the camper?" Mark jokes. "Or that we won't have to go to church anymore?"

"No. Not anymore. We're asking for religious freedom."

"Just like the Pilgrims," Warren says.

"How long were you planning this?" Mark asks.

"From the day Betty beat up Faith."

Mark slaps the seat. "Fuckin' knew it. That's why you wanted me to be cool, wasn't it? That's why you yelled at me all the time. I thought you were on their side. John, why didn't you tell me?"

"Because we couldn't afford to have you tell Betty when you were angry at her."

The front light comes on. Faith walks out with Maria. They take forever to get to the car.

"It's bad news," Mark says. "We're not free."

"We'll see."

"I want to live here," Rose says.

"Maybe they can't take all of us," Mark says. "Maybe they only want a few."

"We go together or not at all," I say. "No one splits us up!"

Maria and Faith get in the car and sit in the front seat, closing the door.

"I told 'em," I say. "What's the verdict?"

My older sisters turn around in the seat.

"They have to think about it," Maria says.

"They don't want us," Mark says.

"No, Mark, they'd have to make the house bigger and contact their lawyer," Faith says.

"Fuck you, Betty," Mark yells.

Maria touches his arm. "Betty can't know. She might split us up or start a legal battle. And you have to behave."

"Did they say when?" I ask.

"By the end of the summer."

The car becomes quiet as Bobby walks from the front door. He climbs in and looks at our smiles, then turns on his opera tape.

"Can we live with you?" Rose asks.

"After we get some things taken care of," Bobby says.

We drive back across Armenia Mountain and Sylvania, reaching Betty's just before ten. I brush my teeth in the bathroom off the kitchen, then go to the camper. I sit in the dark, just listening to the highway all night and wiping my eyes 'cause I finally did something right.

Spring Hill

Look!

There's another UPS truck in the driveway! It pulls right past the contractor's truck and the tractor-trailer that's delivering concrete blocks. Hell, they haven't even dug the foundation yet, and those building materials are already arriving!

"I'll get it," I yell when the doorbell rings. I run down the stairs and open the front door. The driver is holding a big box. It's so big that it hardly fits through the door! The twins and I pull it through, then carry it upstairs.

We're in paradise! Bobby and June have Mark, Warren, and me sleeping in the basement until the contractor finishes the addition. They're building an addition to the house that includes two bedrooms and a full bath next to a new garage!

For us!

I'm getting my own room in the basement with guess what? Paneled walls and a big picture window that looks out over the hills and the cornfield down below our new house!

That's what!

Every day more packages arrive from Sears! We're all getting new clothes: new school pants, shirts, sweatshirts, windbreakers, underwear, socks, shoes, boots, sneakers, gloves, hats, and jeans!

School starts in two weeks and they want us to look nice!

We don't have to go to church if we don't want to and we don't have to wash windows all day!

We're free! It's like everything that Mom ever wanted for us is happening!

For real.

Everything is suddenly better!

We did it!

Us Biggies did it!

We got our family to safety!

It makes me cry when I think about it.

Spring Hill overlooks Mansfield. It's a residential area. The Royers live in the big white house on the bottom.

Guess what? The Royers' garage is big enough for their brand new motor home! Across the street from them are the Walters: they're music professors at the college! Next to the Royers are the Dills: he's a college professor! He has a big ham radio antenna outside his house! Next to him are the Philibins; his father built this subdivision.

Next to the Philibins are the Bishops: he's a dean at the college! A dean! There's so many really smart people who live in our new neighborhood!

Across the road from the Philibins are the Rourkes: he's a foreman on the Tioga-Hammond Dam project and then there are the Wheelers: he's a math professor at the college.

Up from him and next to our house are the Wilmonts. Get this: he's the freakin' President of Mansfield State College! The President!

Across from him are the Findleys on the top of the hill. They have a fully-equipped Winnebago because Mr. Findley was crippled in World War II. Across from them are Bobby and June.

Our house sits back in the woods, so no one can see it in the summer. Our other neighbor is the Raricks: he's a geography professor at the college!

"That's Snob's Knob," some Mansfield kid told me when I said where I lived. I don't care about that. All I care about is that we got out of Columbia Cross Roads.

And just in time too, 'cause Faith is going to college in a few weeks. Maria is goin' stay in Troy school 'cause she's a senior this year. She can ride into school with Bobby because he teaches there!

Bobby and June buy us everything we need. Day after day, more packages arrive from Sears.

I have three more years until I'm in college. Shit, I never even thought about college before.

I never thought I was that smart.

At night, I listen to the radio Bobby gave me, grooving to songs like *Rock Me, Baby*. Because we're on a hill, I can listen to radio from way upstate New York. I can't get WENY anymore, but I don't care. Sometimes, when I'm all alone late at night, I cry because we got out together.

Letters

I write a lot of letters now. Hell, I'm always writing letters to my friend David in Troy. I write him all the time about all the things I miss.

Like hanging out with my friends.

I don't really write about Mom or shit like that.

I like writing letters. He always writes back.

Felicia and Angel

What a pair! I don't think they belong here. On my first day at school in Mansfield, Felicia comes right up to me and introduces herself.

"My name's Felicia. Who are you?"

"John."

"I'm Angel," her friend says.

Get this: they're both in my homeroom. We're ready to say The Pledge of Allegiance and they both stand there!

I mean it: they stand there without saying The Pledge.

The teacher gets mad and glares at them, but Felicia and Angel stand there and say nothing.

The other students glare at them.

But not me: I try not to laugh out loud at the narrow-minded idiots all around us.

Get this: Felicia and Angel are intelligent. I was listening to them making a point in Ecology class and it freaked me out.

Not only that; they're beautiful! Felicia is tall and sexy. I mean it. She's got blond hair and fantastic eyes.

And Angel is this sexy Italian who is funny as hell.

They don't really belong here: they're too smart for this place.

Felicia knows June: her father is a professor at the college though he's nothing like June.

NYC

It's cool. We're in the back of the Ninety-Eight as Bobby drives the car out of the Holland Tunnel into Manhattan.

It's been years since I've been in the city.

Decades.

My life is measured by little lifetimes, events involving the same people, events with the same group of people.

Nothing stays the same.

Little lifetimes; I like that.

The little lifetimes end and make me change what I do because everything else changes.

The last time was in '65 when Dad brought me in for my fifth birthday. We went to the top of the Empire State Building.

Before the Mafia broke into our home.

They were Mafia.

Maria says that they visited Mom after Dad died.

Dad wasn't Mafia.

Bobby and June come to New York for musicals and plays. Bobby is talking, all the time talking and teaching us.

"People should write down their first impressions of the City, so you can look back at what you wrote years from now," he says.

That's a good idea, writing down things.
I've been in NYC before.
During another little lifetime.

We go everywhere: the Museum of Natural History, Central Park, and Broadway for the shows. My brothers and I share a room at the hotel. The girls are in an adjoining one. Mark and I stand at the hotel window watching the street action. We're at the Holiday Inn. It's cheap, but it's safe and clean.

No trip to the Empire State Building.
Not in this little lifetime.

Playin' with Trains

Look at that Christmas tree; it's beautiful! Bobby and June took us out to a tree farm in Wellsboro and we cut it down. Bobby took pictures of us trudging through the woods with an axe to chop it down and bring it back to the house.

When we returned home, June told us how to decorate it. Bobby and June have a lot of rules and the Christmas tree is no exception. We can only put on one ornament at a time and if June doesn't like where we put it, she'll move it.

Bobby takes pictures with his Olympus camera. He likes us to smile while he takes pictures and reminds us by saying, "Say cheese," or something like that.

And, when we're done, the tree looks like it could be in a display or something because it's that beautiful. And perfect.

When it's time to open presents, we have to follow another rule. "People will open one gift at a time while everyone watches," June says as Bobby is ready with his camera to take the next picture.

When it's my turn, I open a small box. It's an HO Scale model of a diesel engine.

"It's just what I wanted," I say, smiling as Bobby takes a picture.

Hell, this life is just what I wanted.

"I hope you're not disappointed," June says. "I know you said you wanted a layout, but this way you can build one a little at a time."

"That's cool."

Christmas morning lasts forever as everyone opens their presents one at a time and Bobby takes pictures. Afterwards, we all get changed into our school clothes and sit for a group photo. Bobby sets up his tripod so he can be part of the family portrait.

I play with trains differently now. I still have the Lionel train set, but my foot stool was sold at the auction, so I don't even think about the gallows anymore.

All that crap is gone.

It's funny how different I've become. It's odd to feel safe at night and not worry about feeding my siblings. It's strange to not worry about hit men or kids on the bus or Betty beating up Faith.

I don't have to be a soldier anymore.

I'm now a kid. Just a kid in the tenth grade.

No, it's like I'm Wally Cleaver after completing a couple tours of duty in Vietnam.

1976

Bucking Fuss

Faith is sitting in her room.

Excuse me, I mean Faith is sitting in one of Bobby and June's guest bedrooms. Faith doesn't have her own room because she's doesn't really live here. She's quiet as she sits on the bed. Her suitcases are packed and she's just staring out the window. I sit next to her.

Somehow, my sister became beautiful. She's no longer an old lady but instead a pretty coed with a wicked sense of humor. She talks quietly, but her wit is sharp.

Faith's studying art because she's talented.

"I have to take the bucking fuss," she says. "I have to take it back to college."

"Why?"

"Bobby and June said that I can't stay here over the summer." She says, smiling, "so I'm going to take the Bucking Fuss until they let me come back to visit for the next holiday."

"Christmas?"

"Whatever holiday they decide on. So, I'll just be on the bucking fuss."

"Why do you call it that?"

"Stop and think about it," she says.

I do, realizing that she's switched the first sounds of each word so that she can say it without swearing and still get her meaning across.

"You need any money?"

"I'll take your money," she says, smiling.

"No, I mean, are they going to pay for anything?"

"Oh, Bobby and June will pay for the bucking fuss," she says, laughing. "So, just put me on the bucking fuss and send me the hell off."

"You can come back, right?"

Faith shakes her head.

"They said that I'm on my own," she says.

"They can't do that to you."

"They don't want me to come back for the summer unless I have a job up here."

"There's no jobs in this area."

Faith smiles.

"That's why I'm riding the bucking fuss!"

I just sit there. I don't know what to say because Faith's not saying how upset she is right now. The afternoon drags on forever mainly 'cause I know Faith's gonna be gone. We don't talk about it. Bobby and June act like it's no big thing that my oldest sister is going away forever. They sit around upstairs and talk as Bobby sips a beer and June enjoys a glass of wine. Bobby has a Puccini opera playing and it's all very nice.

Later, I go with Bobby when he takes Faith to the bucking fuss. June stays home and has another glass of wine while reading *The New York Times*.

In Mansfield near the town's only traffic light, I give Faith a hug before she gets on the bus.

"Have a safe trip," Bobby says. He makes a couple of quips about her meeting boys. He makes me laugh 'cause that possibility adds another meaning to Faith's term.

Faith just stares at him. I can't blame her; she's being flushed out. It's not fair. She wanted to have a home, too; I'm sad for her.

"Well, have a safe trip," Bobby says, shaking her hand.

"Nice to meet you, too," Faith says.

'Well—,"

"Yeah," Faith says as she climbs aboard the Continental Trailways bus. I stand on the sidewalk, waving and watching as the bus heads south on Route 15 toward Harrisburg.

That's three hours away.

Three hours too far.

Japan

We're at the Airport. Maria is smiling.
Hell, we're all smiling because Maria is going to Japan!
Bobby and June and Maria set it up.
She's going to school there.
It's cool: We're all dressed up in our nice clothes.
It's exciting for Maria and everybody; she's gonna be an
Exchange Student for a year.

Breakfast of Champions

Shit, can you stand it!
You can do this in a novel?
I like the way this book develops. I like the way the
narrator grabs my attention and leads me through this world of
his, through this mind of his.
With drawings even.
I want to write like this. I want people to talk about my
writing like this. I want them to argue about what I meant and get
the little—and big—jokes.

The Brief Case

*Honey, the men were here again today. Don't worry, My
Dearest, I told them that all my dark secrets were going to die
with me. They said something about you and the kids, trying*

to scare me, but they said they wouldn't do anything as long as I stay quiet.

I put down my father's letter.

I am sitting on my bed, looking out the window. In front of me are my father's handwritten letters. Each is folded and in a carefully-opened envelope. The postmark reads April 1969.

He wrote these on his deathbed.

My Dearest,

I love you too. It's just that our luck has been so bad and the cancer has spread so fast. The doctors don't talk to me much anymore. They just come around, take my pulse, listen to my heart, and tell me to hang in there.

The men come at the start of visiting hours. They are always nice, always quick to tell me what the children wore to school. They don't say much else.

They promise me that you and the children will be safe if I don't say anything. I have assured them that I have nothing to say.

I find another one.

My Dearest,

I know you can raise the children. John will:
1) Attend the Naval Academy.
2) Become a career Naval Officer and take assignment in any armed conflict.
3) Memorize "If" (I've written a copy that I enclosed) before his 10th birthday. (This is very important because it will help him be a man.)

I see another neatly folded page that contains that poem. I read it, then think about it for a few moments.

I find in his papers a letter from a psychiatrist that says that Dad can't buy a handgun. It's dated 1955 and says that Dad has severe shell-shock.

I find something Dad typed on the Olivetti. It's filled with mistakes, though I accept this as Dad graduated with only G.E.D.

I realize that he was starting a book filled with clichés and run-on sentences. The book was about his life. In it, he wrote about being put in an orphanage immediately after being born and having no parents until he was adopted by the Highams when he was three years old. I read that his mother was a showgirl and his father was a Boston physician. I read that Dad had another name before he was called Harry David Higham.

But, there's nothing in there about what he knew.

Nothing in there about why the Mafia was after him or why Mom was afraid of hit men.

The hit men were real! Maria said they were and that they robbed the house in Stanhope.

Were they watching the house in Fassett?

I find a journal from Mom. It's handwritten on a notebook page.

At two ten on April 21, Dale English pulled his truck up to his gate for approximately fifteen minutes. During this time, he got out of his truck, opened the gate and walked into his pasture after closing the gate behind him. I don't think he saw me watching him, though he looked at the house four times. He then walked along the fence that borders my property acting like he was checking his fences, but looked at my house several times each minute. After about ten minutes, he walked to the gate, opened it, closed it behind him, and climbed into his truck. He sat in it for about a minute and half, then started and drove toward his house.

I find pictures of Mom's first husband, Frank Deparisis. He was in the Army Air Corp and had Multiple Sclerosis, dying shortly after the war. I find papers involving Dad's first two marriages.

I find a letter from the Veterans Administration Board of Appeals dated December 13, 1957:

Dear Mr. Higham:

Appellate review has been completed by the Board of Veterans Appeals on your appeal for an increased rating for your nervous disability. Your designated representative, The American Legion, is being advised of the Board's determination.

The Board carefully studied all evidence pertaining to your disability, noting in particular the report of your hospitalization from September 1956 to May 1957 and the report of official examination in July 1957. In studying the evidence, consideration was given to the reasons advanced as to why you believe you are entitled to an increased rating. It was determined by the Board, however, that your nervous disability does not warrant the assignment of a rating greater than the 70 percent currently in effect therefore and the appeal was, accordingly, denied. The Board found the medical evidence of record is adequate for evaluation of the issue under consideration.

I find letters that Dad typed to President Johnson, asking for help with raising six children.

"John, it's dinner time," June's voice says over the intercom. I put the papers back in Dad's old briefcase that Mom kept in her closet in Fassett.

I am quiet at the table.

I am not the man Dad wanted me to be. It's not my fault. Mom never showed me the letter. Never showed me any of the letters. How was I supposed to grow up that way when she didn't let me read these letters?

"How was your day?" Bobby asks. He is eating mashed potatoes and meat loaf. There's a large bowl of salad in a wooden bowl.

The Little Ones are at the table, eating.

I am the last Biggie.

The whole world is eating, not knowing what sort of person I haven't been. My crazy father, who took secrets to his deathbed, had something that he ordered my crazy Mom to tell me.

Mom kept secrets, too.

It's really not my fault, but I can't be that man now. I find the idea of killing someone upsetting. Having hated others so strongly, I'm now sickened by it.

"Okay, I guess. I started going through those papers June wanted me to."

June looks up from her end of the table.

"Any discoveries?"

The Little Ones look at me. They don't know about the Mafia, except the stories Mom told us. Anymore, they thought it was just Mom being crazy. Everyone but me thought she was crazy.

"There *were* men," I say, taking the meatloaf and putting a slice on my plate. Bobby and June always make sure we eat well. They buy us cereal and get us good food for lunch and dinner. They have lots of food downstairs.

"Men?"

"Yeah. The hit men visited Dad at the hospital. He was on his deathbed."

June lowers her fork.

"What did they want?"

Bobby and June know everything about Mom. Bobby talked with Faith and Maria about her when they asked him to live here.

"They didn't want Dad to say anything. Apparently, he knew something and they didn't want him to say anything before he died."

"What did he know?" Bobby asks, cutting off a piece of meatloaf. "He witness a crime?"

"I don't know. He didn't write it down anywhere and Mom never said anything about it. But they were watching the house, telling him what we wore to school and all that stuff."

"That's quite a discovery," June says as she resumes eating mashed potatoes. "Was there anything else?"

"No," I say, putting butter and salt on the potatoes.

It's later that night and I'm in my room. I'm sitting on my bed, the letters scattered around me when I see June standing in the doorway.

"John, was there anything else?"

"Well…, I'm thinking about Mom's papers."

June sits on the edge of my bed. She's young; in her thirties. That's gotta be tough for her to go from zero to six kids in a couple of weeks. I'm thinking about telling her everything. I mean, *everything*. Like, how I played with trains every day for over a year, how I almost shot Mom, how I wanted to kill Betty, and how I would beat up Mark whenever I wanted to. I'm thinking about telling her because those things bother me and sometimes I really want to tell somebody about everything I've been through.

But I don't tell June. Not now, anyway. I don't want to upset her. Besides, my life is much better now. It's stupid to bring up the past.

"Why are the letters bothering you?" she asks.

"Dad wanted me to be in the military. Left some instructions for Mom, but she never told me about them."

"She wanted you to be your own person."

"But I'm not the son *he* wanted."

"Don't you think your Mom wanted you to be your own person?"

"I guess."

I stare at the letters. June touches my shoulder.

I'm thinking that I'm gonna tell her. I'm thinking that I can trust her and she won't think I'm crazy for everything I did. I'm thinking that she'll help me.

I can't believe how good it feels to talk a little bit about me and all this stuff. I'm thinking that I could talk to her some more and it would be okay.

"Well, I have clothes to fold," she suddenly says, making me feel stupid inside about wanting to talk to her. She's got more important things to do.

"Yeah, and I have to study some more."

"Don't stay up too late."

"I won't."

June gets up from the bed and folds some clothes in the laundry area just outside my door. I put the letters away, take my shower, and go to bed.

The Interpretation of Dreams

This afternoon, I'm sitting in my bedroom reading this really cool book by Sigmund Freud: *The Interpretation of Dreams*.

It makes sense: unconscious desires come alive and express themselves in dreams. That is the playground of wish-fulfillment, where the Id runs and plays naked.

I can see that in my own dreams. I dream of Mom because I want her to be alive. I dream about the house in Fassett because I want to go back there and make everything right. I dream of school because I want to make it different.

"John, it's dinner," June says over the intercom.

"Coming."

Everything has a symbolic meaning, a set of meanings beneath the surface. Dreams allow us to see with our true eyes into what we really think. The symbolism of the intercom, the sending of one's voice, one's presence, to another place, to the remotest part of the house.

Like an omnipresent voice of authority standing near the door, ready to summon, announce, or direct. It is the ambassador and soldier of sorts for the powers that be.

And, consider the steps leading upstairs, what a thought! This house is arranged according to power. The children remain on the bottom two floors until they are summoned upstairs by the omnipotent voice! There, there they become enlightened in the place where all that is good and right!

"John?" June asks over the intercom as I am passing her bedroom door.

Aw, the bedroom where intimacy has many levels of meaning. Those we sleep with are those who we feel safest with, correct?

"June, I'm right near your room."

"Good, I have a meeting tonight. People have to hurry and eat dinner."

And consider the floor, the layouts of the room, the amount of space. It's all done for power. Those with the most space have the most power. The same for proximity to the bathroom. Those who are closer to it and move about unencumbered by their nudity, their nakedness, and their vulnerability are the most powerful.

Look how they sit at the table. Bobby is at the head. June is across from him. But, at times, where she sits is the head as that position indicates power. I am always on the sidelines, watching.

"How was your day, Mark?" Bobby asks.

Ah, the evening summation. The review of the day's activities over a meal! It's so amusing!

I take a salad bowl.

Everything moves clockwise.

Clockwise, the sweet symbolism, the house running like clockwork, living by the clock, the importance of time, being on time like the table is a giant clock face, the food pacing the sweep-second hand!

I like that image.

Bobby and June are time-oriented, precise in their actions and words. Particularly their words!

"Was stupid. We did some math."

"Why is math stupid?" Bobby asks.

I take the meatloaf, the broccoli, and the bread. Bobby lifts his beer.

Cuckoo clock?

Yes.

And Mark, the candid boy of many passions, will now present his case for Stupid Math! Or, is he doing something else? Is he rebelling against Bobby and June?

"It's stupid 'cause I don't need it."

The floor plan is open.

Bobby and June are open.

Not like Mom's house where everyone hid in their rooms except to come out and fight.

Hmm, never thought of that before.

"Airline pilots use plenty of math," June says.

"There's wind speed, altitude, velocity...," Bobby says.

Mark desires to be a pilot. He wants to fly 'cause life on the planet's surface leaves him wanting!

But wait, look at the plates!

Why are plates round? Completeness? Shaped like the sun?

Oriental plates are square. Does that represent preciseness? Or, the ability to calculate?

"Naw, you just get in it and start the engine," Mark says.

Planes, looking down on everything, rising above it all: transcendence and serenity. Not being held down.

"It just looks that way," Bobby says. "It's much more complex than that. Would you like to talk to a real pilot and see what he or she thinks?"

Mark nods, eating his salad.

Bobby trumps passion with logic, with planning, with research! Lots and lots of research!

I quite like Freud: I'll have to read more of his work.

Life is so different now.

The Experiment

Every ten minutes.

No matter what.

Fortunately, I have no tests or quizzes or I'd have to explain my experiment and these unenlightened teachers would undoubtedly argue with me. They'd go into some dreary explanation about how I have to focus on schoolwork.

Schoolwork enslaves the mind. I suppose there's no other choice because the school routine and procedures are designed to enslave the body.

Every ten minutes, I mark this sheet I devised. I'm doing a study on myself to see if my moods change during a typical school day. This involves rating my mood from one to five, one being depressed and five being ecstatic.

At ten-minute intervals, I put a mark in the box.

The preliminary results indicate that I'm happiest toward the end of the day just before going home.

No surprise there. Except for Felicia and Angel, this place is filled with a bunch of immature kids who have strange ideas about what life is about. They talk about dating, sports.

And the adults? They're not really adults, just teachers. Teachers are children trapped in adult bodies who never left school. They are best left in such an artificial environment.

Sears Clothing

That's me. Look at my helmet head hair. June says I can wear it this long provided that I keep it clean. So, I wash it every day. In the morning, I let one drop of water at a time out from my bathroom faucet because June says that she doesn't want the sound of running water to wake her; we're not allowed to run any water before she wakes up. After I wash my hair, I comb it until it dries. Her bedroom is right above mine, so I have be quiet.

If I wake her, I figure that she'll order me to cut my hair.

Yeah, I know it's a leisure suit. It's the first suit I've owned since Dad took me to *Dad and Lad* in Hackettstown in '67.

It's okay, I guess.

I don't really like plaid pants, but that's okay. It's nice having clean school clothes. Sometimes I pick out a plaid shirt and June tells me to get changed because it doesn't match, so I put on a solid shirt with my plaid pants. I try to remember what goes with what, but it's not that interesting so I don't pay that much attention to it.

I prefer to contemplate Jung. His writings are interesting. I'm reading *Man and His Symbols* and though I agree with the general idea of archetypes, I'm curious about who decided upon these specific ones. I mean, where's the research? It just seems that someone has determined all these meanings by conducting their own observations and drawing their own conclusions. They haven't conducted any research to determine if other people assign the same meaning to those archetypes.

When we get home from school, June told us that we can only have two graham crackers each and a juice glass of grape juice. We're not allowed to have more than two crackers.

They count them: they know how long a box should last.

June and Bobby have so many stupid rules.

They've never had kids before. They never call us "kids" or "children," instead saying "people," as in "People have been leaving the side door open."

People.

It's okay.

I stopped being a kid a long time ago.

After snack, we have to do our homework.

I rather enjoy reading and studying. School work is easy.

Fucking easy.

Even Chemistry. I'm the only tenth grader in that eleventh grade class. Sure, I have an *A*, but that's only because I study it every night, even if I don't have any homework.

After I finish my homework, I take my shower and have a little time to watch TV, but that's pretty boring. I have to set out my clothes for tomorrow and make sure that everything is ready so that I don't have to rush around in the morning.

A few weeks ago, June asked me what I wanted to do after I graduated from high school. I told her that I wanted to be a railroad engineer.

That was weird 'cause nobody ever asked me that before; guess I was too busy to think about it.

I like trains.

They seem magical.

June conducted some research about the job and determined that I couldn't do that. I'm color-blind and would never be able to correctly read the signals.

I guess I'll study psychology.

I'm not interested in helping other people. I just don't want to end up like Mom or Dad. I want to know what to look for so that crap won't happen to me.

Don't want to be manic-depressive.

Rourke

My room is dark.

Shit, I'm not sure what to do about my light. Fuck, I'll keep it off. Where are the other kids?

It's hard to think right now.

Real hard.

Things are messed up again.

Things are fucked up.

There's a lot of shit goin' on right now.

Fuck! Think, John!

Everything is goin' so fast right now.

Okay, Rose is in her room and Warren is in his. June is at a conference until tomorrow night.

When I walk from my room past the laundry area to the bottom of the stairs, I can hear Bobby and Mark arguing.

THUD, THUD, THUD!

I can hear Bobby punching Mark.

That son-of-a-bitch! It's Columbia Cross Roads all over again!

I hear Bobby yelling at Mark and my brother swearing at Bobby then Bobby punching Mark again.

Shit, it's just like the time when Betty beat Faith. Only thing, Bobby's hitting Mark because of Rourke.

Rourke is Mark's age. He lives down the road. Bobby and June don't like him because he rides a mini-bike and likes to hunt.

They don't like him because his father is a supervisor at a construction company working on the Tioga-Hammond Dams.

They don't like him because Rourke isn't like anyone else on Spring Hill. He says what he thinks.

Mark made friends with Rourke. Bobby and June told Mark he couldn't hang out with him.

"It's not fair," Mark said a few days ago. It was in the afternoon and we were sitting in my room right after we finished our homework. Bobby and June were still at work.

"He didn't do anything to them," Mark said.

"You should tell Bobby that."

"Really?"

"Yeah, look at everything they've done for us. I'm sure they'll listen to you."

"You really think so?"

"Yeah, why wouldn't they? They're pretty open-minded."

I hear furniture moving upstairs. Actually, it's the sound of Bobby slamming Mark against the sofa.

That son-of-a-bitch, that fucking son-of-a-bitch!

I hear the sound of Bobby's hands grabbing Mark, of his hands slapping Mark, of his fists punching Mark. I hear Mark yelling and swearing at Bobby and Bobby slapping Mark. I hear Mark sobbing.

Bobby runs down the stairs to the ground floor.

Fuck, who's next?

I hurry to my room and turn on the light. I jump on the bed, grab my Chemistry textbook, and try to look busy. I look around the room, but there isn't anything I can use as a weapon if he attacks me.

Fuck, I need to buy a knife the next time I'm in town! Fuck, how did I let this happen! Should I stay in here or meet him in the hallway? I don't have a single fucking weapon in this room and he's bigger than I am!

Fuck! Dad's rifle is all the way upstairs and I have no idea what Bobby did with the ammo.

Fuck!

I hear Bobby turn the corner at the top of the basement stairs.

Shit, go to the hallway. Now!

I run out of my room toward the bottom of the stairs.

This way, if he tries hitting me, I can retreat to the room, block the door with my bed, and escape through the window.

Bobby runs down the stairs to the basement.

Fuck, I have no weapons to defend myself, not even a fucking baseball bat!

Hell, I don't even play baseball.

I make it to the bottom of the stairs.

Bobby stops a few steps above me, staring at me. He's sweaty, his hair disheveled. He's breathing loudly and he glares at me. His nostrils are flared and he looks as though he will leap on top of me.

If you jump toward me, I'll run out the basement door.

I stare at him.

"Are you... afraid of me?" he yells, struggling to catch his breath.

I stare at his face.

"What?"

I hear Mark crying and swearing upstairs.

"Are you... afraid... of me? Do you think... I'm gonna... hurt you?"

I stare at his eyes.

To my right is the family room and a small workshop.

There's hammers and screwdrivers in there, but he's so mad right now that if I make any sudden moves, he'll pounce on me. Shit, he tossed Mark around like he was nothing.

"No, I'm not afraid of you," I say, lying.

"That's good..., because... if you're afraid of me..., I don't want you..., I don't want you living here."

"I'm not."

I continue looking him in the eyes to prove it.

He knows how to fight. Escaping is my only alternative.

Bobby stares at me for a long moment as I hear Mark sobbing upstairs.

"Good!"

Bobby storms back upstairs and pauses near his bedroom door, watching me and glancing upstairs.

"Get your ass to bed," he yells at Mark. Mark *thumps* down the stairs.

Bobby goes upstairs to the living room and turns on the TV set.

I climb up a few stairs and watch Mark trudge toward his room. He looks like he's in pain. He stops in the hallway and glares at me.

"You fuckin' said he would listen," he whispers. "Yeah, he really listened."

That fuckin' son-of-a-bitch!

"Mark, take a shower and get your ass to bed," Bobby yells from the top of the stairs.

Mark gives the ceiling the finger, then glares at me.

"Fuckin' said he would listen," Mark says. He retreats to his room.

I go to my room, close the door, and sit on the bed.

That fuckin' son-of-a-bitch!

THUD! THUD! THUD! I punch myself in the fucking chest until my hands ache. I don't know what else to do. Faith is at college and Maria is gone. I can't kill Bobby and I know June will believe any story that he tells her.

The fuckin' enemy has penetrated the inner perimeter! I should've fucking known!

Wanna yell right now. Wanna yell out loud, but I can't. Can't say or do anything. I have no weapons and I'm in the enemy's territory!

That night, I sit up all night, waiting for Bobby to attack the kids.

I can't win this war. No one will believe me. We're the orphan Higham children from that broken home. Hell, two broken homes!

In the morning, Bobby is joking around like nothing happened.

Mark glares at him.

Bobby makes jokes about us all having a good day, then he leaves for work. We watch him pull out in his Duster.

"You said he would listen," Mark says. "Said I could talk to him."

"Thought you could. You okay?"

"What do you think?"

Mark lifts his shirt. His chest, back, and sides are covered with bruises.

Bobby's really smart.

He's a real smart coward.

He didn't hit Mark in the face 'cause that would have left bruises that everyone would have seen.

We are trapped, prisoners. Maria and Faith escaped, but the rest of us are caught here. Why does my life keep turning back into Hell?

The Good Parent Show

What a crock of shit!

Whoppie, we're on TV!

We're seated in our chairs and the asshole social worker is videotaping us. We are supposed to be in therapy, but we're really just a TV show.

It's The Good Parent Show!

It's my fault we're here.

About a month ago after Bobby beat the shit out of Mark, I went upstairs and told Bobby and June what I wanted. Told them that because I was so tired of beating my chest every night and trying to figure out what I was going to do. Was even thinking of disappearing, but I didn't tell them that shit.

Fuck that, I don't trust them!

I was wrong about them being open-minded.

I was wrong about them caring about us.

I was right, however, about June buying Bobby's bullshit story about Mark.

I didn't even get into that with her: they make me sick.

Anyway, I didn't tell them everything.

These assholes'll put me away if they find out that I was thinking about suicide or that I was beating myself up every night. I'm not going to a nuthouse for kids. Fuck that. I just have to go away. I have to disappear and the best way to do that is to leave, to go live with another family.

On my own.

That way, I don't have to worry about anyone being put on

the Bucking Fuss or being beat up.

"Bobby, June," I said. "I don't want to live here anymore."

"What's going on that you don't want to live here anymore?" Bobby asked as if he didn't know.

You'd think it was the end of the world or some shit.

Stupid fucking assholes!

"I just don't think I belong here," I said. "I just want to leave. I want to live somewhere else."

"Where?" June asked.

"Anywhere else."

There is a video camera on a tripod across the room. The camera is pointing at us because we're the show. All of our chairs are lined up, like we're on some sort of game show, talk show, or *Meet the Press.*

Fuckers. This is what they did; June called someone at the college's Social Work department. Now we're on Candid Camera*. No, it's like it's* The Bobby and June Show*. No, I get it,* The Good Parent Show*.*

We're on TV! Bobby beat the shit out of Mark and now we're on The Good Parent Show*.*

The rules are simple: We all agree with Bobby and June!

The social worker is an asshole. Can't he see what's going on? Bobby is so full of bullshit saying, "I can see how people might think I'm intimidating."

And the social worker doesn't say anything.

Mark isn't going to say anything. He doesn't want us to get split up. Besides, he's just a kid and shouldn't have to worry about getting beat-up by his guardian. These assholes said they would listen to us, but they're just like Betty and Jack.

They're worse because they lie about what they do. Betty was at least was honest about wanting to break our spirits. Bobby is a fucked-up, lying, manipulating, son-of-a-bitch!

My life is a TV show.

All we need now are the families from Columbia Cross Roads—they can be part of the studio audience—to bring in their casseroles.

I can see that.

*Mark, Warren, Rose and I would be sitting here, combing
nits out of hair while church families brought in their casseroles.
That would make this TV show complete!*

*Wait, I've got an idea; why not bring in Betty and Jack?
Hell, why not bring in Mom and Dad, too? They could all sit here
and tell the camera what great parents they were. Then, all of
America could all gather around their TV sets and watch* The
Good Parent Show *as they congratulate themselves for being such
good parents!*

*Shit, I can see that as each one steps up to the
microphone.*

*"I just wanted my son to be a man," Dad says. "That's
why I called him 'Poop,' and punished him when he shit the bed."*

*"I wanted him to keep the men in the woods from killing
us," Mom says. "That's why I taught him the meaning of terror."*

*"He didn't have a personal relationship with Jesus," Betty
says. "That's why I tried to break his spirit and treated him like
my personal slave."*

"Betty's right," Jack says.

*"People wanted religious freedom," Bobby says. "That's
why I intimidate him and tell him that if he's afraid, I'll shit him
out of my house and my life."*

*"And, people need to follow the rules," June says.
"That's why I'm cold and distant."*

I can see this shit in my imagination as the therapy session
continues. I'm trying not to laugh as I see that sketch in my mind
while Bobby is spewing some fucking bullshit about being a
father. He doesn't know shit about parenting: he thinks he does
because he read about it in some books.

Big fucking deal!

I'm grooving on my TV show idea. It's neat. So neat to
see them all in the same room, this room, telling the world what
wonderful parents they were while the dumb-fuck social worker
points his camera at each of them. I'd love to see that on *Monty
Python* or *Saturday Night Live!*

*Wait a minute, that's not really fair. Mom was psychotic,
poor, and had six kids to look after. Plus, people were out to get
her; really. She had built her life around Dad and when he died,
she had nothing again. For her, adulthood was probably just*

*like her childhood after her mother died and she was put in an
orphanage.*

And Dad? Shit!

*Dad had no parents for the first three years of his life! He
had no one to love him and teach him how to feel. He had to
learn about love on his own: that had to be tough. Then he was
in the war and developed shell-shock. Not only that, he had the
Mafia watching him. Dad knew that he was being watched 'cause
he knew something. No wonder he threw shit-fits and broke
things. Plus, he was in a psychiatric hospital for eight months
back in the 50's: he must have had some severe mental problems.*

But the rest of them? Betty, Jack, Bobby and June?
They're just so fucked-up!

I keep punching myself every night before Bobby and
June go to bed so they can't hear me. And, I'm thinking of
disappearing.

I get tired of *The Good Parent Show*, so I tell Bobby and
June that I changed my mind and want to stay with them. I don't
tell them about the TV show idea or anything anymore because I
don't want to be on another show ever again, especially with
them.

*Life is about having secrets again. I can't trust anyone.
People are disappointing and dangerous. Why did I even bother?*

A few weeks after I tell them that I changed my mind, *The
Good Parent Show* is cancelled. It doesn't matter, because I keep
imagining all sorts of funny stuff about Bobby and June. I'd write
it down, but I don't want them to find it. It's better to just think
about it in my head. I write down other stuff, but not that.

That's how I disappear now; I think of the funniest shit.

Funny stories are safer than my home.

Schwinn Super Le Tour

It's cool, man.

I'm mowing the neighbor's lawn for five bucks a shot,
doing chores around their house, and making money babysitting.
I clean one of Bobby's co-worker's place at the St. James'

Apartments. When she's not around, I drink some of her whiskey.

Man, I'm making money and it's great. I'm making so much money, in fact, that I've decided to buy a ten-speed!

A Schwinn with a chrome-moly frame!

It's cool, man!

It's blue and I ride it all the way to Spring Hill. Hell, I even go up the hills at the college on my bike.

It's faster than hell!

I ride all over town with it.

It gets me out of the house!

1977

Mansfield Junior-Senior High School

This school is stupid.

Everyone here is so fucking stupid, except for Felicia and Angel.

I like Felicia and Angel. I really like them a lot. Hell, I love them, but I'll never tell them that 'cause then they'll just fuck with me.

They'll just disappoint me.

It's not worth it.

I mean, when I went to Troy, I managed to get a few *B's* and mostly *C's*. Here, they moved me ahead a year in science and I'm getting mostly *A's* and a few *B's*.

I turned down the National Honor Society; they can go to hell.

The classes here are a joke. I'm a better writer than my English teacher. All she does is sit up front, chit-chat all class, then run to the lounge for a cigarette. She doesn't know shit about writing.

What a bunch of bullshit.

The students care about stupid shit, like who's going on a date on Saturday and who partied last weekend.

I don't care to socialize with them; they're so immature. I mean, I have lunch with Olmstead, Mc Donald, Jeffers and Rudy, but that's different. I don't invite them over to my house or anything like that. I remember what happened with Ed.

Some of my classmates pick on me. They call me Victor Mature. They probably don't even know who the hell he is.

Oh yeah, Mr. Greer, one of the English teachers, told me

to shut up. I told him that he was being rude. He threatened to send me to the office.

"I'll gladly tell Mr. Boyanowski that you were rude to me," I said.

Mr. Boyanowski is the principal. He stands out in the hall a lot with his arms folded across his chest. He looks like a fake cop in a cheap suit.

Anyway, my comment shut Mr. Greer's mouth.

Does he think that just because he's the teacher, he has a right to be rude?

Fuck him. I want to get the fuck out of here.

Bobby and June want me to make more friends. In fact, one night last week, Bobby came down to my room. Scared the shit out of me. Bobby only comes downstairs to get beer or fold laundry.

"John, June and I were talking," he said as I sat on my bed with all my schoolbooks.

"Yeah?"

"We've decided that you need to be with your friends. We want you to go drinking with them, but don't overdo it."

What?

"Okay."

"You need to socialize. It's not healthy to stay in your room all the time with your books."

"Okay."

Bobby got up and left. He closed my door behind him and I listened to him ascend the stairs.

So, Mark can't hang out with Rourke because he's a bad influence, but they want me, a fucking Honor Student, to go drinking because studying all the time isn't healthy?

Can you stand it?

Mr. Palmer's Office

Mr. Palmer is sitting behind his desk. He's quiet now. Bobby and I are sitting in chairs on the other side.

We're not taking any of his shit!

The nice thing is that I don't have to do any talking because Bobby is pissed-off at Mr. Palmer. See, Bobby is a teacher and a union rep. He knows what to do with people like Mr. Palmer.

Look at how Bobby uses his words and his demeanor to push Mr. Palmer out of his way.

Two weeks ago, Bobby and June called me upstairs to the dining room. I was in the bomb shelter, listening to The Bee Gees. See, Bobby and June made a room for us in the bomb shelter. It's not a bomb shelter, but it's this room in the basement that's underneath the garage where Bobby and June have us watch TV and listen to music on an old stereo. That's where we hang out.

Anyway, I was listening to The Bee Gees when Bobby and June called me on the intercom, summoning me.

I sat at the dining room table.

"John, how would you like to go to college early?" Bobby asked.

"You think I can? Think I'm that smart?"

"Yes. It's early admission. You'll move into a dorm and take your senior year on campus as your freshman year."

I couldn't believe it! I mean, I won't have to deal with high school shit. June can get me in because she's an administrator up there and she has connections.

It's all about who you know, I guess.

Not only that, but I'll be with Felecia and Angel! Angel is also taking her senior year as her freshman college year. Felicia is already taking classes on campus.

So, Bobby and I are in Mr. Palmer's office, the Guidance Counselor. He's got dumbfuck posters for the Army on the wall and shit like that. He has the balls to look right at Bobby and say, "I don't think John's emotionally ready for it."

Can you stand it? He thinks I'm not emotionally ready for college! He thinks I should stay at fuckin' high school and listen to these assholes talk about who they got drunk with last weekend!

That I should go to fuckin' pep rallies and cheer for the

308

basketball team and all that fuckin' shit! That I should join the fuckin' Honor Society and pick up litter or help with the fuckin' blood drive and shit like that!

Not ready, Mr. Palmer? Have you ever stayed up all night defending your house against the enemy, figuring out how to find a home for your brothers and sisters, secure food for your family or protect your brother from a beating? Have you ever contemplated killing anyone? Have you ever attempted suicide, you stupid fuck?

Fuck you!

I know what I want to do with my life: I want to be a psychologist.

I want to analyze people! Hell, I do that now! I take notes on these kids and watch the boys drive around their phallic symbols and the girls move in their cliques.

High school is not real life. These assholes wouldn't know what real life was if it slapped them in the face.

I want to tell Mr. Palmer how wrong he is, how fucked up he is, how fuckin' stupid he is, but before I can say anything to this so-called Guidance Fuckin' Counselor, Bobby looks that son-of-a-bitch right in the eyes.

"If you do anything to prevent John from getting the education that he is legally entitled to, I will drag this school district into court."

"I was just saying—"

"I know his rights," Bobby says, standing up.

And, fuck it, I want to cry because no adult ever did something like this for me before. I'm so happy, I could give Bobby a hug, but I just keep it all inside and kind of groove on it. He must think I can handle college or something. And, even though he beat the shit out of Mark, he's being nice to me right now.

Why? What's he up to? What are he and June planning? Who cares; he's not gonna be intimidated by this asshole.

Two weeks later, Mr. Palmer gives me some sort of vocabulary test from Harvard. It's from the thirties or some shit like that. I take it, but it's pretty fuckin' tough. I think it's funny, because he's trying to keep me from going to college early.

Fuck him.

Bobby will sue his ass if he tries any shit. I'm not pissing him off or anything, but I know that Bobby and June are looking out for me.

Kitchen Cabinets

Aw, fuck, I did it again.

Sometimes, I get so fucking angry that I just have to fight Mark or hit something.

Have to hit something or somebody hard.

Really hard.

I always feel bad about it afterwards, but then something gets me so fucking angry all over again and I have to punch or kick the shit out of something until it breaks.

So today, I got so fucking angry while Bobby and June were in New York. Got so fucking angry that I kicked the kitchen cabinets and broke the fucking little plastic tabs that hold in the decorative inserts.

Shit, shit, shit!

Sometimes, I get so fucking mad about nothing and I have to punch the fuck out of myself until I'm exhausted. Feels like I'm suddenly mad as hell and have to fucking take it out on myself or something.

June and Bobby are gonna be so mad. Shit, maybe they'll make us go back on *The Good Parent Show.*

Shit, I know. I'll take a little bit of Bobby's Elmer's Glue and fix it.

Okay, I was fucking angry.

Why?

How the hell am I supposed to know? I don't know why; it's a sunny day, it's nice outside, and everything is so beautiful. I'm even going to college a year early: I should be happy.

Sometimes I just get so fucking angry about shit.

I'm such an asshole for getting pissed off on such a fucking nice day.

Cedarcrest Dorm

You hear that?

It's Cedarcrest Dorm.

Because it's all electric, it hums. Some of the other kids who are going to college have so much shit that they need a moving van to haul all their stuff.

Not me.

I packed all my books and clothes into the four small liquor boxes that Bobby and June got at the State Store. It's kind of funny because there's no alcohol allowed on campus. Bobby, the twins, Rose, and I each carry a box into the building. I stop at the front desk and get my keys to my room.

June's not here. She said goodbye at the house. She was reading *The New York Times* and enjoying a glass of wine like she does every Sunday. My leaving for college is no big thing to her.

She did, however, hug me.

"Stop by my office in Alumni whenever you want to talk," she said.

"Sure."

Cedarcrest's hallways are crowded and there's music playing on the expensive stereos that some of the guys have in their rooms. My room is on the first floor, my window looking out at the rear of the building and the loading dock. It only takes Bobby a couple of minutes to place the boxes on the floor and shake my hand.

And then he and my siblings are gone. Just like that, I'm in college.

Can you stand it?

I sit on my bed and take out *The Interpretation of Dreams*.

I listen to the other kids in the hallway. Their parents do all sorts of shit like hug them, wish them good-luck, and shit like that. Some even act like they're going to cry when they say goodbye to their kids.

Not Bobby or June, man.

They're not my parents.

My parents are dead.

I said goodbye to them a long time ago.

Hell, I've had three sets of parents, none of 'em that great.

Bobby and June are my guardians, nothing more.

Hell, I'm seven-fucking-teen and I'm in college now!

Randy's Blazer

Shit, man, can you stand it?

Randy gives his Blazer some gas and it shoots up over the dirt pile that had been right in front of us, kicking rocks everywhere. He slams on the brakes so hard that he almost flips it right the fuck over.

Can you stand it?

He gives it a little gas, then taps the brakes, but we slam across a ditch and—BOOM—he nails the muffler. Shit, when he pushes his foot on the gas, it's like there's no muffler anymore and Blazer's ass end roars!

Fuckin' cool!

"John, go see what it is."

I open the door and jump into the dirt. Underneath the truck, I see that he must have broken the muffler lose from the exhaust pipe when he hit that ditch. Only thing, it's not completely broken away, just separated.

I tell Randy. He can't get to it 'cause the left side of his body doesn't work that well since he totaled his Trans Am two years ago and had a brain injury.

"Hit it with a rock, man," he says.

"Hit what with a rock?"

"The tailpipe clamp. Hit that with a rock."

He climbs out of the truck. He's a big guy and limps when he walks. He can't bend all the way over 'cause then he'll fall.

"Okay."

I grab a rock and start tapping it.

"Hit the fucker harder," he says.

"Okay."

I roll around in the dirt so that I can swing my arm all the way from my side to above my head and wallop the fucker a couple times until the pipe goes back to where it belongs.

"Can you fuckin' stand it?" I yell as I stand up and look at Mansfield. The town is on the other side of the Tioga River. Randy and I are on the west side of the Tioga on the hill behind Brooklyn Street. It's all torn up because the Army Corps of Engineers are building a dike through town as part of Tioga-Hammond Dams that are about ten miles downriver.

Randy jumps back into the Blazer and floors it, making the exhaust blast through the muffler.

"Got it!" I yell. I jump back in the truck and we ride back to Cedarcrest. His friend Graveyard shows up: Graveyard is called that because he looks like a dead man. His face looks like a corpse.

A corpse, man!

Anyway, once Graveyard shows up, Randy gets weird. I mean, Randy does all this weird shit. He and Graveyard take a towel and put it along the bottom of Randy's door. Then Randy takes out some incense and lights it, closes his curtains, and puts on some Led Zeppelin. He takes out this weird little cigarette and lights it, inhaling the smoke. The smoke smells pungent and makes me gag.

"I don't smoke that marijuana," I tell him.

"You sure?" Graveyard says.

"I don't do drugs, man. They fucked up my mom with drugs."

"Your mom smoked pot?"

"No, prescription drugs fucked her up. All drugs are bad, man."

"Not bad for me," Randy says.

"John, that's cool for you," Graveyard says.

"You're not gonna narc on me, are ya'?" Randy asks.

"No, but I don't do drugs."

Randy and Graveyard sit there, listening to *Stairway to Heaven* and smoking Randy's marijuana. They look pretty fuckin' stupid sitting there and staring at the record on the turntable, but they're still pretty cool.

Little Daddy

My roommate is an asshole.

Brian parties all night, then sleeps all day. He never goes to class and he goes home every weekend to his little mommy and daddy. He thinks that he's a great party dude, but he's just an asshole from Athens, Waverly, or Sayre. He lives some place in the area that they call "The Valley."

Asshole.

He's just a dumbass kid who was never on his own before. Every Friday, his little daddy comes and gets him. I take my notebook out and write about him when he's gone.

Little Daddy comes and gets him. Takes all his dirty laundry home. Little Daddy brings him back on Sunday night. Then little Brian runs off and parties all night.

Brian doesn't know what to do with his life. Little Daddy tells him what to do.

When I'm done writing about him, I put my notebook away.

The Ninety-Eight

Somewhere beyond the shiny dash, the clean windshield, and the waxed sky-blue hood of June's Ninety-Eight, the men wait to slit my throat. Though they hide behind the trees surrounding June's house on Spring Hill, I can smell their Right Guard over the scent of the fallen leaves.

"I'm not getting out," I tell June.

"You're not ready yet?"

314

June is Lane Bryant pantsuit perfect dipped in Secret. She is Avon foundation, blush, and fingernail polish.

Me? I don't know: I smell the men.

"If you try to hurt yourself again," Mike said, "I'll have you committed. I don't mess around with suicide. Now, why are you here?"

He put his feet up on his desk, watching as I sat with my back against the wall of the therapist's office. Off to one side, deserted toys surrounded a table. I saw checkers and chess. I heard June listening from the waiting room down the hall.

There is a distinctive sound the ear sends when it's eavesdropping: most people can't hear it because they're distracted.

I live without distraction, the world pumping into my brain a million thoughts a second. To explain takes that long because I have to pause the synaptic clefts to translate electrochemical biology into English when English has nothing to do with it.

Mike is graduate school Gary playing Carl Rogers and we're all I'm Okay, You're Okay. One hundred and twenty-one percent pure. Won't find a Jungian trace in his blood.

"I'm…, I'm a non-conformist, Mike," I whispered. Whispering stops my hearing, keeps my mind from knowing when nothing feels. It's like a collapsing universe, only involving the self. In that way, it's like standing at the crossroad of faith and magic.

Mike understood this because he was my universe, the knower of all truth and Wednesday, goddamnit, and seeing truth and light knew the mind could only be understood within the compressed world of his unused chessboard.

"John, can you look at me?"

It's Pantsuit Perfect!

Goddamn the bastard men in the trees with their knives waiting while Pantsuit plays taps with her fingernails on the polished steering wheel, her face showing real Rogerian empathy.

"You… ready to get out of the car?" she asks.

It doesn't matter because Pantsuit Perfect trains herself to hear my thoughts. She does what Bobby tells her. That's why she brought me back to the house. It makes sense: Bobby the

Child-Beater and his men will attack once I leave the Ninety-Eight thought bubble, drag me into the woods, slice my throat like it's an Easter ham, then toss me into the trunk like an old suitcase.

It's so goddamned clear: I could kill Pantsuit's face. But killing is bad. Suicide is not as bad because no one really suffers when the self-disposal unit takes itself from the Rubbermaid garbage can in the unheated garage to the curb for the garbage men.

The biochemicals of my brain make a movie in my mind of the entire process like a 1950's instructional film of the kind I never watched because I wasn't even alive until the sixties. But I know such things and nobody can stand it. That's why the trees smell of Right Guard and the men are here. I smell Bobby's Right Guard.

"No, I'm not... safe."

"John, why aren't you safe?" Mike asked, playing with a pencil. Number two. Dixon Ticonderoga in Vermont is the leader manufacturing center of the goddamned world. You could go there on a plane, you could go there on a train.

"I will not eat them, Sam I am." I yell.

"John, there's no need to yell," Pantsuit says, her fingernail against my collar.

It's all so clear! It's a matter of rearranging the molecular structure of the synaptic cleft in order to increase the amount of serotonin. That increases the number of times the brain fires, allowing thoughts to drip from the wound.

I am wounded..., I am wounded..., I am wounded..., I am so fucking wounded... by this life... why am I still here?

Pantsuit needs to be quiet. That way I can formulate another hypothesis.

"So, you're a non-conformist. That mean you shit on the floor or what?" Mike asked. He stared at the wall. When he spoke, he turned his squat head toward me, expecting an answer.

"I..., just see things... differently. Can't accept... what's on the surface."

Had to be careful, because everything gets knife to my throat real fast. People haven't been understanding me. I can tell

316

by the words in their eyes when they smile. Can't see anything, blinded bastards caught in their own caramel-coated reality. Worse than Baskin-Robbins.

"What's on the surface?" Mike asked.

"Words. All words. People say things they don't mean. Bullshit."

Mike wrote something down.

"What are you writing?"

Mike paused, then smiled.

"Words."

Someone made my leg bounce on the floor, jackrabbit jumping like shit. I wanted to tell Mike about Bobby the Child-Beater planning to kill me right then, but I made the leg stop and behave. I made it behave in the bad world.

"Don't screw with me, please."

"You're a very sensitive guy," Mike said.

I'm in the label factory as Pantsuit sat down the hall making plans with Bobby the Child-Beater. They won't do anything in front of Mike. Mike is a good guy. They don't come any better to your door to start your day off with a smile on your face and a song in your cold, cold heart. He might be a garbage man if he would just wear a gray uniform and spiffy little hat.

Pantsuit hands me a tissue and I confess my sins.

"I'm sorry nothing's making sense. I'm sorry I fucked up."

She taps my shoulder because Monday is garbage day and she took the garbage can to the curb. That's what they're going to do with my body.

"Are you taking your medication?"

Medication? The slow-motion pills stopped all my goddamned work and screwed everything up. Goddamn me for taking one of those sweet beauties that paved over my soul. The pills didn't stop the world from being bad: I just didn't care anymore.

Fuck, I let the toilet in the dorm eat them and made myself wait for me, made myself wait for my body to wake up. I sat on the floor next to it, grooving on the water hum because I was so free then. Purely biochemical, the cascading flushes clearing my mind so I could stay up again. Without them, I would stay up another year. That's all I needed. It's strong to go without. It's strong for my legs to bounce and the Ninety-Eight to shake 'cause I'm going to explode. No one will hurt me.

"No one will hurt me," I yell.

Pantsuit takes the key out of the ignition. She doesn't matter as I lock my door.

"John, listen to me: have you taken your medication?"

Pantsuit's face is death. If I listen real closely, I can hear the trees breathing outside the windows, but June is death. I could outrun the trees, but not the leaves. The goddamned leaves are falling and burning the shit right out of me.

"The pills make me sleepy. They slow me down and make me not care."

Pantsuit loosens my seat belt. It creeps across my chest like a loose rope. No, like a power-pack cord fashioned into a slip knot.

Playin' with trains…, wanna play with trains again. This time, I'll step off. Please? I promise to kick away the foot stool this time. What is June saying?

"But they helped you. Why'd you stop? Don't you want to get better?"

Good, better, best. It's all good, better, best. She doesn't know it and I don't have the time to tell her about how it relates to the idea of the trees growing into the ground as they reach for the sky while belonging to neither. Goddamn, she doesn't understand anything about leaves.

"Remember what Dr. Wineberg said?"

Last week or yesterday, Mike sent me for testing. I looked at inkblots of dead animals. Of explosions, of blood. My God, too much blood and dead things.

But, God, I loved card ten.

I cried inside so hard right when I saw it. It reminded me of pretty scenes and stories of lush jungles where the leaves were nice and trees didn't need Right Guard.

I sat in my chair and watched blot after blot. I drew houses with smoke coming out of broken windows, broken trees, and broken people. Stick people with big smiling faces, faces ten times bigger than their bodies.

Dr. Wineberg in his plaid Sears pants and Made in Taiwan plastic-rimmed glasses sat behind his desk and smoked a cigar. It couldn't be Cuban because President Kennedy stopped the Surgeon General from smoking. Everyone knows Castro became pissed-off and put a hole in J.F.K.'s head. It all had to do with taking up too much primetime.

Wineberg doesn't care. He's sucking on sometimes a cigar is just a cigar and telling his little patient the news.

"Unfortunately, you have strong tendencies toward being manic-depression with psychotic features. At times, your mind takes off and it becomes difficult for you to slow down. When this happens, you have trouble knowing what's real."

Real?

Real is my M1 Garand rifle against my shoulder, my finger on the trigger, and almost firing point-blank at Mom. Real is hearing Bobby beating Mark, hearing Betty beating Faith, and feeling my fist beating me.

Real is believing that if I fall asleep my family will be killed, assassinated by hit men hiding in woods. It's me holding Betty's hands apart on the stairs and telling her not to hit me, knowing that if she does, I'm gonna beat the living shit out of her until I not only kill her, but obliterate her.

Real is me standing on a mahogany foot stool with a power pack cord tied around my neck and trying to convince myself that today is the day I take that Neil Armstrong one small step for John Higham.

Doesn't anyone know what's real for me?

Why the fuck don't they know what's real for me?

Real is shell-shocked Dad flipping dinner tables through the air like a wrecked Ranch Wagon 500 on Interstate 80.

Poop is real.

I was Poop.

I am Poop.

Dad called me poop: it's the first memory I have.

I was real. Was real poop.

The tests say that I have trouble knowing what's real? Fuck, real is what's been giving me trouble ever since I can remember!

Real is ugly and real is painful.

Real is a mess.

Real hurts me so fucking much and real is killing me 'cause it won't leave me the fuck alone!

I nodded to show I'm real. Mike's the Wizard of Oz standing behind the curtain and Dorothy tells me not to pay attention to him. He's pulling levers, the shit's hitting the biochemical fan and the scarecrow is really pissed because he wants my brain.

Cigar is just a cigar continued. "The good news is that you're not as involved as your mother was: you're quite bright and creative," he said as he waved his cigar like a Freudian magic wand. "But first we have to slow you down. Medication can help you do that."

"Which one?"

"Right now, you're what we call manic. Librium would slow you down. Help stabilize you."

Freedom multiplied by medication equals stabilization, itself totally equivalent in 1977 society to I'm-not-okay-devastation: that's how they plan my demise. Someone gets too close to the truth and they have to destroy him because it makes everything else too clear. The best way to do this is through entropy, winding his soul down against the grindstone of biochemical synaptic cleft re-uptake regurgitation central nervous system depressants.

It's molecular homicide.

The last night I slept in Cedarcrest dorm was because of Librium. It killed my brain.

When I ran silent, deep and awake, I grew so strong. Goddamn it, I couldn't fall apart because sound waves bounced off my supersonic skin at the edge of the atmosphere and the sonic boom caught Pantsuit in Rhode Island after Felicia told me to call her and tell her that I wanted to step off the foot stool by riding my Schwinn Super Le Tour right into a truck. Told June that I knew, that I knew with all my might without a question of a doubt that Bobby the Child-Beater wanted me dead. It fit together nicely in the middle of the night when everything was quiet and I sat up, writing papers, studying and crying because I felt so fucking wonderful. I was hungry for the scent of my blood splattered against the front end of a truck. It was a craving and I went out on my Schwinn Super Le Tour at dawn looking for Mom and Dad before Bobby the Child-Beater realized that I was afraid of him.

I told Felicia everything and she invited me to stay over at her house until June could arrive safely from Rhode Island because no June is an island.

I, on the other hand, am a rock.

No, I'm just a messed up psychotic manic-depressive son-of-a-bitch right now.

Can you stand it?

Clarity is a moment of truth stringing across the fiber of the soul. It's something people don't quite know because they're too caught up in surface things.

I can't explain how strong I feel not needing sleep, not needing food. I can't explain how clear everything seems or how I pump myself up. Everything makes so much sense I just want to die before gangrene invades my clefts.

Most people have the wrong idea about suicide, thinking it's good, better, best for the depressed. It's not. It's that final moment of total systems failure when all the biochemical synaptic clefts explode at the moment of ecstasy. That's when it should be savored and enjoyed; when the self is freed and allowed to move away from the bullshit. It's a fucking celebration!

It's depressing to be different. It's so fucking depressing to be different. To be this fucking different and know it makes me want to die. I'm too tired to make myself want to die.

"John, where are you?" June's voice asks.

In the day beyond Pantsuit's hood, the leaves fall, sizzling as they cool in the wind.

"If you take me back the dorm, I'll go back on my medication," I tell Pantsuit.

Her stiff hand touches my shoulder.

"John, remember what Mike said?" she asks.

"Testing indicates that your thinking becomes disorganized—," Mike said, his feet on his desk.

"Delusional, Mike. I'm a psych major: I know the terms." And I pushed full-speed ahead at the electro-plated skin, wedging myself back into the can of spinach so Popeye the sailor man didn't come out to play chess in Mike's office. I could wipe his ass on the chessboard. He's a King's Pawn to King's Pawn Four Opening guy and no good at the long game. That was obvious.

Mike smoothed his pant leg.

"Yeah, you do. Because you're so sensitive, you've got a lot of control over your nervous system. Not like a leaf falling. When you're out of control, you become delusional and your thinking breaks down. The best way to stay in control is to sleep each night."

Mike lived pure Jungian motif trotting out at the fashion show. Motifs on the runways, archetypes in the audience. I knew it, goddamnit!

Goddamnit, there are two Pantsuits. No, one stands in front of the trees. The other one is gone. Her key is in my door and the shiny plastic faux chrome lock tab shots up, up, up so magically, so wonderfully that all I feel is love.

Motifs are love: they transcend the clefts, really.

"C'mon, it's time," Pantsuit says, Avon fingers easing me from the seat.

I'm out of the car, my feet dragging in the gravel as she moves me toward the house.

"See, you can do this. No one's here to hurt you."

I don't know how I get on June's deck. There is a gap in my life, even though I see the Ninety-Eight and the skid marks my feet made in the gravel leading to the steps. I was wrong, they aren't going to slit my throat.

Bobby the Child-Beater will push me from the deck. Pantsuit won't stain her upholstery. They can say I jumped. I haven't been taking medication. The dean will write a note to my professors saying, "Please excuse John, he's a delusional manic-depressive. And disorganized: he shits on floors."

Can hear the world thinking. Bobby has become the trees, communicating with Pantsuit through the birds.

"See, you're fine." she says.

"Fine," I repeat.

To understand fine, you have to be able to live through its opposite. Not fine exists just beneath the surface.

"Let me stand here, please," I say.

Her arm hugs my shoulder.

I listen to birds talking. The conversation lasts a few minutes as the grosbeaks gather at the feeder. I'm smiling because I want them to think that I can't hear them.

"Are you smiling?"

It's hours before I answer June.

"I'm not sure... why I want to die when things... feel so perfect." The skid marks remind me of crooked amusement park railroad tracks. "Will it ever go away?"

June stares at me, touching my shoulder.

"Did you come down? Those thoughts gone?"

I nod.

"Take me back to my dorm ..., please? I'm really tired."

I pat June's shoulder and stagger toward the Ninety-Eight, ignoring the trees.

Cedarcrest Dorm

Can you stand it?

I'm pretty fucked-up right now. I'm on my bed, trying not to puke 'cause of all the shit I drank right after dinner. It's all so fucked up. All the stupid jocks are standing around my door, those fucking assholes.

It's Craig's fault.

No, it's Jimmy's fault. That stupid son-of-a-bitch asshole.

You know what he did? Huh? That little asshole came down here and told me right out that he wanted to..., said he wanted to...

Shit, I can't say that!

Shit, wait, said he's been thinking about doing that ever since he saw me, before he even introduced himself. Said he's been thinking about it a lot. Like, all the time. Been watching me.

Watching...

That was too much. I asked him to leave my room.

Fuckin' watching me, man? I almost killed myself last month, man; I don't need to be afraid all over again. Don't need you playing head games with me, man.

I don't want people watching me, man. That's scary shit.

At dinner, I told Craig and my other friends, Buddy and Joe. They were more upset that Jimmy wanted to do that other stuff than that he was watching me.

Fuck, man, he was watching me.

That reminds me of Fassett, Mom, and the hit men in the woods.

Why are people watching me? Why are people watchin' me? I don't want people watchin' me.

"I got just the thing for you, John," Craig said. We all went back to his room and listened to *Year of the Cat*. He opened a foot locker and took out all sorts of liquor. They made me drinks and got me drunk.

Real drunk.

I drank straight through five until seven o'clock tonight. Got smashed in two fuckin' hours, man!

I call Felicia and Angel. The guys all liked them, but I got sick and puked out my guts.

Who else is watching me? What the fuck?

And now the guys from my floor are standing in my room, laughin' at me 'cause I'm drunk and yelling at them.

Are they watchin' me? They walk by and punch my door, calling me "faggot" when I'm trying to study. Stupid fucking assholes. Fuck them!

I'm not a faggot. I didn't let Jimmy do anything. Who the fuck are they trying to tell me who I am? Fucksticks!

Fuckin' watchin' me! Fuckin' watchin' everything I do! That just fucks me up!

Elmira-Corning Regional Airport

The nice lady next to me is smiling. She doesn't care that it's too snowy to take off. The plane's engines are straining and I'm trying not to freak out.

I'm going to Philadelphia, then on to Orlando. There, Bobby and June are waiting with the twins and Rose. We're going to Disney for Christmas vacation and then to Miami to visit June's relatives.

"You need a haircut before you go," June said.

It's a month ago and I'm in my dorm room on the phone with her. Brian is all gone. I wrote about him in my notebook.

Little Daddy took Brian home for good 'cause Brian flunked out of college. Now, Little June wants me to cut my hair.

Yeah, June called. We talked about the trip and just before she hung up, she mentioned my hair.

"Oh, and make sure you get a haircut before the trip," she said.

What? It's my hair. It's thick, wavy and black. It's shoulder length and it's mine. I wash it, condition it, and dry it every day. It's who I am.

"I don't want to cut it."

"Bobby and I discussed it. We want you to cut your hair before you go on your trip."

"I don't think so. I'm living on campus and I want to wear my hair the way I want to."

"We want you to cut it."

"No. If you're going to insist that I cut my hair, I just won't go. I'm not cutting my hair. I keep it clean and neat. I'm not going to cut it just for a two-week trip. It's not worth it."

June hangs up.

The engines are straining as the plane struggles to rise above the floor of the valley. The lady next to me is smiling and giggling. I'm trying not to yell 'cause I'm freakin' out.

The stewardess approaches me. "Sir, is *this lady* bothering you?"

The lady keeps smiling. In fact, she's the only person smiling on the whole plane. She looks excited.

Why are you smiling? What brings you such joy?

Her smile makes me think about relaxing, though the stewardess is pissing me off. *This lady* is not the problem.

"No, she's not bothering me."

I look at the lady.

"Are you bothering me?" I joke.

The lady nods her head, smiling the whole time. I look at her: she's in her thirties and keeps clutching her purse and nodding her head.

"No, she's not bothering me: I've never flown before and the bumps are making me nervous."

"Well, if she's bothering you, we can move her," the stewardess says. "We can't do anything about the turbulence, but if you don't like having one of these retarded people next to you, we can move her."

One of these "retarded people?" Move her? I'm the one freakin' out. Who the hell are you, you fuckin' flying waitress? Fuck you, you charm school dropout!

I look at the lady. She looks at me and smiles widely: she's groovin' on it.

"No, she's okay. I'm just a little nervous about the turbulence."

"We'll be above the storm in a few minutes," the stewardess says.

The lady smiles at her, then back at me. The lady's cool, so I make myself smile at her. It relaxes me.

June called back in a few minutes.

"If you promise to keep it clean and neat, then you don't have to cut it," she says.

"I always keep it clean and neat."

"Okay."

So, this is the plan: I'm flying down to meet everyone, we'll vacation in Orlando and Miami Beach, then I'll take a train from Hollywood, Florida to Philadelphia on New Year's Eve. Faith and her boyfriend Dave will pick me up in Philly. I'll stay with them in Reading for a few days before I take a Bucking Fuss back to Mansfield to be at home for the rest of the break.

It's cool. I've never flown before and I've never taken a train. I'll have a roomette on the Silver Meteor. I leave Hollywood, Florida on New Year's Eve and arrive in Philly on New Year's Day.

And, I don't have to cut my hair.

1978

Reading Railroad

Hard black snow crunches when I stumble along the sidewalk toward the phone booth. Darkened cars shoot out from alleys without honking. Somewhere a siren wails, it approaching rapidly from behind as ambulance lights flash on the storefronts and illuminate part of the street.

I pull the shattered door and step inside the scratched, dented booth as the rescue vehicle cleaves traffic. Inside, I tuck my hair behind my ear and hold the receiver close enough to talk through the pitted plastic.

"Bobby?"

"John? Fan-tastic hearing from you! How was your trip?"

A man runs past, his steps uneven.

"Okay, I guess. A lot of people got drunk— "

"Did you join them?"

"Naw…, I don't do that."

"Why not? You look twenty-one. Besides, after midnight, I bet everyone was loaded. Why should they care about some seventeen year-old?"

A freight roars across a nearby overpass, the diesels belching smoke and the steel wheels screeching along the rails. I turn to see it, the corners of the cars catching arcs of streetlight above shuttered apartment buildings. As it builds speed, the horn blasts an echo.

"Hold on, Bobby," I yell. I cover the mouthpiece to keep the train's thunder from reaching his ear.

Yesterday afternoon Dave's swearing echoed in Broad Street Station. He addressed a pair of Mennonite ladies blocking the vestibule.

"Hey ladies, could you please get the fuck out of the way?" he yelled.

The Silver Meteor smelled of toilet water splashed over unwashed skin and flatulence. It gave way to the Brut my brother-in-law-wore as he stood capable in the station.

The Mennonite ladies wore thick legs under their dresses and covered their mouths in embarrassment.

"It's alright, you chicks can pray for me. Need all the damned help I can get," Dave yelled.

"Happy New Year," I said, lowering my backpack.

Dave shook my hand and I kissed Faith's cheek.

The couple took me to their car.

"How was your trip?" Faith asked as she stared at the train yard through the windshield.

"Beautiful," I said. "Really beautiful."

"You get laid?" Dave asked.

Faith slapped her husband's shoulder. "You and this laid shit. Always goin' on about it."

Dave laughed. "Hey, it's important, okay?" He looked in the rearview mirror. "And we both know it."

Faith covered her laughter with her hand. The three of us laughed during the drive from the station to their apartment in Reading.

Tonight, Reading becomes quiet for a moment when the freight ends, its caboose bobbing on the jointed track. Not really quiet, but still. More still than it had been. Another siren wails a few blocks away, then stops.

"John?"

"Yeah, Bobby, I'm coming home… like we planned."

"You can't."

"What?"

Someone staggers past, his feet crunching in an awkward rhythm. I smell his liquor and vomit as he slams against the booth. He swears, then stumbles toward the intersection and disappears down the street.

Bobby keeps talking.

"...send you money. You'll return to the dorm the day before the semester starts. June and I will keep paying for college, so there's nothing to worry about."

I put another quarter in the phone.

"When can I come home?"

"You can't."

A cop car crawls past, then stops. The back-up lights cast a glow and a flashlight's beam hits me in the face.

"You, what are you doing?" a cop voice yells.

I raise the phone to my temple.

"Officer, I'm speaking with my father. He lives upstate. In Mansfield."

The beam drops over my purple parka and my polyester Sears pants and galoshes, then back to my face. A moment later, it searches the empty storefronts as the car makes its way down the block.

"Well, John, this is costing you money. I better let you go."

I deposit another quarter.

"John, you're wasting your money."

"Why can't I come home?"

"It's... just not a good time. You take it easy, okay?" Bobby's voice disappears just as it had three days earlier when we stood on the platform in Hollywood, Florida. He wore light clothes then and looked through me as a passing freight shook the earth.

"Have a good time and take it easy, John," he yelled, waving at my outstretched hand. He climbed into the Ninety-Eight without looking back. Rose, in Mickey Mouse ears, waved. The twins half-smiled. June sat in the front, placing a pillow against her window so she could sleep before taking her turn to drive.

Then, Bobby would sleep against the window.

Later that night, I met someone on the Silver Meteor. He endured a miserable coach seat. While the adults became drunk, I showed him my roomette with its overstuffed chair and picture window.

"My guardians wanted me to have a roomette," I said. "Told me I deserved it."

We stood facing the roomette's big window in the car's dimness and watched the night cover the sky. For miles, we were quiet as the Amtrak train made its way north through the Carolinas.

"This is beautiful," he said.

"Yes, it is."

When I rang for the porter, he arrived before I thought to turn on the light.

"You kids newlyweds?"

The old man in a white uniform smiled in the hallway's light until seeing my mustache.

"Sorry, I..., I thought you were a girl. With your hair...," he said. "Young man, can I help you?"

"Yes, we'd each like a grilled cheese sandwich, please."

I gave him a five-dollar tip when he returned with plastic-wrapped sandwiches. My friend and I sat in the dark and ate in silence before walking to the club car.

As drunks pinched each others' asses and intermittent red flashes of crossing lights punctuated the night, we drank Seven-Up between giving confessions and toying with the idea of renting out the roomette by the half-hour.

My friend disembarked in Washington shortly before I opened a shade in the club car and saw the New Year's Day beginning. I watched him shake his father's hand and kiss his mother. The family smiled and waved at me, then embraced on the platform alongside the Southern Crescent occupying the adjoining track in Union Station.

A vestige of rail's golden age, that train exists separately from Amtrak.

The Reading Railroad died a few years ago and was absorbed into Conrail. The overpass, I can see in the lights of an ambulance running sans siren, reads "LIONEL" even though I now stand in the railroad's namesake city.

A half-block stumble path on the black snow leads me back to Dave's apartment. I knock once and wait.

"We don't open the fuckin' door if someone knocks more than once," he told me yesterday. "They'll hurt you real bad if you let 'em in."

Bucking Fuss

I wave at Faith and Dave through the dirty window. My sister finds me and waves back, yelling, "Enjoy the bucking fuss."

I'm just like her now. I've been shit out by Bobby and June.

The thing is packed and smells of cigarettes and fast food. That's 'cause a guy behind me is smoking while he eats a Big Mac and fries. He belches when he eats, but I don't care.

I'm going home. I take out my notebook and my pen. I push on the light above my head and settle into my writing, staring at the blank page.

Darkness comes quicker on the night bus, the night surrounding everything and isolating it from the world. Right now, there's only the smell of unwashed humanity and diesel dirt. We're a bunch of nobodies sharing an aisle that comes from—and goes—nowhere. Now, I'm a nobody going homeless.

It takes forever for the bus to get away from Reading before it cuts through central Pennsylvania, violently shuddering as it crosses long stretches of ruptured pavement. It follows some piece of shit highway through Centralia, that place a collection of warning signs and boarded up houses.

"Mine fire," the guy behind me says to himself. In the dark, his voice doesn't belong to anyone. I smell the smokers in the back as their scent mingles with the sulfur and diesel dirt.

"Whole ground is on fire," the voice says. "Started in an old mine and just spread under the town. Government is buying out the town."

The bus hits a piece of broken asphalt as we see some vent pipes sticking out of the ground.

"It's burnin' everything. Can't fight a mine fire with water. Have to dig everything up and suffocate it. It feeds on the leftover coal."

I see slagheaps and old coal tipples when I look out the window. There aren't very many streetlights, though lots of warning signs. Just north of there in Shamokin, the driving rain turns to wet snow that whitens both the night and the dark heaps of wounded earth.

"Not even the snow can stop the mine fire," the man behind me says. "Nothing can stop it. It started decades ago and it's just burning through the ground under everything. Can't tell it's there unless you know what to look for."

The inside of the bus is dark and quiet except for the talking man. Passengers are draped over their seats. Every once in awhile, I hear them fart or sneeze.

My pack is on the seat next to me.

"Not even the snow can stop the mine fire," he says. "Nobody knows what to do except run away from it."

Not me. I am running toward it, toward the epicenter. This hole that has devoured my life. I have no family now, no home. It's all gone. My room in the basement, my place at the dinner table, and my bed are all gone. Not destroyed, but removed from my life without anyone asking me about it.

Hell, I have no life. It's like someone put a gate up and said I can't go there.

I've been removed 'cause it's not a good time.

I imagine a clock on the wall of Bobby and June's living room. But, instead of having numbers, it has the words "Not a good time" in the twelve o'clock position.

"You can fuckin' stay here," Dave said yesterday when I returned from the phone booth. I sat on his sofa and looked at TV, my pack leaning against my legs. A pizza box was next to me, a bottle of *Cold Duck* next to it.

"No, I have to go back. Missy says I can stay with her."

"Who's this Missy chick?" Dave asks.

Faith laughs.

"Always wondering about the chicks," Faith says. She punches the floor next to her and pours another cup of Cold Duck into a plastic cup.

"No. I mean, is she a friend, a girlfriend, or what?" Dave asks, taking another slice of pizza.

"Went to school with her."

Dave laughs at Faith.

"Probably helped you with your homework," Dave says.

The bus sways over the highway as it approaches Shikellamy, its headlights illuminating the deserted station. There is a small overhang at the end of the pavement. The driver's voice interrupts the night.

"This stop is for anyone going to Mansfield, Corning, or Buffalo. You have a two-hour layover."

I am the only one standing as we approach the empty building. By now, the snow has accumulated a few inches and the shitty little town is all white, save for the tire tracks.

The man continues talking about the fire.

"Someday, the fire'll spread up here. Then the state'll have to do something," he says.

The driver turns on the light as I stumble up the aisle. Absent-mindedly, the people move their arms and legs from the aisle, sit up, and remember their manners. The driver watches me in the mirror.

I carry my pack in front of me. I figure that it's too easy to get ripped off if it hangs behind me and it's a pain in the ass to turn around with a pack on.

I pause at the top of the stairs and look out the windshield at the darkened station.

"Excuse me, sir, but this station is closed."

"That's right, son, it closes at five."

"You sure the Mansfield bus is coming?"

"That's what I said. You can have a seat on one of those benches," he says, pointing to one tucked beneath the overhang. "Your connecting bus will be here in two hours."

"But I don't have a watch. Does the driver know to stop?"

"Son, we always stop. Have to. The ICC won't let us skip a stop unless it's a flag stop. Now, that driver will see you if you sit right there."

He points at the bench.

A cold blast opens the door when I step out. Diesel dirt and snow fill the air and my parka is unzipped, so I pull it tight. The wind kicks up and the bus pulls out into the town and the rest of the night.

I have no gloves, so my fists find pockets and stay there after I put on my pack. It's never a good idea to sit still in the cold, so I walk the ten paces under the corrugated steel roof. After awhile, a cop car pulls up.

It's a local cop and he throws his spotlight on my face.

"Miss— "

"Hello, Officer."

No matter fucking what, always be polite. No one wants a longhaired hippie-looking freak with a backpack fucking up their town, so always be polite.

"Son, the station's closed."

"I know sir," I say, shaking as I hand him my ticket. "I'm waiting for the Mansfield bus, sir."

He looks at the ticket without reading it.

"You a student at that college?"

"Yes, sir. Goin' to see my family for a few weeks. Was in Reading... seeing my sister."

He hands me back the papers. "Got any I.D.?"

I reach into my back pocket and take out the wallet Bobby gave me for Christmas two years ago.

The cop looks at it. He flips through the pictures in the wallet and shines a light in my face as he glances at the license. He hands it back to me and shuts off his light.

"Well, stay warm," he says.

"This parka's pretty warm."

He backs away and disappears into the night.

"You can stay here until the semester starts," Missy said on the phone. Dave stood outside the booth, his back to me as he watched the street. Faith was in the car with the engine running. "Reginald says you can stay in the dorm with him."

"Good."

"Why don't they want you to come home?" Missy asked.

"Said it wasn't a good time."

"That doesn't make sense. Thought you lived there."

"So did I."

Missy was quiet as I hear an old Chevy screeching past, its belts way too tight.

Shikellamy is quiet except for the snowy wind that covers everything. The white snow pelts the ground and creeps over the curb toward my bench. I grab my notebook and pen.

In the bus station are empty benches where other people have sat, waiting to go somewhere. No one is sitting in them. The benches are always empty, even when people are sitting on them.

It's not a good time to have a home.

I am no one now, a snowflake cast out of the sky, falling to nowhere.

I am in nowhere now.

Nowhere now and forever.

My legs are cold, so I pace.

After a long time, I hear a muffled diesel pusher engine as it brings a bus across the Susquehanna River Bridge into the town. Its tires splash in the slush as I stand, its headlights bathing me in white light as the vehicle approaches the overhang. Without thinking, I step into the slush and squirm as I try to get a footing toward the door. When it opens, my lungs fill with treated air.

The driver turns on the light and I step into a warm, empty bus. I take off my pack as he examines the ticket.

"You don't want this bus," he says, handing my ticket back.

"Why not?"

"We're goin' south. To Harrisburg. You got another hour."

I back down the stairs and into the snow, looking at "Harrisburg" on the destination board as that bucking fuss retreats into the night.

I am wet now, the sweat inside my parka having reached the nylon shell. I am chilled by the wind, even though I re-tightened the purple faux fur around my face. My hands retreat to their pockets and I think of Missy.

"It'll be okay. Dad said you can stay with us as long as you need to," Missy's voice said to me in Reading.

Dave and Faith were sitting in their car on the street. Dave watched a passing bum, then got out of the car and knocked on the phone booth's door.

"This isn't a social call," he yelled.

"I have to go," I said to Missy.

"I love you," she said.

"I'll see you tomorrow night."

We got back in the car and Dave took off. Faith handed me a bus schedule. "Your bucking fuss leaves at six. You know you can stay."

Shit, I didn't know anything. Just wanted to get home. Or, to anyone's home.

Missy said she loved me; she's probably just being polite.

The bench waited to be free from its burden. It watched the snow suffocate the city and beat down the remaining signs of life, the isolated glowing TV sets that flickered in the living rooms and the Christmas lights that flashed at the numerous flakes drifting down from the night.

I don't trust the bus that pulls in, waiting until its doors open before I grab my pack and walk toward the source of the treated air. I stare at the driver as he reads my ticket and closes the door. He starts backing out even before I drop into my seat.

The landscape outside the window is white, but the bus is dark as it rocks back and forth northward through the hills. It's long after midnight when the bus pulls into Mansfield. I walk three blocks from the intersection to Missy's house on Academy Street. Her home is about three miles away from Spring Hill, but I don't live there anymore.

She kisses my cheek and shows me a room off the kitchen, sitting on the bed while I take off my sneakers and my parka. She hands me an envelope.

It's a necklace and a card. The writing is all in red ink and the letters are big and fancy.

"Thank you," I say to her, giving her a quick hug before she goes to her bedroom. I'm alone in her guest room listening to her fridge running.

I really didn't want her to go. Wanted to ask her to stay for a little bit and just hold me. Wanted her to tell me that everything is going to be all right. I just want to cry and feel safe again.

Shit, I'm seventeen and I'm homeless.

A refugee in my own town.

It's not a good time to have a home anymore. It's not a good time to have a family.

Alumni Hall

The administration building smells like melting snow and perfume. I hear numerous Selectrics working in the offices as I climb the stairs to the second floor waiting area near June's office.

"Good morning, John," June's secretary, Anne, says. "June tells me that all you kids had a great time in Orlando!"

"Yeah."

"It must have been nice to be in the warm weather! Have you ever visited there before?"

"No."

"So, it must have been very exciting for you!"

Anne's from Rose Terrace below Spring Hill. Her desk is in June's outer office just outside the door to June's office. On it are smiling pictures of her husband and her daughters. Everyone seems to be smiling in her pictures.

Anne is asking me all the questions right now. Questions about flying, about the hotels, about Miami, about Cypress Gardens, and about the Florida Keys. She's asking me about all sorts of vacation shit but I can't say anything except "No" and "Yeah."

Why?

Because I'm tired, having slept for only a few hours last night after my bus ride from Reading.

This place seems surreal.

The door to June's office is closed, but I know that she's here: her Ninety-Eight where I had my psychotic break a few months ago sits in the parking lot out front.

"Is June in?"

"Have a seat and let me check," Anne says. She takes forever to push the extension, then turns partially away from me to talk in a lower voice. She looks at me and smiles the whole time, then hangs up the phone.

"June will be with you in a few minutes," she says. The secretary goes back to work as I sit and wait. There are no sounds coming from behind June's door, no sounds coming from anywhere except for the rattling of the Selectrics from down the hall.

Finally, Anne's phone buzzes and she answers it.

"I'll show him in," she says, then hangs up the phone.

Anne stands and opens the door. "John, this way."

She closes the door behind me and I see June sitting behind her desk, a piece of paper on it. June holds a pen in her hand, looking like she's going to take notes.

"I'm here in Mansfield now," I say.

"Good. Where are you staying at?"

"I'm not gonna tell you that."

She emphatically lowers her pen, stands, and walks toward the exit door. Her office is twice as large as Anne's and has a back exit. June opens that door, motioning me toward it.

"Well, it's good to see you. You can see me here anytime that you want. Anne will let you know my schedule if you want to make another appointment."

"What's going on?" I ask.

"Didn't Bobby tell you?"

"Yeah, but—,"

"Well, don't worry. We'll pay for your school, your Social Security and VA checks will go right into your account that has your inheritance money, but you'll have to find a place to stay between semesters and during holidays. Oh, and we'll make arrangements for you to get your furniture."

"Yeah, I know all that stuff. Why are you doing this?"

"John, I have another appointment."

We shake hands and I walk into the hall. June closes the door behind me and I'm alone in the hallway listening to Anne's Selectric for a few minutes. Soon, I hear other Selectrics. I open my notebook and jot down a note.

Listen to the song of the secretaries' Selectrics, their droning drowning out all signs of life.

I walk downstairs and back to Missy's house. I'll stay there tonight, then sneak into the dorms so that I can hang out with Reginald until the semester starts.

Cedarcrest Dorm

Look, I know it's illegal. The college handbook says that only International Students can stay in the dorms between semesters.

It's illegal for anyone else.

Me, I'm an anyone else.

That's why I have to sneak in every night. It's cold as hell, but I don't mind hanging out with the guys. Reginald is from Singapore; Lawrence and Victor are from Chad. We make dinner every night in the kitchen after the security cop makes his rounds.

It's kind of funny 'cause I'm breaking the law in the very place where June works: fuck her!

During the day, I have to leave because the guys are working on campus and I can't hang out here because the college has maintenance people working in the building. Those guys will get in trouble if anyone finds me here.

So, I take really long walks all day until after dark when one of the guys lets me in. Sometimes I visit June, but she only talks to me for as long as it takes her to walk from Anne's office to her office's exit.

Walker Man walks all around the town that he once called home. Walker Man talks to himself without saying a word.

Composition Cowboy

What a get-up: Dr. Hindman is wearing cowboy boots, a hat, and all sorts of cowboy stuff. He's got silver-colored belt-buckle and a western-style vest and dress pants.

He's a Composition Cowboy. Got his Struck and White tucked in his boots!

I don't care how he looks. I'm clenching my copy of E.B. White's *The Elements of Style* and listening to him talk about clarity in writing. He's got white hair, wears glasses, and doesn't look like any English professor I've ever imagined.

After class, I write my essays on white sheets of paper. I've got shitty handwriting, so I have to take my time. It's frustrating because my brain works faster than I can write.

He's a Composition Cowboy.

I stole that. Somebody called him that. It's not original, but it is funny.

Bob helps me write. He's my new roommate. He's friends with Felicia and Reginald.

Gaf

Bob calls himself Gaf. When he swears, he says, "Zeke, biff-baff-Gaf." He's a professional student or something. I met him through Reginald. He's old enough to be my father, I think, but he's funny as hell and Felicia really loves him.

He's a minister who never married. He's from Coudersport: that's about an hour west of Mansfield on route six. He has degrees in English, music, psychology and divinity. He's working on a degree in social restoration.

I told him some things about me. I told him about Mom, Dad, the Mafia, the kids on the bus, Betty and Jack, Bobby and June, Mike and Dr. Wineberg. Told him about playin' with trains and my psychotic break last year.

It felt good to finally tell someone about things. Never did that before. I didn't tell him everything, though, 'cause it's just too much.

"Zeke, biff-baf-Gaf, you managed to get yourself through a lot of really rough stuff pretty much on your own," he said. "It's a good thing you write."

Guess he's right, though I never thought of it that way.

He calls me "the boy with the hair," 'cause I take an hour every morning to wash it, dry it, and style it. It's feathered, layered, and naturally wavy. He likes to pick on me 'cause I like the way I look. I'm the guy with the longest hair on campus.

Pinecrest Dorm

It's all soft and wet inside Julie. She's on top, her thighs straddling me. Her roommate is asleep on the other side of the room. It's late and she said it was okay 'cause she's on the pill. Hope I don't get syph or the clap: the pill doesn't stop any of that.

I don't move, though I want to.

This is what everyone talks about?

This is the big thing?

It's okay, but all I can think about is walking down an aisle with her and that makes me stop.

Penis in vagina: this is sex? Smelly, sticky, gross penis in vagina sex.

She moves a little and I can see her smile.

Julie moans. I lift her hips up and pull myself out of her.

You ain't my girlfriend. I just put my penis in your vagina. That's all. Now I smell like vagina. Your vagina.

The Ninety-Eight

I see Warren.

He's in the back seat of the Ninety-Eight, waiting at the end of the day. Normally, I don't see him anymore. June was going to invite me to the house for sweet and sour pork, but she and Bobby couldn't schedule a time. Also, I'm usually in class, but I missed class because I had to see Warren.

Felicia told me what her sister said, told me what her sister said about Warren.

About what Bobby did.

I tap on the car's window and Warren lowers it.

That's when I see the marks. His neck is all red and everything. It's a mess.

"What happened?"

"Bobby did it," he says.

"Is there more?"

"Yeah," he says, pointing to his chest.

I'm in my dorm room, calling Maria. She's in Hawaii now, attending college.

"Bobby beat Warren," I tell her. "Can't we get them out of there?"

The next day, I'm in June's office, sitting in a chair. She is behind her desk in her big swivel chair.

I'm listening to her explain, making myself listen to her defend Bobby. June is talking to me as if she has rehearsed everything and is giving a press conference.

"Warren just didn't come home. Naturally, we were very worried. Bobby went out looking for him, but couldn't find him anywhere. We even considered calling the police. Anyway, when Warren finally came home, finally came home so late at night, Bobby gave him a chance. He gave him one opportunity to tell him where he had been and what he had been doing. We were naturally very concerned about Warren."

I look at her. She is in full make-up and wearing one of her Lane Bryant pantsuits.

"And Warren didn't say anything. He just sat there and remained completely quiet. Naturally, because Bobby and I were so worried about Warren, so worried that he might not ever come back, Bobby felt frustrated—"

"And beat Warren—"

"Bobby feels absolutely terrible about having struck Warren. He continues to be unnerved about his reaction to Warren's defiance. It's very upsetting to everyone. Incidentally, Bobby apologized to Warren."

"He left bruises. All over him."

June stands and moves toward the exit.

"As I said, Bobby feels terrible about having hurt Warren, but he gave your brother a chance to admit to everything. Warren said nothing."

June opens the door and motions for me to stand.

"Now, if you excuse me, I have another appointment."

I leave her office, though stand outside the door for a few minutes listening as I hear June joking with Anne.

Two weeks later, Bobby's standing in the doorway of my dorm room as I sit on my bed. "June and I will take every legal measure available to us to keep the children," he says as I sit on my dorm bed. His anger reminds me of the night he beat Mark and the day he yelled at Mr. Palmer.

Fuck you, I'm not afraid of you, you fucking coward!

"I lost all respect for you when you beat Mark," I calmly tell him while I look him in the eye.

He glares at me. "Well, I've lost all respect for you, too," he says. "You're so negative all the time. Maybe you should find the good things in people instead of judging them."

"Judging? You beat up Mark and Warren."

"I apologized. You need to let go of the bad things in other people and move on."

He glares at me.

I'm not afraid of you. You're too much of a coward to try anything here. Besides, I'm 18 and I'll have you arrested if you touch me, fucker!

And I'm thinking that I want to tell him that maybe he should find good things about kids instead of beating them up, but instead Bobbie walks down the hall without even saying goodbye.

The cowardly lion retreats to his home on Spring Hill.

Allen Hall

I'm staring at artwork.

It's a sculpture.

Of a guy.

Bending over.

It's interesting, but that's all. It doesn't talk to me or anything like that.

Phil sculpted it.

He's older.

He's a friend of Bob's.

"Stay away from him," Bob told me one night while I sat at my desk in Pinecrest.

"Why? He's nice."

"You don't want his kind of nice," Bob said. "He's got a real darkness about him."

"What's that supposed to mean? Is he evil or what?"

"Just watch out."

Phil stops by my room often. We eat lunch together all the time. We talk. He's got a different way of looking at things.

I like him.

First Citizens National Bank

It's fucking cool, man.

See, I turned eighteen last week, so I went to the bank and got some money.

All my inheritance money!

I have about three thousand dollars in cash in my pocket: can you stand it?

But you know what? There was this lady at the bank: a teller. You know what she said? She said some shit like, "Son, you should keep that money in the bank where it's safe."

Fuck her! It's my money, I can do what I want with it.

People's Place

I hate Sears clothing.

I hate polyester, plaids, and stripes.

Missy's taking me to Elmira. She says she'll help me buy clothes. Cool clothes. I like the look of gauze and French jeans and clogs. I want to wear real clothes, not polyester.

I've been reading about androgyny; sounds cool.

Look, Tommy Hilfiger owns People's Place.

He's got real clothes.

The store is vacant when we get there and he's in the back in the head shop. They've got all sorts of glass pipes, but I don't use that crap. I mean, it's okay that people get high, but I'm not into it.

I'm high on cash and cool clothes!

Tommy and Missy help me decide what to wear. I pick up a couple pair of clogs, some French-cut jeans, and some gauze shirts. I pay for it all with cash and I can hardly wait to get rid of my old clothes.

My Sears jeans have ironed creases! I can't believe I ever wore them.

I give Missy a big hug when we get back to her father's Audi in the parking lot.

She kisses my cheek and we groove to a cassette all the way back to Mansfield. She takes State Route 549 and I feel so good that I want to throw away all my crappy clothes.

"Should give them to Santa's Gift Bag," she says.

It's such a good idea that she helps me fold all my Sears clothes and put them in old State Store boxes. I gave away my polyester pants, my plaid shirts, and my stripe shirts for somebody else to wear.

I suppose it's better than having to skip and go naked.

The Econoline

It's a beauty!

Look at that perfect green paint!

It's perfect for conversion. It's gonna look nice when I'm done with it. I'll buy a kit and convert it.

I'll be able to live in it.

"Why'd the dealer park it in the weeds?" I ask Randy. He and I took the day off from classes to look for a van.

"I don't know. Body looks good on it," Randy says. "That's a nice wax job." He pulls his Blazer to the main building and I get out.

We're just outside of Scranton at a Ford dealership. When we walk in, the salesmen are sitting at their desks. I'm about to make someone's day!

"Can I help you?" one asks, a cigarette hanging out of his mouth. He's an old man.

"Yeah, how much is that Econoline at the back of your lot?"

He moves to the glass and takes a puff.

"How much ya' got?"

I take out my wad of cash and count it right there in front of him. He tries not to be interested as he watches me, but he knows that I mean business.

That's how I am. I don't play games.

"Eighteen hundred."

"Jim," he yells, "Go get that green Econoline and bring it here." Jim hurries to an office. A minute later, he runs from the building with the keys to my Econoline.

Randy looks at a Mustang on the showroom floor. I walk over to him.

"Is that a good price?"

"Yeah, man, that's a great price."

We're looking at the Mustang for ten minutes until Jim walks back into the showroom. The van is outside. Someone had towed it from the lot to just outside the door.

"The battery's dead," Jim says.

"We're not paying for a new one," Randy says.

"Yeah, so fix it," I say.

"And the hinges broke on the hood when we looked at it last week."

"Not paying for that either," Randy says.

Jim inhales, then stares at us. I bet he's ready for retirement. He's too old for this kind of shit. "Guys, we don't run a charity here," he says. "Look, I'm giving you a great price on the van, but you're gonna have to pay either for the battery or the hinges. Otherwise, I'm not making any money on the deal."

Randy walks over to the van and looks at the engine. He goes inside and sits in the seats: they look brand new. The box is real clean and in great shape. It's a beauty alright.

"How much are the hinges?" Randy asks.

"One fifty-five."

"And the battery?"

"Thirty with the old one."

"We'll pay for the battery," I say.

Randy nods. It's cool.

When the battery gets fixed, they let me drive it in a small circle in the parking lot. It runs well. I'm impressed with it. When I come back in, Randy is sitting in a Thunderbird on the

348

showroom floor and Jim is at his desk.

"Where you boys from?" He asks as he motions to his seat.

This is cool. Making deals is no big thing!

"Mansfield."

He nods as he takes out a bunch of forms that have an *X* on them. "That's quite a ways away."

I laugh. "Well, we've been lookin' for that perfect van to customize. There's not much out there."

He takes a pen and hands it to me.

"No, those vans are pretty popular. Ford makes 'em to last forever. You need to sign here, here, and here."

"What's this?"

"Oh, it's for the state. Says you've bought it. The good thing is that because you're payin' cash, there's no financing. That's the way to buy them."

Randy is back to checking out that Mustang. He's got the hood up and is talking to another salesman.

I sign some more papers: then *my* van is ready. The repairman spray-painted the hinges black. It looks real cool. I wave to the dealer when I drive onto the highway. I never drove a van except Billy's.

Billy's van is so cool! His mother paid to have it customized and it's real nice. It's dark blue and has mag wheels!

And a sunroof!

Inside, it has carpeting and a bed in back! Not only that, he put in a fantastic stereo system!

My van is loud.

So loud that it sounds like the engine is gonna come right through the cowling at me. Another thing, the faster I go, the louder it sounds.

Must be a van thing, I guess.

Another thing, I'm sucking up gas big time. Randy said it's only got a six in it, so it shouldn't be using this much. By the time we get to Tunkhannock, I've used half a tank. I pull over where the highway goes back to two lanes and flash my lights at Randy.

He makes a U-turn in the highway and pulls up alongside me.

"Seems kinda loud," I yell. "Can you take a look at it?"

He waits a minute and shuts off his engine. When he gets out of his Blazer, a brochure drops out. It has pictures of Mustangs. I pick it up.

"Nice car," I say.

"Maybe I'll get one. What's going on?"

"It's using a lot of gas and it's tough to get it over forty. Seems like it's straining."

He sits on my seat and moves the column shifter. It's called three on the column 'cause it makes a *H* of reverse, first, second, and third.

"Makes the noise no matter what gear I'm in. If it's first, second, or third."

Randy makes a face as he tries moving the shifter.

"Said you got it into third?"

"Thought I did."

He shakes his head, swears, them shimmies under it.

"Fuck, get your ass in the seat and move the shifter to second when I say so."

I tug the lever and it goes right into second.

"Randy, it just moved farther than it ever did before. You fixed it!"

He shimmies out from under the van and stands near the opened door. "Shit, I should've noticed that. Your linkage is broken. Can only use reverse and first or second and third. The linkage that takes you through the gate needs replaced. You've been running in first. Lucky you didn't blow the engine."

Randy takes the brochure and gets back into his Blazer.

"I fixed it so you'll start in second. That's easier on the engine for a long trip. Make sure they fix that." He pulls over and I push in the clutch while letting off the brakes. The vehicle rolls forward and bucks like crazy when I let go of the clutch and give it gas. Then, all the dash lights come on and it stalls.

It's embarrassing, but Randy doesn't care. He glances at me in the mirror as he flips through the brochure. It takes me about ten minutes to give it just enough clutch to get it rolling without stalling it. I know it's working okay when the engine runs smoothly and the van only jumps a few times.

It's okay, I can still fix it and use it as my home between semesters.

Black Dog

It's morning and I'm sweating as I sit on my bed, writing.
Dream Note: April___, 1978
I'm in Pinecrest in my dorm room. It's day, maybe morning, and everything is quiet. Still.
I hear a dog running up from South Academy Street, so I go across the hall to the lounge. I hear the dog. It's outside. The window is open and I can hear the dog running. I hear it growling.
I look out the window and see a large black dog running up the college drive from South Academy Street. As it moves closer, I realize that it sees me. It growls and runs faster toward me. Its teeth are bared.
I close the window and it's growing larger, scarier as it approaches. I know, however, that I'll be safe in the dorm.
It reaches the dorm and is now twice as large as it was when I first saw it.
I hear it smash into the basement wall beneath me.
I run into my dorm room and close the door.
I lock the door and jump onto my bed, cringing as the black dog chews through the concrete block wall.
It chews its way through and rushes into my room.
It's even larger now, maybe eight times larger than it was the first time I saw it.
I'm unable to move.
The black dog leaps toward me, baring its teeth to attack.
I wake just as it lands on top of me.
Shaking, I close my notebook and get ready for class.

Hemlock Dorm

I tried staring at the concrete wall or the bunched up pillow as Phil kneaded my ribs with his left hand, twisted my black mane around his right, and dug his elbow into my spine. His textbooks poked against my chest, the covers making indentations through my gauze shirt. I wedged my arms close to keep them from moving while I waited for him to finish.

"Don't make me kill you," he kept repeating in a secret voice at odd intervals. His vow lurked beneath the songs playing on his black plastic stereo just beyond his easel and scattered acrylics.

I tried recalling our conversations, counting the concrete blocks or watching the lazy string of incense smoke escape through the window. Once upon a time in a far away land, I sat; a freshman whiz kid, a handsome young prince whispering stories to myself as an April sun set in the magic woods above the dorm.

Now, I tried not being at all so that Phil might hear my body louder than my futile words.

His sweat dripped onto someone's gauze shirt, adhering it to my back. It would be the only sensation I felt for years as he pulled away and slumped onto the floor in the corner. The room went still and I waited.

I tried not to know if he gazed upon me with a satisfaction that he had previously shown when talking with me. I tried not to see the smile I had felt long ago when we joked in the cafeteria. Our eyes would never meet again, be it across the dining hall or a coffeehouse.

I went away in my mind.

From far inside my body, I watched as someone who I once was made me presentable, then coordinated my arms and legs so that I could walk against air made of invisible wet cement.

"Look pensive," I heard him say as his feet filled my clogs. I had not left my body, but submerged so deeply into to it that I felt as if dreaming.

In the television lounge at the hallway's midsection, this kid's body passed a couple of jocks. They had been watching television while Phil finished.

"How's it going?" the kid asked.

"It's cool." One said.

"What's on?"

"*White Shadow.*"

Pinecrest Dorm was empty as the music majors were practicing at Butler Center. The kid's roommate, Bob, sat at his desk and listened to Chopin. A long time ago, they had joked about mispronouncing it 'choppin'.

"You eat yet?" Bob asked.

"Naw. Go on ahead."

How clear this kid's voice was just then. Feigning strength and confidence, he grabbed clean clothes and soap just like I would. In the bathroom, he found the corner shower. There, he carefully removed my soiled garments and placed them in a garbage bag he took from the bathroom's trash can. He set the water temperature and I watched him wrap a soaked white towel around my wrist.

When he placed me under the stinging water, the kid cried, forcing himself to weep softly. The hot spray stung and percolated his skin with Phil's stench: it made his body remember. The kid tried to burn away my skin. He tried holding my arms tightly against myself so that I embraced the tiled wall. He tried to be brave. He tried so much.

If only...

But I failed and now I am soiled, my skin stained.

The hot water gradually brings me back into my body. I clench my fists and press my face against the shower stall. I stand and shiver, sweating. It is now my aching.

In this timeless shower, my tears wash my face and I stand with my legs wide to avoid stepping in the water that touches my skin and becomes raw sewage.

"John, you okay?" Bob yells in from the outside world.

Startled, I reach out, checking and double-checking the stall door, adjusting the lock and not wanting anyone to see my filth. My wrinkled hands fumble with the chrome lock that secures the steel door. I pull the inner fabric curtain tight against the seams, wedging it into the crevices and trapping me in Phil's stench.

I turn off the cold and still my tears with the burning water, standing with my back to the wall, and waiting for Bob to tear me away from my tile and steel womb.

"John? You've been in here for over an hour."

I am weeping now as my hands shake like an old man's. I try to make a voice.

"Yeah, just thinking." I finally shout over the spray. "You eat yet?"

"No. Thought I'd wait— "

"No, no. Go on. I'm not hungry."

Dinner is a half-dozen Seven and Sevens and movie scenes. This is me, punching the concrete wall next to my desk until Bob and two other friends grab my arms and legs, pressing my chest against my textbooks when they throw me onto my bed.

"You got really quiet," Bob said the next morning. "It freaked us out."

Men are so stupid. So fucking stupid, but I didn't tell Bob that.

I can't tell anyone anything anymore.
I instead write that lesson in my notebook.
It is the only friend this pauper has left.

Homework

I smell Phil. I smell him when I bleed, crap, and breathe. I taste his soap on my skin and I can hear his whisper in my sleep. Sometimes, I can see him watching me in the cafeteria, even when his table is empty. His friends all stare at me.

354

I can feel their eyes on me.

And I hear him.

I hear him whispering so loudly that I can't sleep, knowing that he's waiting at his desk, that little smile on his face.

Fuck me to hell. If I was stronger, I'd beat the living shit out of him with an aluminum baseball bat and turn his head into a mass of blood. If I was stronger, I'd go into June's office and tell her what happened. I'd tell her everything about my little friend Phil.

Fuck me, fuck me, fuck me.

Step right up, ladies and gentlemen, and see the Living Coward.

I see him in the classrooms acting like it's no big thing. He's going to classes like it's no big thing. Like it's all supposed to happen like this. He's not sitting in the bathroom stall between classes, shaking like a shit 'cause someone comes into the bathroom, afraid of who it might be.

Fuck, I can't even shit without thinking about him.

"You okay?" Bob asks. He sits at his desk, his back to me. It's because I smell of Phil. I reek of him. No matter how often I shower, he's in my pores.

Bob knows. Hell, they all know. There's a giant sign on my ass that tells everyone.

Fuck, I need a drink. I call Randy and he runs me to the State Store. He gets me wine and more *Seagram's 7*. Shit, I like the way that tastes. I'm back at my desk in no time, knocking down a Seven and Seven.

"Shouldn't you study?" Bob asks, turning around. "You okay?"

"Yeah, I'm okay. 'Sides, one won't hurt."

The whiskey is cool against the ice and the glass ends everything.

I can't kill him 'cause I'd have to admit it. And I can't tell anyone about that shit.

I mix another. *Shit, you can get two drinks from one can of 7-Up.*

Bob stands next to my desk, his eyes bulging out in shock.

"Biff-baf-Zeke-Gaf," he says. "What's going on with you? Another drink? Don't you have a test tomorrow?"

"Yeah. I studied for it."

Hell, maybe Bob will know what to do; shit, he told me to stay away from Phil. Warned me about the fucking bastard.

No, there's nothing he can do about it. He'll want me to press changes. And who's gonna believe me: I wasn't in prison.

That shit doesn't happen to men.

"You eat lunch today?"

I laugh at Bob.

"No, but I had a pretty big breakfast."

"Why aren't you eating lunch anymore?" He looks at me. He means well, but I can't tell him shit. He'll want to get the cops.

"Maybe we can go to lunch together sometime," he says.

"I don't need you to look after me. I'll be just fine," I say, laughing as I open another can of *7-Up*. After all, I've got a whole six-pack and an almost-full bottle of *Seagram's*.

Alumni Hall

I hear someone walking in high heels on the linoleum as I climb the steel and concrete steps from the front door up to June's office. The sun is over the western hill. My coat smells funny and my eyes hurt. When I look out, I see the Hill House. It is across the street from Alumni and, on the other corner, Lambda Chi Fraternity. Both of those places were built in the 1800's and still have wood siding.

Alumni is a glass and steel block building, its front entrance looks like it's puking concrete ramps and steps toward the parking lot.

I walk into Anne's office.

"John, she's busy," Anne says as her fingers dance on her Selectric. Dentist office music comes out of a clock radio, though it only exists if I strain to hear it.

The sound of the high heels is much louder.

I lean back in my chair so that I can see whose feet those shoes belong to. It's Adrienne, one of the secretaries who spends all of her state wages on her outfits. Her clothes are tight against her spreading body.

Body denial is when someone needs to buy larger-sized clothes but refuses to.

"Would you like to leave June a message?" Anne asks.

Before I can answer, the phone rings once, makes her hand swoop up the receiver, and make her mouth move so that she's talking.

"Office of the Vice-President of Student Affairs, this is Anne," she says into the phone.

When I lean out, the heels and Adrienne have disappeared. When I look back into Anne's office, June's door opens a crack and a woman's hand reaches through. As if on cue, Anne picks up a thick file and allows the door hand to take it.

Anne holds up a finger when I take a half-step.

"Wanted to talk about mid-terms," I say to her hand.

"Excuse me a moment," Anne says, covering the receiver.

"Said I... just wanted to talk... about midterms."

"I told you that she was busy."

The door opens.

"Just a minute," Anne says. She turns to June, who leans out far enough for me to see her beige pantsuit.

"John was wondering if you could see him."

June waves me in. "For a moment. I'm awful busy. I have appointments all afternoon."

"It's just about midterms."

I rapidly duck inside. June closes the door as Anne returns to the phone conversation.

June's desk faces away from the sun, giving her a view of herringbone wallpaper and Sam Dee Thomas' paintings.

I met Sam. He's an art professor who lives in Blossburg. He has his own studio.

A transparent curtain of hanging plants catches the window. African violets or some shit, I can't be sure.

June escorts me from the inner office door past the chairs in front of her desk. That piece of furniture is covered with opened manila files. There is a small picture of us kids in the far corner, but she probably can't see it.

"The Walking Parent: A Primer for Those With Appointments." I can imagine that ad.

"I know your grades already. I always see them before you do."

"I'll bring them up."

She opens the door to the hallway.

"I know."

"Parenting by Appointment: A Primer for the Unemotional Parental Figure." That ad has June staring at me with that uninvolved look that she probably takes into meetings.

I stop just inside her door, throwing her off.

"Was there something else?" she asks.

"Yeah, how's it going?"

She touches my shoulder and I'm looking in at her from the hall. I hear Adrienne again.

"You know, we'll have to have you at the house for dinner," she says as her hand closes the door.

I follow Adrienne down the stairs, her steps echoing in the foyer. She sees me at the bottom when she turns toward the Registrar's office.

"Excuse me, are you June's son?"

"No, she's not my mother; she's my guardian."

Adrienne touches my shoulder, her hand resting there.

"How do you like school?" she asks, smiling and gently nodding. She's pretty.

I never realized that before.

"It's okay."

"I understand that you're studying psychology?"

I nod.

"Does that mean you analyze everyone?"

I laugh.

"No."

"I always wondered that about psychology majors."

Adrienne walks away.

I go outside, walking along the concrete sidewalk toward the frat house. I stop, turn, and look up at June's window. When I do, I see June watering her plants. She takes her time to carefully position her chair, climb on it and carefully lean so that she can tenderly water each one, the whole process lasting about a half-hour.

Felicia's Room

Diamond Dogs is playing on Felicia's radio. She and her roommate Debbie are passing a joint back and forth.

"Little Johnny Higham," Felicia says, laughing at something, "we have to go to a hall meeting." She hands me the joint, then lights a cigarette.

"What do I do with this?"

"Hold it between your fingers and inhale."

Debbie giggles as she stands in the mirror combing her hair.

"Yeah, real fuckin' deep."

Felicia puts drops in her eyes. "And hold it in. It'll burn at first, but just ignore that. Then exhale through your nose."

"Okay."

Felicia looks at me. She looks stoned 'cause her eyes are all messed up and everything's funny.

"Little Johnny Higham in Sears pants is gonna get stoned," Felicia says.

"I don't wear Sears pants."

"Used to. And you're little purple parka. Maybe I should call June and tell her."

Debbie punches her shoulder. "Don't be makin' him paranoid. Let him get stoned first."

Felicia and Debbie leave. I close the door behind them, lock it and towel it.

Toweling a door involves precisely positioning a folded-over towel so that it covers the entire gap between the bottom of the door and the floor, thereby significantly decreasing the amount of cannabis-laden air that reaches the hallway while simultaneously decreasing the possibility of undergoing arrest for getting high on state property.

In Felicia's mirror, I watch my hand bring the joint up to my lips. It stays there as the tip grows red and big. I freeze as my eyes water, then the smoke seeps out my nose.

Again, it grows red.

Again, it grows red.

Again, it grows red.

Again, it grows red.

Again, it grows red.

Again, it grows red.

Now, the mirror's face is sweating, but the radio is playing and music comes from everywhere. Soft, gentle stuff, but I can't quite make it out.

The chair is made of warm wood and warm vinyl upholstery. My feet rest on Feicia's warm bed. My head drops and it kicks back up again in a WOW 'til I nod back down to sleepy land in the land of giants 'cause it's gonna rain outside on the radio noise that's the way I like it, uh-huh, uh-huh.

Felicia is giggling. Somehow she and her roommate got back in here without me knowing anything about it.

"Little Johnny Higham is stoned."

It doesn't matter. Nothing matters anymore. It just doesn't matter. It just… doesn't matter… it just matters… doesn't. Matter doesn't just… it.

I want to see how this stoned makes the world look, so I stand up and make my way to the door. It feels like it takes me a few hours to get there, but it's cool.

I'm out in the hallway, closing Felicia's door behind me.

I walk by Phil's room.

Hey, who are you raping tonight?

The hall is quiet, *but it matter doesn't just anymore.*

I walk through the lounge.

My dad is dead. My mom is dead. But, I have Bobby the Child-Beater Dad and June the Mom by Appointment. I can see her anytime I want when she doesn't have an appointment to water her plants. Hey, look, there's not "White Shadow" playing on the TV set. That must mean that all the good little boys and

360

girls are under the haystack with Betty and Jack, having a
personal relationship with Jesus.

Amen!

Now, that makes me laugh, ha-ha!

Pinecrest Dorm is the same way. I'm in the bathroom
mirror there, smiling as I take a shit. I crap with the stall door
open.

Wide fucking open!

I like to shit. Like to feel all the toxins leaving my body.
They slide the out and splash into the lukewarm waters 'til I flush
and the dirt gets sucked away.

Pot makes me braver in bathrooms! No more freakin' out!

When I get to my room, Bob sits at his desk, writing a
paper. His face gets Picasso-like when he joins my eyes from
across the floor. His shit slides out, I bet. Everything slides out
of him.

"Where were you?"

"My dad is dead," I whisper because I don't want to wake
anyone. It's funny as hell, but Bob doesn't get it.

Screw that: the joke is on him.

Bob holds his pen still and above the page.

That point of contact is small. So much comes from the
union of ballpoint to paper. Words, man; words. It's all in the
words. If you don't understand words, you can't even begin to
understand the basis for thinking. It's all so pretty deep, man.

"You been thinkin' about him?" Bob says.

"Man..., how'd you know?"

"You just mentioned your father."

"Yeah, he was cool."

My bed is so incredibly warm. So incredibly soft. It
wraps me all up in the blankets. I like the linen service pillow and
sheets. They hold me tight enough to stay asleep.

Bob's face is playing Skylab with mine. He's too close,
but he's just drifting toward me.

"Breathe out," he says.

I might hold it in for the next five thousand years. Might
never exhale through my nose again. Never gonna talk either.
Where's my notebook?

"C'mon, breathe out."

I suppose his feet are connected to the floor, but I can't see 'em. Someone put my sneakers on, but I better slide them off. Should untie them so Bob won't yell at me.

Bob scrunches his face like a dried tomato that's been out in the sun too long.

You know, the ones that are sun-dried and the sun casts a red glowing shadow on the table for the people in the art museum to contemplate on Sunday afternoon when the world is on hold and lovers hold hands? Not because it's the thing to do, but because they love each other so much that each understands dried tomatoes. Not only as individuals holding hands, but as minds overlapping so that the tomato has a new meaning.

Dad was the sun once: Mom said so. Maybe to her, but I never looked directly into the Dad's eyes 'cause, man, that's just too much. You know.

The covers are...

"You're stoned!"

Bob sits on his bed, making me sit up.

"Dad is dead."

"John, you have too many issues to be running around getting high. This isn't good. Running away from your problems isn't the way to deal with them."

Is this a bad trip? No, wait: that's what happens on LSD. Acid. Not the heartburn kind, but the other kind. Yeah, this is a bummer. That's what potheads say.

"This is a bummer."

"See, you're already taking like a pot head."

"I only smoked one marijuana cigarette, man. It's cool. Let me go to bed."

"You smoked a joint?"

"That's right, I'm a marijuana pot head after just one... marijuana... joint... pot head... cigarette! Tell my Dad. Wait, he's dead."

I'm laughing like hell 'cause I can visualize Bob and me standing at Dad's grave confessing to my having smoked one marijuana joint pot head cigarette making me a marijuana joint pot head!

"Why are you joking about that?"

"It's just another bummer, Bob. Bummer Bob. You're Bummer Bob."

Bob's essay waits for his pen. The blank page needs his pen.

I should really write. I'm more comfortable on the empty page than any other place in the universe. The blank pages are full of so many wonderful possibilities, the blue lines numerous invitations for my thoughts. It's like a big warm fluffy bed on a cold morning, the only source of heat in an unheated house. Why can't Bummer Bob shut up so I can find a pen and write down some stuff? I need to write.

"You're making a big mistake."

"Yeah, you're right, but Dad is still dead."

"Why do you keep saying that?" A little giggle escapes from inside me, but it pisses off Bob.

"'Cause, Bob, if I want a dad, I'll go to New Jersey and dig mine up."

"Zeke-biff-baf-Gaf."

"Is that your full name?"

The bed sheets open and I let them wrap me like a giant present on Christmas day.

I'm underneath the tree and it's snowing outside. Can see it beyond my fireplace in the silent night. It's some really cool stuff right now, man.

I like Christmas. It's all warm and fuzzy stuff. And, you get great presents!

Garry's Hardware

I'm here to party. It's early and there's bag of weed in my pocket. I knock on the door and wait for Carrie to open it. Shit, she's such a fucking asshole. She thinks that she's a fucking writer, but she can't write for shit.

And instead of Carrie, there's some mousey chick standing there instead.

"How ya' doin'?" I say to the chick.

"Hi," she says, looking at the walls, then the floor.

She's not a stoner. I can tell what stoners look like.
They've always got that look in their eyes.

That stoned look.

On their faces.

You know, it's like they know you're a stoner, but they
are too, so it's all okay.

And nice. Fuckin' nice.

Not this chick. She's got fuckin' long brown hair and
wears gray cords. She's cute, man, but I don't give two shits
about her if she's not gonna party. I'll be cool about it.

"I'm John." I say, waving my hand at her.

"Bev," she mumbles.

Shit, it's my outfit. It's my purple parka and my French
jeans and my clogs and my long hair that are freakin' her out.
She's straight, man. Probably is a Jehovah Witness or some other
weird shit.

Well, fuck her.

She's looking at me and she's probably thinking that I'm
some sort of faggot or shit even though my penis was in Julie's
stinky vagina.

Stinky vagina!

For what that's worth.

Or worse, this Bev chick thinks I'm some sort of a freak.
People used to look at Mom like that when she was acting crazy.

Bev leaves.

Fuck her, man. People don't like what I am, they can go
to hell.

Carrie and I sit on the sofa. Her place overlooks
Mansfield's intersection. It's above Garry's Hardware, next to
Jupenlez's Saddle Shop and the Health Center.

This is downtown, downtown, downtown Mansfield!

Carrie gets to listen to the trucks all day as they blast
diesel dirt and make everything dirty.

There's a string of incense smoke going from the plate on
the table to the ceiling. It's a white string that keeps the ceiling
from floating away. I open my pocket and remove my baggie
filled with pot. Actually, it's filled with a bunch of joints I rolled.

My dick's getting hard. Carrie's not that pretty. Bev's prettier, but she's not cool. Not cool at all.

"That Bev chick party?" I ask while sucking the life out of the joint.

"No, she doesn't," Carrie says.

"Too bad." I take another hit on the joint. "What's her major?"

I hand the joint to Carrie.

"English. And secondary education."

I crack up.

"Shit, English teachers don't get stoned. Fuck that shit."

"I'm a secondary ed major in English."

"Yeah, but you're a writer."

I try sticking my tongue into Carrie's mouth, but she turns away. She moves to the window and pulls it open. The stink that is Mansfield pours through the window and I'm feeling like I could jump out because the pot is that good.

"You better go," she says.

I roll up my baggie and zip my parka. It might get to fifty today in the sun, but I don't want anyone to see me, so I pull the hood tight.

It's all fucked. The good-looking chicks don't party. The ugly chicks who do party don't fuck. Partyman can't party with anybody.

The Econoline

Holy fuck!

The interstate twists and turns everyway and the drivers don't care. They zoom their cars around everything.

The Econoline engine whines as I floor it. When I shift lanes 'cause I'm in the Exit Only lane, all my stuff gets thrown around in the back. My books hit the flashlight and something slams against the doors.

Driving is what makes me go right now. See, I can get into the van and drive for hours because nothing else matters but the four lanes, the eight lanes or the ten lanes going right from the ground straight up to the sky.

And, I'm not coming down until the Fourth of July!

Driving is the only thing that feels real right now. Shit, I love the road, I love the highway. I love everything about driving down the road right now even though everything is moving so fast.

It took me twelve hours to drive here, not including the six I slept in the truck stop. Yesterday, a couple of the guys helped me borrow a mattress from the dorm. I'll bring it back when I'm done with it.

Never mind that, I'm in Chicago.

Maybe I'll go on to Denver tomorrow and return in time for the first day of classes during the summer semester.

As long as I can drive, I don't think about the fact that I'm homeless.

Hell, I'm not homeless.

Homeless people have nowhere to sleep.

I have a mattress in the back I can always use.

Being homeless is pretty fucking cool.

Maple "B" Dorm

In the hall with Deb and Eve, I'm takin' turns Frenchin' with each of them.

Deb's mouth is warm, but she pulls away.

"Hey, this is college," I tell her before pulling her close again.

Eve wraps her arm around my neck and closes her eyes. Her tongue is hard and pushes at mine.

"I've got a boyfriend," she says just before she inhales.

"That's great. He must be a nice guy."

And then we're tonguing again in the stairwell. I'm rubbing her bra through her polyester shirt. She's wearing one of those flowered tops that shows every seam of her fiberfill cross your heart or I hope you die bra.

I gotta smoke a joint.

"You ladies want to join us? In my room where we can partake of some herb?"

They giggle 'cause they want to party.

In my room, Graveyard sits on his bed, talkin' some bullshit 'bout The Tower of Power. He's okay though because he's just tryin' to impress the chicks. He's too old for them, but he doesn't care. He's got 'em listenin' to him as if any of it matters.

Oh yeah, Graveyard is my roommate. I couldn't live with Bummer Bob 'cause he didn't party and he's such a bummer to be around. Man, all he did was piss and moan about my partying. He became such a downer to hang with, man.

Anyway, it' summer semester. That's when the college admits Academic Opportunity Program and Economic Opportunity Programs freshman on campus. I'm suddenly very popular.

That's cool.

I'm in my room and the guys are all here: Anthony, Munchie, and that big rich prick, Henry.

Fuck him.

Hell, I don't mind his ass sittin' on my bed, smokin' my stash.

"John, man, you mind if we smoke it in my room?" he says when he wants to get stoned.

"No, Henry. We'll smoke it here."

Deb and Eve look at him and my pants get looser 'cause I'm losing my erection. He's an asshole, but, God, he's funny as shit. Once, he made me laugh while I was takin' a hit on my bong and made me blow burning weed and bong water all over the place.

Right now, he's trying to get laid by impressing the chicks. "I play in a band," Henry says.

"What the fuck, don't you have a gig tonght?" Graveyard asks.

"Naw," he says. "We have one tomorrow."

"That's cool," Anthony says; he's doin' the same thing as Henry, but nobody says shit for a long time. Everyone watches my bong move around my room. It goes from Graveyard to Anthony to Henry to Deb and Eve. I'm at each step, giving it an added boost to the bowl between each person. You know, I can't stand that shit at some parties where the host sits on his stoned ass. His job is to keep things goin'. That's the whole point of having a party!

Not only that. At my parties, I use a party bowl as a single hit bowl. Can you stand it? You know, they call me *Iron Lung* for a reason!

Deb and Eve stare at Anthony. He wants 'em, I can tell. Stupid punk. It's my room: he should respect me.

Hell, I don't care.

I don't care much for pussy 'cause pussy can't buy me love.

"*So Very Hard to Go* is their only real hit," Graveyard says grabbing the album cover. "I mean, c'mon."

"Fuck that," Henry says, "You got any Stones? Our band covers their songs."

"Really?" Eve asks. Good thing she's got a boyfriend. She hands me the bong. I stand at attention waiting for the stoners to look at me. It takes the assholes a long time 'cause they're so fucked up. Eve looks first, giggling and tapping Deb's shoulder. When the chicks look, the guys follow.

Fuckin' penisheads.

Felicia calls them fucksticks 'cause that's all guys think about.

Anyway, I go into a comedy spiel like I'm a drill sergeant.

"Men, this is your bong. It is your friend. You treat it well, it will treat you well. You will eat, sleep, shit and piss with your bong. Do you understand me?"

Henry salutes me.

Deb and Eve are laughing so hard that they're crying.

Graveyard is on the floor laughin' that silent laugh of his. He looks like he might upchuck, but I know him. Never seen him upchuck.

"This is your bong," he mimics. When he does that, his fair-skinned face looks like a corpse that was somehow brought back to life by bong hits and Genny Cream Ale.

Munchie covers his ears with his hands.

"I'm so fucked up," he screams. "I'm so goddamned fucked up." He steals the bong from me and takes a long hit, sucking the pot smog from the Plexiglass tube into his mouth and out his nose like a giant vapor snake. It's humungous. Like a goddamned smoke hard-on or some weird shit like that.

368

Anthony and Deb are holding hands.

I don't care. They're just kids. He'll probably come just after enterin' her.

Fuck them.

Henry is sorting through Graveyard's albums. There's nothing there 'cause he ain't got shit.

"John Fucking Denver?"

"Son, don't get Graveyard started on John Denver," I say in my drill sergeant voice.

Henry looks at the album and the girls get that look in their eyes. You know, like they just saw *someone* worth a shit. It's as bad as playin' anything from Bread. It's not party music, it's Sunday-afternoon-in-T-shirts-and-panties music. Ain't got no place in this party.

"No, fuckin' no," I yell. "I order you to put that shit away."

Everyone laughs, but it's too late.

Graveyard gets the look, but he don't wear panties. He'd play anything from Bread when he wants to remember some feel-good shit or he's feeling mellow.

"Play it," Deb says, laughing.

Henry looks at her.

Fuck, fuck, fuck.

We could have screwed in the stairwell, but now she's gonna get all weepy and shit.

"No, it's gonna bum everyone out," Graveyard says.

"No it won't," Deb says. Anthony puts his hand on her ass. He's definitely gonna get her. Seen this shit before.

Fuckin' big man.

"My dad owns a Chevy dealership," he says. "He let me have my own Monte Carlo."

That's his line.

I load the bong.

Fuck 'em all.

Henry puts on the John Denver shit and the stupid fucks all sit there, zoning out to the goddamned tune. My dorm room turns into a funeral parlor.

369

Deb leans back in Anthony's arms. He's probably got his hard-on against her back by now. His hands are underneath her bra.

Eve leans against Henry.

Munchie just cries, but he's got no tears. It's a stoner cry. Seen it before when some dude just stares and feels sorry for himself.

Graveyard takes a hit and puts the bong on the linoleum floor. The smoke comes off the bowl and pipe. Everybody watches it and feels real sad as *Annie's Song* plays.

Anthony rubs Deb's breasts through her blouse, then those lovers stumble out, leaving my door wide the fuck open.

"I'm pretty fuckin' stoned," Henry says. He stumbles away into the hall without Eve. She's into the song.

Munchie looks at his door across the hallway.

"Gotta crash," he says as he takes off his sneakers and throws them into the hall. He follows, almost tripping over them.

Eve straightens her hair, then stands up and sways for a minute. She leans over and kisses me, leaving her tongue in place for a long time. I like the taste of her mouth, but I'm getting too pissed-off to stay in the room.

I stand... and she disappears out the door.

I drop back onto my bed.

Graveyard and I zone out as he reaches over to his black plastic phonograph and makes the song play again. We sit on our beds and stare at the dying bong, then I grab my van keys.

"What's up, John?"

"Gotta disappear for awhile."

"Why don't you hang out here?"

"Because I don't play games. Don't play fuckin' games."

The Econoline

It doesn't matter why I'm driving to Jersey.

I need to disappear for awhile 'cause I don't play fuckin' games!

Interstate 80 is busy this morning with truckers and vacationers going somewhere. I'm going with them, or at least pretending to. Paul McCartney and Wings are singing about a little luck on the radio and the engine in the van shakes the whole rolling metal box.

Anthony thinks he's big shit!

I'm rested because I slept at the rest stop outside of Bloomsburg last night. I felt safe in the van across the comfort station from a line of tractor-trailers. I slipped off my clogs, put my feet up on the engine cover and slept a good three hours.

Now, it's raining like hell. So badly that the sunrise is a gray tint on the horizon as the blackness fades.

I'm going away from Mansfield and the dorm ants. I'm disappearing for awhile.

Around me are sedans and station wagons filled with commuters. They're doing what they always do as they make their way from the Poconos across Northern Jersey to the city. The big city is like Mecca to them.

Near East Stroudsburg, I sit in traffic. It's hot and muggy. My black shirt—it's one of Mom's blouses with billowy long sleeves—sticks to my skin. My feet hurt in my clogs and my French jeans are tight.

It's a long way 'til breakfast. If I were in Mansfield, I'd be sitting in Developmental Psychology right now, listening to Professor Forbes talk about adolescence.

Someone made a road through the hay fields and cities so that all these people could pass through without ever meeting anyone. Without ever knowing anyone.

Finally, I get across the Delaware Water Gap and enter Jersey.

"Enter Jersey" sounds like a title to bad porn movie.

An hour later, I take the Panther Valley exit. The construction men cut it out of the side of the Allamuchy Mountains in '72 when they finally completed this part of the Interstate. Before that, all east-west traffic converged on Hackettstown.

I drive past Vern's Gulf station. I remember it from before they built the Interstate bridges right near it. Once, Dad pulled in there when we had a flat tire. We were going to the shore on vacation and Dad picked up a nail. All of us waited while Vern fixed it.

In '65 Dad bought toy U-Haul trucks that he gave us for Christmas. He bought then from Vern. It was the same Christmas that he bought me racecars.

We rode on those trucks, even when he yelled at us not to.

"You're gonna break them," he said.

We did, snapping the back steel axles.

Mark had a toy Econoline van until I broke it in Fassett.

I broke a lot of things in Fassett.

It's about seven-thirty when I drive past the general store and go onto Jane's Chapel Road. Supposedly, there was a chapel here, but it's long gone.

The empty fields are gone and developments are encroaching the area. All the barns are empty. I don't see any cows.

I pull into Chuckie's driveway.

His mother comes out in her bathrobe and curlers.

"Is Chuckie here?" I ask.

She looks at me, not recognizing me. It's the hair, the blouse, the clogs, and the French jeans that throw her off. Never dressed like this when I lived up the street.

Hey, Chuckie's Mom, I know that I look like a girl! It's my androgynous look. Sandra Bem wrote about it. Look it up in any good intro psychology text!

"Tell him it's John Higham. I used to live up the street."

Her eyes make the translation and I'm the little boy in worn clothing running across her lawn. Or, I'm standing at the back door with a brand new baseball glove in my hand. Or, I'm wearing swimming trunks with a towel wrapped around my neck.

"Well, come in," she says. "I'll wake Chuckie up."

Chuckie's gotten fat, his sister Cindy is now sexy, and the house remains neat though there are boxes piled in the living room. His Dad is at the police barracks.

"Look at you," Chuckie says as he steps out of his bedroom in a pajamas and a bathrobe.

I shake his hand.

"What are you doing here?"

"Have a few days between classes and decided to do some driving."

He looks out at the van.

"Wow."

"Yeah, I'm planning to customize it." I look around the house. "Where you going?"

"Ohio State. Majoring in Engineering."

I laugh. "You always did like building things."

We talk for a little bit about my brothers and sisters. I tell him about Maria being in Japan then going to Hawaii, Faith being in school, and the twins being in Mansfield with Rose. The three of them want to hear all the stories.

I only tell them the good shit. They really don't want to hear the bad shit.

No one ever knows how to deal with someone else's bad shit.

"Would you like some breakfast?" his mom asks.

"No, I want to get going and see some other people."

"Butchie moved," Chuckie says. "Butchie Senior died a few years ago and Harriet moved to an apartment in Hackettstown. I think Butchie joined the Army."

"I see. Well, I better get going."

Chuckie walks me out to the van. I open the door and show him the empty inside.

"You don't have any luggage," he says. "You staying at a hotel?"

"Naw, I just catch some sleep in the passenger seat. Besides, it's just a day trip."

"I see," he says while looking at the walls and floor. "Well, take care."

We stare at the van for a few moments, then I close the side door and climb into the driver's seat. I wave to him as I back out of his drive and head up the hill. I watch in the van's side mirror as he stands in his bathrobe and pajamas on his front lawn.

This is fucking surreal.
Why did I do this shit?
What the hell was I expecting?
Goodbye, Chuckie.

Up the road, my old house looks like hell.

It's a squat box on top of the hill with ugly blue paint.

No one's done anything to it: the driveway and garage floor are still dirt. It looks like someone recently mowed the lawn.

When I stop my van in the road, the people inside ignore me for a few minutes, then peek through the curtains. I take my foot off the brake and roll down the hill past the new houses and the Knapp Shoes man.

I drive past the Gun Club entrance and stop at the fire station. There, I turn around and go back past all that shit that was once my childhood so that I can drive toward Cemetery Lane.

The van stays on the slow road even as commuters rush past. They whisk past in their Fords and Chevys, listening to WABC with me.

Yvonne Elliman is singing, "If I can't have you, I don't want nobody, baby" as I approach the cemetery gates and turn.

Ten minutes later, I find my parents' place. When Mom died, we paid to have a headstone made. I stare it for awhile.

This is where I go when I need to disappear.

My shirt sticks to my back and armpits, the wind blowing my hair as I stand and look at the double headstone. On the lane, more cars shoot past on their way to Route 46.

Each car has a single commuter, a single moron who doesn't know why he's going anywhere. They do it because they have to and won't know what to do once they get there. They'll do all the same shit they did before.

I can hear Yvonne singing, her song leaking through the opened van door as I stand like a lost asshole on Cemetery Lane. I want to go back to Chuckie's house and tell him about Betty and Jack, about Bobby and June, about Phil and getting high in Felicia's dorm room. I want to tell him about the Lionel power pack and hunting down Bitch and almost killing my mother one night when I thought she was an intruder. I want to tell him about Eve's mouth and Deb's full lips.

Hell, he's got his own life.

I don't belong with Chuckie, Eve, Deb, or anyone. I belong here. This is my family, this is my home. I don't want to leave.

More cars speed past on the lane.

374

I return to the van and turn off the radio. I open the glove box and take out my notebook and write.

The headstones stand quietly, the dead waiting for the morning visitor to leave. He slowly climbed back into his van and returned to his own cemetery that others mistakenly called his life. He has many headstones to read.

When I swing around in the seat, I see the empty van.

I'm just as empty as this van.

No one else lives here.

I'm so pathetic.

I return my notebook to the glove box and drive back to Mansfield.

Memo Boards

Okay, I can't help it.

I see the blank white space, the beautiful blank white space memo boards, and I have to fill them all up. I have to take the marker and write whatever is going through my mind at that exact moment.

No matter how strange it is.

I have to write it down on the memo boards that are stuck to the doors in the dorms.

I just have to, man.

I do it when I'm straight, I do it when I'm stoned, I do it when I'm bored, I do it when my mind is moving at a thousand miles an hour and the words come out of me before I even know what I'm saying.

Shit, my mind is always moving that fast.

I like giving away my writing on erasable memo boards.

I like writing on the boards when I'm depressed. I never tell anyone that I'm depressed: that's none of their business, man.

Anyway, guess what?

Sometimes, people write my shit down on paper and want me to sign it.

Can you stand it?

Like they think it's worth something, like they think it means something, like they think they want it to keep.

Hell, they're just being nice but I always sign them anyway.

Sayre

"Daddy…, Daddy!"
I am naked save for a moist sheet and my erection.
"Daddy…, Daddy!"
A small hand grabs my foot.
Pussy breath is all over my face. I find a cigarette from someone's night table and sit so that the little voice won't see my hard prick. The utterance belongs to a boy, a toddler in Star Wars pajamas.

It's not much of a bedroom, more of a living room, though it has no TV; just a bed, a dresser, and a night table. The furniture doesn't match and the carpeting is old. Everything looks clean though worn. This area is set off from the rest of the house by a pair of curtains hanging over the doorway that appears to lead to the actual living room and stairs that lead to the house's second story.

I don't remember coming in here, undressing, or falling asleep. I don't remember how I got pussy breath, though I can easily figure that part out.

I hold the ciggy joint style, pinching it between my thumb and forefinger. Inhaling it recalls the taste of Florence's mouth.

"Daddy…, Daddy!"
"Dude, I'm John. I'm not your dad. Go away!"
The doorway curtain flies open as Florence runs in wearing a bathrobe. She is older, much older today than she was last night. She looks to be about forty.

Think she said thirty-six, but I can't be sure.

I'm surprised that my head is clear. That makes sense, 'cause I didn't really drink. I do remember smoking a lot of pot, however.

"Watch TV, Todd," she says.

The boy dashes into the next room as Florence opens her robe. She finds me with her mouth and pushes my back against the headboard. I consider the occasional gray strands among the brown mass that covers her head and reaches over her shoulders.

Her stained panties are on the floor, though I don't know where my clothes are.

"I love you," she giggles just before I climax.

Last night, people sat in chairs as I tasted cigarettes in Florence's mouth. Dennis sat with his girl, Tina, on his lap, his hands pulling down her Playtex Cross-Your-Heart-Bra and wedging his hand into her Levi's. Florence's breasts sagged onto the carpet when she rolled over and I lifted her sweater to her chin. Somewhere music played and I tasted Miller beer and pot.

"Fuck me?" she asked.

I nodded, trying to get up on the stained carpet. The living room filled with bodies and I drank someone's beer. I heard someone pissing in the next room. Dennis heard it too as he spanked Tina's pantied ass before biting it.

I could do her, too.

Florence grabbed a beer and loosened my pants.

"Not here," I said.

Earlier that evening in a bar, two old women drank whiskey and threw shot glasses at each other. They took out their teeth and soaked them in beer glasses. The other patrons didn't really give a shit.

Then they started wailing on each other.

"Cat fight," Dennis said, hiding a joint in his hand. "They're fighting over fresh meat."

"Who's that?"

"You," he said, laughing.

One gouged the other with her nails. Outside, a train roared past. I took a hit and watched the Conrail freight dissect the town as it occupied half of the old Lehigh Valley main.

Dennis followed me out.

"Cover that shit; I don't want the cops to take it."

I put my hand over it like he just showed me as the caboose bounced past. I watched the gates open and cars pour across.

"Fuck 'em," Dennis said. "Fuck 'em all night long. The bitches in this town fuck forever."

Inside, the old bitches fought, pulling each other's hair and slapping each other's faces.

"This isn't cool."

Dennis held the pot in, forcing it through his nose.

"Do you realize... that you're walking... away from a good thing? They both want you. Could go back in there... and be the king of their worlds. In the... fucking toilet."

"I don't want to be their king. Especially in the toilet."

Much later as the night was ending, I drove my van through Sayre as Florence partially unzipped my jeans and pinched at me until she made a lump. She leaned over in the seat and tongued my ear as my headlights bounced around the streets.

"Watch for the cops," Jean said as she sat in one of the dorm chairs that Bob and I had borrowed from the college before we left for Sayre. She wore a tight polyester shirt and a pair of cheap jeans. With too much eye make-up, she smelled of Charley and lip gloss. She's Florence's younger sister.

"Leonard is in the City," Jean said. She drank Riunite in a plastic glass and put her bottom against the dash as Florence stepped over Dennis and Tina. Dennis and Tina now messed around on the blankets I had thrown on the floor before Dennis and I had left Mansfield earlier that day: the blankets were meant as carpets.

The trip was Dennis' idea. Earlier that afternoon, he, Graveyard, and I were sitting in my dorm room, smoking pot when Dennis, a freshman art major, came up with the idea.

"Let's go to Sayre. That place is one continuous party," he said.

"No shit?"

"No shit."

Florence's hand played in my jeans, her gray hair smelling of smoke in the dark van.

Sayre slept and Jean stared at the lights of Robert Packer Hospital when I drove past.

Mom died there.

378

"Can you drop us there?" Dennis asked near midnight when I crossed the throat of the old Lehigh Valley freight yard and came up to what I thought was a deserted house. It wasn't much of a place. The paint was long gone and there was an abandoned truck in the front yard.

That was Tina's house.

I stopped and the pair of them slid from the van, their hands continuing to grope each other as they staggered toward the building. Jean, Florence, and I watched them and laughed like stoners until I put the van in gear.

"Twelve more streets," Jean whispered.

"You have them memorized?"

"Lived here all my life."

Florence smiled and played with my hair. Her free hand gabbed the door handle and she pulled herself upright for moment, then slumped back and grabbed my hand.

We crossed the tracks. Here, the houses were closer, their back yards facing the broken fence that had once separated the rail yard from the neighborhood. Now, everything smelled of booze, piss, and pot.

"Here."

When we climbed out, I saw the abandoned railroad shops. Across the train yard downtown Sayre stood, that place leading right up to that side of the tracks by Newberry's.

"I like to sit out and look up to town right here," Jean said.

The three of us went inside and drank more beer from passed-around bottles. Jean cried for Leonard.

"He don't beat her," Florence said after pulling off my jeans while we sat on the couch during *The CBS Late Movie*. "Even takes her to Binghamton for ice cream."

My body ached and Florence guided me through the stained curtain hanging over the doorway. Somehow, my clothes were gone.

Florence's bedroom was at the bottom of unpainted stairs. There, someone had placed what appeared to be random pieces of furniture along the walls.

Jean said goodnight in the dark while Florence made sucking noises and tried sticking her fingers up my ass.

She winced when I grabbed her wrist.

"Hey, be careful," she said.

"Maybe you should be careful." I released her hand.

"She'd do you," Florence whispered about Jean. "Said she really likes you. Want me to get her?"

"Naw, she's got Leonard."

Florence kissed me.

"You're so nice."

Sometime later, I passed out.

Maple 'B' Dorm

"Stay on the wall," Susie screams.

I'm stoned, but I listen to her 'cause she's standing right near the window at the other end of the residence hall. The halls in Maple 'B' are straight, with a window at each end.

She's having some sort of bad trip.

She's all fucked up.

She's messing with the window at the end of the hall like she trying to squeeze through it and jump three stories to the ground. That would probably kill her.

I'm at the other end of the hall, near Deb's room. The hall is otherwise empty.

Susie is panicking and says something about needing to jump out the window.

That's not cool.

"What's your name?" I ask as I make my way toward her.

"I'm Susie. Stay on the wall!"

"Susie, I'm John and I'm stayin' on the wall. Susie, you gotta help me 'cause I'm really stoned right now and nothin' makes any sense. Tell me why I gotta stay on the wall."

Deb is watching from her room, a couple doors behind me. Susie screams.

"There's people all over the place that are gonna get you! Stay on the wall."

"Okay, Susie, is this how I stay on the wall?"

I'm squeezing myself against the wall, sliding over the painted blocks as I make my way toward her.

Susie screams again and slams her head against the cinderblock wall.

She slams it again.

She slams it again.

And again.

Deb, Eve, Anthony, Munchie, and I were hanging out in Deb's room, just smoking a few joints after studying like we always do when we heard Susie's door slam shut and her screaming in the hallway.

Then we heard Reefer. Reefer is a garbage-head prick who I simply don't trust. Man, he knows how to get a good high and has been known to hitchhike all day just to party for ten minutes and crazy shit like that.

But, he's an asshole. He's an asshole because he only cares about getting high and getting off.

Anyway, Reefer was yelling at Susie to shut up, as in, "Shut the fuck up, will ya'?"

THUD—THUD, we heard Susie slam her head against the wall as she ran down the hall away from the garbage head prick. A garbage-head is an asshole who does any drug, or any shit, to get high. Garbage-heads huff fucking gasoline, man. I hate garbage-heads. They're a fucking waste of time.

Anyway, after hearing Susie beating her head against the wall, I jumped up and opened the door without thinking. Shit, I was holding a fuckin' joint in my hand. I opened the door, and there was Reefer standing in his briefs sporting a hard-on.

"You gonna hit that joint?" he asked.

"Never mind that. What'd you give her?"

"Nothin', man."

I gave the joint to Deb, then walked up to Reefer. He drew back as I approached him. I passed him and kept moving toward Susie who by now was at the middle of the hallway. She was crying and I figured out what Reefer was doing.

I turned around and moved toward the asshole.

"You better fuckin' tell me what you gave her or I'll beat the fuckin' shit out of you."

"Be cool, man. It's all cool."

THUD! Susie slammed her head into the wall.

"Are you gonna fuckin' tell me?"

"Just a little Panama Red, man, really."

"Liar."

Reefer cowered.

"Okay, well it had a little PCP in it. Maybe. Not much, but a little PCP." He looked right at me for the first time that night. "Uh, you're not gonna tell anyone?"

THUD!

THUD!

THUD!

I walked toward Susie, watching Reefer.

"You need to get your ass off this floor right now!"

"Man, you're not gonna—"

"Get your fuckin' pants on… and get the fuck out of this building!"

"You mind if I grab my stash—"

I gave him a look.

"John, it's cool. Okay, you can have the PCP. It's not that bad, really. It's a really good high. Chicks dig it."

I ran toward Reefer, freaking him out.

"I'm goin', man, I'm goin'."

By now, there were other students standing in the hall. They watched Reefer run like a fucking coward back into the room, throw his pants on and escape down the staircase.

"Get on the wall," Susie yelled.

I looked at Deb.

"Get everybody out of here," I said, "she's freaking out."

Deb chased away the onlookers and stayed in her doorway as I started down the hall toward Susie.

"And flush the shit that's in her room."

Deb complied, then watched me from her doorway.

Susie is fucked up.

PCP?

I heard what that shit did to some chick last week. She was hallucinating and thought the dorm was hell. Thought Satan was holding her onto the floor. She was totally screwed up. I think it took six of her friends to restrain her for eight hours or some shit like that.

THUD!

THUD!

THUD!

Susie's screaming at me.

"Get on the wall!"

"Susie, I'm really messed up right now. The only way I can help is if you look right at me without moving. Can you stand completely still so that I can see you?"

Susie freezes and stares at me.

Her makeup is a mess; her mascara has run all over her face and her hair looks like hell.

Fuckin' Reefer; I know what he wanted from Susie.

"Susie, how am I doin'?"

"Stay on the wall."

"I am."

I'm sliding my head along the wall, my hair acting as a cushion as I slide along the wall toward her. Finally, I'm across the hall from her and we're looking at each other.

"Ohmygod, you're not gonna be able to get me," she screams, pointing at the floor.

"Susie, I can't see; what's down there?"

She screams.

"It's some sort of hole. Goes on forever."

"Susie, I'm kinda messed up right now, but I've got my hand in the wall right now and I can reach across and get you. You have to put your hand in the wall too."

She stares at her hand as she presses it against the wall with all her might. There isn't much to Susie—she might weigh a hundred pounds—but she forces all of herself into her left hand.

"Grab my hand and I'll pull you to this wall."

Her shaking hand finds mine in the middle of the hallway.

"Susie, I'm gonna pull you to safety, but you have to look right at my face. Can you do that?"

"Yes, John."

I gently tug her over to me and she wraps herself around me, shaking.

She holds on as if she's a thousand feet in the air, her fingers clenching my gauze shirt and I slide back along the wall to Deb's room. Once there, we sit on the floor.

"Susie, we're gonna stay with you until you come down, okay?"

She nods.

Deb and I kneel on either side of her. The three of us practice relaxation exercises for an hour until Susie falls asleep on Deb's floor.

During the next six hours, Deb and I talk. She talks about her sister who has Down Syndrome and I talk about Mom, Betty and Jack, and Bobby and June.

She talks about growing up in Bradford: I talk about New Jersey, Fassett, Columbia Cross Roads, and Mansfield.

We talk about everything except Phil. I can't tell her that because I don't want her looking at me the way she stared at Susie after she figured out what Reefer had tried to do.

At sunrise, Susie wakes up and looks around the room.

"Thank you," she says, then goes across the hall to her room. I slip on my clogs and go downstairs to get some sleep.

Roaring Run Road

The morning after the New York State Trooper woke me by knocking on the side of my van, I drove out of the W.T. Grant Plaza parking lot. I went south on Route 14 over the border into Fassett. I turned right at The Rancho and drove along Roaring Run the three miles past my old house and turned onto Kinney Road.

It was hot by then. I drove to the turnaround near Kinney's cornfield, took off my jeans and slipped on a pair of shorts. I grabbed a dirty towel and located my soap dish. Somewhere under the mattress I found my razor.

The van was getting hotter and I smelled of asshole.

Behind a thick line of trees, I stripped everything off and walked into a pool of creek water. Colder than hell, it still felt good. I washed my hair with the soap and shaved, then washed the rest of me.

I held off pissing as long as I could, then slipped on my Nikes and ran downstream where I peed over some rocks.

It was beautiful.

384

When a truck raced by and kicked up a trail of dust, I stood still behind the tree. The driver turned his head toward my van on the other side of the road without slowing down. I found a large rock and reclined, letting sun warm my body for a few hours. From where I sat, I could see Point X and the place where the twins and I had built our cabin five years ago.

Around noon, I got dressed and went back to the W.T. Grant parking lot. It's just this side of the Erie Lackawanna Railroad tracks that run from Buffalo to Binghamton. The plaza is on the Elmira's Southside. By afternoon, the lot was filled and the van was hotter than hell, so I took out my bike and rode around Elmira until around sunset. Then I treated myself to a Happy Meal at the same McDonald's Mom once took me to when I was in the seventh grade.

That's the important thing about eating: never go to the same McDonald's two days in a row. It's better to catch the meal of the day at a different place so that people don't think you're a bum. I don't take the van, instead bicycling up like I'm visiting and need a quick snack.

When I got up to brush my teeth in the bathroom, I left the toy behind on the table.

Kids like surprises like that.

The State Troopers always wake me after midnight. I wait for them, leaning against the back of my van while sitting on the mattress. I see their cruiser's headlights, then their flashlight dancing around my windshield.

They always knock and I always open the double side doors.

Tonight, it's an older Trooper from the Wellsburg Barracks. He wears his hat and holds the light on me as he asks for my license and registration. He is quiet as he reads them.

"So, we're babysitting you," he says. I don't blame him. After the department store closes for the night, I'm the only one in the lot. "When does the fall semester start?"

"Next week," I say.

"Your parents know you're living in this van in this parking lot?"

"Sir, my parents are dead."

"Then who lives at this address?"

"My guardians."

He reviews my registration card. They always look at that.

"Do your guardians know you're living in this van in this parking lot?"

"Sir, they don't really care where I'm living."

"Son, why's that?"

"Don't really know, Sir."

He hands back the license and shines his light right in my eyes. I lower my head and watch the beam as it moves over my psychology textbooks and my dirty clothes. I try to keep the place neat, but it's hard because everything slides around whenever I move the van. The covers on the books are bent and some of the pages have been torn out. Some of my clean clothes are in the backpack, but most of them are dirty and scattered around the back of the van.

My van.

My house.

My own little world between semesters.

"Where do you go during the day?"

"Sometimes, I go to Fassett, Sir. I have friends there who don't mind if I shave and take a shower."

He holds the light so that it falls on my long hair.

"Why can't you stay there?"

I'm looking toward the parking lot lights, but I can't see anything.

"My friends don't want me there."

He chuckles to himself.

"Son, those are not your friends." He turns the light back on my clothes. We both look at the wrinkled French jeans and gauze shirts.

"You should get to the laundromat."

"Yes, sir."

He turns it back on my eyes.

"You're fully aware that you're not supposed to be here."

"I know, Sir. It's only for this week. Then I'll be living on campus for the fall semester."

I put the license back in my wallet.

"I know your story," he says, leaving the light on me. "Everyone at the barracks knows that we're babysitting you."

He stares at me.

"Thank you, sir."

"Get that laundry done soon."

"Yes, Sir."

He turns off the light and gets back in his car. I leave the van's double doors open and listen to the American La France plant down the block. After a few minutes, I close the door and head for the all-night laundromat. The cruiser follows me as I pull in and grab some clothes.

Because I only have money for food and gas, I wash my clothes in the utility sink, scrubbing each piece with the bar of Ivory soap.

The cruiser sits outside the place, the trooper watching me as I lean over the sink and wash a few of my shirts. I scrub them with the bar and rinse them in the sink.

In the morning, I'll take them to Fassett and let them air dry on the big rock.

Pinecrest Dorm

My pants got tight when I was smoking a joint with Graveyard, Billy, Henry, and Gina. She starts playing with my thighs and sticking her tongue in my ear. Billy inhales deeply and watches as she turns me on.

Billy's cool. I like his van 'cause it's all customized and everything. I want mine to look just like his.

I stand up. "You, you, you; go," I say, pointing to the guys. They laugh at first, then realize that I'm not fuckin' with them and stand up like dumbfucks.

"You want me to leave?" Gina asks.

"You, stay."

The guys quickly pull their shit together and get their asses out of my room.

After the guys leave, I lower her onto the bed and pull down her jeans. I slide up her T-shirt.

Her crotch smells of Dove and her breasts become firm in my mouth.

"I always thought you were cute," she whispers, "and smart."

I knew Gina in elementary school in Gillett. She was a year behind me.

Her pussy makes my pecker slide all around and she's slipping off the bed. Her legs keep her from falling onto the floor. She's got her fingers in my hair, messing it all up. I'm not thinking about anything. My tongue licks her teeth.

You smell like pot and Newport's.

I grab her hips and squeeze her.

She holds the side of the bed and the room's built-in desk light that's next to my bed. Before she can fall off, I'm done and my pecker goes limp. She grabs my ass and sticks her cigarette tongue in my mouth, but everything's gone.

She climbs out from underneath me, then pulls her shirt down and pants up.

"Thanks for *that* party," she says, laughing as she opens the door.

Country Roads

It's a couple days later when Pam is sitting cross-legged on my bed, her Nikes on the floor. We're tickling each other as we smoke a joint and giggle. When I tickle her, her shoulder-length red hair flies around and temporarily obscures her face.

"I never know what to expect from you," she says.

She laughs, then pinches my armpit. I grab her thigh and squeeze it tightly, making her squirm as she flops around.

Graveyard comes in and looks at us, but we're too busy wrestling on the bed to notice. Pam reaches into the back of my jeans and yanks, giving me one hell of a wedgie. I try to get even, but I can't find her waistband.

"I'm not wearing panties," she yells.

Graveyard sits on the bed and takes a joint.

"I can smell you guys," he says.

"I didn't fart," I say. "Pam, did you fart?"

"I'm not talking about that," Graveyard says.

Pam reaches back down my pants, but I grab her arm.

"Time out," I say to Pam. "Man, could you smell it in the hall?"

Graveyard nods. "When I came into the building."

"Fuck. Can you tell it's from here?"

"John, it's the middle of the day. It's not that hard to figure out."

"Aw, fuck."

I disentangle myself from Pam and grab a towel. There's already one on the floor, but it ain't doing the trick. Shit, shit, shit!

"Carmel-coated fucksticks!"

"Oh, relax. It's cool," Pam says. She straightens her hair and lies on the bed.

Graveyard makes his eyes bug out, shaking his head as he takes the joint. He holds onto the hit, then lets it out his nose as he speaks in falsetto.

"The caramel-coated cocksuckers! John, remember the first time you said that?" He hands the joint to Pam, who watches him. "John was at a party when someone mentioned his R.A. Remember, Henry said, 'Who's that skinny little guy with the big head who has the private room down the hall?' and you said, 'That's the caramel-coated cocksucker R.A.' Remember?"

I re-towel the door, then jump back on the bed. Pam rests her head against my chest and I take the joint. I like Pam. She's fun to party with 'cause she likes to hang out.

Graveyard stands up to do another imitation.

"You, you, and you, leave. You, stay."

I hand the joint to Pam.

"No, man, that's another time. That's not the caramel-coated time."

Graveyard laughs and rolls his eyes. He approaches the end of the bed and touches Pam's bare foot, making her giggle.

"The caramel-coated cocksuckers are everywhere, the caramel-coated cocksuckers are everywhere," he says, getting more excited as he repeats it. He says it a few more times, then flops onto his bed. He giggles.

"John, you're the funniest guy I know," he says.

Pam agrees.

"He's funny as shit," she says.

"Never mind that shit; let's party!" I say.

I pull out my wedgie.

"There's a better way to do that," Pam says.

"You're not gonna see my underwear," I say.

Graveyard takes out a John Denver album and puts it on the turntable.

"Graveyard!"

"C'mon, man, I like John Denver."

"You're killing my high."

"Shut up, man," he says. "They're gonna hear you. I don't want to get busted." He puts the needle on the record and John Denver starts singing.

Graveyard stands and bounces to *Country Roads*, singing along. Every so often, he blurts out, "caramel-coated cocksuckers," and laughs to himself.

Pam holds me close and watches Graveyard's floor show. We wrestle on the bed. I almost flip her to the floor, but I save her from falling by grabbing the front of her shirt.

"Shit," I say. "You have a lot to hold onto."

"Yes, I do," Pam says, smiling.

Graveyard puts the needle back at the beginning of the song after it finishes. He sits on the floor and takes the joint, laughing at himself. He doesn't notice when I put on Fleetwood Mac.

"Good choice," Pam says. She pulls off my socks and tries tickling my feet. I almost kick her in the crotch, but she puts her hands down there.

"Off limits?" I ask.

"To feet, yes. I only allow a few body parts near that."

She butts her head into my chest, slamming my back and my head against the wall. I hit it hard, making my teeth hurt.

Pam sits up, gently holding open my mouth and checking my teeth.

"Shit, another drug-related dental injury," she says.

Graveyard laughs and stands.

"Okay, all you caramel-coated cocksuckers," he says, "I want all of you caramel-coated cocksuckers to leave. John, you fuckin' crack me up."

Buttonwood

After U.S. 15 leaves the Williamsport valley, it runs along Lycoming Creek. At Trout Run, the highway turns away from the creek and heads through Steam Valley toward the summit at the Turkey Ranch. Professor Yacavissi told us in Geography and Regional Planning class that in those eight miles, the elevation rises 500 feet.

In the van, it seems like a mile straight up. Jill and I listen to the engine rev as the poor vehicle tries to stay alive for another twenty miles to Mansfield. Everything I own is in it.

We are coming back from Long Island. Jill's boyfriend, Terrance, lives there. I volunteered to take them out to drop him off. Terrance lived with Jill in her room for the semester.

They're a cool couple and really love each other.

The van is dying. The engine revs like it did when it didn't shift out of first, but we're in third. The clutch is shot, I'm sure.

Jill misses Terrance. She's joking and everything, but she's quiet when she's not responding to me. I don't talk with her about her lover because I'm here to drive. It would be cool to love someone the way, though.

After reaching the summit, the highway drops down into Buttonwood. Without the exit sign, the place would be unremarkable. There are a few houses on the East Side of the highway and an old truck stop that some guy uses to store his tractor-trailers.

I push the clutch in and let the van drift down toward the exit sign. We arrive quickly at this nowhere place. When I try putting the van in gear, the engine only revs.

Our trip is over.

"I'm sorry, Jill."

"We can hitch," she says.

That's what I like about Jill; nothing stops her. And, she always speaks her mind. Earlier this summer, when a bunch of us were getting stoned in her dorm room and she saw me writing in my notebook, she stopped the party.

"Higham, what are you doin', man?" she asked. "You've always got that notebook with you."

"I'm writing," I said.

"Oh, yeah? Is that what you're always doin?"

"Yeah."

"Well, you better not write about me or I'll kick your ass. Then, I'll sue you for everything you own. Not gonna write about me."

She's now gathering her suitcase and purse. I put my wallet in my pocket and hide my pot in the vehicle's frame near the roof. My other shit is scattered all around the back of the van. The semester is over and I'm homeless again for just another day. That's okay, 'cause Jill said I could stay at her house until tomorrow.

Outside, it's hot. I mean, the van doesn't have any air conditioning, but at least the windows make a breeze when the vehicle is moving.

Jill and I walk a hundred feet toward the exit, our thumbs popping out when cars and trucks roar off the hill. A state trooper pulls up and gives us a lift. It's cool because we haven't smoked anything today and, besides, it turns out that he's moving to Spring Hill.

I'm glad that I left my pot in the van and that Jill and I aren't stoned.

It takes a few weeks before I can afford to pay for the repair bill. The state police call my dorm room and get all pissed-off about it, giving me a ticket for abandoning the vehicle. June drops me off at Ralph's Ford when I get it repaired.

"You need any money?" she asks as we sit in the front seat of the Ninety-Eight.

"No, I got it." I climb out of the car with five hundred dollars in my pocket from my Social Security check and some savings. It's all I've got, but I don't want her money.

Don't want anything from her.

Hell, I hardly ever stop by her office anymore.

Mister Donut

Man…

I'm sitting…
Alone…
In a booth…
At Mister Donut…
In Mansfield.

I'm getting into…
A glazed doughnut.

I'm tasting…
The glaze flakes…
On my tongue.

The orange walls…
Are decorated…
With large pictures of doughnuts.

Everything is bright…
It looks like Technicolor…
In a movie.

I smell coffee…
And doughnuts.

There are rows of doughnuts…
In the glass case…
Rows on the racks…
Behind the counter.

There's a few truckers…
Sitting on stools.

Man…

It's cool in here…
Cool in my head…
Everything is slow.

My thinking is so slow…
Real slow.

Instead of having…
A thousand thoughts…
Bombard my mind…
Like they always do…
I am so totally…
Focused.

Never felt this way…
Before.

Did Henry really…
Give me two…
Black Beauties?

Or…
Did he slip me…
Some 'ludes?

"John, you want some speed?"

That's what he asked…
An hour ago.

In his dorm room…
We were listening…
To Boston…
More Than a Feeling…
On his Kenwood.

"Sure."
"How many you want?"

"What will they do?"
"Give you energy, man."

"Really? I always have energy."
"These'll make your mind work really fast."

"Shit, Henry, my mind always works really fast."
"Well, these'll make your mind work faster."

"Cool. I'll take two."

That's the entire conversation…
Really.

He handed me two…
Black capsules…
I swallowed them.

Henry was wrong…
My brain never picked up any speed…
My brain slowed down…
I slowed down…
Way down.

Better than Librium…
I'm wide awake…
Wide alert.

Librium without…
Sleep.

Speed isn't supposed to…
Work like this.

My brain is no longer running…
My brain is walking…

My brain is crawling...
My thoughts are crawling inside...

I feel relaxed...
Really relaxed...
So totally relaxed.

Man...

My brain is working...
In slow...
Deliberate...
Motion.

I'm calm...
I like this...
Serene...
Never felt...
This relaxed...
Before.

Focused...
Extremely focused...
And slow...
And Technicolor.

This must be...
How other people...
Live.

Man...

The Econoline

There is snow on the highway and the windows on the van
are frosted. I have to scrape them because I can't afford
windshield washer fluid.

Someone stole my gas cap.

The insurance payment is due next week and I don't have the money.

Shit, I'm flat broke.

"What are ya' gonna do?" Graveyard asked as we hit bongs in the room and partied with Henry last night.

"That's the problem with a car," Henry said. "It's always an expense. Can never make money on a car. Have to realize that it's always an expense that can make you poor."

What the hell does Henry know about being poor? He lives in Cherry Hill; that's a wealthy area of Jersey. His father works as a lawyer. A corporate lawyer. Henry told me that his dad wrote a single check that covered all of his college expenses.

All of his college expenses.

On one fuckin' check!

"Yeah," Graveyard said, taking the bong and inhaling. He holds the hit for a long time, then lets the smoke out of his nose.

"Maybe I'll pay to have it blown up."

Graveyard laughed. He's stupid whenever he gets stoned: everything is funny.

"I'll do it for a couple hundred," Henry said. "Stick a couple wires in the gas tank and attach the other ends to a battery. Throw a switch and BOOM!"

Henry laughed.

Graveyard laughed as I took a hit. He kept talking, moving to the edge of the bed.

"Shit, that way, you'll have all that cash. What would you do with it?"

"Go into business," I said. "Can you stand it?"

I coughed really hard and deep.

"This pot is shit."

It was shitty pot. In fact, that's all I can ever find anymore on campus. Either someone wants to sell me that PCP-laced shit or they spray it with water or add plastic to it to cheat the weight. *Nobody has any ethics: their product is shit!*

Henry looked at me and says, "Shit, that's a good idea, man. I could be your partner."

Graveyard handed me the bong. My mouth fit over the smoking end and I inhale, making the water bubble as the pot turns red and the acrid smoke filled my lungs.

"Iron lung," Graveyard yelled, laughing.

A couple of days later, I take the van to a local dealer just south of Mansfield in Covington. It's right next to the State Police barracks. The man comes out and looks at it, playing with the shifter and adjusting the clutch. He's an old man in gray work clothes. His Carhartt jacket is worn on the elbows.

Just a nice redneck.

He sits inside my van. Shit, I can remember when I was gonna customize it. Hell, I lived it in between semesters and took baths in the creek by the house in Fassett. Drove to Chicago and New Jersey. This van is my home and I can't afford it anymore. The tires are bald, the engine is dying, and the only nice about it is its body.

The dealer toys with the column shifter. He puts it into reverse, the new clutch making it shift smoothly.

"The linkage and the clutch are new. So is the pressure plate," I tell him as I stand outside, shivering. I only have lace-up dress boots because my clogs got wet in the snow. I've got a cheap pair of winter boots, but their soles are cracked.

"You've taken really good care of it?"

"Yeah."

He drives it around the lot twice, then climbs out. "Why are you getting rid of it?"

"I don't need it anymore."

He walks into the piece of shit office. It's small, the chairs pulled tight against the wall and a solitary desk between them. He takes out a worn copy of the NADA Guide and flips through the pages, handing it to me with his finger on it.

"Seven hundred is what it books for," he says. "That's a fair price."

"Shit, I bought it for eighteen in the spring."

He allows me to look at the guide, then takes it back. "This your first car?"

"Yeah, how'd you know?"

Two hours later, I'm sitting in Pinecrest with Henry and Graveyard. It's a bummer, man, 'cause there's nothing going on. We're smoking some Columbian shit that Henry scored, but we have to sort out plastic shavings that the asshole dealer put in it to give it weight.

"Fuck him, man," Graveyard says, yelling as he exhales.

They're bad joints. Graveyard can't roll for shit and a ton of weed drops out when it burns.

"You'll have to look somewhere else," Graveyard says. "This area is bad for cars. You need to sell in a city."

Henry slaps the wall. "Fuckin' yeah, there's this place outside of Philly called Reedman's. They have a ton of cars. You can go there and they'll put the car on the lift and tell you exactly what they'll give you for it. They'll give you the cash on the spot."

I take the joint, snuff it out, and tear apart the motherfucker. I grab my rolling papers, then take half of the weed and place it along the crease. I then hold it in my hands, rolling it tightly between my fingers and my thumb. Not too tightly though, because joints rolled too tightly are difficult to smoke. The trick is to allow just enough air to flow through it. I wet the new joint slightly by sticking it in my mouth and pulling it out in a twisting motion.

"Dude, try this."

Graveyard lights it. None of the shit falls out and it burns like it should.

A good joint never calls attention to itself.

"Only thing, there's no negotiation," Henry says. "Have to take it or leave it."

"Sounds good to me," Graveyard says. "Totally cool, man." He giggles as he falls backward into the wall. He's too stoned to care.

A couple hours later, I'm driving behind Henry's beater Torino. The roads are slick with rain that fucks up everything.

At least it's not snow. I wouldn't be able to drive 'cause the van is too light and I can't afford snow tires.

I watch Henry and Graveyard pass a joint back and forth. It's a sweet deal for them. I bought Henry a full tank of gas and gave the guys five joints for the trip. I spent my last ten bucks on gas for the van. I've got some change, so I can wash it before we get to Reedman's.

It's a long drive and Henry drives like an asshole. He runs lights and all sorts of shit.

Reedman's is huge. We pull up and go toward the used car section. They have a garage there. Henry and Graveyard pull over and get out.

"We'll ride with you," Henry says.

Some guy in a trench coat waves us over and I pull the van up.

"Good afternoon, gentlemen, can I help you?"

Henry comes forward. "We want to sell this van."

"Who has the paperwork for it?"

"I do," I said, waving the pink slip. "It's mine, free and clear."

The man squats down under the doors for a minute and I watch his hand run along the side.

"The body is in good shape," I tell him.

"Uh-huh."

He closes the door really gently, then walks around to the front and looks at the title, checking the serial number on the dash.

"Pull into that garage," he says, pointing at an opened service bay.

The guys are happy as shit. Fuck that, we're all happy as shit!

"I'm going take this money, start a business and work toward buying a brand new van," I say.

Henry laughs. "See how he checked out the body? You're headed for the large cash-out, man."

"Fuckin' cool," Graveyard says.

Inside the garage, a guy in dark trench coat directs me onto the lift. We sit in the van while he's shouting at us.

"You have to get out of the van and stand over there," he says.

400

We scramble from the van and wait by the door. He raises the van. It spins a little bit when the wheels break contact with the concrete floor.

Graveyard laughs like a stoner. He's wasted. Henry shoves him a few times. "Don't lose it, man," Henry whispers. "Don't lose it."

The man takes a service light and looks in the wheel wells. He moves along the frame and pokes at the floor near it. In the bare white light, I see grey steel flakes fall from his finger. He pokes some more near the wheel walls and more flakes fall. His hand makes a crunching noise.

He turns off his light.

"Son, is this your van?"

I step toward him and he blocks my path to the van. I can see the large flakes on the floor.

"Yes, sir."

"I'm sorry, but we can't buy it. You've got bad rust on the frame and the floor. The wheel wells have been Bondoed and the rust never went away. Just spread. Like cancer."

I look at the large rust flakes on the floor.

"I gotta sell it."

He turns off the light. "Sorry."

"But, I don't have any more money. Mister, I don't even have enough money to drive it back home." The other buyers stare at me. "'Sides, a dealer in Mansfield said he'd give me seven hundred for it."

The trench coat man turns back on the light and looks again. "Bet he didn't put it on a lift."

"No…, can't you give me *anything* for it?"

He pokes at the frame and more large rust flakes break off. He turns and looks at me. He sighs. "Son, four hundred. Take it or leave it. We won't sell it. We'll scrap it. Can't go any higher than that."

"Thank you, Sir."

I take the money and we leave.

Henry's Torino is quiet on the way home; we're all bummed out. Henry, feeling sorry for me, stops at a State Store and Graveyard buys us some cheap whiskey. Henry stops at a McDonald's and I spring for chocolate shakes. We pour some whiskey in the shakes. When we finish those, Henry stops at another McDonald's as he drives on the turnpike toward Scranton.

"I'm never gonna be this poor again. Fuckin' beggin' to sell my van," I say. "Man, that's just bullshit."

Graveyard sips his drink, then pours in a little more whiskey. Henry keeps shaking his head. "Being poor is just not cool, man," he says. "It's just not cool."

"Well, I need money and this is going to be my seed money. I'll go without food for a month and cash out my Social Security check. I need some cash. I've got nothing to live on."

Henry nods his head. Being drunk makes him slow the fuck down, but he still drives like a fuckhead.

Everyone's a fuckhead right now, especially me.

I drink some whiskey and chase it down with the shake.

It's dark by the time we reach campus. Henry and Graveyard look like they could crash. I go to my room and figure, smoking a couple joints and sitting down with paper and pencil. I sit at my desk and figure all sorts of shit until just about morning.

Then, it all comes together.

Christmas is about six weeks away and I have nowhere to go. I no longer have the van and I need cash. I'm definitely goin' into business.

Pinecrest Dorm

There are state police cars at one of the tollbooths, their lights flashing.

"Just be cool, man," Henry says. "Just stay cool."

I'm freaking-out in the front seat of Henry's Torino. Years ago, he tossed it into a ditch after his father bought for him. The accident bent the frame and now it tracks funny going down the road.

See, this business is my idea. I figured it all out.

I told Henry about it the day after I dumped my piece of shit van.

"We'll put all our money back into the business," I said. He was cool with that idea. "And, we don't get greedy. When we're done, we'll split the earnings."

"Fifty-fifty?"

"Fuck, yeah," I said.

"It's cool. But, we'll need one more person."

"Billy."

Billy and his girlfriend Hannah are cool. He drives a customized Ford van. He's a Chemistry major. Henry and I talked to him about it in my room.

"I'll do it for free," he said. "I'll just party with all the chicks."

"We'll maximize our profit and minimize our risk," I said.

We all agreed to the terms and shook hands 'cause we're businessmen.

Henry slows down his Torino. We're just coming back from Philly. That's where we had a meeting to pick up some product.

"Just stay cool," Henry says, moving toward an open lane. It's one with a catch bucket and he throws the quarter. "Don't look at the cops," he says.

"I'm gonna look. You don't look and they think you're stoned. I'm not getting' busted 'cause I look paranoid."

Henry smiles.

"You're right."

In Pinecrest, we accidentally wake Graveyard when we divide the product. See, that's how we maximize profit; we buy a large quantity and sell it in the smallest units.

Graveyard bitches for awhile until Billy comes over and handles everything. We bust ass for a half-hour, then Billy takes a couple handfuls of packages and goes away.

Graveyard rolls over in bed.

"John, I have a test in the morning."

"Okay, okay."

I turn off one of the lights. Henry sits at my desk while I'm on my bed, leaning against the wall. We're smiling like dumbfucks.

"I'm gonna retire," he says.

"Thought you wanted to join the Marines."

"Yeah, I'll do that first, then retire after four years," he says, laughing.

Graveyard rolls over. He's pissed.

"Guys, could you be quiet?"

"Sorry, man."

Henry and I sit in the dorm, waiting for the big bucks to come rolling in.

About an hour later, Billy knocks on the door. "I wanna rock and roll all night," he sings when I open it.

"And party every day," Henry says as Billy dumps a handful of crumpled bills on my desk. Billy takes some more product and returns a half-hour later, dumping more cash and taking even more product. It goes this way until three in the morning.

By then, my whole desk is covered with crumpled ones and fives.

"I'll hold the money," Henry says. "For our next weekend."

"That's cool," I say. It takes the two of us an hour to roll the money into a big wad that Henry sticks into his pocket.

"I'm gonna put it under my mattress," he says. "You can see it anytime."

"I trust you, man. I know where you live."

We laugh at my joke and then smoke a joint. Around four, Henry goes back to his room and I can finally sleep.

I'm in business now.

Cedarcrest Dorm

There is…
A flow of air…
Feeling like it's…
From a cartoon word balloon…

404

Flowing...
From the dorm room's...
Concrete block...
Through my nose...
Down into my lungs.

My stomach expands.

"Use your diaphragm," Al says.
"Take the breath in very deeply."

"Cool. It's sort of like hitting a bong."

He remains silent and my mouth stops working.
I am breath in...
Breath out.
Al sits...
Across...
From me...
On his bed...
His legs...
Are folded...
In a full lotus.

I...
I am...
Mirroring him.

I feel my hands...
Resting...
On my knees.

My palms...
Face upward.

My fingers...
Draw energy...
From beyond...
The ceiling...

Beyond the room…
From the sky.

The world.
The spirits.
I am aware.

I can feel…
The electric hum…
Of the building.

The taste…
Of the air.

I am…
In this space…
With Al.

I can see…
OMMMM…
Letters flowing…
Across the concrete walls…
Over the windows…
Through my soul.

"Allow yourself to focus on your breathing. Right now,
everything else is bullshit."

Breath in…
Breath out.

This is…
Better…
Than pot…
Than speed.

I…
Want…
To write…

Visualizing words…
On the walls.

There is…

St. James' Apartments

The blotter takes forever to kick in after Tim and I each take a hit. He's one of Henry's frat brothers, but Henry doesn't drop acid.

"It's not my thing," he told me.

Felicia scored some, but I didn't want to trip with her. She knows too much about me and I don't want her around for my first trip. I really don't want to trip with Tim, but everybody says that you should never trip alone because you can flip-out. Everyone says that it's better to trip with someone so you can help each other if the trip gets bad.

Tim puts on an Elton John's *Goodbye Yellow Brick Road* and sits in his overstuffed chair. I'm on the floor by his bed. He's got a private room. I think his parents are rich.

We listen to *Funeral for a Friend* from the album. I suddenly remember that Phil had that song playing in his room. *That night.*

My eyes find the door in Tim's room.

I smell Phil. It's been awhile since his stench invaded my nostrils, but it's pretty strong right now.

I haven't seen Tim with Phil, but if Tim tries anything, I'll have to kill him. He's taller than I am, but he's a pretty boy and I can stab him with the pen I keep in my notebook. I'll have to go for his throat. Probably only have one chance so I'll have to be quick.

He is giggling, acting like the acid is taking effect. It's not. I'm not hallucinating and I'm not delusional. He's staring right at me, smiling like a happy dumb fuck. He's fucked up and I have to remember that my brain works faster than the world around me.

"You know, you're a really cool guy, John," he says.

Tim is sitting between me and his door.

I'll have to kill you if you make a move. Should I take out my notebook, or will you think I want to read to you?

My hand reaches around to my notebook.

"I said, 'You're a really cool guy, John'," he says.

"Thanks, man."

Tim stands.

If you come at me, I'll drive my Bic into your balls and make a break toward the door.

He looks stupid lifting the tone arm and pushing the needle back over.

"No matter what happens, remember we're brothers," he says, plopping into his chair. He puts on his sunglasses, giggling.

I know what you want: I can just tell. You're setting me up, you motherfucker.

"I'm really... fucked up... beyond all repair," he says.

He giggles some more, stroking his crotch.

What's with that shit?

"I think trippin' is making me really horny," he says. I take in the room. I see a picture of him with his parents on the desk right next to a Thanksgiving picture of a whole group of people who look just like him.

Probably Italian.

Or Slavic: I don't know.

Shit, I can't remember his last name.

I think your family decorated this room. The fat lady in the picture probably hung your curtains and the older guys in the prom tuxedos probably set up the wire rack and the raised platform for the bed. Maybe you have a bunk bed at home.

I don't know where you live.

I don't know shit about you, but I do know that you'll die if you touch me.

I do know that; knowing that makes me feel incredibly strong. Safe.

I'll be cool unless you make a move toward me, then I'll have to stop you, have to kill you. And I will fucking kill you! You're not gonna touch me!

I'll take my Bic from my notebook and jab it as deep as I can into your fucking neck!

You won't know what hit you.

Self-defense, close-casket, protect my perimeter.
You will not touch me!
You will not harm me, you stupid son-of-a-bitch!
I'll listen to your bullshit and laugh at your little jokes, but
you will not touch me!

"Whoa, this is good shit," he yells as Elton John sings
Benny and the Jets. "I'm trippin' off my ass. I can hear colors."

"Cool."

"You feelin' it yet?"

"It's good shit, man."

No, it's not, I'm just playing along, watching you watching
me without you knowing. Just being cool, being mellow as long
as I can.

He leans way over in the chair, but he's still across the
room. He turns off the fluorescent light, so the room is black-lit.
His framed posters of death look funny.

Like Tim: big white teeth and glowing eyes.

He takes off his glasses and reaches for me, smiling.

"Whoa, what the fuck, man?" I ask, drawing back.

He sits back in his chair.

"I'm just feelin' cool," he says. "Real cool. Wanna really
party today. Wanna get laid and have a good time. Can you stand
it?"

"Yeah. I can stand it."

Think I need to stand. He's above me right now.

I stand and fall against the corner, but the floor stays flat.
I know where the door is. That how people get in trouble, they
forget the door so when the flip-out happens they are totally
fucked.

You're not getting anything from me. I'll trip with you,
but you're not getting anything. Not getting shit from me. And, if
you try, I'll gonna kill you. No one's hurting me anymore.

"John, do you like to fuck?"

You better stop your little game. I've handled all sorts of
shit and I can handle you, you fucking little rich boy!

I know I'm capable of killing, Tim. I don't want to, but I
will.

I look around the room.

I'll just stab you in the throat, then slam your head against the wall until I kill you.

"John, man, do you like to fuck?"

I smell Phil. Is he outside the door, waiting? Maybe he is, knowing that I can take Tim. Is Henry part of this? They are in the same frat. Maybe this is some sort of frat thing.

"John, man, do you like to fuck?"

Tim is rubbing his jeans as I reach around to my back pocket. My right hand finds my weapon as I fake yawning.

Man, you don't have much time. Is this how you want to spend the last moments of your life?

"Can you stand it?" I ask, stepping away from the wall.

This way, I can swing my arms without hitting the wall.

Tim laughs.

"Shit, I am so fucked up right now. And, horny."

Okay, tell ya' what? I'm gonna give you a chance. I'm gonna walk to the door. If you touch me, if you reach toward me, I'll kill you. Okay?

You touch me, you die.

You let me go, you live.

I'm not gonna smell you on me.

I smell Phil.

"John, man, you like to fuck? I like to fuck." He chuckles. "Man, I really like to fuck."

I'm being set up.

Time to escape.

"Tim, you said something about goin' to St. James?"

Tim nods, then stands.

I'm at the door, my hand on the doorknob.

How does this doorknob work? I pull at it, but it's locked, tight. Shit. I'm trapped!

Someone's hand is my shoulder. It feels like Phil's.

"Yeah, it'll be real cool. Just remember," Tim says, hugging me from behind, "We're buddies, no matter what."

I push him away.

"We're not buddies. We're fuckin' brothers, man. At least that's what you're saying." I grab the doorknob and twist it.

The air pressure sucks me into the hallway.

Outside, the lines are fuzzy. It's like I need glasses. And, it too bright. It's so fucking bright. Cedarcrest Dorm looks like it's on a TV show.

"It's <u>Cedarcrest Dorm</u>," the TV announcer in his polyester suit says as the audience cheers. The audience members all wear the same polyester ensemble.

And the asphalt smells funny, but I don't smell Phil anymore. I want to grab Tim and sniff him to see if he smells like Phil.

Not really; I really don't want to touch him.

I wonder if he knows how close he came to being killed. Asshole probably doesn't even know. Should I tell him? Naw..., it's not important anymore. Shit, it's a beautiful day.

I feel the heat of the sun warm my face and the air is good to my lungs.

"Don't stare at the sun," Tim yells, covering his eyes.

"Be cool, man. Just be cool."

I check my shoes.

Do I have naked feet? That would look so stupid, walking along the oozing asphalt in my bare feet, the cuffs of my jeans eroding the street.

No, I'm wearing clogs.

From a thousand miles away, I hear Lori and Sally. They pull up in Lori's Impala coupe. It's from the sixties like Dad's company car and like Doug's Impala.

But with two doors and two chicks.

"Hey, hot chicks, we are fucked up beyond repair," Tim says.

Lori looks over Tim with her fuck-me-now eyes. She's in some of my psychology classes. Such a big-fuck smile. It's so big, I could just climb in there and taste her for awhile.

Her mouth must taste good.

Sally's big smile tastes good, too. Her hands are soft, so soft and I like her fuck-me-now scent.

The asphalt smells like fucking. It smells like smegma and semen.

"What are you two chicks doing?" Tim asks. "We're going to a party at St. James. Wanna come?"

Sally lets out a porn star laugh. She looks like a cheerleader, her smile is so big and her eyes so bright. They're from the sun, they shine forever.

And such white teeth. Even whiter than Tim's black light special.

"We dropped some good 'cid and we are fucked up beyond all repair," Tim announces.

"We'll give you a ride, get in," Porn-star Sally says.

Sally leans forward and Tim hops in the back. When I get ready to enter the cruise ship, Sally tugs at my arm and I flop into the front seat between her and Lori.

Tim yells and Sally punches him in the face. Lori opens my pants and goes under my shirt, all the time squeezing my stomach. Sally helps her.

I hear John Holmes porn movie music.

"Hey, we're brothers," Tim yells. He's trying to climb over the seat.

Lori pushes him back into the seat. She grabs at me, fondling me as Sally pulls down my jeans.

The driver's side window melts when I look into Lori's eyes. She's got her mouth in a circle and I'm listening to more John Holmes music. The porn music is playing way too fast and sounds more like circus music.

"Hey, we're brothers," Tim yells. His foot hits my shoulder and I hear his belt unbuckle.

Sally punches him in the face.

Hard.

So hard her fist becomes a cream pie and the Keystone Cops chase the Stooges around the car. Curly, Me, and Larry slap each other on the street just beyond the car's hood. Somehow, I'm in the episode where there's a pen in the blender and when Moe takes off the lid, the pen sticks in his head.

I hate the Stooges. Can't watch a whole episode. It's too stupid. And slapstick is pointless.

Sally and Lori exchange porn-star looks and smiles, fluttering their eyes. They moan and lean back, then Sally punches Tim again.

Lori smiles, then reaches over the seat to push Tim back. "What's so funny?" she asks me.

The circus music is louder. Woody Allen floats past wearing his <u>Sleeper</u> costume. It's the big bag filled with air. He's bouncing on the hood and the police are chasing him.

Shit, where's the Orgasmatron?

Lori tickles my ear. "John, what's the matter?" she whispers, her tongue going right into my brain.

Tim throws his leg over the seat.

"Don't you like this?" Sally asks, tasting my cheek as her fingers go into my briefs.

She's in clown make-up. Lori grabs at me, making porn-star faces as Tim throws one of his Nikes on the dash. Without stopping, Sally grabs the severed foot and tosses into the abyss.

I hear Tim's echo.

"Fucking tease," Lori yells as Sally drives away, taking her friend with her.

I taste sex and motor oil as the Impala glides through the intersection and Lori's middle finger makes a ripple in the air above the car roof.

"Wow, your friends are pretty intense, man," Tim says.

He's standing with his pecker in his hand.

He's a mean mother-fucking and he's doing what he can.

"You better get dressed, man," Tim says.

My clogs are gone. Someone wrapped them in blue denim around my feet. My shirt is hanging out, but my pants are gone all the way down to the pavement.

I don't give a damn if I'm naked: he's not getting anything from me.

"Man, those chicks are fucking hot," Tim says.

I try walking, but my feet have been tied by some sort of denim rope.

If I could find a knife, I'd slice the fucker apart. Someone washed them in Sally. My pants smell of her, but my head is all messed up from all this acid trip shit.

"Buddy, pull up your pants," Tim says.

He's all tucked in like his fat mom used to do before he went to school. She made sure his buttons lined up.

Look, I found my pants!

Somebody tied them around my ankles and wrapped up my clogs.

Those bastards. Who did that shit?

I'm getting all tucked in, too, because I have to.

It's a matter of keeping everything in line, and making sure the seams match. When they don't, that's when New York State Troopers wake you and make you wash your clothes after midnight.

That's so messed up.

"C'mon, I found the way to St. James' Apartments," Tim yells as he runs across Mr. Rathbun's yard. I keep an eye on him as I walk three beats to a measure and don't step on any cracks 'cause my mother's back can't break.

Ten guys and four girls play drinking games at the apartment.

This is like the place I cleaned when I lived with Bobby and June, but there's no Seagram's bottle for me to sneak a couple of shots.

The place smells like someone's old panties, but I don't see any underwear on the shag carpet.

"Hey everyone, this is John," Tim announces like he gives a shit.

The jocks look at me. These guys weight-lift. They're football players and these chicks are cheerleaders. The door moves away and I can't taste it, so I run. Tim puts down his pitcher and he chases me, standing in front of the gate.

Thought there was a door here: who put in the gate?

It's so big, but he's got the keys in his hands.

I smell Phil.

"Everybody, John's freakin' out," Tim says.

They stand around me, the cheerleaders and the jocks.

I'm in the center of the circle, a nucleus to this cell.

They turn off the music and Football Player One guy looks sad. Fuck, my hair is longer than the fucking cheerleaders'!

Mine is nicer, too!

I am so fucked!

"John, what's the matter?" Football Player One asks says to the guy who has such long hair that he has absolutely got to be a faggot.

"He's afraid you're gonna hurt him," Tim says. He wears a white suit now and has some sort of halo. I don't remember him wearing that.

I'm hearing that lyric from the Billy Joel song; something about trying to please me. He's okay just the way he is with his fat mother and Porn-Star Sally.

Shit, what if Tim is a doll?

"He's having a bad trip," Tim announces. "We just dropped some acid."

Fucking asshole. Telling Football Player One and Cheerleader One that John Higham is having a bad trip just because I didn't give you what you wanted! What a fucker.

Shit, be cool. These narcs have figured it out, man.

Shit, did Henry tell them about the business? Fuck, that son-of-a-bitch. I'm so fuckin' screwed. Busted at nineteen.

They'll wanna know my source. Okay, it's just some guy I never saw before, but I'm pretty sure I could pick him out if you give me a photo album.

Like Dylan sang, yeah, there's danger near, so open up the door.

Dylan sing that? Shit, I don't remember anything right now, but I better not say anything. Feel my lips be still.

"It's cool. You can stay here," Cheerleader One says. Her face is perfect. Her skin smells so soft and wonderfully clear: I can hear it when she smiles.

"I'm cool," I say. "I'm cool with that."

Football Player One slaps my back in a good Christian way.

He probably sings loudly in church so that God will hear him.

He lifts his pitcher to pour me a glass of beer. The music gets louder and it's Aerosmith.

Aerosmith?

Fuck! Everyone knows that Aerosmith is narc music! Fuck, totally narc music! That's how they freak you out! They play Aerosmith so everyone will know! The next time it goes off, the place will get busted. They're all cops, including Tim! They'll get me really fucked up so I'll have to talk! Seen this shit before, but I can't remember who warned me about it!

Or, what to do.

Got to stay cool.

I walk ten miles down the hallway on the shag carpet that is so warm that the fibers reach through my clogs and massage my toes. I find the bathroom.

I know there's got to be a trap door somewhere in this castle.

Or whiskey.

I go through the big door that makes the bathroom airtight. I take out a joint and light up, then sit on the toilet, rolling one joint after another.

There's some fucker in an alternative universe reflected in the mirror on the back of the door, matching me breath for breath.

Breath in..., breath out...

No, shit, it's some sort of truth mirror or some shit like that. It's my past present future self. He agrees with me completely, saying things right when I do. He tells me that I should write down all this shit, but if the cops find my body, they'll just say it's another drug-related death.

I think someone's screwing with him too, so we have a lot of shit in common until Football Player One rattles the building by punching the door so hard.

I can't find the fucking seat belt on the toilet, so the re-entry is rough. I can't wedge myself around the lip of the toilet and the shower curtain is too heavy to move. I'm so fucked and Football Player One is breaking through the door.

I look at the back of the door. My dark haired friend says, "Just be cool and open the door."

Whoa, he is me.

I am strong.

I am safe.

I am smart.

I know how to survive.

I open the door.

"Young man, are you smoking pot?" Football Player One, the Number One Narc asks.

He deserves to wear polyester pants: his jeans must be making him break out. And get this: he's wearing Nikes: That's fucking scary.

"Yes, sir, I am."

Busted. I can't follow the smoke up the vent because the fan blades will chop me apart and send my blood spewing all over the place. Busted isn't so bad compared to being chopped to death in an exhaust fan.

"Can I have some?"

"What? Yeah, man. Can you stand it?"

"Fuckin' yeah, man!"

He comes in and towels the door. I nod at my friend in the window mirror to my soul just as Football Player One uses his superhuman strength to pull back the curtain and free the keg sitting in an ice wrap.

God, that's all I have to do; stay cool. Been fucked with, fucked over, fucked up, but I keep on truckin' just like the Dead say in that song.

"Have some," Football Player One says, handing me the pitcher. I exchange my joint for the pitcher.

Shit, beer tastes fuckin' great!

It's cool because the bathroom pushes me out into the empty apartment. For some reason, everyone kicked ass into the toilet, so no one guards the door.

What happened to the gate?

It didn't matter much because the room made the town dark. Not only that, somehow it became a model railroad layout.

Bye, Tim. Maybe one of those jocks will give you what you so desperately need.

Someone had changed things in Mansfield while I was in the bathroom. They took away the sun and wrapped the place in a darkness that permeated every crevice.

I feel... so safe.

The streetlights are dim, the sky smells dark, and the cars whisper. Not only that, but white lights flash through the scene.

It's like a movie. A good movie, an atmospheric movie.

The pneumatic sidewalks mess up my legs, but only when I remember to walk.

It's no big thing, this trippin' shit. Okay, things mess up when I think about it, so why think?

Like the sidewalk; when it's okay I look at it, but when I think about it, it melts and flows like a smooth concrete river.

Let the sidewalk flow! It's not hasslin' me. Hell, I flow right along with the cement into the model railroad layout that is now Mansfield.

It's the people thing: they smell so life-like and move so smoothly. I've never seen this on any layout, not even Butchie's.

I walk down to the abandoned Erie station and wait for the Lionel train.

This acid isn't that much different from how my brain usually works.

These tracks are disconnected, but maybe a giant hand will come down and put me in the boxcar so I can be a hobo.

Or some crazy shit like that.

Pinecrest Dorm

I can hear them in the hallway and see their parents' cars in the street. They are dorm ants carrying their shit from their hives through the snow squall to their cars. I watch them prepare for winter break as I peek through the nearly-closed blinds.

They're all excited about Christmas.

My room is filled with smoke. I scored some opium and felt like celebrating the end of the semester, so Deb and Eve and Pam and I are on my bed smoking it in a hash pipe.

Graveyard left. He's moving into a room off-campus in the Hill House. He's doing his internship. His side of the room is empty and his bed is stripped to its state-issue grey mattress.

The coeds and I are on my bed. The four of us moved it right in front of the window, then we took off our shoes and socks.

We are sitting on the bed, holding each other and watching the snow fall. The wind whips it around the canyon that is between the buildings. The western hill is obscured by the white sky.

The squall is beautiful in its ferocity.

My new footlocker is near the door. I packed everything I own into it. Everyone thinks I'm going to Hawaii for the break to visit with Maria: she said I could.

Pam hugs me as I pass around the pipe.

Dorm ants shuffle around outside as they move their shit in cardboard boxes and milk crates.

We don't talk. Deb gives me a hug as she hands me the pipe. We hold each other as we watch the snow and the dorm ants.

"My parents are coming later," Deb says after I reload the pipe with a ball of the brown goo.

"Only my dad's coming," Pam says. She holds me close for what feels like an hour.

"I'll leave after the snow stops," Eve says. "John, you're going to Hawaii. Shit, that is so cool. I'll miss you."

She hugs me, too. It lasts forever.

Everything is lasting forever inside here where it's safe and warm.

The pipe disappears in a large hug, the warm embraces and sweet tastes of their voices and fingertips keeping me warm and safe while the squall hides Mansfield. They are a living blanket and I want them all to stay tightly wrapped around me, swaddling me with their words and their bodies.

I don't want sex. I just want to be held tightly… forever, please. I'm so safe right now. I never felt this safe before…

I can't talk for a long time, instead inhaling their scents and their breaths. I hear their arms holding me and the smell of their Clairol shampoo.

"I'll miss you guys."

I love you; all of you. I feel like in that song where Jackson Browne sings about staying a little bit longer.

I hand the pipe to Eve. She takes it and inhales steadily, taking off her glasses. Her face relaxes and she smiles. Deb is next. She purses her lips and gently takes in the air. She could be smiling; I don't know.

Everything is cool: the details don't matter when love is present.

I love you.

I love all you right now.
Details? Screw the details.
My whole life is a mess, but I'm fine right now.

No need to tell them that I didn't buy a ticket to Hawaii or anywhere and that I'm actually planning to disappear forever because I have no one and have nowhere to go.

Nowhere 'cause my life belongs to me and I'm no one.

It's easier to say nothing and pretend to be going to Hawaii to see Maria.

Maria will be waiting for my call, but I don't have any flight information. After awhile, she'll forget and go back to her life.

And everything will be good because I'll be gone. I will have disappeared. It will be good to disappear.

That's a relief.

We smoke for a million years, the squall continuing to rage and the sounds of the dorm hall dropping off until we can hear only each other breathing, inhaling, and resting. I want to meditate with them, but instead I load the pipe again and pass it around. We lie across each other as we lean against the window like kids waiting for our dad to come home as we watch the snow.

"There's my parents," Deb finally says. The four of us hug. I smell her Coty on her skin. She stretches and inhales deeply, like waking from a deep sleep.

These women are even more beautiful now, the world not polluting the beauty of their souls as they flow through all they touch. They are so alive at this new wakefulness. Cleansed, refreshed and loved. Snow hides away the world's dirt.

I want their embraces forever. I need them so much right now.

"Don't leave," Deb whispers. She holds me tightly. The others take her lead and wrap me so tightly I can't move.

Maybe I should tell them about disappearing. Maybe I should tell them that I haven't been to classes since I went into business.

Hell, I can't tell them anything: they'll look at me that way and want to rescue me.

420

"I love you," I say as they slip on their boots and coats, then leave.

Suddenly, I am alone in the room, left with the scent of their skin on my clothes as the storm continues outside. I want to hold onto their scents and the safe world that their collective presence gives me: it's better than the one waiting outside my door.

I open my notebook.

The Lonely One is ready to disappear. He is tired of the hoaxes that others call life. The dorm ant nest is empty: it's time for him to take his few belongings and act as though he has a life beyond its walls.

His life beyond these walls is... death.

He likes disappearing, going away without anyone knowing what's really going on.

In his life, everyone else had their chance to disappear. It's his turn.

I slide my bed back along the wall, throw on my backpack, and lift the trunk. It's too heavy, so when I enter the hall, I throw most of my textbooks into the garbage can. I don't need them.

School doesn't matter anymore.

I don't need it where I'm going.

It's getting dark. The hallway is cluttered with piles of student junk left near the brown steel refuse containers. Dorm furniture borrowed from the lounge and now returned also litters the hall. Everyone has left, though the sound of a radio leaks from a nearby door.

The R.A., Pete, sticks his head out of his door. Even when I'm not stoned, he looks weird. His eyes fill the lenses of his glasses.

Aw, fuck that, he's someone's son. At least he has a life to go back to when today is over. That's more than what I've got right now. Hell, that's more than I've ever had. Tonight, he'll probably be asleep in the bedroom he grew up in: that's cool.

"John, I gotta inspect your room before you go," he yells. His whiny, nasal voice echoes in the empty building.

"It's not important."

"No, you have to be there during the inspection. If there's any damage, you have to pay."

"Send me the bill, I'll be in Hawaii."

"But you have to sign off."

He watches me throw my Geography and Spanish books in the trash. I stopped looking at them about a month ago. I was too busy making money with Henry.

I take a pack of razor blades and put them in my backpack.

"Pete, just sign it for me. I trust you."

I walk toward the door at the end of the hall, pulling at my parka. The exit seems too far away and the trunk is still too heavy. I open it and sort through my rubbish, looking for more stuff to jettison.

It's like I'm a boat making my way through choppy waters: I have to lighten my load. There's nothing left in the trunk but my writing notebooks and psych textbooks.

I take a few of my notebooks and slam shut the footlocker, leaving it in the middle of the hall as I walk closer to the door with my backpack positioned on my back.

Pete emerges from his room. "John, c'mon, this will only take a few minutes."

I am dying a few minutes at a time.

Pete carries a clipboard and a set of keys.

"I left my keys on the top of the dresser."

Henry wants me to keep in touch with him after I get to Hawaii. He'll be pissed when he can't find me, but he'll get to keep the money. That should make him feel better.

"C'mon, John, get in here," the R.A. yells. "And, don't leave that damned trunk in the middle of my floor."

Somehow, I'm going back to the room and sliding the footlocker on the floor. It's too big. The lid slams hard and I lock it. I position my backpack and move to the fire door at the end of the hall. I just want to disappear.

"Higham, get your shit off my floor," Pete yells.

"I don't need it now," I yell back.

Pete runs down the hall and gets in my face. With his big glasses, he looks like Mr. Peabody from *Rocky and Bullwinkle*.

"You are not leaving your fucking stuff here. I'm not throwing away your shit."

422

He grabs my hand and pulls me back to the trunk. The doorway seems farther away.

"I'm gonna miss my bus."

"Yeah, so you better get your butt in gear and inspect this room with me."

I'm back in the room: it's so depressing. There's no sign of my girls and our intimacy.

So empty. So empty that it makes me want to cry. All the love that was once here is gone. Faded into oblivion. It makes me want to disappear even more because it's really who I am right now.

Love is so fragile, evaporating in a moment.

Instead of going, I'm listening to Pete as he talks to himself about the blinds, the closet doors, the dressers, the desks, the mirrors, the bed frames, the mattresses, and the ceiling tiles.

There's not much to it anymore. If it's ten by ten, that's large. The dressers are off to one side. Pete takes my mattress and props it on one edge against the wall, exposing the steel bed frame. The desks are bare and the dressers have been pushed off to one side. Pete opens the closets and checks the door tracks to make sure they're working.

"Excited about Hawaii?"

"Yeah."

"Where you goin'?"

"Hilo. My sister lives there."

"That's neat," he says. "Hey, sorry I got pissed at you. You're the last guy left on the floor. When you're done, I can go home."

"That's cool. I'm sorry, man. Wasn't thinking."

I sign Pete's sheet. He walks back out to the hall.

"Goodbye, Pete." I say.

"Merry Christmas, John," he says.

"Yeah, same to you."

I grab the trunk. It's lighter now, but still heavy as I swing open the metal fire door at the end of the hallway. The cold air feels good in my lungs as I make way down the hill past the vacant campus.

The dorm ants are gone.

Soon, I will be.

Bucking Fuss

Mansfield is quiet now. The thing about a college town is
that it dies when school is out. I walk through the diminishing
squall and contemplate Pam, Deb, and Eve. I wonder about their
lives and who they are now in the cars with their parents.

And, Felicia and Angel.

*I miss those two. Fuck, I love them. Should've invited
them to join us.*

I have to leave even though I have nowhere to go.

I once told stories to myself for comfort.

*I've told them to everybody and no one caught me. I like
telling those kind because it's easier than telling the truth. People
hear the truth and all they want to do is help out.*

And they get that look in their eyes.

Fuck, I hate that look.

*Like I'm nothing just because I have nowhere to go and no
one to be with. Like I don't have a life, just my stories.*

My stories are my life.

*I'd rather tell those stories than see that look. Hell, I've
learned to tell my stories before they ask: I've gotten that good at
creating a world they can believe in for me so I can do what I
want without their interference.*

I tell so many kinds of stories.

At the same bus stop downtown where Faith went on her
first bucking fuss three years ago, the nice driver loads my trunk
in the storage area and smiles when he takes my ticket.

*Bobby and June are probably packing for a trip to Rhode
Island.*

424

I climb on.

The bus is packed, but I find two empty seats.

The squall stops and the sun breaks through the clouds. The color brown emerges like a mold from beneath the white-coated landscape as the bus moves away from Mansfield's only traffic light. I watch the college and that part of my life remain on the hill as the packed Trailways coach moves south.

I might go to Philadelphia and call Faith and Dave. It depends how I feel in Harrisburg. I should have thrown away the trunk.

I am listening to people talking, being extra nice to each other because Christmas is coming. They all have family and lives. And, nice things to say to each other. I have an opium buzz and cool memories.

Sometimes, I miss people so much.

I open my notebook.

People have their own worlds. I am just peeking in at their lives. I am preparing to disappear as they prepare to visit their families and eat their turkey dinners. I have my words: these will accompany me into oblivion. They are the crumbs that I leave behind. Words and paper are my companions. They are always there, even when no one is.

Even when I keep everyone away...

The snow on the highway becomes black slush as the Penn Dot trucks dump cinders. My window gets filthy fast. I want it to snow so hard that every Penn Dot truck will have to stop.

I smell it again. It's that putrid rotting smell I started having after Phil finished with me. Everyone can smell it, I'm sure. Thank God someone's smoking, or everyone would be sick. They shouldn't have to be exposed to my stench.

I keep writing as the bus makes its way south from Williamsport.

The highway takes me away from life, from me. I hear people talking and joking. Their words and joy are their language. They are happy. I'll allow myself to get a contact high from their happiness. That's cool.

The snowpack has thinned and more patches of brown poke through along the Susquehanna River outside of Selinsgrove.

Randy lives here. I could drop in for a day, tell him to take care of the footlocker, then get on another bus.

Magic bus.

Magic Bucking Fuss. Where people put up with each other because it's all temporary. Temporary merry. A very temporary and Merry Christmas.

Everyone is temporary in life...

More miles pass as the landscape becomes more brown and gray.

This is how I'm going to disappear. I'm going to the Harrisburg bus station. I'll check my locker and throw away the key. Then, I'll go into the bathroom and pick out a stall at the end. There, I'll kneel by the toilet, slash my wrists, and allow myself to drain into the toilet.

Don't know why I didn't think of that earlier. I have razor blades in my backpack.

It's so much better to have a plan to disappear. Any plan. Just hoping to disappear without working on it is so stupid. It's better to have a plan to go along with the goal.

Yes, I'm planning on slashing my wrists in the Harrisburg bus station. I'll go into the bathroom, drag all my shit into a nice stall, and cut away. I'll slice myself from the wrist to the elbow and back again. I like the part about draining into the toilet: that is going to be so symbolic!

Will anyone understand that symbolism?

By the time the bus reaches Harrisburg, it's dark. The bus station is at the Pennsylvania Railroad station. It's an old building built God knows how many years ago. The columns are stained from the floor to about six feet high.

Stained from people touching them.

People messed them up with their little fingers and dirty hands. People always need to touch things. They fuck everything up by touching it.

My trunk is at my feet; it's too heavy. There are bunches of families and students traveling.

Everyone is in such a damned good mood.

A Salvation Army Man stands outside, ringing his bell and thanking all the assholes who can give only money.

426

People don't understand that suicide is giving away life. It's the most selfless act. Disappearing is the best anyone can do.

I write down all this stuff because there is no one to tell it to and if I don't write it down it will take over my head.

The trunk is too big to check and I don't want to leave it here or with the nice lady sitting with the well-behaved girl next to me on the bench.

Nice lady and well-behaved girl sit on the bench, ignoring Trunk Boy who was preparing to disappear.

She looks like the type who'll get all concerned when I don't come back for it.

I once wrote a poem about the Harrisburg station, but I can't find it in my notebook. June read it and called it interesting. Really, it was adolescent poignant trash. Really not the least bit interesting.

The Amtrak schedule says that there's one last train to Philly tonight. What the fuck, I can disappear easier there. It's at ten or some shit like that. I approach the ticket booth and buy my ticket from a nice lady.

"Have a merry Christmas," she says.

"And to you."

The trunk is heavy. The metal reinforced corners slam on the steps as I slowly go down from the train shed to the platform. The air smells dirty as a train pulls into the station.

It's a Metroliner. Suburban types are in the car, reading their *Philly Inquirers* from the morning.

Not worn like Mom's. I don't see her bed anywhere. 'Sides, I'm not in the mood to tuck her in and say, "Nighty-night."

Nighty-night!

Wish I could be tucked in again like that. I miss everyone.

We're all too tired, though I'm thinking I want to talk to someone, anyone about anything.

I need to hear my voice to keep me awake, to make me stop me from harming me. I don't feel like I don't have any control, like I'm looking for death to happen to me. My stories can't keep me alive or safe; they can only keep people away.

I don't want to die right now. I just want to be dead.

It's really too late.

I'm too far away from anything anymore.
I'm too far away from everyone.
I just want death to come and take me away from all this.

I'm very tired and when the train moves so fast, it scares me. My ass burns and stinks like Phil, but I don't care too much about that because soon that scent will disappear, too.

I'm so tired. So fucking tired of living, so fucking tired of everything but writing.

I look out the window and see big stretches of farms with kerosene lights. The Amish live there, beyond the railroad track and highways. They run their cute little horse-drawn coaches on the paved streets and go back home after every barn-raising.

Big farms with Amish lights should burn away Phil's stench.

This train has to have a toilet. I could be sliced open before Paoli and they would have to hurry their asses at Broad Street if they found me. The conductor would notice the goddamned trunk and recall the hippie in the purple parka and ratty French jeans.

Maybe I could open the vestibule and throw myself toward the Amish.

No, Faith and Dave will come and get me. I'll call Maria and tell her, "I'm sorry but it didn't work out."

She'll understand.

Broad Street Station

"Can't you catch a train or something?" Faith's voice asks through the phone and into my ear. "Or, stay somewhere in Philly and take a bus to Reading?"

I want to tell her how much I miss Deb and Pam and Eve. And, how much I miss Felicia and Angel, how much I miss her and Maria and Mark and Warren and Rose and Mom and Dad.

I just want to be okay right now.

I want to tell her how hungry my skin is for the razor. How hungry my mind is for quiet. That I can't take much more of this drifting, this slow dying. I'm trying really hard not to disappear. I'm trying real hard to live right now.

428

"I'm workin' in the mornin'. So is Dave," she says. "What the hell are you doin' callin' me just after I went to bed? Why don't you stay at a Motel 6 or somethin'?"

"Okay," I say. "I'll call some friends in Elmira," I say.

"Elmira? Why the hell are you goin' to Elmira?"

"Well, you weren't really planning to have me visit."

"Thought you were going to Hawaii."

"Didn't work out. I had to pay some bills."

"Well..., Merry Christmas."

"You too."

And the phone call is over.

What am I doing?

This place scares me. There are signs warning me not to get into unmarked cabs and the speaker is too loud.

A bucking fuss to Elmira. I'll go there. I don't really want to stop travelling 'cause I'll just disappear. As long as I keep moving, keep working toward a destination, I'll keep myself from disappearing. Movement equals life.

Tom Sawyer Motor Inn

It's a nice room. I put my footlocker on the floor near the TV and wash my clothes in the bathtub. I run down the hall for ice, and use the sani-liners to shine my clogs.

I sit naked on the bed with for my notebook. It's been a hell of a night: I travelled in a giant loop from Mansfield to Harrisburg to Philadelphia to Elmira. No one who cares about me knows where I am, though they all think they do.

I like that.

The coolest thing about disappearing is just dropping out of sight, falling away into the world.

In less than six hours, I'll be officially missing if anyone would be searching for me.

Maria might. She'll call the airlines and learn that I never made a reservation. I don't want to call her 'cause she'll confront my bullshit.

It's cool: she'll call Faith who will tell her that I'm in Elmira.

I open my notebook and find a poem.

More Reflections In A Harrisburg Station

On the worn benches
The blood of the weary vibrates.
Gathered against columns,
Today's paper are readied
For tomorrow's trash.

An occasional rumble alerts
Policemen hiding from the cold.
Without a shave the beggar
Asks for kindness,
Meets with disgust and hate
But still manages to get another dime.

Past battered doors
And crumbling ceilings,
I ventured,
Searching for anyone, anything
To take me somewhere else.

A loudspeaker blared,
Startling police and beggar.
Soldier boys and girls
Sat at ease while I
Said goodbye to the lockers,
And made Harrisburg fade
Through the train's windows.

My past day's journey is all there in my mind's eye as I read it; the face of the conductor, the atmosphere of the bus, the fingermarks in Harrisburg, and the speed of the Metroliner.

Writing is better than the rest of my life; these pages can never disappoint the way that people do, the way that sex does, the ways that drugs do, and the ways that I do.

People are a disappointment. They die, go crazy, have shell-shock, are mean for their own reasons, and are hateful.

430

I am a disappointment because I should've killed myself tonight and I didn't. Now, my life is totally fucked up

In a few days, June will discover that I blew off all my finals. I don't have to deal with her right now. I'm alone with my words. I won't let anyone disturb us.

It's great to be alone, totally alone. I wish I could be this way forever.

North Elmira

The nicest thing about my rented room is my backpack. Soon, it will smell of mildew and mold like everything else does in this building.

I've been here for two days, having moved out of the Motor Inn. The landlord of this hellhole knows Bobby—had him for class—but still made me pay a security deposit.

There's a man's voice beating the shit out of a woman on the other side of the wall. Occasionally, he punches the wall or slams her body against it; I can't be sure which sort of violence he's practicing.

It's okay that the steps outside my door creak when someone goes past. I don't want to stay asleep even though I've locked the padlock inside my door.

In the afternoons, I sit in my briefs and smoke a joint. Sometimes, I beat off if I can find something worth thinking about. Most of the time, I sit on the smelly mattress that is called my bed and stare at the rusted refrigerator in the corner, waiting for the compressor to kick off.

The radiator has no knob. The heat makes the window fog over. The man's voice beats the woman at night, so everyone in the building gets just a few hours of sleep.

In the mornings, I wake early and walk all over town, putting in—and checking on—my job applications. It's tough to get work.

St. James' Apartments

On Christmas Eve, Santa chases me from the St. James'
Apartment Building, the bastard waking me when he turns on the
storage area light in the basement. I make myself still as his
singing of *White Christmas* grows louder and his boots hit heavy
against the concrete among the rows of plywood closets.

"Get outta here, you son-of-a-bitch," he yells when he sees
me reclining on my backpack.

"Just passin' through, man," I whisper while grabbing my
pack, parka, and boots. In his anger, he punches the walls.

"Fuckin' bum, how'd you like to spend Christmas in jail?"

He chases me up the narrow steps, his red hat falling to the
dirty linoleum. He grabs my hair and slams me through the steel
door into the night. When I fall, the pack lands hard beneath me
though it keeps me from getting wet in the snow.

I run across the courtyard while Santa stands at the door.

"You fuckin' bum," he yells.

"Fuckin' mutt," a man yelled through the wall that
morning. I covered my ears and pressed my face hard against the
stained mattress of my room as a puppy whimpered and a woman
screamed over the muffled sound of a blaring TV. Outside the
window, a cloudy sky hung over North Elmira. I folded my jeans,
shirts and briefs, placing three of each in the pack.

It's all the clothing I have left.

I wore a pair of briefs and tied a T-shirt around my left
arm. It made the blood vessels in my arm bulge out.

"Fuckin' mutt." A loud thud shook the room and the

woman's shrieking faded. I took my razor blade and practiced sliding it along my bulging vein from my elbow to my wrist.

"Can't have a puppy in the city, you stupid bitch!" the man yelled.

The woman sobbed.

I practiced a few more times, then pushed a corner of the blade into the dirty wallpaper.

"Should've taken him to the fuckin' 'SPCA," I whispered.

The woman sobbed as I spread my last dollop of peanut butter against a pair of crusts and made a sandwich. My arm ached, so I loosened the T-shirt. I winced as blood raced to my fingertips. I heard another man talking in a low voice outside my room as he went into the toilet. I waited until he turned on the shower before I dressed, grabbed my pack, and went to Reefer's.

I lift the pack as the snow fills the night. In Mansfield, Christmas trees illuminate empty living rooms in the apartment buildings. The cold drives Santa back inside. At the first house beyond the complex, I allow myself to inhale. As I do, I feel my coat's sweat and my boots' dampness. The town is still as I trudge uphill on Academy Street past the college.

Reefer opened the door as I moved along his walk. He held a Rum and Coke in one hand, a cigarette in his other. "What are you doin', Bud?"

"Takin' a walk."

"What's with the pack?" He chugged his drink. "Cretin, I need a refill."

Cretin carried a bottle of Bacardi. He's a regular guy with a really big head; that's why Reefer called him Cretin.

"Can always crash here," Reefer said, "but we're gonna drop some 'cid and we don't have any for ya'. Got some good weed we can share with ya'."

"Naw, not in the mood to party—"

"That's cool. Well, enjoy your walk."

A block later, I found a cab. It took me a mile to Southport, dropping me at the Pizza Hut parking lot.

"Where ya' goin'?" its driver asked.

"Mansfield."

"Shit, that's thirty miles away. You hitchin'?"

People don't understand hitching: they think it's about standing and waiting. Hell, that's not asking for a lift, that's expecting one. Hitching is constant movement, each step proclaiming, "Fuck you, I'll get there without you. Help if you want."

It took me ten hours to walk Route 549's thirty-one miles. I followed the road from Southport to the state line, then southward past Mosherville and Job's Corners. The first snowflakes fell when I passed that village, and it got dark just before I reached Matt Butcher's farm outside of Roseville. On the other side of that village, a man in his pickup paced me.

"Son, where ya' goin' in this storm?"

"Mansfield."

"That's fifteen miles down the road."

"Yeah, I know."

"Come on', lemme give ya' a ride."

"Naw, but thanks." I said, walking into the night.

He followed me for a bit, yelling. I ignored him and he went away. I couldn't take his ride: he'd ask what the hell was some kid doin' walkin' alone on Christmas Eve.

Don't want to tell myself that truth all over again.

Or worse, I'd sleep on his sofa in his trailer and watch his kids tear through presents in the morning.

After Roseville, the pack became heavy. Just the other side of Hogback Hill, my sweat broke through the parka. When I stopped to dry heave the first time, I saw a pine tree on someone's lawn decorated with lights. It looked pretty as the wind kicked snow off the branches.

In the night that is now Mansfield, I'm walking on the deserted streets. Hitching, like walking when I'm this tired, takes concentration. I remember what Al taught me in Cedarcrest Dorm and use breath in, breath out to build my pace. I steadily walk as I pass June's office. It, like the other college buildings, is dark except for glowing exit signs that I can see through the windows.

Finding sanctuary will be easy. I'll just throw my pack through Forrest's store window.

That'll land me in the warm backseat of Jim Pratt's cruiser. I'll punch him once or twice just to make sure he wakes Eleanor. The magistrate will ask after my guardians, then arraign me after I spit on her. I'll sit in county lock-up until after New Year, then Rob and Sue would spring me.

No, it won't work that way.

Jim'll talk to me in the cruiser, answering questions I couldn't ask myself as he stares at me in the rearview mirror.

Fuck me for abandoning the razor.

When I reached Mansfield, I went to Rob's house. I met him through Reefer, but he was much cooler. He lived with Sandy. They were both so easygoing, they wouldn't mind if I hang with them for a while. Until I decided what I wanted to do. Last winter, when I told Rob about being kicked out by Bobby and June, he said I could crash at his place.

"Anytime, Dude, anytime."

Tonight, Rob's house was dark. And quiet. I went onto the porch and knocked on the door.

"Everyone, Merry Happy - - We're partying in California," a cardboard sign read. I turned the knob and realized he used the deadbolt.

For a long while, I considered breaking the glass or sleeping on the porch, but instead trudged along Academy Street to the St. James' Apartments. I slipped into the basement around midnight.

In the morning, I'd walk back to Elmira.

Santa changed that. Because of the bastard, I figured I'd be hearing a man beating a woman as I rehearsed with my razor and T-shirt.

Fuck me for thinking otherwise.

On Academy Street near Almuni Hall, I hear a few drunken voices playing. Snowballs break apart on the snow-covered street. I ignore them, building my pace.

Breath in, breath out.

"Higham, is that you?"

I look up from the street and see Hufnagel. He stands in his jeans and sweater, a beer in his hand. "Want a sip?"

I take it.

"Where ya' goin'?"

"Walkin' back to Elmira."

A couple girls throw snowballs at him. He swears, reclaims his beer long enough for a swig, then returns fire toward a tree. Music leaks out of the front doorway when Lorraine comes out onto her porch.

Lorraine. Jill lives with her. She's cool. She was majoring in Special Ed. Partied a little bit.

"Who's that?" Lorraine asks.

Hufnagel hands me his beer. "It's Higham. We took Chemistry together in 11ᵗʰ grade. He's walking to Elmira."

He made it sound fucking stupid.

I move along the street toward Route Six. In another forty minutes, I'd be back on 549. Daylight will arrive just this side of Job's Corners, and I'll be back to my room before noon. I'll disappear just as people are sitting down to Christmas dinner.

"Catch ya' later," I say.

Hufnagel grabs my arm and leads me onto the porch.

"I'll take you back first thing in the morning," Lorraine says. "How'd you get here?"

"Like I said, he walked from Elmira," Hufnagel says as he guides me through the door. The heat of the house burns my face and my clothes feel moist. The party becomes still as the combination of booze, music, and the late hour makes everyone drowsy. The roomful of strangers nod at me and drink their beer.

"Higham walked from Elmira," Hufnagel announces, lifting his beer.

Some of the guys stagger over, pat my shoulder or smile, then half-collapse onto the furniture. I allow Lorraine to remove my pack and parka.

She whispers, "Why'd you do that?"

"Had to. Had to give myself a little present."

After the party evaporates, Lorraine dries my clothes in her dryer. I sleep in Jill's bed; she went home downstate for the break.

My legs ache all night. None of that mattered because Lorraine and her mother made me remember everything when we ate dinner later that day.

436

1979

U.S. Route 15

I see headlights in swirling snow across the Tioga River Valley just north of Mansfield even before I hear the trucks' diesel engines. Automatically, I turn to face traffic. My arm goes up and my thumb goes out as my broken hiking boots make a trail on the highway's snow and cinder-covered shoulder. The plastic bread wrappers that line the boots and insulate my feet crinkle as the semis roar past: those vehicles spray me with a curtain of cinders and ice, the mixture pelting my parka.

The miles pass slowly.

The shoulder ain't the highway, but it's as close as I can get right now. The highway is for cars. It's for going places. The shoulder is for breakdowns, for hitchhikers, and for emergency stopping. It's for all the people who were on the highway, who want to be on the highway, but who can't handle the cars and the moving.

Shouldn't have sold my van. I could have made a few bucks by using it as a taxi and I'd have another tank of gas. Hell, I could've forged the insurance certificate. I'm so fucking stupid.

Earlier today, I hitched down State Route 549: that's how I got from North Elmira to Mansfield. A religious old man picked me up near the state line. He drove a Buick.

"You believe in Jesus?" he asked as soon as I got in and closed the door. The car smelled of clean old man. You know, the sort of scent that comes when a man takes care of things. Too, the car was so clean that even before I sat down on the velour seat, I made sure that I had tapped my boots against the rocker panel to knock off any snow. The highway's shoulders were covered with white snow. The cinder trucks hadn't been out yet.

"Yes, sir," I do. Never mind that I told another story.

To hitch, I have to tell stories. I have to be whoever the driver needs me to be to feel safe about stopping to get me. I have to say and be anyone that makes him feel safe, so fucking safe, that he will let me stay in the car. That's what hitching is about: getting in the car and riding as far as I can. The car is more than transportation: it's protection from the road's world, safety from the crazy fuckers who are ready to pounce on me at any time. The fuckers who see me as an easy target, the fuckers who think it's funny to almost hit me, who honk at me, who throw shit at me, who pretend to slow down before speeding up at the last moment then look in their rearview mirrors for my reaction. I just keep walking, planning possible escape routes just in case they want to fuck with me.

The old man didn't fuck with me. In fact, he let me out at the end of his driveway outside of Job's Corner. There isn't much to that village, just a few houses lining the series of reverse curves sandwiched between the two signs that mark it.

Most of the time, I get let out in the middle of nowhere.

Just as the hitcher fears every driver, the opposite is also true: the drivers never really let me know anything about them. They never let me off at their homes or their jobs because I suspect they fear that I'll target them for a future crime that may not be any more involved than expecting another ride. A ride is a ride: nothing more. There is no further obligation between the driver and the rider.

The religious old man lived in an old wooden house with a big porch.

"Where you headed?" he asked.

"Mansfield. To see my girlfriend on campus," I said. "She's expecting me."

It's always good to state a simple destination that must include an intimate relationship. Gina isn't my girlfriend. Sure, we partied, but we're not that close. I'm going to see her, but that's only because I had to see someone. I had to be held 'cause I was feeling like shit and was obsessed with using my razor blade to rip open my arm.

Didn't tell the old man that.

Saying that I had a person—a girlfriend— waiting made me sound human, loved and expected. Human, loved and expected people aren't looking to kill old religious men and leave their bodies in a ditch along State Route 549. They're also going to be missed if somebody thinks about fucking with them.

He smiled, but still looked afraid.

"I believe in Jesus. Thank Him every time I get a ride," I said. I lied. I figured that telling him that I believed in Jesus just like him was the least I could do to thank him for giving me a safe and warm ride.

"God bless you," he said before I latched his car door and watched him drive away. I walked about a half mile before a *Star Gazette* newspaper van stopped and gave me a ride all the way into Mansfield.

I reached town as the sun set. I walked toward Gina's dorm: she was working with the basketball team, so she moved onto campus two weeks early before the semester started.

Slowly, the miles pass as I make my way north away from Mansfield. Some asshole drivers swerve toward me, trying to scare me as they lean on their horns: those fuckers just want me to jump so that they can get their jollies: fuck them. Most, however, shoot into the opposite lane when their lights fall into my face and my extended thumb hand.

I am walking naked tonight, sans sign.

Hitching requires a sign: it gives the driver the false impression that the hitcher knows where he's going. A destination makes everything safe because people think a life awaits the hitcher. When a life awaits, no one thinks that the hitcher is a threat. What no one realizes, however, is that for this hitcher, my life is only a threat to me to the point that tonight the road is my life: it is my destination, my sanctuary.

I am safest out here. The road keeps me away from my thoughts, my memories, and my blade. It keeps me alive, scared shitless, thinking about some destination, some elusive future paradise that is always so disappointing.

This adventure of the road keeps my mind from thinking about dying. It keeps me from thinking about disappearing. Out here, I am safe because I can't do anything to myself that the solitude of sitting in my room listening to the incessant roar of my own desperation insists that I do immediately.

It's terrible when a string of traffic kicks past and sends snow, cinders and road shit all over me. No one's going to stop, but I can't afford to turn my back on the traffic. Not on a Saturday night; it's too easy to be clipped by a car and left for dead.

I walk backward for miles, until I am on the hillside north of town, looking down as the snow becomes steady and the shoulder turns to grey slush.

After arriving on campus, I walked past Memorial Hall, seeing basketball players shooting pool and the security guard flirting with the student assistant at the desk. The campus, still on Christmas break, was generally deserted except for the teams. I passed Lorraine's house without stopping.

It would be better if she had a party going on. That way I could sip a beer, find a corner to sit in, and watch everyone having a good time.

I really didn't want to go to Gina's, but I had to go somewhere. It would be dark in an hour and I wanted to be held.

Wanted to be touched.

I wasn't hungry, at least not for food. Days of being alone with myself stripped away that sort of appetite. Sure, I made myself eat the peanut butter and butter sandwiches and drink the milk I had bought from Byrne Dairy, but my eating had stopped depending upon appetite when I left Mansfield for Hawaii almost a month ago.

Hawaii. That whole idea felt cool.

Telling people about it and watching their faces light up with all their contrived Hawaii images and shit was worth it.

I like telling those stories and watching people get into them.

A Chevelle pulls up in the dark, slowing down on the shoulder. When the passenger door opens, I see them wearing dresses and nice jeans and sitting boy-girl. Stewart is driving.

"Where ya' goin'?" Stewart asks.

"Corning."

"Get in. We're goin' as far as Green Shingles."

In high school, Stewart once pushed another kid against the lockers and gave him a bloody nose. Taller and bigger than most of the teachers, he drove a hot-rod Chevelle when he was in 11th grade. That was two years ago, but he still has the car.

I found Gina's room in Maple Dorm by listening for Heart. When I knocked, she opened the door, kissed me and grabbed at me.

It was all wrong.

I just wanted to be held, to sit on her bed, fall asleep in her arms and just feel safe.

It was a better alternative to disappearing.

Instead, Gina closed her door and loosened her gauze shirt.

"Man, can't we just... sit and listen to music together?" I asked.

Instead of cuddling, her fingers found her buttonholes as she hurriedly dressed.

"Keep your *fucking* parka on," she yelled, opening the door and pushing me into the hallway.

"Please—"

The door's slam echoed in the empty dorm just before she blasted *Dog and Butterfly*. I didn't bother knocking a second time.

The Chevelle smells of Old Spice and Charlie. It's a party night. I sit in the backseat. The car remains quiet for most of the ride, the Chevelle's ass-end occasionally swinging out toward the double yellow line as Stewart and his friends make their way to Green Shingles' Bar just across the New York border in Lindley. The bar usually sees plenty of kids who want to drink before they're twenty-one. In New York, anyone can buy beer once they turn eighteen. Not like stupid Pennsy, where you have to be twenty-one and prove it.

Gina, shit.

Just wanted to be held for a little while. Didn't want shit from her. Just needed to be held.

She didn't understand any of that shit. Didn't understand anything about my needing to be held or of needing to feel safe if only for a little while.

The parking lot at Green Shingles' is packed, though Stewart finds a space near the north end of the parking lot. By now, the snow is kicking up and covers everything in a white blanket that is interrupted only by the traffic passing on the highway.

"Ya' wanna party with us?" Stewart asked.

"Naw." I said. "Gotta get home to Elmira."

"Elmira? Shit, ya' gotta go all the way to Corning, then take 17! Hitchin' will take ya' all night. Come on in and party, man!"

"I'll be okay, man."

"Well, be cool, man," he says.

"Thanks for the ride, man."

I gotta say all that 'cause when I'm feelin' like this, I don't drink. It's just not cool. Beer can't do what being held does. Instead of making all the bullshit go away, I figure that it will me even more depressed.

I walk back to the highway.

Again, the night highway is mine.

Hitchin' at night is a bitch, especially in snow 'cause nobody sees you until the last minute and then they get all pissed off 'cause they almost slam into the who-the-fuck-is-that-hitchhiker? and don't want to stop.

Saturday night hitchin' is even tougher. The only people who tend to stop are drunks and stoners and perverts.

The perverts are the worse: they talk about sex like that's all there is in the world or saying shit about beating-off and apologizing about saying their sex shit but they just keep talking about it and there's not a damned thing you can do about it except to try to stay cool and figure out how you can escape if they reach for you.

They never reach for you, of course, because they want you to say that you'll party with them. They look at your long hair and worn French jeans and they think they know what you like to do. They want to be that kind of cool 'cause they think that's why you're hitchhiking on a Saturday night like you have a choice and this is what you do for fun. They don't know anything about you being out there because the only other option for you in the whole fucking world is to use the blade and disappear once and for all.

And you can't tell them that you like sex or anything like that because they'll take it the wrong way and think that you're telling them that you want to party when all you fucking want is to get the hell out of the car and go to someplace that doesn't really exist but feels good to think about. And don't bother telling them you don't like sex because then they'll try to teach you that all sex is good, which is the biggest lie in the world.

I couldn't stay in Mansfield. Lorraine's house was quiet and Gina wanted sex. I could probably be with Gina now if I had let her.

Maybe I should have told her how much I needed to be held, how much I just wanted someone in my life right then for just a moment, how much I needed to hear someone else breathing and smell someone else's scent. Instead, I am with the night, the snow, and my broken boots.

A Penn Dot plow truck blows past, it swerving away from me at the last moment though it still flings heavy slush at me. The cars that follow it spray me with cinders and salt. All of that crap stings my face and probably stains my clothes: it's too dark to tell. After the line of cars behind it ends, the traffic fades.

Hitching means walking: that's all there is to it. I'm not a lazy hitcher. I won't stand alongside the road like an asshole, waiting for the ride to stop.

I do math when hitching. I can walk about three miles an hour. Lindley is fifteen miles from Corning, I think. No more than five hours.

Seven plus five equals midnight. In about ten miles later, in Corning, the bars will be closed and the drunks will be driving!

At Presho around one AM, there is no traffic. Here, the highway opens to four lanes like an interstate. I hear nothing but the sound of snowflakes falling and my boots. I'd probably have had a better chance of getting a ride if I had brought a backpack.

444

Without one, I'm just another drifter, another bum, another hobo, another serial killer, another party boy. At night, a hitcher becomes everyone's worst fear as each driver makes up the perfect reason to keep that right foot tucked tightly against the gas pedal. And those fuckers who stop are looking for fun.

A station wagon fishtails across the northbound lanes. If it keeps swaying, I'll jump over the guardrail: that'll protect me.

I should've fucked Gina: I'd be safe and warm in her room. I'd be stoned and used, but she'd be holding me and I'd be asleep in a warm bed tonight with her next to me.

I'm so stupid.

The station wagon stops right next to me, its front passenger window creeping downward. I can smell the cigarettes and booze as the stench escapes the car and pollutes the winter air.

"Where ya' goin'?" the man's voice says.

"Elmira."

"Through Corning?"

"Yeah."

"I'll take ya' to Corning, but I'm headed toward Bath."

I open the door, not kicking the rocker panel as I climb in.

The car is warm. So warm that my sweat starts in my armpits and crotch, then travels along my sides, back and front until I'm taking a bath in my clothes.

It's too late: I smell of asshole. And Phil. It's fucked up: I can smell him at odd times; his scent is all over me. I smelled him this morning right after my shower, his stench was in my nostrils even before I toweled off. There's nothing I can do when I smell Phil. I can't escape his stench.

When hitching, I usually remember to loosen my coat, but I walked so quickly in the snow that I forgot to protect myself that way: shit!

Now, I smell of asshole and Phil. The car reeks of alcohol and cigarettes, but it doesn't cover my stench. Nothing ever does. In this moment I am sewage and if I were alone, I would instantly disappear in the flash of my blade before the stench choked me.

"Was playin' in a band," the driver volunteers.

He wants to fuck me. I can tell.

Drunks are scary when they drive. The one I trust to drive is me 'cause I know where the fuck I'm goin'.

A drunk musician!

Everybody knows how much booze one of these guys can absorb. That's part of being a musician: he's the good-time-Charlie up there, so let's ply him with drinks. Then the fucker climbs into a car and becomes my problem.

I grab the seat belt and fasten it.

I've got no identification, so it'll be days before anyone figures out who I am. It's so fucked right now and the stench of asshole and Phil has me almost puking.

He's talking about playing. Talking about living in Bath and having to drive all the way down to Tioga to play at some bar.

Then it starts.

He's talking about sex.

Sex, sex, and more sex.

He's talking about his favorite positions, his favorite party girls, and his wife.

He's drunk horny.

He wants it all but will take what he can when he can and where he can, no matter what: that's what he says. He sees my long hair in the glow of the dashboard and he starts talking about what he likes and what I probably like: man, can you stand it, doing it like that, man? He's talking real fast and spending more time looking at me. He's talking about his wife waiting for him in Bath and what he's gonna do to her when he gets home. He's telling me all about her, about what she looks like, about what she tastes like, what she does and what she likes. He's telling me that he's always wanted to watch her with another man. That he's really into guys, but he's never told her that.

He's talking so much. I try not to notice the car sliding all over the northbound lanes.

I have no weapon. Hell, all I own is a blade, but I don't carry that. I don't want to even think about disappearing like that while hitching.

If he makes a move, I'll act like I want to party and talk him into stopping the car, only to jump over the guardrail and run like hell into the night.

And he keeps talking about all sorts of sex shit and chicks

at the bars and all sorts of parties, do I like parties 'cause parties are so fuckin' cool? He's so drunk horny right now that he can't stand it, have I ever been so horny that I couldn't stand it, that I was just gonna explode if I didn't do it right there and then? Did I? Did I, man?

And all I smell is asshole and Phil and I'm thinking that I'm gonna tell this asshole to stop the car right now 'cause all I wanna do right now, man, is party right here on U.S. Route 15 on a snowy Saturday night so that I can leave him playin' with himself on the road's shoulder while I escape over the guardrail.

"She's waiting for you," I say. "Take her, man. A woman like that, man, needs all your lovin'. Save it for her, man: fuck her fuckin' brains out. That's fuckin' cool."

"Fuckin' right," he says as he keeps talking about what he's gonna do with her and to her. And he's pissed off 'cause he hasn't got a picture of her so he can't show me how fuckin' sexy she is, do I want to party with him and her? It's okay if I don't 'cause we can party by ourselves before we get too much farther down the road and he'll never tell anyone 'cause it'll be our secret.

I don't want any more secrets.
Secrets are killing me.
I don't know this guy, but I smell Phil.

I smell the stench of asshole and this guy is slowing down the car and keeps sayin' if I want to he can find a place for us to party or I can meet his wife. He's saying it's all up to me.

I'm seeing the lights of Corning and I'm not saying anything.

He stops the car. We're in Corning.

"What do you want to do, man?" he asks.

"Uh…, man, three-ways just aren't my thing."

"You sure?"

He reaches for me and I climb out of the car, jumping back.

"It's cool, right?" he asks.

"Yeah…, it's definitely cool."

I'm standing on the sidewalk in five inches of snow, nodding at him as he heads west on New York State Route 17 toward Bath and smiling because I know that when he gets home, he'll pass out on the sofa.

It's after one A.M. and I'm a thousand years away from me, but at least that fucking stench is gone. Gina is probably hitting bongs right now. I'm freezing in my parka as the cold air seeps in and chills me.

It's never a good idea to hitchhike while in any town, so I walk along Main Street toward the sewage plant.

Corning is laid out along the Chemung River. When Tropical Storm Agnes tore through here, one of the dikes gave way and flooded the place. The Corning Glass tower stands above the town not far from the river. The factory is humming as I walk past the lights that turn colors for the trucks waiting to get back onto the limited access highway.

Here, New York State Route 17 cuts through town. There's a Seven-Eleven open along the snow-covered four-lane main street, but I stay outside. My feet are cold and wet. My parka is soaked. In the streetlights, I can see that my coat and jeans have been stained by the salt and the cinders.

I ignore the rigs that drift through the endless intersections before they pick up speed on the eastern end of town. It's better not to call attention to myself because I have no identification, no money, and no life. I'm a vagrant if the cops stop me. They can do what they want; I have no rights here.

I don't blame them.

I look like hell, but at least I'm not disappearing in my room tonight. I forget... how far it is to Elmira?

About six or seven hours. I'll be getting home around nine or so. I think. Maybe earlier.

I can't do any hitching math anymore; I'm too fucking tired. Swinging Guitar Man from Bath tired me out.

It seems like hours until Corning's streetlights end and their memory becomes cloaked in the night. I'm too tired to make good time walking backward, but too cold to take off my hood in order to listen for traffic.

It's safer walking backwards anyway. I don't want to be hit. My legs hurt from all the walking, but that's okay because it gives me something to think about. It's too bad that it's so cold or I'd just jump over the guardrail and sleep on the embankment. Just for a little bit.

I walk for miles. It doesn't matter that I don't see any vehicles after I leave Corning. I'm almost home and figure that I'll see North Elmira by dawn.

At least I wasn't alone tonight. That would have been fucked. Fuck it: a wasted day is better than disappearing. Thank you, Gina, for giving me a reason to go somewhere away from me for a little bit.

About three or five miles east of Corning the plows have stopped. My aching legs are cold. My feet are soaked. When the still night finally surrounds me, I hear the sound of a dying car running too fast on bald tires and watch it as the flow of its lights dance in the snowflakes.

I move toward the guardrail: it's always there when I need it.

The car's wheels lock up and the vehicle slides, fishtailing. It's an old station wagon.

What, is this the night of the old station wagon?

It's a Kingswood Estate Wagon. A GM product with a clamshell gate. Only thing, this one has all sorts of Bondo and rust. It slides right past me, its red taillights blinding me as the vehicle stops hard on the road.

The passenger side door in the front opens. Some kid stumbles out, hitting his knees against the pavement. He pukes and pukes and pukes. I can hear him above the disco music that pours out of the Kingswood. I can smell the alcohol in his vomit as the puddle's steam drifts up to a shaft of dome light escaping from the wagon that illuminates him. The kid wipes his sleeve over his mouth.

"Ya' wanna a ride?"

"Yeah."

The car smells of booze, vomit, and piss. He and his friend are messed up. Very messed up. So messed up, they're too afraid to drive faster than twenty on the highway. It takes too long, but it's okay 'cause they're too messed up to talk.

I don't care. I'm not disappearing tonight. I'll be back in Elmira to see the new day. I'll visit Gina again the next time I don't want to disappear, but I'm not fucking her. Not gonna ever fuck her again.

You know what: I'll go see her the next time I'm thinking about disappearing. She can go fuck herself! I don't care if I have to ride in some booze-smelling, puke-smelling, piss-smelling Kingswood Estate: it's better than fucking Gina or disappearing!

I'm going home.

Home.

I feel like I have one again. That's cool. When I get back there, I'm going to open my notebook and write a little bit until I can fall asleep.

Alumni Hall

Lorraine helps me move back to Mansfield. The spring semester is starting in a few days and I have to return to school because I haven't found a job in Elmira.

I see June's shiny Oldsmobile when I stand near the window in Anne's office inside Alumni Hall. I saw the car when I walked into the building, the clean vehicle contrasting with the cinder-covered ones in the parking lot. It looks like Bobby took it to the car wash: the paint is all shiny and the vinyl roof looks clean.

Anne is typing, waiting for June to open her door and give me my five minutes before she escorts me to her exit.

And now, another episode of "Parenting Between Appointments" or "Parenting Between Exits" starring June. Technical support provided by Bobby the Beater!

Anne tries not to stare, but I catch her looking at my lace-up boots, stained jeans, and cheap vinyl coat: my parka is ruined. I bought this coat from a used clothes store.

I'm freakin' out Anne! That's funny. She's probably wondering where Little Orphan Johnny went!

I want to laugh, but I instead pretend not to see her eyes as they take me in.

It's okay. I know what to expect from the Alumni Hallers. They don't know shit about Phil or disappearing or Hawaii. They have their own little world where all the cars are shiny and clean.

They live… in a… happy and shiny and clean world!

The door opens. June smiles and I go into her office.

"The Oldsmobile looks nice," I say.

Start with an obvious compliment!

"Bobby took it to the car wash yesterday," she says.

She's taking the bait. June really knows her lines!

"How was your Christmas?" I ask.

Good job keeping it superficial, Little Orphan Johnny!

"Nice. We went to Rhode Island to see my parents and Bobby's parents. Then we went to New York and caught a few shows."

Ah, the family holiday vacation. It's always so much fun!

"That's great."

"How was your Christmas?" she asks.

June is so good at this. It makes me want to kiss her!

"Good. I stayed downstate with some friends. It was very relaxing."

Great response, Little Orphan Johnny! She's not asking about the rags you're wearing while simultaneously feigning interest!

"Good."

We approach her exit door and she rests her hand on the door knob. She is blocking me from leaving as she clears her throat.

"Professor Yacavissi told me that you didn't attend your finals," June says.

Yac? I took two classes from him last semester. Both in geography. No, one was regional planning?

"No, I was… dealing with… something."

Good job being concerned and vague. Remember, she really doesn't care about you, just about how your behavior makes her looks, Little Orphan Johnny!

"I hope you don't mind me calling him. I did so because I wanted to know why you failed both of his courses. You didn't leave me a phone number. I've reviewed your grades and they are quite disturbing. You also failed Spanish."

"I failed Yac's courses? I had an *A* in each going into the finals."

"John, you didn't go to any of your finals. And, your Q.P.A. went down. You're at a two-point-oh. If it drops any further, you'll be put on probation."

"He failed me? Twice?"

"John…, is anything… wrong?"

June makes a funny!

"I can't believe he failed me. I had an *A* in both courses."

June looks at me, then touches my shoulder. It's one of those what's-the-matter touches, but it doesn't mean shit.

C'mon, this is June.

She's worried about how this looks. Shit, this means that she'll be talking about me during those little cocktail parties that Bobby and her host once a month. People won't know how to deal with it and she'll be awkward about it. I'm the problem child now.

A problem child they can't beat into submission.

"Look, I missed my finals because I had something goin' on. I'll pull up those grades. I'll retake those courses."

"John, they're not offered this semester. They won't be offered until next fall."

"I'll take them then—"

"John… is something wrong? Your other professors said that you just stopped going to classes immediately after mid-terms."

She gives me a long look, like she did when I lived at her house and was part of her life. One of those people-need-to-talk-about-it looks.

It's too late for that, June. I'm not gonna tell you about the stench and Phil. Can't tell you about how I wake up and smell Phil on me, how I can't get clean anymore, how I'm obsessed with using the blade, and how I'm trying anything and everything to keep myself from disappearing, to keep myself alive. Shit, if I tell you any of that, you'll call Bobby, the state police, and the nuthouse.

"John, do you need to see Mike again? Do you think you need therapy?"

Mike?

Shit, that would only make it worse. Another round of tests and more medications? This time, Goldberg would make me see a psychiatrist and I'd have to live on fuckin' meds. Shit, I'd probably see the same assholes who fucked up Mom. And, it

wouldn't matter: I'd still end up telling them everything and I'd
have to tell everyone about how dirty I am. Shit, it's bad enough:
why can't they all leave me the fuck alone?

"I don't need to see anybody."

"You sure?"

"Yeah... I'm sure."

June gives me a weird hug. Hell, she knows I'm really
fucked up, but doesn't know why. I'm not telling her shit: fuck
that. It's funny, but I'm fucked up in so many ways that she can
just think I'm crazy without me having to say anything about Phil,
the stench, disappearing, hitting bongs all day, or doing business.

"John... sometime... Bobby and I would like to have you
come up for dinner. I know I've mentioned it before, but you
never followed through— "

Oh yeah, it's my fault. Okay, I'll play along. I'll play,
"Let's Try to Make a Dinner Date!"

"Cool, when's... a good time?"

"Well, Bobby plays poker every Monday night. On
Tuesday, I have bridge. Of course, on Friday we're all too tired to
entertain. And, our weekends are scheduled through the
summer." She laughs.

What a strong opening, but I'll hang in there.

"Uh, Wednesday?" I ask.

"I usually have paperwork."

Fantastic!

"Thursday?"

She shakes her head. "Um, I don't think that's going to
work."

Hmm, that's every day of the week. But, wait, I have an
idea.

"That's okay. Maybe during the summer. You and I
could have lunch."

Good job, Little Orphan Johnny! How will she wiggle out
of this one?

"Well, I bring my lunch 'cause I'm on a diet."

"I could bring a sandwich."

"Well... okay. Stop back sometime and we'll finalize it,"
she says, closing the door.

That's not gonna happen. But at least she tried. She won't have to feel guilty about shitting me out.

I button my coat, walk down the stairs, and go outside. There, I stroll past the Oldsmobile.

Damn, it looks good when it's clean.

I fight the urge to spit on it, instead walking away. I have to get fucked up before I kill myself.

Manser Hall

Fuck, when did it get so fuckin' dark outside? And so fuckin' cold?

Listen... I am... so ripped, so... totally wasted... that I just puked my guts out in the Alumni Hall parking lot. I think it was where June parks her fuckin' Oldsmobile.

Fuck it, man. Fuck, in the morning, she'll fuckin' step in it! It won't be steaming then, man! Today, she saw me! Tomorrow, she'll see my puke!

That's so fuckin' symbolic!

Shit... I was drinkin'... some shit. Forgot... to fuckin' eat. Should've... fuckin' eaten. Fuck.

Fuck the Alumni Hallers! Fuck all of them! Fuck 'em... for suckin' in my air and polluting it! Fuck my professors! Fuck them!

I am not fuckin' manic-depressive. I don't need a fuckin' shrink, meds, or Mike. Fuck June for even thinkin' that. She fuckin' thinks I'm crazy.

Fuck her.

Fuck Bobby.

They shit me out, man.

They can go fuck themselves.

After puking everything feels so much better. Maybe I'll go to Laurel and hang out with the Delta Zetas. They're cool.

I get my ass toward Laurel Dorm.

454

See, I know lots of people, but they don't know shit about me 'cause I'm not gonna tell them any of it: it's none of their fuckin' business. Besides, I don't want them lookin' at me like that. I don't want them lookin' at me the way Anne and June did today, like I'm so fuckin' fucked up that I'm worse than fuckin' crazy.

Hate that fuckin' look.

Now I know why Mom only talked to me about the hit men late at night: she probably hated that look too.

In Laurel, the Zetas' floor is dark.

Fuck, they're probably at some fuckin' mixer with the Lambda Chi boys. Fuck, I don't know where they all went.

A police car drifts past.

Fuck, it's the cops. Campus Security. Like someone is insecure and needs them! Being cool here, Officer Friendly. It's… fuckin' cool, man. Just being cool. We're all cool.

I'm hungry. Don't want dry heaves again. They suck. It makes me feel like I'm gonna puke out my heart. Puke it out my fuckin' mouth.

I try the doors at Manser Dining Hall; they're locked!

Fuck, fuck, fuck! When did it get so fuckin' dark? I want Manser food. Gotta eat or I'll dry heave again. Hate fuckin' dry heaves, man, they hurt so fuckin' much. Tears right through me, man.

Fuck you, Manser!

Shit, I know.

I sit near the Manser door that faces South Hall. I'm looking at the brushed aluminum letters that spell out M-a-n-s-e-r H-a-l-l.

When I lived in Cedarcrest, the jocks trashed that place. Tore the living shit out of everything and nobody ever got

455

in trouble.

Fuck the jocks!
Fuck Manser!

A group of sorority girls walk past: they're not Zetas. These bitches smell like they were dipped in perfume. Fuckers move in herds.

I smile at them, though I don't know 'em and don't want to.

Fuck it: it all makes sense now.
Fuckin' letters.
Fuckin' aluminum letters that everyone looks at every day and don't think a fuckin' thing about it.
People don't think anymore. Just fuckin' do shit without thinkin'. That's not fuckin' cool. Not fuckin' cool at all.

I grab at the letters on the dining hall sign.

Fuck! The letter M *comes off when I wedge a piece of wood beneath it. Fuck, it's huge! The* H *pops off and I read this new fuckin' message: "anser all" it says to everyone.*

"Answer all, you fucksticks; answer all!" I yell.
Some girl walks past me. She's goin' to Cedarcrest.

Fuck it, she saw me. Maybe she's a narc or some shit like that. Fuck that, she's no narc.

I follow her.

She's all pretty and shit, but she's not fucked up. Who's not fucked up on a Monday night? What's this shit?

"Hey, what's your name?" I ask.
She looks at me, man, like I'm totally fucked up.
Fuck that shit.
Gotta stay cool, man.
She doesn't know me, and I'm freakin' her out, man.

456

"Melissa."

"No shit?"

"Really."

"Fuck, that begins with an *M*!"

"Yeah!"

"Fuckin' cool, take this." And I fuckin' hold it out to her 'cause it's a fuckin' gift. "Take the *M*, Dude!"

"Thanks." She takes it.

"It's an *M* like in Melissa. It's all yours."

She picks up speed.

Fuck, I don't want to freak her out. Just want to give her the fuckin' letter.

"Melissa, you take it easy."

I run away with the other letter. I throw away it in the field behind Cedarcrest where I get an attack of the dry heaves. It's all fucked 'cause I can't bring anything up and I hurt like fuck.

Business and Bongs

So, man, it's like this. Henry and me are doing business. Me, I'm doing bongs. I get up in the morning and I do a few, then decide to cut classes. Sometimes at night, I drop some 'cid on my own and watch *Saturday Night Live* or *Twilight Zone*.

Every Sunday, I go up on Armenia Mountain with Derek from Troy and we smoke pot all day. When I get back, it's too dark and I'm too stoned to study.

Man, when I'm out of pot, I meditate with Al and that's totally cool.

The Counseling Center

Can you stand it: it's April. I haven't gone to many classes this semester and I think I'm flunking everything. Everything! Now, I have to see this nice old man at the Counseling Center.

This nice old man, he played one...

The nice old man's not stoppin' me. Even though I'm wearing my sunglasses, this room is still too bright. Who taught this nice old man anything about having a therapeutic environment? His fluorescent lights belong in a supermarket, not a therapist's office.

And he's too old for this kind of counseling.

Dude should be sitting in a rockin' chair and smokin' a joint at some fuckin' retirement home.

"John, what brings you here?" the old man asks.

"I'm quitting school. I want to work for awhile."

It's been a good semester. Henry and I are in business and he's sitting on our shitload of cash. It's in his dresser in Pinecrest. He's got a private room, so it's all cool. When he found out that I didn't get to Hawaii, he was cool about it. Shit, he said we can even keep it going after he graduates in a few weeks. Said I could have my half of the money then. I'll live on that. School is such a bummer.

It's time to get out of here. I mean, I haven't even been in the mood to read a textbook! And, now that spring is here, it's party time!

The old man writes some notes.

This nice old man, he played two...

Shouldn't he be telling me what he's writing? And, why hasn't he asked me about my sunglasses? I'll tell him that my eyes are bloodshot. From allergies. Maybe it's his way of being cool about the whole thing. Who knows?

Betcha he's gonna be on the phone in no time, telling June everything. She'll probably read all his notes. He hasn't even discussed confidentiality with me.

"Do you have any work lined up?"

Yeah, I'm a businessman! Look at me, man, I'm a stoner sitting in your office and I'm wearing sunglasses.

Dude, put two and two together!

I'm broke, failing all my classes, and partying all the time. Can you stand it?

"Uh, yeah, I'm planning on working at McDonald's. In fact, I went to high school with the manager, Erin. They're gonna train me. I'm eager to make a few bucks."

"It's good to have a plan," he says, writing.

458

Probably noting, "has a plan," and "working at McDonald's."

"Uh, yeah, once I get back on my feet, can I come back? To school?"

"Well, you'll have to reapply and, depending upon when you come back, you might have to take some tests. And, of course, pay off any unpaid balances."

He flips some pages of shit.

"Says here that you owe approximately twenty-two hundred dollars. You have the money to pay that off?"

"Uh, yeah. I'll... save it up."

I'll just payoff the two grand I owe the college with some of the money Henry owes me from our business, then use Mickey-D as cover for my real income and stash my cash for awhile. When Henry reports for basic training in September, that'll be cool 'cause we'll have an import-export business. Didn't Mark Twain write something about not letting college get in the way of obtaining an education?

Or, some shit like that.

"I think it's good that you're taking a break. Seems like your grades took a tumble," the old man says.

This nice old man, he played three...

"Yeah, I lost interest. Not sure I want to be a psychologist. Need some time to think."

He takes out a form, studies it for a moment, and then fills it out.

"John, I need your ID card." He hands me a form. "This just indicates that we discussed readmission and your plans."

I sign everything.

"Now, the classes I'm taking, what happens with all that stuff?"

"You'll just get a *W* on your transcript. It will say that you withdrew from school: that's effective as of today."

I sign the form.

"You living on campus?"

"No, I have a place in town. Renting a room from John and Benita Butts. Went to school with their son."

"Good."

He gives me a copy of the form and stares at me.

"Yeah, is there… anything else?"

"Yes, I need your ID card."

"Cool." I hand it over. The edges are green from scraping pot on album covers.

This nice old man came rolling home!

Pinecrest Dorm

"Man, I'm sorry," Henry says like he gives a shit.

He stands in his robe, his mortarboard in his hand. A black and red tassel with '79 hangs from it. He doesn't wear an honor braid as he stands in front of the door in his dorm room. He fills the doorway as he picks up a shoe brush to clean his Hush Puppies.

"I gotta know," he says "if you're, uh, gonna do anything about all this?"

"What can I do? You lied. And, you're gonna be a Marine."

I'm sitting on his loveseat. Henry's family brought furniture for his dorm room: it looks like a real bedroom. His bong sits on the floor, empty and cold. He brushes his shoes, then grabs a comb and fixes his hair.

"John, look at you. Man, you look like shit."

He's right. My clothes are worn and I need a shower. My breath smells like vomit 'cause everything I eat makes me puke. Hell, I'm puking all the time, even when there's nothing in my stomach. I'm not sleeping much anymore: I'm just not tired.

And I smell Phil all the time.

"Dude," he says, "my parents are coming. Real soon. Think you can get going?"

"I need that money to live on. We agreed—"

Henry puts down his comb. "Like I said, John: It was my car, my transportation. I used my gasoline, my oil, plus wear and tear on my car. It's a business expense."

"I was gonna live on that over the summer. Giving me back my initial investment won't be enough for me to live on. And, what about our business?"

"John, I'm goin' into the Marines. I don't have time for

that shit. I have to think about my career."

"But, we agreed—"

"John, we only talked about it. We never made a legal agreement."

"Henry, you're fuckin' me over."

"Look, my father's a lawyer—"

"I know what your father does. We were partners. You agreed."

"Not in writing. You show me something that I signed and I'll give you more."

I get up because I'm pissed and I have to get out of here. Have to go and figure out what I'm gonna do with my life.

Henry stands in front of the door, blocking me.

"You gonna do anything about this? I have to know if you're gonna try coming after me and *my* money."

I look at him. He's a big fuckin' guy from Cherry Hill. He once owned a Corvette and knows all sorts of rich and powerful people. His father's a lawyer.

A corporate lawyer.

Henry can kick my ass physically… and legally.

And me?

I weigh about a hundred and ten pounds, have dry heaves, and wear rags. June lets me talk to her between *appointments* that usually involve her watering plants or calling my professors. She would probably have me committed if she knew about this shit.

I'm screwed and everything is just a bummer.

"I can't come after you; you know that," I say.

He moves aside.

"Take it easy," I say, going out into the hall. I hear some other graduates talking in the hallway and see the flash of cameras as their excited parents snap pictures.

"So, no bad feelings?" Henry asks.

"No, man, no bad feelings. Actually, even better than that is that I have no feelings at all."

"Cool! I'm glad."

Henry extends his hand and I shake it.

"Good luck," I say.

"You too. Stop down and see me if you're ever in Cherry Hill."

I feel him watching me as I walk down the hallway. I smile and nod at the students dressed in their robes that are adorned with honor braids as they mill around with their parents in the lounge area.

"Congratulations," I say to them. "You've earned it."

They smile back at me.

The Butts' House

It's Monday morning, I smell Maxwell House coffee, and I've got to bleed. I've got to take the corner of the razor and push it into these arms while the birds chirp and the children walk to school.

I have to disappear.

Should I dress in the torn, stitched, and re-torn sweat pants? The faded Arrow shirt will be for the ceremony. Can't expect Bobby and June to buy one: that would be a waste.

I smell Maxwell House coffee and it stinks. Benita made John Senior eggs, probably over easy with bacon on the side.

The hand has already sliced the skin on this arm again along the veins, but the wound is oozing, not squirting.

The blade hasn't touched the vein yet.

I smell the blood.

Just cut the flesh is all. It's the opening act, the glorious climax is yet to come on the empty stage that has become the remnant of the life.

I don't want the ceremony. It's finally time to disappear… forever. I'm so tired of being such a coward.

Buses on Route Fifteen pass through the intersection at the end of the street.

All the kids' horses and all the kids' men win, win, win. Why don't they know it?

It's too beautiful outside to pull out the corner and wrap up the arm. At least I can hear birds and excited children. I'd play with those kids, but the bleeding arm would gross them out.

I'm a freak.

I'm sitting on the bed, a T-shirt tied around the left bicep. I'm wearing a grayed pair of briefs. Oh yeah, the corner of a razor is stuck in the arm, making me bleed. I'm broke, out of food, out of pot, and out of time. I keep having dry heaves, but I don't know why. I mean, I've only had water for the past week.

All I know is what I don't know.

I don't know how to eat any more.

I don't know how to feel any more.

I don't know how to live any more.

Yesterday was Mother's Day, but that doesn't matter.

The mother is dead.

The father is dead.

Soon, the son will be dead.

I hate that holiday. There's so much to hate right now...

John Senior is downstairs in the kitchen with Benita, his wife. They're both laughing at her joke. That old man slaps the table, then slides his chair a bit on the wooden floor. The boards creak when he walks to the Mr. Coffee that fills the house with that stench.

I'm sorry they'll find me: they're cool people.

I had contemplated walking into the woods yesterday, stripping down, and slashing everything open, draining while inhaling the forest's scent. It was that pretty outside and I felt that ugly on the inside.

Shit, I couldn't do anything yesterday but look at old photo albums.

The scent of the woods penetrates the room. This skin is sweating and bleeding, the wound stinging. After the razor blade plunges into the vein and follows it from the wrist to the elbow, I understand that the body will become really cold after awhile.

That's why I'm going to the bathroom and running a hot bath. I'll put a lot of soap in the water, so I'll be clean. I won't let the water run over the tub and ruin the Butts' floor.

Fuck, I'm crying. I haven't even started to die yet and I'm crying.

Fuck, I never cry.

The tears sting the wounded arm that wipes the face, but it can't stop anything anymore.

I have to do this: I've been trying to do this for the past six years and I'm tired of failing.

John Senior walks up the stairs. He passes the room without pausing, slipping into the bathroom without making the spot in front of that door creak. The ears hear him brushing his teeth at the old sink. He gargles with *Listerine*.

In this room, the hand slides the razor out of the arm, the eyes admiring the fingers holding the bloody blade in midair.

Everyone, it's time for a celebration! You all won: Dad, Mom, Phil, the kids on the bus, Betty, Jack, Mr. Palmer, Henry, Bobby, Gina, and June.

Everyone's a winner!

I am Subservient Man, Pestilence Man, and this is my final act. No more stories, just a little slice.

The razor doesn't need the body; the body needs it. It needs the sensation of the steel parting the skin, slicing the veins, and freeing the soul.

The notebook is on the floor.

I haven't written in over a week.

Maybe the hands should destroy that damned book.

The hands grab it and write.

Pretty Boy

"Pretty Boy"
You thought of yourself.

"Pretty Boy"
You loved to hear those words.
Repeated until euphoria was
Yours.

"Pretty Boy"
How you loved your face,
Mind, body, and soul.

"Pretty Boy"
Wanting to share none of it,
You broke your trance
Of Self-enchantment
And your pretty neck.

The ears hear John Senior walking downstairs. He pushes in his chair, coughs, and hugs Benita.

"I love you. Have a nice day," he says as he walks out the door.

Nice days are for someone else to accumulate. They are filled with kids skipping to school, warm spring air rushing into school bus windows, and birds chirping.

I've only the razor. They'll say that I was crazy… like my mother who couldn't be helped. Like his mom, the crazy son threw away everything… and everyone.

That's what they'll say.

No, they won't even say that.

I'm not that important.

The ears hear water running through the pipes and flowing into the kitchen sink. Benita turns on the radio and listens to country music, but the brain can't make out the tune. The ears aren't listening to that world anymore.

The razor feels large in the fingertips, its steel warm. This is what I've done to myself today?

The eyes look around at the room at the photo albums and the journals. In the dresser are the crazy son's three changes of clothes and the canvas Nikes. Everything that he owns and everything that he is can fit into a backpack.

A backpack; that's what they'll remember.

The eyes consider the razor. The right hand has cut the skin on the left arm from the wrist to the bicep. The arm is now bleeding, but the hand still hasn't sliced the veins that are bulging between the tourniquet T-shirt and the wrist.

The eyes continue to consider the blade and prepare for the final slashing. The crazy son's body will be cold for awhile, but then it will be forever still.

And, Phil, Betty, Jack, Bobby, June, the Mafia, the kids on the bus and Mom and Dad will have won.

Won it all.

The razor is part of the hand, part of the body. It's who the crazy son is. See the sweat and blood mixing together on the steel?